Bringing Up the Rear

Other Books by S.L.A. Marshall

On Tactics and Leading

Men Against Fire
The Soldier's Load
Vietnam Primer

The Armed Forces Officer
The Officer as a Leader

On War

Crimsoned Prairie
The War to Free Cuba
Armies on Wheels
World War II Story
Swift Sword

Blitzkrieg
World War I
Military History of the Korean
  War

On Battle

Battle at Best
Battles in the Monsoon
Island Victory
Sinai Victory
Night Drop
Ambush
Bird: The Christmastide Battle

The River and the Gauntlet
Bastogne: The First Eight Days
Pork Chop Hill
Makin
West to Cambodia
The Fields of Bamboo

On Operations

Hill 440
Critique of Infantry Weapons and Tactics in Korea
Problems of the Defense in Atomic War
Guide to the Use of Information Materials

Bringing Up the Rear

A MEMOIR

———————————★———————————

by S. L. A. Marshall

EDITED BY CATE MARSHALL

PRESIDIO ⌶ PRESS

Copyright 1979 by Presidio Press

Published by Presidio Press, San Rafael, California

Library of Congress Cataloging in Publication Data
Marshall, Samuel Lyman Atwood, 1900–1977
    Bringing up the rear.

    Includes index.
    1. Marshall, Samuel Lyman Atwood, 1900–1977
2. Historians—United States—Biography. I. Marshall,
Cate. II. Title.
D15.M34A32   355'.0092'4 [B]   79-14949
ISBN 0-89141-084-8

Book design by Hal Lockwood

Jacket design by Mark Jacobsen

Printed in the United States of America

With love to my Shipmate, Cate
Who taught me to sing about
Mrs. Murphy's Chowder

Contents

By Way of Warning

A brazen conviction that, while winning more ground in my old age than I lost in my salad years, I at the same time led a more exciting life than any American in my century may not be a sufficient reason for writing these papers, but I can think of no other way to defend the claim.

With one exception, an article that appeared in the old *Infantry Journal* during the Korean War, no biographical sketch of me that has made print is an accurate reflection of my person or my work, to say nothing of completeness. Such obituary notices as follow in my wake cannot be expected to improve on portraits done while I lived. One thinks of obits only to recall what the Sphinx replied when asked by the Anzac for the digested wisdom of the ages: "Don't expect too much."

Skepticism is the child of experience. During my many trips to Israel, for example, two differences between the approach of the average newsman there and the good reporter in this country during the interview process have invariably impressed me.

The Israeli is interested in the roots of the individual life, the making of the person, the diverse influences out of which character and career are shaped. If the life itself makes a story, the mission of the visitor or his lack of status as a gold-plated VIP may be given passing mention but is never made the main theme.

No American newsman that I have ever seen in action takes this tack unless he is dealing with a personage in the forefront of public interest and has been assigned to write exactly that kind of story. To the pattern of a life he is generally indifferent, and while he would always prefer to interview a VIP, of his own choice he would rather come up with a startling quote on a hot topic or a news break that will win an eight-column streamer than dig for pure gold in the field of biography.

That kind of work is left mainly to minor clerks in pressdom's morgues who make a routine task of it, mailing out forms studded with questions

xi

most of which are less imaginative than those asked by the Census Bureau, and none of which is aimed to get better than a surface reading of the individual. For instance, no man is asked whom he rates as his most cherished friends, which are his favorite books, or what he means when he speaks of success, though such questions would beget revealing answers.

Still, our correspondents simply reflect the superficiality of the society. Educators are not more interested in the processes by which career and character are formed. Except for my departed friend, Dr. Nelson Glueck, that many-sided man, I have never had an educator express the slightest interest in why my life took such an eccentric course, though I have spoken on several hundred campuses. Fourteen universities have written requesting that I will them my papers or my library. None ever sent a missionary to determine whether any such papers existed or of what the library consisted.

By way of contrast, I have had many army officers raise the question: "How could it have happened?" The story of the life I led is much too complicated to permit a simple explanation. Some things happened to me through fate's whimsy. Changes also came of my own decision coldly resolved. Other turns to right or left had neither reasoning nor accident behind them. Enough to say that they eventuated and I cannot account for all of the motor forces. Still, it seemed worthwhile to sort things out, if only because so much that is misleading or flattering has been written, in particular what I am credited with having achieved for dear old alma mater.

The salient facts that make (I was taught as a cub reporter that only lard is rendered) difficult the summing-up are easily enough stated:

• For approximately one-half century I have lived two roughly parallel careers, one as a newsman-author, the other as a soldier.

• Though a reservist, I have always had my direct support from the regular army.

• I won my star though I was a high school dropout and subsequent to commissioning was never sent to any army school.

• I am the only American to know combat in both World Wars, Korea, and Vietnam.

• So being, I am the only person to figure in half of the wars of the United States.

• At age twenty-two I planned my professional life and did not deviate from that plan thereafter.

• The army was my university; it never gave me a bad assignment and it afforded me opportunities far in excess of my formal qualifications.

The book is begun around Christmas, 1969, as I turn toward seventy, feeling every year of it. Once that age came to the late Barney Baruch, every birthday made a national news story, with the invariable assertion that he had been close adviser to several presidents, which might have been said of Woodrow Wilson's pastor or Cal Coolidge's barber. I have known several presidents; to mention it is like playing the game of Touch Hemingway. They had their councilors and guideline-makers, and when I was consulted there were always laminations of committees and palace guardsmen between what I said and the ultimate decision.

My dealings with high military command were usually much more direct. Without doubt, I have known well a larger number of high military commanders, and had personal experience with more troops in the field, by the tens of thousands, than anyone in our history. This is said thankfully and not in boast; fortune favored me.

The title of the book comes from such an experience. On May 20, 1968, I sat with General Bill Westmoreland during the cocktail hour at his residence in Saigon. It was on the same night that the immediate area was first heavily pounded with 122-millimeter rockets. Dr. William G. MacMillan, his scientific adviser, and the theater surgeon, Colonel Bill Hall, were also present. Someone made a proposal. It went like this: "Whichever one of us first writes a memoir dealing at all with the military must title it *Bringing Up the Rear.*" It seemed like a good idea at the time and so we shook hands on it, which leaves me with no option.

In this work there is a minimum of combat reporting and description. It is limited to those episodes which require telling, either to explain myself or because they are significantly related to our history, though as yet untold. The reasoning behind this decision to use the broad brush and exclude the detail is elementary. I have written too much about combat and am tired of the subject.

S. L. A. MARSHALL

Dherran Dhoun
Birmingham, Michigan

Chapter 1
Early Influences

I was born in the beginning of the century in Catskill, New York. Luck and only luck enables one to be born in a year that makes all following events, whether cataclysmic or trivial, simple to remember. Dates become fixed without any need to add or subtract, and I do not merit credit for having a long memory. Like most memories, mine is uneven and sharpest on matters in which I was personally engaged.

Catskill was a small village, but to the mind of a child it seemed almost without limit. The school was at least two miles from my home and I was forced to trudge that road every day. The Catskill Mountains in the distance imposed an insurmountable barrier. The Hudson was a great inland sea. Hop-a-Nose, the promontory on Catskill Creek, was a glaring monster. Or so I thought.

In 1927, when I returned to this environment for the first time since age seven, everything had shrunk. The school was less than one-half mile from the old home. The Catskills were foothills, and all of the other massive images were dwarfed in proportion. In that same year I returned to Boulder, Colorado, which I had not seen since age twelve. There everything was in exact perspective, congruent with the images impressed on my brain. So I learned for myself what no one had ever told me, that at some point between seven and twelve, and short of arriving at full stature, we all grow up in this one particular and view the physical world with as much dimensional exactitude as our minds will ever acquire.

The weather in the Northeast fed my tendency to be accident-prone. In Catskill I received two concussions in the 1907 winter, the first from being hit by a streetcar, the second from skidding down an icy stairway in the storm and dark and hitting my head on a water plug. Dad found me an hour later, unconscious in the drift. A bobsled spill split open my face and I still wear the scar. Both arms were broken that year, one in scrub football and the other in a fall from an outdoor trapeze. While keeping my parents in

1

debt, this made me ambidextrous. I also began to suspect what later years confirmed: I felt pain far less than most people. That is not to say that I could bear it more easily, but that I did not hurt as badly. One of our daughters, Catie, is similarly blessed.

Of the early recollections that stay in my mind, one is of the village churchyard in Killian, South Carolina, where we moved when I was just about to turn five. Dad, who was something of a genius among brickmakers, kept moving on to where the job looked better. On Sundays Dad preached as a layman in the little wooden church.

I played outside, enchanted by the quiet, moss-covered, mildewed, and lily-grown graveyard. One day it occurred to me that, by copying the writings on the tombstones in God's orchard and carrying them to Mother for translation, I might learn the alphabet. Some of it was done by the process that is now called rubbing. Using wrapping paper, I finally completed copying my first epitaph. It read: "Here lies Eli Eisenhower. He was kicked by a mule who caused his death." I give thanks to Eli and his mule for making me a man of letters before the age of six. (Strangely, I never heard that name again until the years—the great ones for me—that culminated in my directly serving the president-to-be as his chief historian in the European Theater.) I learned then that you can learn to write anywhere, even from the grave. Moreover, I began to understand the joy of learning things fairly on my own. On this I have no theories about what might be best for another person, but I am sure that, for me, getting my thoughts and ideas published would have brought me small satisfaction if I had worked from a cell and tried to imagine the stress and challenge of strife and adventure without having been able to experience it first. The writer, like the actor, is frequently never quite in reality. He is part of the world's make-believe. I have always been part of the action. As a youngster, I was much too easily dared to try things that were either ridiculous or absurd as well as dangerous. When later this foolishness abated, the residuum was an understanding that security is not the end and all of living.

By the Christmas of my seventh year we were living once again in Catskill. I mark that holiday for a particular reason. Mother's gift to Dad was a seventy-five-cent copy of Conan Doyle's *The White Company*. I was awakened at 6:00 A.M. by his voice reading to her from the book. It was the scene where Sir Nigel and Hordle John are trapped in a castle by the Little Men. Listening on my pallet, I was transported. I remember distinctly telling myself that if such wondrous things were to be found in books, then books I must have. (I would like to note that in Washington, D.C., in 1950, I was at a cocktail party with eight former members of my military staff and their wives. I suggested that we play a game. Without consulting each other, each person would write a list of the five authors whose work had real meaning and influence in his or her personal life. The only names to appear on all lists were Doyle's and Rider Haggard's.)

Actually, I loved candy much more than books and fortunately in 1906 it cost a penny a bag. The country still had a good five-cent cigar. The hot dog, which had its genesis in that season, was hawked door to door by peddlers who pushed bright steam carts and sang out: "A loaf of bread, a pound of meat, and all the mustard you can eat for one nickel," a cry not heard since.

I was never very good at children's games that required finger dexterity—of which I had practically none. I could not learn to fly a kite, spin a top, or play a decent game of mibs. Out of that frustration, more than all else, I turned immediately upon entering school to contact sports: football, baseball, wrestling, the whole works. This twist had as much to do with what ultimately became of me as my premature fascination with reading and writing. Every pivotal turning in my life developed out of one impulse or the other.

Some of this may sound like rationalizing after the fact, though I am sure that it is not. If in those early years the mind is so plastic that lasting inhibitions derive from painful experience, likewise must positive drives be initiated, and possibly fixed, by sensations that are rewarding.

Relishing most sports, I never tried to learn to swim. This inability gnawed at me during the campaigns in the Central Pacific 1943–44 when during landings I had to descend a cargo net in the darkness combat-loaded. I knew that if anyone stepped on my fingers and I lost my grip, I would drop like a plummet to the bottom and stay.

My early years in Catskill on the whole were good. I have seen it written by several eminent psychiatrists that childhood is a time of anguish, uncertainty, and great trial. For others, possibly—it was never so for me.

The time came to pull up stakes. Father got a call to a better job in Boulder, Colorado, that magnificently situated city crowding the Rockies just below the Arapahoes. It was the most fortunate thing that ever happened to me and the least fortunate for the family.

The thrill for me was in the great open spaces, the magnificent distances in any direction. There were only two houses on our block and the closest built-up area was half a mile distant with little but prairie between. We lived right next to Base Line Road, where the fortieth parallel was marked to the extreme eastern horizon. It was this sage and tumbleweed country, with its shades of silver gray, buff, and dun, that drew me.

Boulder in that time was a place of great winds that would come down from the Rockies with such force as to blow the roof or porch from a well-built house. So my older sister, Alice, and I saw the wind and the base line in combination as a challenge to flight. The urge had been whetted when we saw a crude bamboo mockup of the Wrights' Kitty Hawk plane at the county fair. With father's tool set we fashioned gliders fixed with large canvas sails and handholds at either side, then tried them in a thirty-mile-an-hour wind, only to fall flat on our faces. Some weeks later we tried them in a sixty-mile-an-hour gale that blew away the Finks' front porch—and that experiment truly got off the ground. Heels kicking, we soared out and away just above the mullen tops for all of seventy feet, where the wind slackened slightly to let Alice make a violent two-point landing that spun her head over heels while the sail whipped on its way straight along the fortieth parallel. I oozed down in the middle of an irrigation ditch, thereby ending our try for a niche in the aeronautical hall of fame.

By this time I was in the fourth grade. Geography was my love; I devoured poetry and also feasted on Gulick's *Hygiene* for no good reason that I now recall. I had no real gift for the Palmer method of handwriting through muscular control, but, amazingly, that way of writing without more than minimal strain stayed with me through life. That alone enabled me to write millions of words in my field notebooks during World War II, Korea, and Vietnam.

The only subject in which I excelled, however, was music. Colorado's method of instruction was exemplary at that time. One had to learn to read music at a very early age, a faculty that helped me fifty years later to help save the Eighth Army in Korea in the darkest possible hour.

It was not my voice, however, but my arm that brought me the big dividend in Boulder. Living close to school, I was on hand when the football team, formed of eighth graders, scrimmaged on Saturday morning. They needed opposition, and I was it. I already knew that the quintessence of the game was in the tackle. All other technics could be acquired, provided one had the nerve to go straight in and hit the ball carrier around the knees. The bigger they were the harder they were certain to fall. So, out of sureness in tackling only, as a fourth grader, I became the center of an eighth-grade football team. It was my first awareness of the fact that size counts little, and my first assurance that willingness to risk yields the big payoff in most of life's endeavors.

The peace of our lives in Boulder and the satisfactions of our home tucked away in the Ben David orchard were probably too near perfect to last. Yet the blight descended much too swiftly and the family's life was never the same again.

Wilbur, the youngest, sickened and died of pneumonia. Then Teddy, the brilliant and favored, the rugged little nonpareil, was stricken. The doctors said it began with ptomaine poisoning and that the illness went straight to his heart. That was the only diagnosis ever given. If it makes little sense today, there is still much that medicine doesn't know. After one month of terrible agony, he died. Mother was never the same thereafter.

My own feelings I am at a loss to describe. Death in the family does not numb children in the same way that it affects parents, and for that, thank heaven. My sister Alice and I had our playmates, our studies, our private puppy-love interests, and we shortly returned to our accustomed rounds, she to go on to the eighth grade, I to the seventh. She stayed at the top of her class; I remained among the also-rans. Mainly what changed was that Boulder never seemed the same again. The light had gone out. There was a great emptiness in the place and too little laughter. Father quit Boulder to go farther west, hoping that the displacement would ease the pain of remembering. The aim was not more beautiful than vain.

We went to Niles, California, then as now a modest village next to the hills between Oakland and San Jose where the Southern Pacific line branches toward Stockton and Tracy. In 1912 the Essanay Motion Picture Company, one of the Big Four that virtually monopolized the film industry, was resident in Niles. I was screen tested along with the other eighth-grade boys and got the part playing opposite Danny Kelleher in the Snakeville Comedy series. My pay when I worked was seven dollars per day, which made me more affluent than my father.

During the next two years I attained all of the height I would ever achieve, fleshed out, and became better coordinated than before. I was relatively mature physically at age fourteen, having known none of the pangs that supposedly attend adolescence.

My entry into high school coincided almost exactly with the beginning of World War I. Though I never suspected that the latter would in the end contribute more to my higher education than all other influences put together, I followed the news. Toward the war I had little more than an average American youth's interest in Mons and the first Battle of the Marne, but I scanned page one after devouring the sport pages and loathed the kaiser from the word go. Still, it was a poorly informed emotion.

My life went on . . . rugby, football. I would ride over the railroad cutoff to the far side of the Bay to roam the redwoods. I didn't lose my heart in San Francisco until the 1915 world's fair. At the Exposition I found the real world of power, beauty, and excitement and loved it. My horizons suddenly went way out yonder. Oddly enough, enchanting me above all else were the Portuguese galleries in the Fine Arts Building. Color had fascinated me since kindergarten and here I had glorious color. It was color, possibly, more than anything else that drew me to study maps in depth, which hobby—for it became that—greatly shaped my life.

Winter baseball in this era in the San Francisco Bay area was spectacular beyond anything known since. Towns like Petaluma, San Rafael, Burlingame, and Pleasanton had clubs studded with stars. Major-league talent wintered there and the price was not too high. Duster Mails, who became a star with the Cleveland Indians, pitched for Livermore, and Herb Kantlehner, later of the Phillies, for Pleasanton. The players on the Niles Club, some of them Pacific Coast and Northwest League pros, were given odd jobs at the studio.

I played in the outfield in practice against the studio team and for the first time traveled in fast company, getting to swing against Joe Corbett, brother of Jim and teammate of John McGraw on the old Orioles. For me the Essanay team was a great pick-me-up. They treated me more as an equal than a junior nuisance, which to a kid is more steadying than giddying.

Things were happening to my home as well. My father had decided that Niles wasn't the environment in which to rear what remained of the family. We quit the land of the Native Son and went for one small piece of America that was a community apart, a little kingdom on its own, and good enough for its people. Though El Paso has long since lost its fierce frontier flavor, simple geography keeps it uniquely blessed, a city without a rival, unimpressed by wonders elsewhere.

Father went first, and I followed in two weeks. I worked at the brick plant that summer, hard manual labor ten hours daily, running a pugmill or a dry press, this as I was turning toward my fifteenth year. To save money, Dad and I slept on army cots in a small office above the dryer, which made us hotter than the hinges of hell. I saw little of El Paso. Most nights I was far too tired to move about, and my hands and fingers became so contorted from handling the brick that I would have to massage them through the evening to restore some suppleness.

The compensations were beautiful. Set right next to the International Brick plant was Camp Cotton, the base of the 16th Infantry Regiment and my first meeting ground with the army. Father and I took all of our meals in the tented messhall of F Company, which was to become not only my favorite outfit, but a unit of renown, the first to be hit by the Germans in World War I, the first to lose men: Privates Enright, Gresham, and Hay. The army ration in that day was twenty-seven cents, though the meals were ample. We became attached to that mess because my father had formed a close friendship with its commander, Captain "Mickey" Michaelis, the first army officer I ever met. By massive coincidence, it was his son, John, who thirty-six years later introduced me to Cate, the mother of my three daughters, at the Imperial Hotel in Tokyo.

My main contacts, however, were with enlisted men: First Sergeant Sholes; Spike Wintermeyer, the head cook; Nick Mulhall, the dour corporal who was to become the first prisoner of war lost to the kaiser; Private Floyd Smith, whom I would meet again as a fellow officer in France; Sergeant John Baxter, the moneybags of the outfit, a loan shark who would become a rifle captain in the American Expeditionary Force (AEF); and many others. I enjoyed the association with those old pros all the way. They did not talk down to me or seek to embarrass me, and I enjoyed their friendly conversation over the following months. While associating with them did not really draw me to the military, it had the residual benefit that at age fifteen I lost all fear of being in the infantry. Whereas nearly every youth regards the army with a little awe and trembling, though he is loath to admit it, the men of F Company helped make my putting on a soldier suit a quite natural thing.

Pancho Villa—in person, not a motion picture—was just across the Rio Grande and the attraction was irresistible. Though it has galled me that most of my life this brute has been treated as a modern Robin Hood by the mythmakers, whereas he was in fact a low-grade criminal with charisma aplenty, he already fascinated me because of the colorful stuff that had been written about him by the war correspondent, John Reed. The urge to see him was overpowering. He was then in control of Northern Mexico, or, to be exact, the State of Chihuahua, and most of his time he spent in Ciudad Juárez.

One could get on a streetcar at Stanton and San Antonio streets in El Paso and for five cents become transported in relative safety to the dead center of Ciudad Juárez, a modern Gomorrah. Bandoliered Villistas thronged Calle Commercio in the evenings, and one could move among them with less reason for fear than attends a present-day nocturnal stroll in Central, Forrest, or Belle Isle Parks. The average Villa adherent was not a *bandido vaquero* but a simple peon, and the average Mexican country fellow is a child of nature with little vice.

I took the streetcar. I already knew from soldiers of the Sixteenth that the main spots in Juárez were the Black Cat Casino and the Big Kid's. Starting at the Big Kid's place and losing a few quarters at chuck-a-luck (I have always figured that gambling was just another form of entertainment as much to be enjoyed for what it costs as the opera or a ballgame), I broke off to get to the Black Cat at 9:00 P.M. Villa personally owned that casino, which was a one-story affair occupying the most prominent corner of the town, recessed from the street and set in a garden of feeble palms.

Mostly curiosity moved me although, since I was hungry, I went first to the cafe and ordered a hamburger and a beer, which became my first taste of anything alcoholic. Before the sandwich could be served, a man I assumed to be Villa entered from the street, accompanied by Brigadier General Rodolfo Fierro. They settled themselves two tables removed from me. Villa was stockier and fatter than I had supposed, and the swarthiness of his face was less impressive than its greasiness; he sweated profusely and just let it roll. The brilliance of the whites of his eyes and the expanse of shining teeth when the mouth opened as he gesticulated reminded me of the great Teddy. He had taken off his stetson as if preparing to relax; so I got the full view. The rogue smile was winning enough. I guessed he was about half drunk. Pancho began thumping on the table with his pistol. Fierro's head came close to his as if to discuss something sotto voce. Then in an instant Pancho leveled the weapon on his forearm and pulled the trigger. The one bullet hit the forehead of a waitress standing within a few feet of me, opening the skull wide. She was kicked backward and fell without a sound. Then both men laughed uproariously, something passed between them, and they left the Black Cat in a hurry. So did I, not waiting for the hamburger. The cantina had magically emptied in a twinkling.

One baldheaded American followed me out. He had been closer to Pancho's gun than I and had stayed fastidiously calm. We caught the same trolley back to El Paso. He sat next to me and introduced himself—Norman Walker, war correspondent (and, oddly enough, an Indiana University classmate and friend of Doc Gilmore, my great chief on the *Detroit News* in later years).

Norman, whom I came to know as Squiggs in the years of our close friendship, told me what had happened. Pancho had bet one hundred dollars that he could shoot a Spanish comb from the girl's head by dead reckoning and had lost the wager. Nothing could happen to Pancho, who was king of all he surveyed; the incident became closed when the girl dropped. Though this was my first brush with violent death, I could so little comprehend what I had seen in those few moments that I was more numbed than shocked. I had seen enough of Villa to know that he was a no-good bastard and a cold killer.

Fall, which is otherwise the best of seasons in West Texas, brought school, and for the first time I went alone. Alice had met Joseph J. Willis, a Southern Pacific railroader, fallen in love, and married. He had grown up in Kansas City, next door neighbor to a younger boy named Maxwell D. Taylor. The latter went to West Point and ultimately became chief military adviser to John F. Kennedy and chairman of the Joint Chiefs of Staff. Our paths crossed a hundred times.

I was in high school. To paraphrase what was said of Philip Nolan, no one ever had a better time in school and no one ever deserved it less. My father had brought me to the right place. The young El Pasoans with whom I immediately became associated were the strongest, gentlest, and most generous teenagers one may ever meet. The city was tougher than nails and vice-ridden. Gunfights were common. A far-extended red-light district was just one block off the main drag. The kids went the other way. They did not drink and they honored women. There was no delinquency problem.

The atmosphere was too congenial. The opportunity to live it up decently was much too inviting to permit room for worry about marks in school. Dates and games were all I had on my mind; so I decided early there would be no homework. To compensate, I would have to pay absolute attention to everything said in class and try to get it down. By so doing, I might pass examination at month's end and squeak through. It didn't occur to me that this defaulting could become an exercise in the power of concentration, and that in consequence most of what I picked up from the little high schooling I had would stay with me through the years, whereas with the average student it does not. That was the bonus out of laziness or indifference.

Through two years I was as dillar-a-dollar a scholar as the school could boast. My record in history was deplorable. I took two courses in my junior year and was flunked in both. It was settled that I would never have a history credit to my name. Still, one of those failures paid big.

Mr. Brown had sixteen boys in his class and one girl. About once a week he would excuse her to tell us an off-color joke. He was all male. He used to say to us: "Forget about the dates and personages. The object of studying history is that we may learn from its processes. Either we do, or we repeat our mistakes." That bit sunk in. I realized it must be true and I never forgot it. Either history had to be a living science or it was merely another amusement. When in the Central Pacific Theater I insisted we use it that way, using our data as the basis for correcting operations, that new departure in military thinking was a debt I owed to Mr. Brown.

Across the Rio Grande, the scene and cast had shifted rapidly soon after my first sighting of Pancho Villa. Out of the pack of self-seeking intellectuals and politicos, along with brigands who had arisen to challenge Victoriano Huerta when that monster usurped power in Mexico City after murdering Francisco Madero, a sufficient number had finally rallied around Don Venustiano Carranza of Coahuila to semivalidate his claim as First Chief of the Revolution. His was a grotesque figure, theirs a lamentable choice, scarcely defendable even on the ground that a more promising alternative was lacking. Carranza was a walking fever, despotic in his conversation as in all else. More absolute than the pope, he was not more pleasant to look upon. Tall, ungainly, and much bewhiskered, he had tiny eyes behind tinted, thick-lensed glasses, making the face remote and flatly characterless. If it was impossible to think of Villa as the standard bearer of an elevated movement, it was not less impossible to believe that this apparition could regenerate and unify a people as volcanic and fury-filled as were the Mexicans in revolution.

Since this is not a history of the Mexican Revolution, Villa's smaller acts of vengeance and the reaction in El Paso will go unnoted. One incident is worth the telling, however. The El Paso county jail also housed federal prisoners, and included in the roster were several dozen of Villa's soldiers, picked up by the Immigration Service while trying to make a sneak entry. Typhus had broken out in Chihuahua. To safeguard the public health, the county jailer, Frank Scotten, proceeded to delouse the prisoners, using gasoline. With twenty or so of them collected, standing naked and well sprayed, someone struck a match. They all blazed and died, human torches in a scene fit for the pen of Edgar Allen Poe.

El Pasoans were horror stricken. When a few days later Villa's raid hit Columbus, New Mexico, the people in my city concluded that it was an act of reprisal for the burning of the Villistas. (There is no reference to this incident in any history of the raid.) The mood changed drastically. I was downtown that night. For the first time in my life I saw the terrible face of the mob, hundreds of Americans pummeling and pistol-whipping helpless

Mexicans. Many of them were bestially drunk. Floundering about on the sidewalks or dragging their hardly resistant victims into darkened alleys, they seemed to have renounced their quality as human beings by the act of coming together. The only sounds that came from this writhing mass were thuds, screams, and curses. When I tried to walk away from what I saw, the echo stayed with me.

The raid changed many things. National guardsmen descended on El Paso by the thousands. The old regiments marched away under Pershing on a forlorn and hopeless errand for which they were ill prepared.

Months later a real war came to the United States. By then the expedition had returned, still under the hand of a commander burning with ambition to lead any force that we might send to France. Pershing's statement that he did not seek the command of the AEF is pure fiction.

James Montgomery Flagg had done a poster portrait of Uncle Sam for the recruiters. The message was that the old chap wanted me for the United States Army. At least I took it that personally, and since the poster seemed to be on every street corner, there was no way to get it behind me.

I took the soft way out, held up my right hand and mumbled the oath, and that was that. Mother and Father were quite willing. Before quitting home I disposed of all my clothing and other main possessions, figuring my future would have no call for them.

Chapter 2
A Very Impersonal War

What I write of myself and the army in World War I is perforce no contribution to history. When one is not a student of the events in one's personal experience, time dims the memory. The trivial may leave a clear imprint on the brain when most of what was truly significant has long since faded away.

I recently spent a week at the Infantry Center in Fort Benning. My main object there was to interview officers of captain's rank or field grade for a book I was writing, *The Fields of Bamboo,* on further details of a battle (Operation Nathan Hale) fought three years before in Vietnam. I could remember the battle vividly because I was there, and getting the campaign documented was my line of duty. Of the twenty-six officers, only two had the photographic memory and recall of detail and conversation that in any way helped me. This is an average percentage and a normal group reaction. The majority of the other twenty-four did not even know where they had been. One field had dissolved into another. This demonstrates why I put no faith in any attempt to reconstruct battle history from what survivors say many years later. Such works are at best enthralling fiction.

Enlisting in World War I at Fort Sam Houston, I won my first bout with official red tape. When the examining doctor told me my feet were flat and I therefore could not enter a combat branch, I argued that I was an all-around athlete, had never felt a twinge in either arch, and was absolutely certain that my feet would carry me any place. He told me that he was merely repeating what the blotter had told him and had no choice but to follow regulations.

I said: "Look, Doc, after today you'll never see me again. If I break down, it will not be your funeral. What have you got to lose by letting me take a chance?"

He opened his mouth, closed it, reached for the form, and okayed me for unlimited service. I felt proud as punch. During my whole military life my feet never gave me the slightest trouble.

11

The taking of the oath was a watershed in my life, though not because I was throbbing with patriotism. I know that the average young soldier of yesterday or today does not feel that same way. It is more often a traumatic experience, especially if he goes into a combat arm. Not fear of death but fear of failure is the emotional preoccupation that makes army service abhorrent to the majority of young males. To the uninitiated, the military business usually seems harsh and forbidding. Literature makes its characters ogreish. On TV, if they are not portrayed as villains, they are dolts or clowns.

In the army I did mainly what I was told. My course ran smoothly. I adapted with ease to all army technics, with no need for adjustment. I found that the skills and coordination I had developed in body contact sports applied directly to the requirements of basic training: the handling of objects smoothly, hitting the dirt, the hard grind of the bayonet course, and even the stentorian use of the voice. Any seasoned ballplayer is better prepared for the transition to soldiering than a dead-shot rifleman who has that one specialty.

Having rejected study in school in favor of fun and games, on entering the army I did the opposite. Today my bumptiousness in that time seems incredible. Knowing nothing of what lay ahead, on enlisting I had shortened my name to Sam L. Marshall on the brassy assumption that I would rise to a command spot and a lengthy signature would waste my time. At seventeen that was pure egoism.

Reveille was abhorrent to me. I just couldn't get enough sleep. Scouting for some way of beating the bugle, I found that by getting school duty I would avoid all formations. I began applying, and since no one else was volunteering, I got what I wanted—school after school. The first was grenade school, a three-week stint for officers and noncommissioned officers (NCOs). In those days being a bombardier was a real specialty. We made our own jampot grenades and used live ones in bombing out traverses in a model Western Front trench system.

Disaster hit me in the classroom. During a class break, I sat idly at a table next to one Lieutenant Frankenstein. There were half a dozen grenade shells on the table. He pulled a pin from a citron, thinking it a dummy. So did I until it exploded and blew corrosive liquid in my eyes. I went to hospital blinded and stayed there for a month, bandaged, not knowing how much sight would be left. The trauma of that experience I have wholly forgotten. But when twice later in my life I was temporarily blinded, the accident in youth had so conditioned me that I felt no shock.

I returned to the outfit sans eyebrows and eyelashes and with the upper left of my face distorted from injury to nerve and muscle. After two years of massage and eye treatment my face became workably normal. There remained permanently, however, one hangover. My visage was fixed in a scowl that, especially in bright light, became a cross for others to bear.

I went next to demolitions school, and after that, reconnaissance and topographical school, where for a time I found my niche. Map-making was so much my dish that I became sergeant-in-charge of recon-topographical teaching at the division school.

Eventually I went overseas to attend the Infantry Specialist School at Châtillon-sur-Seine. The training area into which the division staged was north of Dijon in the Côte d'Or mountains along the plateau that divides the valley of the Seine from the valley of the Saône. One of the relatively poor sections of France, this rolling country was admirably adapted to combat refresher training, though it had not been garrisoned at any time during the Great War.

My outfit, when it arrived, still seemed green as grass, and it was served by a general staff and logistical backup that was not much better. We were based in a village named Bure-les-Templieres not more than two miles from where the source of the Seine bubbles up under a limestone cliff. Rumor told us that the village name meant "burial ground of the Templars." True or false, no soldier had set foot on that ground since the last Templar was planted there or elsewhere. Every cobbled street was encrusted with a five-inch paving of vitrified manure. The Roman road had not been lost longer to France under a millenium of debris. Still it was wonderfully springy to walk upon, something halfway between a crepe sole and a trampoline.

We troopers would have kept it that way for posterity, there being all too little bounce in life. Down came that hard foot of oversensitive higher authority. Before we were permitted to drill, goldbrick, or fire a Chauchat (that evil French light machine gun was ironically nicknamed "Sure Shot") we had to fall to with picks, drills, and shovels to divest the billet area of that overlay. It was like trying to spade a sea of rubber. But by the end of one week we had it made, all in the name of U.S. Army sanitary standards. Bure-les-Templieres began to shine and smell like a gardenia, though the cows kept coming, and for our work of destruction, the villagers, from the local idiot to the mayor, continued to glower.

Though there was entertainment, no Hopes, Bennys, or Dietrichs stormed our way to amuse the troops and make work easy for their press agents. There was only Elsie Janis. While the fight was on, the only music heard by the troops was our own singing as we slogged the dusty road— "Pack up Your Troubles," "Long, Long Trail," "Lulu," "Frankie and Johnny," and "Mademoiselle From You Know Where." We always marched carrying spiked canes because it seemed to help, though no Hollywood picture ever shows the AEF as an army of ash-swingers. When we passed a national guard outfit, we broke out with "I'd rather be a bulldog in a whore's backyard than be a brigadier general in the national guard" to the tune of "Casey Jones." They were no less ready with a flattering comeback. We were almost unspeakably gentlemanly.

Our uniforms were about as unsightly as anything the mind of man might devise, and we each had only one. Our rifles were poorly made and inaccurately sighted. Our other weapons were almost nonexistent, and had it not been for help from our Allies, we could not have fought. We many times had to bury our own dead after battle. We were never carried to any point that was within maximum walking range. Not knowing any better, our superiors kept as much weight on our backs as possible, hoping to build muscle, instead of lightening the burden to refresh the spirit. Despite such small woes, there was respect in us for higher authority and full belief in the sanctity of an order.

In studied retrospect I can honestly say of Pershing's AEF that I saw no better American fighting men until Vietnam. That first one was a crude army by present-day standards, unreasonably self-confident, high humored, boisterous, cocky, almost vulgar, but within it we strove mightily to help one another.

This is not a book about combat other than to outline the way it pivotally influenced my thoughts and my course through life. Though I participated in the Soissons, St. Mihiel, and Meuse-Argonne campaigns, except for certain graphic incidents that stayed in my brain I cannot write factually of either my unit's part or my personal role. Any attempted reconstruction would be a brick without straw.

I doubted that I could stand fire and at the same time was curious to know. Over the years since, from the study of many men in many wars, I have concluded that anticipatory doubt is normal in the emotionally balanced male, and the soldier who acts cocksure is the almost certain failure.

It surprised me to discover that fire of any kind did not unnerve me. I had no reflex inclination to jump, duck, or run. From the start I learned that losing myself in my work was anxiety's antidote. I had four and a half months in the fire zone with three different regiments. The passage of time and repeated experiences with artillery, machine gun, and mortar did not change me or wear me down, though to keep going I would flatten or seek cover like any other soldier. In 1918 I was mystified about my own reaction and wanted to know more. Was it because, being a kid, with no family responsibility and not even a girl back home, I had less to worry me than the others, or had something that I little understood so conditioned me? Even the question reminds me that I am more conditioned than Pavlov's dog.

To that questioning of self I attribute the pattern of my professional career. I wanted to know if a man's reactions, given fair health, stayed the same. Exactly fifty years later I was under fire for the last time, for thirteen days running in Vietnam; I was not simply moving about in the fire zone but under bombardment of one kind or another. Wherever I moved with my escort officer, U.S.N. Commander Billups Lodge, the well-known commodity hit the electric fan. My reaction was no different from 1918. I had work to do and stayed with it. The tour was exciting, not grueling. Courage is not the word for what I am talking about. Call it ease of adjustment.

My qualifications had moved up two notches before the Armistice came. In midsummer I had been detailed to the Theater Gas School at Gondrecourt to qualify as a gas defense NCO. I got to be one of those "experts" who in later years became more irritated than amused at the mock horror with which the society and its politicos view chemical warfare. We who were in the game did not feel that way. We had a main chance to beat poison gas if we acted sensibly, but common sense could not neutralize a bullet or a shell shard.

Graduating with top honors and first place in the knock-off-balance game called cockfighting, I proceeded to let the school down. My next time out at St. Mihiel I got gassed from playing wise guy. While walking through a small valley called the Stumpf Laager not far from Thiaucourt, I could smell phosgene but figured there wasn't enough to hurt me; so I didn't put on my mask. I knew better when I began retching, and then I stopped dead still and waited for an ambulance, or else it might have killed me.

For that bit of stupidity compounded, the down payment was eight days in the hospital, and the price went still higher some years later.

I finished the war at 11:11 A.M. on 11 November as a lieutenant of infantry* in a foxhole not far from Stenay. It was the day that I had never expected to see. A brigade commander from the 89th Division, Colonel J. H. Reeves, happened along.

He said: "Young man, have you anything to drink?"

I said: "Water."

He said: "Let us drink to it in water."

Though the canteen stuff was chlorinated, water never before had tasted half so sweet.

At the time the last shot was fired, we who were there within kissing distance of it reckoned that all our grief was gone with the echo, and henceforth life in the AEF would be one sweet dream.

Once one comes out of a combat situation a bit surprised and many bits overjoyed, he does not continue long in euphoria, thanking whatever gods may be for his unconquerable soul. The satisfactions of today do not stay in deep freeze for use tomorrow. As with the big thrill of getting done with a war, it is the same with the first landsight of America or passage past the Statue of Liberty after long absence abroad. The overpowering surge of

---

*Marshall was commissioned from the ranks and at age seventeen was the youngest commissioned officer in the AEF.

emotion is felt only the first time. The climbing of any mountain thereafter cuts it to the level of a plateau, as Sir Edmund Hillary might have discovered had he tried Everest again. The second view from the top is never as good, and the lack of satisfaction brings an ache to the soul.

As the Sioux say, it takes more than snow to turn a black dog white. Our winter of discontent in France befell the AEF not because of tired men sweating to get home, but due to high command blunder. The brass truly believed, for example, that the way to maintain discipline in a combat army once it stacked arms was to resume drilling the hell out of victorious troops. Such utter ignorance of the true nature of man within the military is not easily excused. The time had come to relax, and general headquarters at Chaumont did not even know the meaning of the word.

Of these undue pressures on a mighty host, I was not a victim but rather a sideline benefactor, powerless to supply a cushion to anyone except men close to me. I learned more from my post-Armistice experience than from all that had gone before. It was in those months that my ideas about the leading of men became fixed, and from that period came the beliefs applied in the writing of *The Armed Forces Officer* and the restoration of a demoralized Historical Division in the European Theatre of Operations (ETO) some decades later.

Chapter 3
An Uneasy Civilian

There was no GI bill for returned soldiers in 1919. The weary trooper home at last got absolutely nothing. But if he had not completed high school, and had become too aged from the wars to return thereto with any dignity, and especially if he had been an officer, college would admit the poor benighted bloke. In no other way might the pearly gates have become opened to me.

Simply to get a reading of these prospects, I had visited the high school my second day home. I was saddled and bridled, a rifle looie wearing a Sam Browne and Russian horsehide cavalry boots, bought in France from a Cossack captain who was running out of funds with which to stable a blonde. It was very dashing. In the lobby of the school, I saw two of the school beauties first off and in a few minutes of conversation, counting eeny-meeny-miney-mo, picked the one that I would ask to go dancing that night. Just that lightly it was done. So we went dancing. Later I married Ruth Elstner. We were just right for one another while the orchestra played, Vernon Castles in miniature, Veloz and Yolanda before their time. Everyone said so. Yes, we were just right. We couldn't miss. How idle now to look back and lament that, when two persons are so very young, it is not only possible but natural to assume that success in that which counts above all else in life—marriage—may be founded on the altogether superficial.

Drifting from job to job, I reminded myself only of Robert Louis Stevenson's description of the man who imprinted all things with his own incompetence. I tried brickmaking again, only to burn enough kilns to convince Father and myself that I had better take to the tall timber. Employed in a mine at Bisbee, I did all right until the price of copper hit bottom and the work force was curtailed.

On the morning of November 11, 1922, I stood watching an Armistice Day parade go by, my thoughts black as night. I was workless, three thousand dollars worse than broke, and sick at heart because I could not care for my wife and child.

Four years had passed since that foggy but otherwise utterly bright morning on the Western Front when the guns went silent and we felt exaltation beyond expression. That memory simply mocked me as the parade passed. My thoughts went like this: What's wrong with you? Not only did you make good in the war, which is the toughest game of all; you went over with a bang. Yet as a civilian, you're not worth a damn.

Though two days earlier I had wired Phelps Dodge Company, applying for a mining job in Tyrone, New Mexico, I was wholly without prospect. The confidence with which I had quit the army, that I had some talent as a writer, had swiftly withered and faded away.

Now, as the parade tailed out, something stirred. By chance only, I happened to be standing in front of the *El Paso Herald*. Two minutes later I was inside, asking G. A. Martin, the managing editor, for a job.

Martin was agreeable. He said he would take me on trial as a reporter. A few minutes earlier, on the same basis, he had hired one Nathan Lapowski, who was not without newspaper experience. There would not be permanent room on the staff for both of us. The pay range was from twenty to forty-five dollars a week, depending on experience.

"Mr. Martin," I said, "I'd like to start at forty-five."

That brought him from his chair.

He waggled a finger at me and shouted: "Are you crazy? You have just about talked yourself out of any chance to start."

"No," I answered him, "I'm remarkably sane at this moment. I happen to be three thousand dollars in debt and have a family to support. If I start at twenty-five or so, my creditors will be on my neck and will be pestering you. That will finish me. But at forty-five, I can begin paying off, and they'll see the wisdom of easing off. If I haven't made good in thirty days, I'd expect to be fired. So the most you can lose is less than two hundred."

He pondered for all of two minutes. "It sounds like a sporting proposition. You're on. Just don't tell anyone what you're making."

"When do I start?"

"Right now."

Hallelujah! I had become a reporter.

It was then noon. The home edition was already out and the staff was clearing away for lunch. Feeling like I was walking on air, I went to the street, bolted a sandwich, and strolled over to San Jacinto Plaza, one block from the *Herald* and the very heart of El Paso. At the center of the square in those days was a well-populated and crowd-gathering alligator pond, where I pulled up.

The Mexican caretaker was cleaning the pond as I watched quite idly. Then in a twinkling it happened. A 'gator lunged, grabbed him by the left leg and jerked it off. No screaming rent the air. The leg was wooden. I had my first story, which made the front page of the afternoon edition, a natural as we called it in that day, unbeatable suspense and the surprise ending. Later on the same day I was assigned to write a comic story about the meaning of the symbols and elisions used in cattle market reports at the local brokerage offices. That first day saw me off to a flying start.

The second day all my seniors had gone off on a big story about a maniac killer who had boarded the Southern Pacific train bound for Los Angeles. Big stories are not for cub reporters. So it was that I got the call from a deputy sheriff from El Paso who had the news of how the killer had been shot by the sheriff of Dona Ana County, New Mexico. And it was I who managed, ignorant as I was, to get out a slightly lopsided extra—but it was the largest-selling extra in the history of El Paso.

Other unbelievable breaks favored me during the weeks before the year ended, and I cannot honestly say that diligence or intuitive reasoning had much to do with them. As with my much later book-writing years in and out of the army, time and again I chanced to be the one man at the *right spot next opportunity's forelock*. Though I had ceased to be a cub in the first forty-eight hours, fate had to be extraordinarily kind to make me a veteran reporter within two months. My newspaper life was not unlike the political career of Cal Coolidge, for I would maintain that any literate person pondering his autobiography must regard it as wholly illogical that he should have become president of the United States. Consider that two months before he was hit by the lightning of the Boston police strike, his native Vermont published an honor roll of a thousand or so of its distinguished sons. That is a large list and Vermont is a small state. Several blanket manufacturers and a dozen buggy whip makers made the list. Cal didn't. His life was as if at an early age he had been placed on a moving belt bound to deliver him to the White House. Working in a far less consequential field, I too was unable to avoid the breaks that came my way.

Beyond doubt the beginning of style came from my lack of experience with the typewriter and the consequent habit of thinking things out painstakingly. It is my firm belief that having a keen intellect or learning how to think are much less important than the power of concentration whereby all that one knows about a given problem may be brought to bear in a given moment. That holds true of newspaper work, book writing, a command job in the military, and almost any field except waving a danger flag at the opening of a detour. The payoff is not in learning as such but in practical and positive application.

My guidelines on how to build what became my writing career were handed me by one person on a very special day. Arthur M. Lockhart was a big man in our town, president of the Rio Grande Oil Company, clubman, sportsman, and an amateur writer with no mean talent. About one month after I had turned reporter, he came to the office and handed me a clipping. "Read it. I think the guy's got something."

The sense of that piece was that the real newspaperman is the all-around writer. He can do a better job of sports writing if he can also write politics, and he's superior as an editorial writer if he has handled markets, society, the police beat, and done a humor column.

Without doubt, the principle was correct. The field was surfeited with specialists who usually limped when they tried any other subject. Therefore the true roustabout or all-around writer was bound to be the superior craftsman.

But in order to make money, in addition to trying for all-around excellence in news writing, a writer needed to have certain specialties, subjects that he had mastered and could write about reasonably well.

Within the next hour on that same day I had my formula, my plan for my professional life. In foreign affairs, instead of following the crowd and educating myself on Europe or the Pacific, I would specialize in Mexico and the Central American states. That way, I would get a crack at a revolution more or less regularly. Finally, I would train myself to be a military critic. The goal would necessitate much home study and the building of a special library, but once I made it, I would have practically no competition in this country.

So at age twenty-two I set my course and did not thereafter look back. Several months after the talk with Lockhart I was in Ciudad Juarez having a beer with Tad Dorgan, Hearst's justly famous sporting cartoonist, originator of *See What The Boys in the Back Room Will Have.*

"You do a slick sports column," Tad said. "But that name's no good. Sam Lyman Marshall. Who would remember that?"

"That's not my name. I shortened it when I went in the Army to cut down my signature-writing time. My full name is Samuel Lyman Atwood Marshall."

"Good God," Tad yelled, "You must be dumber than I thought. Your initials spell SLAM, and you don't realize that's money in the bank? It's perfect for a sports editor. It's perfect for anything. Nobody can forget that name. You start using only your initials tomorrow and never change."

I followed his advice in the next day's paper and ever thereafter. Dorgan was right. Next to what Lockhart said, it was the most valuable counsel ever given me. Many strange and wonderful things came of it. In World War II, I was the only soldier permitted on orders to travel exclusively under my initials because the commanders knew me that way and were better prepared to receive me. In cablese it looked too sweet for words, almost devilish, coming out Sugar Love Able Marshall. Years later a president of the United States was responding to a talk I had just made on a night when life peaked splendidly. This was Ike exactly ten days before he left the White House.

He was being awarded the Hoover Medal by the engineering societies of North America, and I had spoken about the magnitude of his achievement in the European Theater. Ike arose and said: "You may think of him as General Marshall. To the army he will ever be known as Slam and no other name would seem to fit. Slam, I'm glad that you didn't tell me how big that job was while the war was on. You would have scared the hell out of me."

Chapter 4
The Journalist's Trade

Writing sports for the *El Paso Herald* was for me a romp and a frolic with none of the tedium of other newspaper work. While I wrote sports, in my spare time I was sedulously pursuing the study of war. My approach to military studies on my own was deliberate, systematic, and strictly derivative of my own thinking. For instance, while I was watching polo, a transfer of thought began, unconsciously at first. As I watched the game, I began to think of the study and management of war. The fundamental simply had to be in the organization and maintenance of superior defense, since sound, practical offensive operations could only be launched from a secure base.

Looking back, I know that it was careful observance and analysis of the game of polo that turned me in the right direction. Through the years, when analyzing a military operation, or assisting in the guidance of a proposed maneuver, I pointed ever to the defense. Make sure of that and the attack must almost inevitably fall into place.

Reporting sports, I could knock off about four thousand words daily, which more or less continued to be my pace later in the book-writing years and even during military service. I believed then, and still do, that writing is not a gift or an art but a willingness to accept the required self-discipline. One must go at it every day, either to determine that the well is temporarily dry or to stay until fatigued. Nothing but the hard try determines what may come forth.

When I was moved up to the city desk, I worried mainly about whether the holiday from writing would vitiate such style as I had acquired. H. D. Slater, the publisher, shortly relieved that doubt by starting a morning paper, the *News-Herald*. He proposed that I write a full-length humor and light verse column to run every day down the left of page one—this in addition to my duties running the *Herald,* the post of managing editor having been abolished. Again, I was the only one who profited. The newspaper was for him a disastrous experiment, while my paragraphs and verses became quoted over the country and ultimately brought me a job offer from the *Detroit News.* This was fortunate since my job with Slater rapidly came to an end. He had financially overextended, and the *Herald,* one of the truly great newspapers in its time, expired, to be memorialized only in a hyphenated name on a Scripps-Howard masthead.

----------------------------★----------------------------

Detroit was to become in most respects simply a less exciting extension of my El Paso education in journalism, in some minor ways an improvement thereon, in major particulars, a letdown. In my personal life, my shaky marriage was coming to an end and I was glad of new horizons.

The journalism game was still exciting, but never soul-satisfying. It left an empty feeling, being a mirror of life and not the living of it. Above all, from first to last, I objected to most of the members of my craft because they were sideliners rather than activists. Community participation—in fact, contributing anything to the well-being of the society apart from the daily outpouring of information—is not for them. They really take the fourth estate idea seriously. Even were there not so many of them who think of the business as glamorous and setting one apart, their bosses are loath to let them figure prominently in any other activity. The *New York Times,* as one example, objects to any staffer taking leave to serve in the armed forces during wartime. The lordly attitude is that writing for the *Times* is more important to the nation.

At the *Herald* in El Paso, while we sweated out an edition, we raged and we fought, and the city room sometimes became bedlam, but when work was done, we were friends and our families associated. At the *Detroit News* there was none of this. Gentility and quiet were pervasive at edition time. The paper was overstaffed and so highly prosperous that tenure was virtually assured for all hands. Talent so abounded that too little of it found adequate expression. After hours, there was little or no friendship. The move was like jumping from a three-ring circus into an old soldiers' home.

Its compensations were in the few great men on the *News* who became my associates and whose scope was not merely that of professional competence but also included the human spirit. One of the saddest commentaries on life is that one meets so few along the path of whom it can be said in utter honesty: "That person touched me; he did something for me; I am so much better because I knew him."

George E. Miller, the editor of the *News,* was one of those. He was at that time a man of seventy, handsome, immaculate in dress, with very twinkly eyes and snow-white hair. His first gesture was to offer me a Blackstone cigar. Later I learned that when George was expansive or particularly pleased about something, out came the box of Blackstones. It was as automatic as was his expression, "Oh, shit!" when he wished an editorial writer, or any other person, to know that an argument had been heard, lost, and finished. His one other idiosyncrasy was to reach for a blue pencil before he picked up any piece of copy, a habit most discouraging to a writer, as I later told him.

In that first talk, Mr. Miller asked what I could write other than a humor column, or possibly editorials.

"I'm very good at writing sports," I told him.

He positively glared. "Mr. Marshall, sports writing is trivial and will get you nowhere. Don't waste your time that way."

That was the time to pull in my horns. "Mr. Miller, I can do any kind of writing that a newspaper requires. I've worked at it."

"Good! We don't have anyone here like that. Everyone specializes. You will be allowed to write on what you please when you please, and I'll put you on the street for thirty days just so you will get to know the city."

Mr. Miller kept his word. Following my month "on the street," though I sat in the paper's inner sanctum among the group that H. G. Salsinger, the irreverent sports editor, called "the parsley boys," I was encouraged to range far and wide, and on one particular Sunday I had articles in eleven different departments of the paper.

Sardonic Salsinger, his executive editor Harry LeDuc, and the Texan Sam Greene, who as a writer was second only to Sal, were a triumvirate extraordinary. Salsinger and Greene were not simply first-class sports reporters; they were distinguished writers and studious analysts. I chose to continue writing sports as much as I could in my outside hours, feeling that worthwhileness in the company I kept was of greater value than my technical progress as a writer. Never in my life have I had any doubt about the relative worth of these sometimes conflicting choices.

Detroit and the *News* were a desert as far as the watering of my military interests went, though Mr. Miller was agreeable to my attending small revolutions now and then south of the border. My adventures in Mexico became many and my travels covered the length and breadth of the republic so that I knew every state and territory. Just before he retired at age seventy-five, George called me in one day and said: "Now I am going to your beloved Mexico. You just go ahead and make all the arrangements."

I tried to shake him off. He had gone through two recent bouts with pneumonia. I asked: "Mr. Miller, do you think your ticker will stand it?"

He laughed. "Does it really make any difference?"

Shortly he was on his way. Pneumonia hit him again in Mexico City, and he died in the arms of his friend, Josephus Daniels.

W. Steele Gilmore, his successor, possessed the same warmth and extended to me the same measure of confidence. My newspaper career continued.

There had been a prolonged oil strike at Tampico and negotiations were getting nowhere. The talk of the day was what government would do about it. The chief arbiter was one Mr. O'Connor, a vice-president of Standard Fruit Company. We had met and warmed to one another in Villahermosa, Tabasco, out of a common liking for the dictator, Garrido Canabal, an enthusiasm we shared with George Creel. Garrido was hard but also incorruptible.

Arriving in the capital on a Friday morning, I called O'Connor. He said: "Meet me in the billiard room of the University Club at five and come in the back way." I knew something big was coming and cabled the *Detroit News* an attention-getter.

O'Connor came straight to the point. "As you know, Cardenas will be on radio Saturday night. There's a big buildup about it, much mystery. I know for certain what is coming. He will announce the expropriation of the oil fields. I am certain of it."

I cabled the *News* that I had an exclusive, a real grabber for the Sunday paper, forecasting what Cardenas would do on Saturday. I thought I had a sure-fire exclusive. Within four hours came the return message from W. S. Gilmore: "Forget the story. No interest in expropriation story here. Roosevelt's attempt to pack Supreme Court concerning everyone." Almost incredulous, I said a four-letter word, and doubtless some more, and took a taxi to Cuernavaca to brood over a lost weekend.

If nothing else, the turns and encores in Mexico furthered my conditioning for work ultimately far more important by giving my nervous system repeated workouts. As to health otherwise, I will not eat uncooked vegetables abroad, save in a few states of western Europe, and so I have avoided Montezuma's revenge and related indignities to the bowels. As a foreign correspondent, I found other forms of risk vastly preferable.

One such risk was flying when all things were uncertain. Around 1932, the CAT airlines, headed by C. E. Hull, with headquarters in El Paso, were trying to make Mexicans air-minded. Hull wired me that in addition to his passenger flights he was going in for freight business in a very adventurous way, and that I should come on down. That being the time when my first marriage had finally foundered, it was my dish of tea.

The line flew Lockheed Vegas, and their landing speed, compared to what I had known, made one's brisket curl right next to the bronchial tubes. Very shortly I was with Lowell Yerex in El Paso, he being a one-eyed ex-Australian ace who later would organize and command the Honduran Air Force. Yerex was a stunter and ex-barnstormer, a delightful companion, and as reliably durable as they come. Our job was to pioneer the transport of freight into remote mining camps and bring out bullion. I believe we were the pathfinders, blazing the trail for a kind of operation now fairly commonplace.

The February weather was impossibly bad after we cleared El Paso. Soon we were flying just above the rails of the Mexico Northwestern. Twice we clove through telephone lines without crashing. Twice we made forced landings on the desert and waited for the fog to lift. With these delays, we got to Chihuahua City after dark, and Yerex made a perfect landing, without lights, on what was supposed to be a field adequate for the plane.

We barreled not more than 250 yards and seemed hardly to have cut our speed when the landing wheels of the Vega violently crashed into some object that first spun the ship, then threw it nose down, wrecking the prop and the fuselage. That we could walk away from that one with nothing worse to show for it than Yerex's bloody nose was luck fantastic. There was no help at the field; we extricated ourselves alone. Then we looked for the cause of our debacle. The general commanding the Mexican garrison was a polo nut and had ingeniously given the flat a dual purpose. The obstacle that had flipped us was a line of raw pine sideboards revetted here and there with adobe brick. Next day we bucketed back to the border and were given another Vega.

On the next try the weather was clear. Our object was the San Luis mine at Tayoltita, Durango. That property had been worked since the early seventeenth century, and through all that time its supplies and people had trekked upward from the west coast through the sierra, the pack train journey taking five days. Once we made our landing, the camp would be within forty-two minutes of civilization. It seemed well worth doing. Owned by W. R. Hearst, the mine was a bonanza, the ore body being as rich in gold and silver content as any on earth. Also, as I was to learn during the next several days, despite its isolation, the camp itself was idyllic, its health, social, and recreational programs being beyond fault, as were its schools. Tayoltita stayed that way until the Revolution and the unions washed out its harmony and beauty.

We had no chance to scout the landing field to see if it was practical. We had been told that it was a strip of stamp sand or tailings about 500 yards long by 40 wide laid deep in a canyon. The camp was connected by telephone with the supply point at San Dimas just above Mazatlán. Yerex told the *mozos* to put in about one-quarter ton of cargo so that we would go in loaded. He left the choice of material to their judgment.

At 11 A.M. we were set and ready to go. Then came a call from the mine manager's wife, Mrs. Swent. She hadn't tasted seafood in fourteen months. Would we please bring along at least two large lobsters? Anything to oblige a lady.

A half hour later we were airborne and headed for the sierra. I gripped one large lobster in each hand, there being no other place to put them. The boxes had not been strapped down, and if the cargo shifted, Mrs. Swent's dinner would be crushed. To take my mind off the lobsters I began reading the markings on the boxes to either side of me.

Then I yelled at Yerex. "Do you know what we have here?"

He yelled back. "No, what?"

I gulped. "Four cases of dynamite and six of cyanide."

He considered, then called back: "What about it? If we hit that mountain before we drop to the canyon, it won't make a damned bit of difference to either of us."

A most practical view of realities, though from that point forward I forgot the cases and concentrated on the lobsters.

Well, we made it. The day was sunny, the air satin smooth, the landing without incident. Every last person in the camp was present for our arrival. The next two days at the camp were fiesta compounded. All operations were suspended at the mine. Care took a holiday. Only one other time have I known such mass delirium—August 25, 1944, when we liberated Paris.

Nevertheless, after a few days I wanted to leave. One afternoon, after Swent, Yerex, and I had gone hunting together in the heights above the camp, I told Lowell I wanted to fly to San Dimas the next morning.

He said: "What's the rush? I like it here."

"I just thought of a girl in Detroit I'd like to marry, and I want to get up there as fast as I can."

Swent asked: "Do you know her very well?"

"Not really, not well enough to call her by her first name. But I have seen her face and noted her grace and I would gamble on her above all others."

Yerex picked up his rifle and said to Swent: "He's an odd one, so let's get back to the camp. We fly tomorrow."

Accordingly, we headed for San Dimas and Mazatlán, whence I enplaned on a much more vital mission, one that before the end almost overwhelmed me with a sense of life's goodness, beauty, and tragedy. My marriage to Ives Westervelt lasted twenty years. The first three we lived on the summit and were exquisitely happy. Then multiple sclerosis hit her while she was touring Europe, and she returned with her left side partially paralyzed. For seventeen years I watched her try to bear up against her terrible affliction with its gross indignities. She had almost superhuman courage always and the will to sacrifice for my well-being. Most friends fell away. Few mortals care to be embarrassed by the presence of an invalid. She kept her radiant smile and her facial loveliness until death took her, the body ravaged, the mind clear, the spirit undismayed. Of these things it is so hard to write that enough has already been said.

★

By the late 1930s my private military studies had begun to pall. There is a decided limit to mental and imaginative stimulation that can be drawn from re-reading books and doing exercises on paper. Deprived of professional contact, there is no proving or testing ground for such new ideas as come along. The last army chief of staff I had known well was Charles P. Summerall, and we continued to correspond; he was ever ready to encourage and confide in me. Except for annual visits at Fort Bliss when I made El Paso, my only contacts with the military throughout the decade were with the army polo players who came east for summer.

Then Harry Bannister came to the *News* to direct the operation of WWJ radio. Harry was a big lumbering hulk with a jovial manner and a deep bass rumble. We found one day in chance conversation that we had both been commissioned second lieutenants of infantry in France on the same day. With this common bond, we started lunching together, debating military science in the *News* cafeteria. More than we could imagine came of that.

Another main prop to my career was Colonel Joe Greene, editor of the *Infantry Journal*. Here again I race ahead of my story to tell one anecdote. When my first book *Blitzkrieg* was published in 1940, Greene personally reviewed it and praised it as the "soundest and most concise analysis of the Hitler war machine and the war problem confronting the United States to appear in print." In the same mail came a review from the *Nation* written by Freda Kirchway that read: "Mr. Marshall wastes much space on patriotic fustian and editorial platitudes. Perhaps his mental processes are themselves in a dangerous state of inefficiency. One suspects that he knows nothing about military tactics." Not knowing the meaning of fustian, I decided I could do without the word. As to the rest of it, you pay your money and you take your choice.

It was in the late thirties that I wrote for the *Infantry Journal* my first paper ever on the outlook for armored forces and their role in any great war of the future. The thesis was organized around three central ideas that were at variance with theories of the period's most inspired advocates of armor who foresaw tank masses operating in virtual independence to ensure swift movement.

By that time I had already become convinced that General Hans von Seeckt's much-publicized doctrine on "lightning war" was a calculated hoax, and that he well knew it. It was too simple to be true. In fact, his own writings invalidated his theory.

I believed that tank columns, bent on deep penetration and supported by air power, threatened the very heart of government. Nothing but a nation fully armed, with total mobilization, might block them. Therefore any nation making such a move must be fully prepared. The nature of the weapon itself foreordained that war could be staged on a vaster scale than ever before.

Strange as it now seems, these were unorthodox ideas even in those years, when the fighting in the Spanish Civil War was casting a long shadow, for they were not self-evident. The war in Spain proved nothing about tanks. Seeckt, no chump, was at the same time writing secret memoranda to his General Staff emphasizing the general conclusion I had reached.

Of this somewhat disembodied concept came my first paper on an armored future, wherein I advanced several radical propositions:

• Armor would never obsolete infantry. Should a great war come, we would see infantry decline and go into eclipse for a time. Then it would have to bound back in stronger form than ever before with its own tank-killing weapons.

• Fortresses were not dead, as some prophets said, due to the rise of armor and the building of a more mobile artillery. They had simply changed character. Every great city, directly menaced, would become a fortress. Attacking tanks dare not defile into narrow, stone-walled streets, and the defenders thereof would be debouching on radial lines, ready to hit armor in flank when it attempted to bypass.

• Unlimited horizons, such as the Ukraine afforded, were not the best tactical opportunity for tanks in that armor would be tempted to go on too fast and too far, outrunning its support and supply and finally becoming beached.

Some weeks after the article appeared I was astonished to receive under British postmark a letter from Major General J. F. C. Fuller, the great military writer and theorist, indeed, the Clausewitz of this century. He wanted to know where I had gained my knowledge of armor. I replied honestly that I had only thought about it, that I had read his books, especially *FSR III,* either to agree or disagree. Where I took exception, I wrote it out in marginal notes. If my points in disagreement were enough to comprise a theme, I wrote one, mainly for my own amusement. While this process cannot be called original thinking, in any case it was what I did.

Fuller's next letter to me started off: "My Dear Boy, so far as I know you are the only person in the United States or Britain who is taking me seriously." Continuing, he said that it would take another great war either to validate my propositions or disprove them, and that, while he hoped it wouldn't come, he feared the hope was vain. The letter closed: "If I can ever do anything to help you, I am at your service."

Few things more needed than these kind words ever came my way. Shortly afterward he dedicated a book to me, his *Machine Warfare*; I couldn't believe my eyes. Over the years and almost to the day of his death, I called on him many times; always he responded and lifted me. The same must be said of my other dear friend, Sir Basil Liddell Hart. Because these two Englishmen took my military writing seriously in the early years, helping me with suggestions for improvement and providing me with guidelines from their own writings, it mattered less that so little encouragement came from within our own shores.

Few Americans, least of all authors, are generous in this same way, though my close friendships with Sherwood Anderson, Carl Sandburg, and Stoddard King, in years before I thought of book writing, buoyed my hope of achieving something solid some day. We all need that feeling along the way and it comes like a benison, the thought, the startling realization that older men with intellect respect one's mind and spirit. Harry S. Truman, Dean Acheson, and Frank Murphy are among those who, through their letters, have exalted my being and made existence seem more radiant. The late Laurence Stallings, whom I never met, made one day glorious by writing me at the time *Pork Chop Hill* came out: "It's what I tried to do with *What Price Glory,* but I failed."

Though I have always tried to help young writers, I have otherwise been neglectful about paying back for all that was given me. Of that I was reminded during a visit with Basil Liddell Hart at his place in Buckinghamshire shortly after World War II. We were on his croquet green. Midway in the game I began telling him how digging into his books in the 1920s had given me the urge to do a little prospecting on my own. He looked down at me from his great height and said almost mournfully, "Slam, why in heaven's name didn't you ever tell me? I had no idea you drew anything from my work. I thought it was all Fuller." I felt sudden shame. He was right. I had never said one word in praise.

Apart from the effort already mentioned, I did no military writing in the thirties worth recall. Had there not been a world cataclysm, the odds are that I would never have done a worthwhile book on battle or military history.

Chapter 5
War Correspondent to Military Analyst

Throughout my life as a correspondent, I have known no restlessness. Most of the way I relished the excitement of the highly volatile and complex environment that war generates and the reckoning of its factors: first, the personal ones of getting along and cultivating the productive contacts, and next, describing the nature of the struggle while estimating the prospects for both sides and what will finally come of the conflict.

As I see it, these are the essentials for a war correspondent. There are other approaches to the work, and beyond doubt mine was conditioned and narrowed by the fact that I was a military tactician first and later drifted into writing. The journalist who sees all war as a feature story and can pound out hot copy may have little trouble marketing his wares. People may in time hail him as a great war correspondent. But if his knowledge and experience are so limited that he cannot analyze what he sees, while he may entertain, he will not inform. His kind remind me of Iago when he vents his spleen against Cassio:

> Forsooth, a great arithmetician
> That never set a squadron in the field
> Nor the division of a battle knows
> More than a spinster.

From the beginning of the Spanish Civil War, I knew that I would go, and I anticipated a stimulating tour that would last long. My sympathies were wholly with the Loyalist or government side.

The revolt that had begun in Morocco on July 17, 1936, was less than a week old when I came out of Mexico via Cuba for a visit with my wife, Ives, at Key West. The first afternoon we went fishing in the Gulf with Ernest Hemingway aboard the *Lady of Pilar*. Another guest was Harry Sylvester, the novelist.

33

Through the afternoon we cast and cast and in the end caught nothing except the measure of how different were our views of the struggle then beginning.

I said I expected to head for Spain shortly, and that I would go in on the Republican side because my emotion and sentiment favored it.

Hemingway said he had no interest in the war and would not go. He explained it this way: "I have dear friends on both sides and so I am neutral."

Then, as an aside to me, he added: "If you wish the key to my apartment in Madrid, you may take it along."

Sylvester was shocked and saddened by what Hemingway said and so expressed himself. Being a devout Catholic, Harry was committed to the insurrection and disappointed in his great friend.

Though I felt no surprise or other reaction then, what did astonish me later was that after Hemingway changed his mind and went to Spain, he wrote as a passionate crusader for the Loyalist side, blind to its increasingly red coloration and uncompromising ugliness.

My own dispatches may still speak for themselves, if they are of any interest.

I was in Aranjuez when General Emilio Mola, who had just taken command on the Madrid front, spoke to a group of correspondents about the "fifth column" of Nationalist adherents within the city who would help deliver it to him quickly. A few of us who heard him on radio helped give world circulation to the term that on that day became the synonym for treachery and espionage.

At the same time, I had concluded that Madrid for the time was impregnable, that the siege would go on and on, and likewise the war. The Loyalists in the end must lose it, however, for that side was already gravely short of basic supplies such as cotton, petroleum oil lubricant (POL), and road transport, and the pinch would steadily tighten. Whereas Hitler and Mussolini were solidly supporting the Franco forces, the Russians were wildly exaggerating their contributions, and the Spanish Communists were greatly overestimating their material resources.

Seeing the logistical imbalance between the two sides as devastating and final, that is how I wrote it. Once I had made my estimates, however, I wanted out of Republican Spain. One could not work with any ease of mind there. Until Vietnam, it was the only war-torn country I had known where one felt more secure up front than in the rear areas. The law-keeping forces having been almost eliminated when the Guardia Civil swung over to the Nationalist side, the war became a facade for private assassinations, muggings, kidnapings, looting, and reprisals between rival political gangs.

The official attitude toward correspondents almost inevitably became one of suspicion and semihostility. The censors were surly and sadly incompetent. The border watchmen were belligerent and hard as nails. Nothing redeemed the situation except the generous help given me by Lawrence Fernsworth, the brilliant correspondent of the *London Times.*

My mouth went dry when I thought of going out through Port Bou. It had been rough enough entering. The anarchist committee had grilled me for half an hour. The *Detroit News* meant nothing to them; none but the chairman had ever heard of Detroit. I was finally passed because that worthy decided I talked "the language of the people," meaning that I spoke border Mexican.

My heavy sweat about the exit came of a determination to smuggle $500 out of Spain. One of our U.S. consuls was rotting in the Port Bou brig for trying that stunt with a lesser sum, when the law said that the limit was fifty pesetas. I knew that I would join him, if caught. But I had not been advised of the money embargo when I entered Spain, and I didn't care to be cheated of my hard-earned cash when I left.

I had a plan, the elements of which were a multiflapped wallet, five already-dead tickets on the Irish Sweepstakes, and my guesses about the Spanish temperament. When I entrained at Barcelona I felt fairly confident. By the time we paused at Tarragona, I was shaking all over and knew I had to risk confiding in someone. The device looked just as simple as ever, but the hazard was almost choking me.

Across the aisle was a man mountainously fat, of uncertain age, and seemingly jovial. I chose him because he smiled, and thus I met a seventy-two-year-old Basque who was one of Basil Zaharoff's lieutenants for forty years. He had been in Spain for three weeks working out a munitions deal with Francisco Largo Caballero, the prime minister.

He listened to my scheme and said: "I think it will work. Being an old man, I'm going out with only fifty pesetas. What you're trying is worth the risk. I'll be watching for you."

At Port Bou, he preceded me in the passenger lineup and caught the rail shuttle to Cerbère in France. Some of the passengers, including several women, were stripped by the committee. One man ahead of me was taken by the police.

My turn came. I was frisked from top to bottom, but the inspector let me take out my own wallet.

On one side of it were the allowable fifty pesetas.

He fingered the inside of the next flap, came out with the worthless Sweepstakes tickets, and fairly shouted: "Prohibido, contrabandista."

I started laughing, showed him the date on the tickets, began shaking my head about what a fool I was to bet on horses, and said I hoped he'd never waste his money that way.

When he joined the laugh, I put the wallet back in my pocket. The good money was in the flaps on the other side.

Though the controlled tension ended when he waved me on my way, as I boarded the shuttle for Cerbère I was shaking in every joint and pouring with sweat, but I felt happier than the man who broke the bank at Monte Carlo.

The Basque waited for me at the railway cafe in Cerbère with two bottles of champagne already on ice at his table.

"Marshall, I was quite sure you would make it, so I made ready the celebration."

"Mighty generous of you, and I need it."

It was his turn to laugh.

"Not generous at all," he said. "This evening is on you. Who has all the money? I am a pobre with only thirty pesetas. I gave the other twenty to a beggar at Port Bou."

"And to think," I answered, "that they waste a name like Largo Caballero on that guy in Madrid."

When we arrived in Paris, we both made for the Hotel Continental, by coincidence my favorite resting spot in the city and his habitat off and on for many years. The moment he reached the front desk he was out of hock. Everyone knew him.

My wife had already come up from Nice and checked in. Late in the evening my Basque friend called on the telephone. "You must come to my room. Good news! Something new to celebrate."

Ives and I went down.

In his room, the table was spread with iced magnums, pâté, caviar, several cold birds, and other goodies galore.

I said: "Well, hallelujah, but what's the good news?"

"I just got it over the radio. In your country, Mr. Roosevelt has been re-elected."

Then he added: "There'll be another world war. You'll see. That's a man who will stand up to Hitler."

---------------------------------★---------------------------------

During the summer of 1939 the storm clouds thickened over Europe. I continued to do my editorial stint, run the travel pages, and keep track of sports and horses. The day after Warsaw was bombed Harry Bannister of radio station WWJ opened another portal for me. Believing, as a result of our luncheon conversations, that I had special insights on war, he invited me to start doing a fifteen-minute daily analysis of developments, ranging as widely as I saw fit. I began that same night, explaining why I thought Poland would be defeated within thirty days.

Two weeks later, Mr. Gilmore of the *News,* taking note of the broadcast, decided that a daily column along the same lines might attract a few readers. Neither assignment lightened my load of other editorial responsibilities. It was just something extra added to my work, which shows what little importance was attached to military writing.

The tasks were not overly demanding, inasmuch as I had been studying for twenty years to prepare myself. I knew the military geography of Europe better than I knew the roads of Wayne County. Military criticism is not the same as reporting or commenting. The prerequisites are professional knowledge and field experience. One must know enough about the possibilities to be able to anticipate and forecast accurately. Unless that can be done at least 85 percent of the time, one should not try. The work may be likened to one person estimating capabilities and intentions with as much accuracy and more relevance than a fully manned general staff.

Still, there is no simple explanation of how one develops this sixth sense. Beyond knowledge is required a vivid, but practical, imagination. To attempt factoring, when that is lacking, leads only to errant guessing. Wholly to the point are the words of Lord Macauley: "No past event has any intrinsic importance. The knowledge of it is valuable only as it leads us to form sound calculations with respect to the future."

My first opportunity to prove to myself that my approach was valid arrived with the march of Hitler's armies into Poland. In my broadcast on the third day of the invasion I foretold when the campaign would end in a total Nazi conquest and the surrender of all Polish armies. When I missed by only twenty-four hours, I knew it wasn't dumb luck.

All along, however, my immediate colleagues took the opposite view of it. In their view, my guessing was simply better than theirs in the early rounds; since the laws of chance applied, they would even the score further along. Though that is one of the less amiable characteristics of human nature, it didn't get under my hide. It was to be bracketed with the mistaken assumption so common within the military that on any given project two half-wits will form a whole wit, whereas in fact they make a quarter-wit. For what it is worth, I simply pass along the observation that through my lifetime I have known few news writers or TV oracles who did not believe that their opinion on any military question was just as apt to be right as my own. American war correspondents in general are so certain of it that they shun professional military knowledge as if it might pollute them.

My own type of war broadcasting was slam-bang and devoid of ifs, maybes, and on-the-other-hands. Whether vice or virtue, there is deep rooted in me the feeling that in all communicating my fellows are entitled to know what I think as clearly as I can express it. What I was taught as a child was confirmed by my teenage experience in leading troops in combat. The business of being accountable for the lives of one's fellow men should impose an abhorrence of double-talk and equivocation. In that situation, it is imperative to talk straight and let come what may; to be ambiguous or to be misunderstood due to vagueness is the cardinal sin. Yet it has long appalled me that many otherwise able commanders will wittingly publish operational orders that may be interpreted several ways, not to give latitude to a subordinate, but expressly with the object of being able to shift the blame if the show goes badly. In my book, this is despicable weakness and unpardonable selfishness.

But back to the war. Though Poland had been swiftly overrun and enchained, American society and the majority of the "experts" that had popped up like mushrooms had settled back to enjoy a complacent view of the war. Everything was bound to come out all right. The Western Front was in sitzkrieg, with nothing interrupting the calm of the nonengaged armies except a little shelling and a few minor patrol actions.

On the vulnerability of France, my conviction was not based upon any nice calculations of the contest between massed armor and a heavily fortified belt. It was obvious the Maginot Line had the irreparable defect that any one rupture would be fatal, since the very existence of its deep works tied the mass of French soldiery to fixed positions. Also, its left flank dangled in air beyond Sedan, and the historic line of invasion through the Low Countries was relatively weaker than in 1914. As a military man, I have never entered into, or had patience with, the scholarly arguments over whether the defensive or offensive is the stronger form of war in any given period. It is a fictitious approach to hard reality. Preponderant military power generates from a judicious balancing of offensive and defensive strength, which precept is more honored today by the Soviets than by the Americans.

Furthermore, while Foch's dictum that the morale counts thrice more than the material in warfare is one more attempt to unscrew the inscrutable by launching a chestnut, men do count more than machines. Otherwise modern Israel would have been snuffed out long ago. I had looked over the French Army carefully in 1936–37 and had concluded it was poorly trained and demoralized. Too much bleeding in the Big War, and too much Pétain, had gutted it. Also, I held the dimmest possible view of the character and ability of General Marie Gamelin, though he was being portrayed as a second Bonaparte. I wrote to my friend Edgar Ansell Mowrer in Paris: "Quit touting Gamelin and the French Army; you are dead wrong." Edgar, unlike my colleagues, did not question my sanity when I reiterated that the might of the Maginot was a myth.

My mail in those days was tremendous; it came by the bagload, as many as four thousand letters in one day, provided what had been said or written a few hours earlier was disagreeable. The bulk of it abused me as a Hitler agent or Communist fellow traveler. Here is the best gauge I know of the rise of tension in America in time of stress: the vaporings from the lunatic fringe begin at once and build up steadily. But it was for me a winter of hard and constant work.

When I had relieved myself of writing the daily estimate, I had approximately three hours free out of what had been a fifteen-hour work day. Lest time hang too heavy on my hands, I sat down at night and began writing to myself. Why was I so certain that the Allies were lost in Norway before the fight was well begun? How did I know that Hitler would next turn west and his armies would prevail? While I had written many pieces tangential to these questions, I had never reasoned the problem through from first to last.

For seven straight nights after my day's work was done, I stayed with this study for six hours at a stretch, usually quitting around 3:00 A.M. because my brain would give no more. When it became tied in knots, I unwound with several shots of scotch. By the end of the week, I had written 60,000 words, all in longhand, and there were still only twenty pages of manuscript. I wrote in a script so small that I needed a magnifying glass when putting the work into typescript, having discovered along the way that this miniaturizing was an aid to concentration.

With little reference to texts and depending mainly on memory, I traced the development of French and British military policy in the two decades following the Great War and analyzed the reasons for the false assumptions that they carried into the new conflict. Then I wrote out the tactical considerations that would make a debacle of the Norway venture and sketched the invasion of France and the Low Countries as if it had already happened.

By week's end, the manuscript that finally became my first book, *Blitzkrieg,* was 85 percent complete. I hadn't the faintest notion that my life had taken its largest turn. When the fall of France was followed by some smaller disasters during the summer of 1940, it was necessary only to go back over the paper as a whole and work in the more superficial details, names of battles and leaders, dates, pivotal actions, and so forth. While it was much like updating a play, far more than a blueprint was already there. I had a fairly accurate picture of the war, the problems that it raised for the United States were set forth with clarity, and I felt satisfied that I could continue to anticipate the war's developments without committing significant blunders. The "I can do it" feeling is like the starting gun in a race; all else is preparation for that moment. *Blitzkrieg* has stood the test of time.

I was just nicely out of this compound nightmare—doing the book and knowing that France and the Allied cause were on the verge of disaster—when Hitler's bullies smashed into the Low Countries. The outlook seemed so unrelievedly black that I felt compelled to write it that way. This is not the custom in a business that leans toward what is called balance, meaning that little rays of sunshine should be inserted here and there if only for the sake of keeping the readership happy. After the entry into Sedan I knew that my estimate of the Battle of France would be confirmed by events. No other newspaper was publishing what I would call a realistic appreciation of the battle's progress. My mail increased in bulk and vituperation. There was every reason why my chief should have felt some alarm about the rising protest that I was trying to win the war for Hitler. Gilmore kept his hand on my shoulder and I felt comforted.

I needed that touch. Those were dismal days. Because of my role and my radio programs, I was called to do a great deal of public speaking in Detroit. Two days after the German penetration at Sedan, my audience was the Wayne County Medical Association. The occasion, I thought, called for frankness. Many of my listeners had patients with nervous disorders affected adversely by the inordinate pressures and anxieties of the period. It seemed best that they know the worst of the ordeal that lay ahead. I leveled with them. When I concluded one hour later, these men of medicine gave me no applause, some booed, and others arose and turned their backs on me.

One lone physician, deep in his cups, followed me into the lounge and offered to buy me a highball, which I needed. "Marshall," he said, "you're an idiot. Your mistake lies in assuming that MDs are realists and intelligent. Like hell! They're naive simpletons with no real knowledge of the world. They're snobs, overloaded with false sentiments, and as wishful as children."

From that hour I was prepared to believe, and as I went on I found it to be true, that bankers, lawyers, and engineers respond best and with greatest understanding to a hard, objective presentation, while teacher and press audiences are down the totem pole, with MDs the lowest of all. Dentists, on the other hand, are surprisingly receptive.

After the day France surrendered, the fire against me from the flanks suddenly died. Still, I felt no peace. The event had shaken me as none other. I adored France with the love of an adolescent. Veterans of the Great War remembered the French poilu in retreat. I recalled mainly the fierce feeling for freedom and for their cause which burned in the average Frenchman after four years of conflict. The 1917 mutinies meant less to me than that Frenchmen could still rally. Too early I came to believe that that spirit was imperishable and that earth knew few greater hopes. When in the thirties I saw how badly the French army had declined, there came only a partial awakening. While writing one thing, I prayed nightly that my estimate would be proved wrong. I went right down to the wire hoping for the miracle that could not happen.

During the weeks that followed France's capitulation, I went ahead with *Blitzkrieg*, making those changes essential to giving the analysis the authority of events completed and already become history. It was truly astonishing how little rewriting was required. When at last I was satisfied with the manuscript, I sent it out simultaneously to three New York publishers, which is a measure of how little I knew of the proprieties of authorship. My embarrassment was considerable when I received three acceptances.

Two of the acceptances, however, were highly qualified. The great Max Perkins responded for Scribner's that he thought the book was grand, but that, as he viewed the war, the Germans would certainly have to invade England, and that, since such an event would wash out my theme, he would have to mark time and see. A very gentle and encouraging reply from W. W. Norton expressed much the same apprehension. He wrote that he had just lunched with Max Perkins and that they agreed in their analysis of the military situation. It was my first tipoff that book editors imagined they could think like G-2s.

The earliest publication date that anyone promised was six months hence, which delay riled me, since time seemed to be of the essence. I believed the book—written in warning—should get to the market with all speed. I wrote William Morrow and Company, which had proposed the shortest wait, and told them that prompt publication was my interest above all others.

I expected a rejection, and in August and September of 1940, coincidental with Japan's adherence to the Rome-Berlin combine, I went on a tour of Canada's defense installations with half a hundred American and Canadian publicists and military from both countries. For a fortnight we moved about by special train. My stateroom mate was Angus McDonald, Canada's navy minister, and a more engaging companion than this frail Nova Scotian would have been hard to find. We spent our spare time together competing in writing doggerel.

At Quebec I got a telephone call from William Morrow and Company. They had accepted the challenge and would publish *Blitzkrieg* in two weeks, without fanfare or publicity, provided I would come at once to New York. The book hit the stands faster than any work I knew except the latter-day quickies on the death of John F. Kennedy. So launched, the commentary went six editions.

That same fall Congress passed a selective service law and the United States semimobilized. Had it done so in the spring of 1939, when the storm warnings were clear, there would probably have been no World War II. So saying is not to blame Mr. Roosevelt for anything except his unwillingness to risk his personal political fortunes; had he done so, he doubtless would have failed. When much too late the issue was raised, all seventeen members of the Michigan delegation voted against the draft, chanting as one, with Arthur Vandenberg acting as chorus master, that "we want to make the volunteer system work." That was too much for my stomach. In November they were all re-elected. That night I said on WWJ radio: "Now I want to tell you about these hypocrites. They say they would make the volunteer system work; yet they must know that throughout the national history Michigan has been last among the forty-eight states in providing volunteers to the fighting forces in peace and war. If all others volunteered at our rate, the standing forces of the nation would now be less than one hundred thousand men. So the volunteer system, by the view of the delegation, is getting men from North Carolina, Tennessee, Kentucky, and Texas to do our share of the fighting."

A phone call came from Congressman John Dingell. He was crying. He said: "That's the worst beating I've ever taken. I agree with you. But what would you do if you had sixteen men on your back asking: 'So you think it's better for you to play the smart guy?' I'm not a smart guy but I promise you never to make the same mistake again." Quite incidentally, by his own definition, Dingell was a very smart guy. He didn't repeat blunders; nor does his son, who followed his father in Congress.

When one year later the draft law came up for renewal, I paid my own way to Washington to have a talk with Dingell. Over bean soup I said to him: "I know voting for the draft will be tough, but if you go for it, I'll make six campaign speeches for you in your district." Not batting an eye, he replied: "I keep my promises, so you do nothing for me. John Lesinski [another congressman from Detroit] is already thinking of changing his position. You make him the same proposition and he'll go for it." Lesinski came in a few minutes after that and the deal was made. With the switch of two Michigan votes, the draft was saved, 171 to 170—this three months before Pearl Harbor. That's the story—or a part thereof—behind what is cited as the closest squeak on a critical issue in the history of the Congress and the nation.

★

If I have rushed on, it is toward adding bits to history at the expense of continuity. I had been writing that Hitler and his generals must nerve themselves to invade England or they would ultimately lose the war. I still believe that the German chance of success was much better than even and that the Nazis withheld finally because of their master's awe of British sea power. The Battle of Britain, like the campaigns in North Africa and Mussolini's stab at Greece out of Albania, was not difficult to factor. In each case the outcome was all but impossible to miss. The unexpected is recurrent in battle, even as its frictions are constant, and sometimes determines the result temporarily. Still, in essence, the study of contending sides is basically a study of overextension, its onset and consequence.

For example, when Rommel reached El Alamein, it took no daring to say with finality that he would go no farther, though there was flapping and quaking along the Nile, and by then my rivals in long-term forecasting were writing bogeyman stuff about German and Japanese power coming to juncture somewhere east of Suez. As if that were not too wild a dream, the national bestseller had become Alex de Seversky's *Victory Through Air Power*, which had as its theme that the war had been lost to Hitler and the one chance for recovery was through strategic bombing out of North American bases. The perspective in Washington was hardly better. It was not dismaying but simply absurd.

My second book, *Armies on Wheels,* was written one year after *Blitzkrieg* and covered the war's development until that time. This one required the conventional five-to-six months' incubating period. There was never a more trying hour for a military author. The Germans were well into Russia by late June, 1941, having won their cheap victories around Bialystok and being on their way to others at Smolensk and beyond. My manuscript had to go forward by July 10. Experts at the War Department were freely predicting that the Red Army would continue to melt away and that Hitler's forces would win before the snows came. If they were correct, then Morrow had bought a bad book, for I couldn't see it that way. It wasn't that I had a high regard for the fighting quality of the forces under Stalin; they had performed execrably in the war against Finland, and in the first stages of Operation Barbarossa they looked still worse, having massed too close to the western frontier, which made them easy victims of the panzer columns when they were fully formed and fresh.

But grit would certainly slow the machine as it got in deeper; the Russian countryside was too vast and the people too many for what Hitler was attempting. I expected the Russians to hold out through the first winter, with the Germans being stopped short of Moscow. Thereafter the Wehrmacht would suffer increasingly from the cardinal sin of overextension, since the dictator was fatally stricken with the disease.

That was pretty much how I wrote my prognosis, which by rare good fortune stood the test of events. Just for fun, having already signed my contract with Morrow, I sent a copy of the manuscript to Simon and Schuster to get their curbstone opinion. It duly arrived. The editor chided me that I had underrated the grand tactics of the Wehrmacht and the power of the German armies. He wrote: "I advise you to read the new book by Colonel Foertsch and possibly you will change some of your ideas."

This admonition went unanswered for four years. Then, in the summer of 1945, I wrote my belated reply to my Simon and Schuster mentor: "Now is the time to revise my ideas along the lines you suggested. Colonel Foertsch is among my prisoners. What do you suggest I ask him?" If it was the perfect squelch, it went unanswered.

General Arthur G. Trudeau was then a colonel on the faculty of the Command and General Staff School at Leavenworth. When the book appeared, he wrote me that he agreed with every tactical concept put forth, which was the beginning of a perfect friendship. When some time later the army opened the Tank Destroyer Center at Fort Hood, Texas, the commander wrote me that the main ideas in *Armies on Wheels* had been approved as the center's basic doctrine.

From the time of the Panay incident I felt it inevitable that another great war would see Japan at our throats. The failure of the people, or rather, the press, to support Mr. Roosevelt made it so. The embargo on war materials—particularly scrap and oil—after Tokyo launched the Greater Asia Co-prosperity Sphere, though called a provocation by some historians, was not the fateful turning point. Japan had set her course; war would have come, one way or the other. In mid-November, 1941, I was at the office of Navy Secretary Frank Knox. My old friend, Hal O'Flaherty, now a commander, was Knox's chief of press relations. Hal told me: "In the Pacific our ships have been directed to fire on sight at any unidentified submarine." I took his word and wrote that war was now unavoidable.

On Thursday, December 4, I spoke to the assembly at Wayne University, until then a center of pacifist activity and leftist dissent, though the attack on the USSR had quieted the commies. I wanted to shock them. I said: "I am speaking at your senior banquet Tuesday night. We will probably be at war before then."

Still, I could not get my colleagues at the *News*, other than Gilmore, to believe. Nancy Brown, a columnist for the paper, had scheduled a great gathering of the faithful to dedicate a bell tower to eternal peace on Belle Isle from noon until 2:00 P.M. on December 7. A less felicitous timing of the misappropriate is not on record.

That Sunday morning I went for a walk in Palmer Park with Frank Arnoldy, a White Russian who had soldiered under Wrangel. The more we walked and talked, the more agitated I became, and at last I said: "War is right here—now—let's hit for home and get the noon news."

In the very instant that I flipped on the switch came the first word of Pearl Harbor. At once I called Doc Gilmore and Harry Bannister to alert the *News* and WWJ so that Detroit would be told. The station was tied tight to Nancy Brown's psalm-singing exercise in praise of peace, and it took us one hour to get that act off the air so that we could talk about the world explosion in the news business. I have heard it said early, late, and often that keeping the public informed is a large responsibility. Any belief in it died long ago. The public does not wish to be informed. It likes to be amused. Least of all does the average American desire the truth when it is unpleasant.

Two days after Pearl Harbor I wired Major General Alex D. Surles, chief of public relations of the War Department: "Am available if you need me." My old friend replied: "Wouldn't think of wasting your talents in my office. Sit tight. The army will make the best use of you." No promise was ever better kept than that one.

   With that, I get back to my appreciation of the late Harry Bannister. As I review my life, it strikes me that I have done nothing by myself. I am a leaner and have been one since childhood. There may be such a thing as a self-made man, though I have never met one. Self-confidence is not born in a person. What we have of it, and what it enables us to do, we owe to others. My profile depends on the space that others grant me. Bannister, more than any other person or influence, was responsible for my having become a military critic, a dabbler in history, and a brigadier without school tie. He said the right words in the right hour. He opened one door and it led to many others. In his own memoir, Harry Bannister claimed credit for my launching and he was wholly correct.

Chapter 6
On Becoming an Expert

Following Pearl Harbor I was called to Washington to be expert consultant to Secretary of War Henry L. Stimson.

It is a title conferred on such persons as might not otherwise be willing to stir, there being no secondary allure such as a living wage. As one of his expert consultants, I saw Mr. Stimson exactly once, though not to be consulted. My civilian genius was drafted to establish the particulars of the Army Orientation Program, which was charged with creating morale-building and information materials for soldiers that would also be useful to gobs, leathernecks, and birdmen.

The initial task given me was to write a budget request for $7 million, the first time in my life, and the last, that I ever had anything to do with a budget of any kind or size. The living that spring was easy. Congress, playing like Brewster, was trying to give away millions and even a nonexpert at nothing might have written a satisfactory budget request.

Then I went on to the larger things of life. General George C. Marshall had in person drafted the directive setting forth what might be done under the heading of orientation. It was a paper revealing the breadth of that remarkable mind. His directive gave the operator maximum latitude, pointing out that the movers of the program could accent ideals, patriotism, and post-war objectives or could concentrate on training and technical requirements, along with reports on the war's worldwide developments. There might also be an effective combination of these radically different approaches.

That charter seemed just as felicitous as the company into which I fell. Colonel Lyman Munson, chief of information of the Special Service Division, had made the request that brought me to Washington and had gathered to himself the most illustrious collection of talented men ever grouped in any part of the General Staff. Among my immediate associates

47

were Frank Capra, Anatole Litvak, Paul Horgan, Eric Knight, Hodding Carter, and Irwin Shaw, and they were all wearing soldier suits. Tom Lewis, then married to Loretta Young, headed our infant radio branch, and I was one of his counselors. I followed the others into uniform on August 1, 1942.

In my talks with Tom Lewis, I suggested making a dramatic record out of the platters from such events as the bombing of Warsaw, the London blitz, the Nuremberg rallies, and the Churchill speeches in order to stimulate troops. Together we visited NBC and CBS in New York to get their cooperation. They were enthusiastic and promised to produce the records. Then swiftly they cooled and told us we could have nothing. They had realized that what we asked could be a big sale postwar product.

The continuing experience with figures in the world of letters went well beyond my immediate colleagues. I heard from my old friend Cecil Forester, creator of *Hornblower*, that he wanted a job in the division. I replied that any such job would be a waste of his formidable talent and suggested that I could arrange to get time at sea for him aboard an American war vessel. Instead, he shipped on a British light cruiser. Of that came his book, *The Ship*.

Then I got an application from Stephen Vincent Benét. He wanted in and nothing would satisfy him but active war service. He wrote that he was sick of characters like Hemingway with their pretensions that as artists they had no obligation to participate. Benét couldn't qualify physically or as to age or in any respect other than his attitude. While he was in limbo he sent me one of his verses, which I don't believe was ever published:

> Civilians hate. Civilians yell "Get Tough!"
> Civilians gripe about "a happy war."
> Civilians say there isn't blood enough.
> Civilians seem to want some more.
>
> Soldiers are slightly different about blood.
> It gets spilled out of them, and on the spot.
> And they find certain kinds of hate a dud.
> And they know whether men are tough or not.
>
> Ask the dead sergeant in the broken stuff,
> Just how he'd like some cutie to explain
> The war he fought was "soft" or "just a bluff,"
> And, if he doesn't answer, ask again.
>
> That's all. Oh, yes, I know. In various lands
> Civilians stood and took it by the millions
>
> And propped the leaguered state with their bare hands—
> But, boy, not these civilians!

★

In the summer of 1942 the Pentagon began to buzz with the rumor that the United States was preparing an invasion. Soon I got word that I was to do a special chore in connection with it; forthwith, I was to start writing a brief manual for the instruction of troops. It would inform them about the terrain, the customs of the countryside, and the habits, ceremonies, taboos, and so forth of the people.

The task would have been large enough had I known where we were going. No one came to tell me and my repeated efforts to convince higher authority that I had to know the invasion site if I was to do the assigned work got me nowhere. I could not even learn who knew the secret or had the authority to impart it. When I pressed inquiry along these lines, nothing came back but a wise look.

Then one day I voiced my exasperation to Helen Cane, my secretary. She giggled and said: "I'll tell you all about it," and in the next few minutes she described the general plan for the show-to-be, explaining that she had learned it from another secretary, one Sylvia, who had learned it from her own boss. In this way I learned about Operation Torch, the invasion of French North Africa, and so went about my work. I commented in a memo to the General Staff that this wasn't security but razzle-dazzle. High authority agreed. I was promised that next time out everyone would be more cooperative and communicative.

Eventually, I was notified of another similar task. Two bird colonels from the Operations Division (OPD) came calling and, after closing the door and excusing Helen from the room, said rather heavily, "It has been decided that you are to be admitted to security secrets in connection with some work you are doing."

Ah, here was the real McCoy at last. I said yes and waited, mouth open.

One said: "That's all we are authorized to tell you,"

They picked up their locked brief cases and left. An hour later I got a telephone call from another colonel in OPD who wished to know if the two gentlemen had called. When I said yes, he told me I was to come at once to his office.

We exchanged the time of day and then he said: "Now, I want you to think of the continent of Europe."

"I am thinking very hard."

"Well, don't exactly think of the continent as a whole. Think only of a peninsula jutting from it."

"I am thinking." The fact was I was becoming more thrown every moment.

He went on. "Now don't think any longer about the peninsula. Think instead of an island that is very close to it. Your work is supposed to relate to that island."

"I am thinking all right, but what island are you talking about? It does make a difference."

"That's all I am authorized to tell you. You are to proceed from there."

Such was the extent of my briefing on the plan to invade Sicily (which, as I remember, was named Little Husky). It was an exercise in mental telepathy. Since I put little stock in ESP, during the weeks that followed, while I toiled at the project, one thought plagued me: "Suppose I'm wrong about it. What if the guy was thinking about Corsica?"

Things worked out finally, if only because I have some talent for guessing games. Helen was no longer able to feed me the straight dope. That was because Sylvia had changed jobs.

Above all else, these experiences revealed the small boy streak in so many grown men. Given a secret to handle, they insisted on treating it as if a mystifying personal manner was the best way of safeguarding it.

On one occasion I got a call from yet another colonel in OPD. On his desk was a cablegram from our command in the Mediterranean Theater. The cable requested the writing and publishing of basic guides on twenty-two European and Middle Eastern nations, several of which, such as Bulgaria and Rumania, couldn't possibly become lodgments for our forces. I told the colonel the cable made no sense; it would mean two years' work and most of it would be wasted.

"I agree," he said, "but the cable doesn't mean what it says. Most of the names here are a screen. There is only one area here that really counts." I asked which one.

"I can't tell you, I truly can't," and at that moment the point of his pencil came to rest on one name in the cabled list. He looked up brightly. "Do you get me?" I nodded and went out. The truth is that, almost thirty years later, I still don't get him at all.

To work off my annoyance at these shenanigans, I wrote a bit of verse about how to classify papers, titled "Security," and circulated it strictly for the amusement of my own staff. It read:

> If to small whimsies you're addicted,
> Stamp all you've written thus, "Restricted."
>
> When matters have no great potential,
> Then kindly mark them, "Confidential."
>
> But if you're drooling to some weak wit,
> For God's sake, think to tag it, "Secret."

Major Eric Knight cutely leaked that bit to *Time* magazine, which played it big. The next thing I knew, two sleuths from the Inspector General's Office were prowling our corridors in search of the varmint who had lampooned the security system. I told them I couldn't imagine who would do such a thing. It was the truth; I couldn't imagine who would do such a thing. It was the truth; I didn't have to imagine.

★

I had taken over the preparation of the *Small Guides to Foreign Countries* from the public relations division. That mountain had labored six months to bring forth one mouse, the "Guide to North Ireland." At that rate the war would be over and the troops home before we had worked through the British Isles.

When the transfer was made, Pearl Buck was already under contract, with a large fee prepaid, to write a guide on China. Among other things, her manuscript had set forth how to distinguish between a Chinese, a Japanese, and a Korean by examining the foot. We had visions of our troops standing the natives on their heads to see which ones should be shot. Other scholars looked over Miss Buck's writing and said it was so full of error and misinterpretation that it was best thrown away. We did so and farmed the work elsewhere.

I personally wrote the first five guides in our shop, including Burma, New Caledonia, and Egypt, to set the tone and get things moving. They were ready three weeks after the start. The writing was no problem and caused no drag. It was the interminable reviewing that slowed down everything. Under department orders, what we produced had to be approved by G-2 and Wild Bill Donovan's Office of Strategic Services (OSS). The intelligence people were sticky enough, but the OSS were real nitpickers. Too many of its people dreamed they were scholars and would hold up copy for as much as sixty days.

The one safe way to get rid of this barnacle was to prove its worthlessness. That called for setting a trap. The chance arose with the forwarding to OSS of the manuscript for the "Guide to Java," without signature. Three weeks later it was returned with a sheaf of critical comment. The woman who did the review was especially caustic about the writer's ignorance of the tribes.

I called the head of the OSS review committee to ask: "How much time has the lady spent in the East Indies?"

It turned out that she had never been there but that she was very widely read on the peoples, problems, and particulars of the region.

I said: "That's what I thought. The guide was written by Dr. Van der Plaas, governor of East Java, cited by authorities as the most knowledgeable man on the peoples of Java."

Came a wail from the other end of the line: "Why didn't you tell me?"

Right then, without any approval from above, I dispensed with all review save our own, and no one tried later to skin me for it.

Writing the short guides to foreign countries, preparing the charts and copy for the War Department *Newsmap* publication every week, getting out the daily summary of the war's developments that went to all army units, and taking care of the special writing projects that the General Staff unloaded on us all too frequently, were exacting and tedious tasks.

We were not in any real sense a general staff section. We were a small publishing house, undermanned and underpaid, but our division managed to survive in strength and with some brilliance. Captain Paul Horgan was in the office next to me. His star as novelist and historian has become more lustrous with the passing years, and as I write it shines as bright as any in the national firmament. Fortune is rarely so well deserved. As a soldier, Paul had gentleness, goodness, and generosity. To every problem he brought a fresh mind and a sincere good will. Such minor vices as envy, bucking for favor, or taking a joy tour at public expense were beneath him. When I was of troubled mind or in need of dispassionate counsel, I went to Horgan.

One day I sought him out because I needed a very special kind of man from civilian life to be commissioned major. On his first mission, while still in mufti, he would have to be able to win the confidence of high authority in Canada and Britain.

Paul said: "Get Ted Davison."

The name meant nothing.

Paul continued. "British poet. In youth a friend of Rupert Brooke and Jock Priestley. Served in ranks in the Royal Naval Division in the other war, later commissioned in the Intelligence Division of the British Admiralty. He's now Professor of English Literature at Colorado University."

It sounded good. I called Davison long distance and he said he would come at once. Such was the beginning of one of the dearest friendships of my life. I came to love Ted like a brother.

Edward Davison had everything that good officership requires—forthrightness, charm, voice, language, manner, orderly thought, and faultless nerve. He was the only staff officer I ever knew who could take a paper I had worked half through and complete it in the same idiom and style, with no break in the continuity of thought. We teamed several times in later years on staff papers of the greatest consequence to the army and to the nation, such as the initiation of the North Atlantic Treaty Organization (NATO) and of arms aid.

Ted had the essential qualities of the sportsman: he disagreed fairly, concurred warmly, and participated enthusiastically. Of large and imposing frame, he resembled in a curious way W. C. Fields, though his blocked-out features were somehow handsome. His humor was inexhaustible even amid trial, and when he was in that mood, as when he meditated deeply, his eyes kindled with fire.

If I write of him elsewhere in these papers as if he still lives, it is because thinking of him that way is a comfort. Ted died while I was in the middle of this work. His son, my friend, Peter Davison, whose talents are not less than those of the father, did not send me the word. For sparing me when Ted died, I am grateful to Peter, and I had best close this off with some of Ted's own lines:

> Poet and friend of friends, beloved by me,
> Even as my spirit your steep pathway climbs,
> Darkness is folded round your golden tree.

★

The army, not the White House nor any group of civilian reformers, set about to repair the constitutional hurt to all our people through the enforced evacuation of Japanese Americans from the Pacific Coast. It was General George C. Marshall's own idea and was bucked to the office of Assistant Secretary John McCloy for implementation, but McCloy did nothing about it.

The problem as a whole was dropped in my lap simply because my director had volunteered to General Marshall that I could write the program, including policy, and even the palaver that the field teams would put to the people at the War Relocation Centers. That entailed drafting the scheme for recruiting the 442nd Combat Team of Nisei, putting through the General Staff the inducements we would offer the colonists for their cooperation (such as post-war citizenship for the Issei), writing the White House message on the new departure, and circularizing the national press to win their active support.

The assignment was in a very real sense an absurdity, for essentially it was not a writing task. Rather, it was a highly complex and multifaceted General Staff undertaking in a highly sensitive and volatile area. If it failed, there could be irreparable damage to the national honor and tradition. I had no doubt that I could satisfactorily delineate the bureaucratic and public policy aspects. In the psychological factor lay the rub. I knew nothing of the Issei and Nisei mind; yet if we went wrong there, we would fail wholly.

Knowing I was beyond my depth, I sought counsel of Colonel Rufus S. Bratton, former chief of the Far Eastern Section of Military Intelligence. Rufe, whom I had not met before, is forever identified in the national annals with Pearl Harbor. Through no real fault of his own, he was among those who took the fall for that disaster. In the movie *Tora, Tora, Tora* Bratton's role is dramatized more heavily than that of any other American. Though he must have still been hurting deeply from his misfortune, Rufe received me as gently as he would a long lost kinsman. For six hours we talked things out. By the end I felt I understood the problem in the round, and returning to my mill, I got into the paperwork.

Here was a mountain of toil. The War Relocation Authority, Army Intelligence, and the provost marshal general were supposed to take it from there, either acting together, or with one of them assuming central direction. At the final conference, I found that each was sidestepping and ducking ultimate responsibility out of sheer gutlessness. I volunteered to take charge of the field operation. They were all quite willing and even showered blessings on their pigeon.

When I returned to the Pentagon, my director hit the roof. He had wanted to reap all the credit possible but without risking getting his fingers burned. I told him that was contemptible. Then I went to General Surles and talked things over. I told him I expected heavy trouble at the camps and that I wanted no public information officer along. If trouble came, I'd try to smother it myself and keep it from the press, provided he'd trust me that much. He would.

Those next seven weeks were the roughest I ever spent in the army, and far more trying than combat. I was dealing with mass hysteria, with thousands of sadly hurt people. There was a great riot at Manzanar and then a whole series of nasty incidents in the camp at Tule Lake. Wherever violence broke out, I went as the troubleshooter, and there was no way to put it down but to counter force with force, out-move them, keep them guessing, and make them know they couldn't get away with it. Before I was through, I had stockaded under military police guard almost 400 people who had entered into a conspiracy to defeat the government's program, and not one hint of the trouble had appeared in the national press.

My only mainstay was McCloy's executive, an old cavalryman, Colonel "Powwow" Powell Scobey. Every day or so I would have to call him to report that I had violated a regulation or direct order, seeing no other way to proceed, and would be ready to face a court when I returned to Washington. Good old Powwow would answer: "Go ahead, Marshall, and we will face that court together." Even the FBI bucked me initially, the locals being under the influence of the California realtors and secondhand car dealers who, more than Attorney General Earl Warren, bear the shame for the iniquity of the evacuation.

My part in the affair was finally over. All of my field assistants were given ten days of extraordinary leave because of the strain of the operation. I was ordered to return to Washington posthaste by first plane. Quite incidentally, my report to McCloy on what I have capsulized here ran 231 pages.

My clever director was waiting in his office to tell me what the rush was all about. In my absence, he had accepted from the chief of staff two more next-to-impossible assignments to be bucked to me.

First, and of immediate moment, I was to write a plan for the indoctrination of enemy prisoners of war. He said: "You know, it's just like what you have been doing in California—working out things for the alien mind." I told him that the relevance somehow escaped me. Then I asked how much time I had. He said practically none. He had promised General Marshall to come up with the paper Monday morning. Here we were talking about the business late on Saturday night, and I was feeling mighty bushed.

When I put on my greatcoat and started for the door, he asked: "But where are you going?"

I said: "To Washington to get pie-eyed. By the time I come out of it, what you have been saying may make some sense. It makes none now."

By late Sunday afternoon I was out of the woods. There are tricks in all trades. In General Staff work, when staring at a blank wall, one writes a paper cut like a kimono: it covers everything and touches nothing. Then, before the recipient discovers that he has been spoofed, more time for sweat and study has been acquired and the second and supplementary paper is sent forth: it outlines the hard policy and covers the implementing detail. That is how things were done to meet the Monday morning deadline. It was on the next day that I sought help from Ted Davison, who in the end had to take on the whole program of indoctrinating our POWs.

Later in the week the director gently broke to me the news of the second overcommitment. My shop was to start producing pamphlets describing our battles for distribution to the American wounded in hospitals abroad. I told the director it just wasn't possible; neither in the Pentagon nor anywhere else was there a feedback of information to give body to the narratives.

He looked as if I had hit him, and for once I was ready to join him in a good cry.

He said: "I can't go back to the chief of staff and tell him it is impossible to comply with an order."

I said: "I can, since it happens to be true."

Then he gave me permission to proceed, provided I would promise to "be discreet." I told him I would do better than that: I would wear my one clean soldier suit.

In this, my first meeting with General George C. Marshall, General Tommy North served as the interlocutor. Marshall acted much surprised when I told him that not even the General Staff had dependable data on our fighting operations.

He asked: "Then what is the Historical Section of the General Staff doing?"

I said: "Sir, it is still bogged down researching World War I."

"Then no one from the army is covering this war?"

"No one."

That about sums up the conversation, though he told me I could forget about the pamphlets. He made a few notes as we talked but seemed only mildly impressed. Though courteous enough, he showed no interest in me and asked no personal questions.

I had no intimation whatever that the talk would change not only my military activities but the whole course of my life.

Chapter 7

The Mice and the Mountain

To borrow a few phrases from Ridpath, we three light colonels of the General Staff, John Mason Kemper, Charles E. Taylor and I, felt that June morning in 1943 like a troop of boy scouts ordered to capture Gibraltar.

We had suddenly been relieved of other duties, brought together in a cubicle on the fifth floor of the Pentagon, and told to plan procurement of the history of the U.S. Army in World War II.

We were given no guidance whatever. Every part of the organizational task, every aspect of operations, would have to be plotted from scratch. This was nineteen months after Pearl Harbor. Guadalcanal had been fought through the year before, the same with Buna, Gona, Midway, and lesser battles in the Pacific. Operation Torch, after a slow start, had rolled to a total success with all German power swept from Africa. The hour was so late that we didn't have time to regret what we might already have missed.

John Mason Kemper was a professional soldier out of West Point; Charles Taylor, a history professor from Harvard. To these companions in labor (and the word applies in both meanings) I pay the simple tribute that I cannot now imagine how the historical program could have succeeded without their ardor, energy, and massive common sense. From them I learned many lessons, chief of which was that scholarship is as valuable in the military as elsewhere, but not more so than fellowship.

That first day I was asked to scan a staff paper as thick as a Sears catalog (the work of Generals Twaddle and Bull), analyzing why the history program had failed in Pershing's AEF. I sailed through it in an hour or so, then wrote a staff paper in eight lines. Its essence was that the historians had not been given access to command decisions or to the fighting zone, and that, unless we were given these rights and supported in them, we would fail also.

Two light colonels in the Operations Division nixed that paper on the ground that what we asked would mean interference with combat forces, which was pure nonsense.

Once we had somewhat sketchily concluded our planning, I immediately set about writing the official chronicle of the Doolittle raid on Tokyo for the army, air corps, and navy. An all-service panel had been set up to do the work. My colleagues heaved sighs of relief when I suggested that for the sake of efficiency I'd rather go at it alone. During the research, I made a number of startling discoveries. By checking Tokyo newspapers for the several weeks that preceded the raid and then interviewing American internees, including Ambassador Joseph Grew and Chip Bohlen, who had returned on the *Gripsholm*, I learned that Tokyo was undergoing a three-hour air raid practice alert when our B-25s went at the city. Of that coincidence came their salvation; the alerted city could not be alerted. There was no way to let people know: "This is for real." Furthermore, the Japanese had not been wrong in saying that some of our air crewmen had violated the laws of war. Two tail gunners had lost their nerve in the tree-top-level run across Tokyo and had fired into the street crowd. Then, by ill luck, Doolittle's ship, which carried only incendiary bombs, had wafted a few pellets onto the largest hospital in Tokyo and the fire consumed it wholly.

More tacitly than formally, there was an understanding among us from the start that my role would be that of the homebody, the copy chief who from the Pentagon worked over the material that would (we hoped) flow to us from overseas. That was natural, since I was professionally qualified as a writer and editor.

Kemper, as our chief, figured to do the fronting for us, winning command cooperation abroad and setting up our small task forces. He made his first try in the invasion of Kiska and scored zero, since Kiska proved to be a dry-run exercise. The Japanese had fled. From that deserted island he cabled me: "Bang goes the last of my Aleutians," which was spoken more truly, if not funnier, than he knew, for it was while flying back that he decided that the pathfinding job should be mine.

The switch came of eminently sound reasoning and is a fair sample of how that keen mind worked. I alone in the group was familiar with combat and was known by name, if not in person, to many of our higher commanders abroad.

Calling me in late in October to break the news, John did it with an awkward question: "Sam, do you wish overseas service?"

"No."

"I don't understand."

"Then I'll spell it out. N-O."

The dialogue went on.

"I have never heard a General Staff officer make that answer before."

"That's because I wasn't asked."

"What do you mean?"

"I mean that if you were to ask me if I wish service right here I'd make the same answer. No. I don't wish anything. Now, if you have a tough order to give me, roll it out instead of trying to cushion your conscience. I'll comply with the order, and if you don't support me all the way, I'll burn your ass."

Then we buckled down to business, relatively speaking. I was told that I was to go to the Pacific Ocean area, find the 27th Infantry Division, join it if I could, and then figure out what to do.

That ride west was a full gallop with no time out for lunch or for loafing in San Francisco once the plane came to rest. Heading at once for Hamilton Field, I got my clearance for overseas the same afternoon. Very edifying, that experience.

The gnomelike psychiatrist who wore major's leaves gazed at me mournfully and whispered: "What do you have on your mind?"

I said: "Nothing, unfortunately."

Again he whispered: "About going overseas, you must let me share your anxieties."

"Doctor, if I could think up one, you could have it all. I'm anxious only to get through with this exercise."

He whispered: "You're the queer one."

"You be careful, major, that's a fighting word."

Right then he coughed and gave up on me.

From his menagerie I was ushered into a chamber stacked high with training aids where a sing-song lieutenant was lecturing about twenty officers on procedures when ditching at sea and how to survive by making the best use of Mae West, a life raft, and a few fishhooks. His patter oozed out like molasses from a barrel. I felt outraged that he would merely gabble about such a life-and-death matter and resolved that I would make a squawk to the base commander on the following morning.

About then I heard the lieutenant say all too clearly, "In the event of ditching, the senior officer aboard will be responsible for the safety of other passengers. The crewmen take care of themselves."

I looked about. I was the senior present, couldn't swim, and hadn't made sense out of anything he'd said. Oh, well, it was just an exercise.

He droned on: "Gentlemen, you will now move out that door and board your plane. We have already loaded your baggage."

We exited into the dark. This same meathead was waiting at the ramp. He had a paper in hand, an affidavit for my signature attesting that I had been adequately briefed. I turned chicken and signed, choosing to be a liar rather than make a fool of myself. It is so easy to dupe oneself that nothing is truly at stake. I took the forward window seat on the left next the bulkhead, always my favorite spot.

We taxied to the runway. The motors were revved. The outside motor on my wing glowed white hot. I knew we would not get away from Hamilton that night. Suddenly we were airborne and winging west past the Golden Gate. The motor cooled and lost all glow. All of the passengers slept. I couldn't; that bloody motor was too much on my mind.

Past midnight and about 400 miles past the Farallones, the motor again glowed white hot. Then the left wing caught fire and the flame licked toward me.

I yanked open the cockpit door and yelled at the captain. "Are you trying to kill everybody aboard?"

He yelled back. "What's wrong?"

"Your ship's afire—left wing."

"My God, I can't see it from here!" He came back to my window, took one long look, and jumping back to his controls, gunned the aircraft full speed ahead to blow out the fire. It worked. Once before I had been with another cool head in just such an emergency. That was in 1923 when I was relief driver of the first Chrysler ever entered in a stock car race. We were doing 2,600 miles over the rough mountain and desert tracks of the Southwest. Our chariot's engine caught fire on a serpentine downgrade through the Mescalero Indian reservation of New Mexico with three miles of plunging mountain road still to go. The driver opened the throttle; we hit seventy; the fire died and I came damned near it too from my heart blocking my gullet.

This time, as the wing quit burning, the pilot cut the hot motor (it had been repaired just that day, but not checked out). Already he was turning back to the United States. Vibration intensified and the ship skewed badly as if out of balance. He cut the other outside motor and we began to lose altitude immediately. We jettisoned our weapons, lunches, ditty bags, and some gas. Equilibrium returned.

We were five hours getting to see another dawn and the coastline of the beloved country once again. These were the longest and worst hours I ever knew. Gnawing at me was one thought: "Twenty men are going to die and it will all be your fault."

We ditched in the shallow waters of the Bay just short of Hamilton field, having almost made it. Rescue craft had been following our approach over radio for several hours and we had no difficulty. As we made land an orderly awaited me with a message: "Sir, the others will be delayed twenty-four hours, but you are to leave for Hickham Field immediately by cargo plane."

On the bus getting back to Hamilton, I told my companions of the night that I knew how things would be. Just before I enplaned a lieutenant would come, bearing a lunch for me. I would thank him. He would say that he was sorry but the lunch would cost me $1.60. I would say I was sorry but that I had already paid $1.60 for the lunch, and that we had thrown it overboard to save an army aircraft. Then he would say at last, "Sorry, sir, regulations do not cover that."

The scenario came off almost word-for-word as I had forecast. My friends gave the looie the bird with a blast that almost bowled him over. No one bothered to explain why.

Aboard the cargo plane we had a glorious day over the Pacific, clear skies except for an occasional roll of billowing cloud, good companions, food fit for a gourmet, and an overload of iced beverages. There was also space aplenty for bunk fatigue.

Over Diamond Head we first learned that the landing gear had fouled out and we couldn't get our wheels down. We went in belly whopper—and walked away from it without a scratch.

Breaks like that are money in the bank. Every omen had been right. The rough stuff was all behind me. I headed for Fort Shafter late next morning feeling that I couldn't miss. Maybe my old friend Lieutenant General "Nelly" Richardson, who commanded in the Central Pacific, could give me the information that would dispel the mystery. He happened to be out for lunch as was his G-2, Colonel Kendall Fielder.

While I waited in his shop for Fielder to return, a sergeant clerk asked: "Sir, can I do anything for you?"

"You sure can, if you can tell me where in the Pacific is the 27th Division."

"Well, sir, they are here on Oahu, but still they are not exactly here. They base at Schofield Barracks. Right now they're at sea on a dry-run exercise. In a few days they'll be invading a place code-named Horse Island. I'm not altogether sure, but I think that will be Butaritari Atoll in the Gilberts."

Then he led me to another room and fingered Butaritari (Makin Island) on a large map. Where the whole Pentagon system had failed me, one buck sergeant who didn't know my name and hadn't asked to see my identity card had spelled out my mission. I knew in that instant that the people in Washington had sent me forth to thumb my way aboard the expedition to the Gilberts. Some way it had to be contrived.

My right-of-way could only be cleared by direct invitation from the commanding general of the 27th Division, Ralph C. Smith. I did not know him and he was out somewhere on a cruise. A General Staff officer in my situation is just another huckster who must sell his wares.

Brigadier General Ogden Ross, the guardsman serving General Smith as Assistant Division Commander (ADC), was at Schofield Barracks with the rest of the troops. I called him, explaining that I was at Shafter briefly on a high-pressure mission from the War Department and had something important to discuss with him. Could he come visit me at Shafter that evening? That is not the way light colonels are supposed to behave, but I sought to impress him and asking him to come to me certainly did it.

Over dinner I explained to him that we had something new in Washington—a staff to cover combat operations in such a way that we would dispel the "fog of war." I said I had just heard that the 27th was mounting an expedition and that I would like, with General Smith's permission, to get one of our bright boys out from Washington to go along.

Ross frowned and I thought I had lost him. Then he said: "It's a great idea but it's too late. We only have eight days."

"Too bad, too bad."

Ross was deep in thought. "Is there any possibility they would let you go?"

There was a long pause. "General," I said, "I can't answer that one. I will cable, urging them to let me go along, if meanwhile you convince General Smith that the thing's worth doing."

He went for it, and that is exactly how we got started. When some weeks later I confessed the hocus-pocus, Colonel "Keg" Stebbins, the chief of staff, fairly roared. "You———city slicker, taking us innocent country boys."

The stay on Oahu was just long enough to allow for briefings on the upcoming operation—what lay before Smith's troops on Makin Island and what the marines hoped to do at Tarawa. There was also a briefing on the theory and organization of perimeter defense, of which I knew nothing but could not forbear questioning. Why weren't lights being used by the defense at night? The only answer given me was that things had been done this way since Guadalcanal.

On first meeting Ralph C. Smith, I felt it was the beginning of a life-long friendship and that we would always understand one another, with no small questions being asked. Ralph is rangy in build and breezy in nature. His extreme consideration for all other mortals would keep him from being rated among the great captains; he is that somewhat rarer specimen, a generous Christian gentleman. We became confidants immediately. I was also drawn to one of his staff, Lieutenant Colonel (later Major General) Charles B. Ferris, the finest G-4 I met during the war, a genius among soldiers. The story of how Charley and I weighed out the expedition to Makin, to give the army its one and only such logistical table out of World War II, is told in *The Mobility of One Man.* We at least proved that most data of this kind from past wars are fantasies.

At Pearl Harbor we boarded the *Calvert,* an APA or troop carrier not built for comfort. The cabins had been designed for dieting Singer's Midgets. There was space aboard for a battalion-plus, if we all held our breath. When I dropped my gear, four officer roommates were already bunked in my cell. (Three of the four were later killed in action at Makin.) Then at the last minute we were joined by Lieutenant Joe Giltner, a chaplain from the Disciples. The command had belatedly realized that, although Father Stephen J. Meaney, a former editor of *America,* could minister to about 96 percent of the 165th Infantry Regiment (the former Fighting 69th of New

York), there were a few of us Protestants afloat who might need a little prebattle soul-saving, also.

The first afternoon at sea Giltner set up a small altar amidships and held service for just seven men, including the captain of the *Calvert*. Meaney, the Catholic, had a large deck aft and a swarm of communicants. Giltner, short and chubby, had that something extra fitting the special situation. He knew how to talk to men bound for battle. While quoting the Book, he could appeal both to their manhood and their ineffable feeling about country. He did not orate or dramatize or spring that seek-salvation-now-before-you-die line that guts troops. The word got around that Giltner was worth hearing. Within five days after leaving Pearl he had become head shepherd for most of the ship's company. He was not competing with Meaney; the padre was backing him all the way, as was the Catholic battalion commander, Lieutenant Colonel Gerard W. Kelley. Rarely have I seen such cooperation between clergy of different denominations.

That convoy went thirteen days. By the twelfth day we were astride the equator and the heat was on. The convoy from the Southwest Pacific was about to join us. The radar disclosed pips of Jap bombers coming on. We had "Now Hear This!" and "Action Stations!" Outside of a chattering of teeth, nothing happened. One small landing ship far ahead of us had knocked two of the bombers out of the sky and the others had turned back.

That night our far-spread flotilla came flank to flank with the battle wagons, carriers, and proud APAs bringing the marines who would attack Tarawa. We steamed along under the most mellow of tropical moons and the sea was like glass. Nature was never more bountiful to men bent on a mission of violence.

I was going through the final round of a ten-night poker game with five hardy professionals. The night before we seniors had been invaded by a young doughboy, one Lieutenant Milton, who said he knew nothing of poker but would like to play a few hands for education. On the fourth round, he had drawn a natural royal flush, but not knowing how to bet, hadn't made a killing. This second time around, he did the same thing, after only six hands, and though he didn't win much money, it broke up the game. We gathered around him, pounding him on the back, knuckling his scalp for luck and telling him: "Kid, don't worry about this small fight. With your luck, you'll survive the whole war." (And he did!)

Giltner had scheduled an all-ship service for 2300. The moon was high and so incredibly bright that every face in the crowd stood clear. It was no prayer service; the little chaplain had planned his show as a tension-breaker. Anyone who could sing, whistle, or put on any kind of act was asked to volunteer. I did my turn as a soloist, singing "If I Knock the Hell out of Kelly" in honor of the commanding officer, and "An Irishman's Dream." Stunt followed stunt, the night wore on, and the moon was still with us.

At 0200 Giltner looked at his watch and said: "Fellows, it's about closing time. Will you do one last thing for me? Will you sing *The Old Rugged Cross*"? He had taught them the hymn on the way out. That largely Catholic audience arose and sang it with a verve such as I have never heard in a Protestant church.

As the song died, Giltner said: "Thanks to all of you. We have little more than two hours before we get into the small boats. That will give you time for a snack, shower, or snooze. So long till then. I'll see you in the small boats."

So ended one of the greatest prebattle uplift performances that I have seen in many wars.

Dawn came quickly. The landing craft headed in line for Red Beach 1 while the offshore bombardment thundered. A special word had been passed around the 1st Battalion, and when the troops that were to hit Red Beach 1 saw Giltner come abreast in a Higgins boat, a song went up from the other landing craft: "Happy birthday to you, happy birthday dear Chappie." There have been more melodious choruses in our time but none braver, and I doubt there is any other instance of Americans singing on the way in to attack a defended beach.

The sequel was tragic—the worst thing that happened on Makin—but nevertheless redeemed by the salient courage of the two chaplains. The left flank of the 1st Battalion's attack had been stopped dead by fire in heavy volume, some of it coming seemingly from a blockhouse. One of my cabin mates, Lieutenant Daniel T. Nunnery, moved up for a better look and was shot dead. An enlisted man accompanying Nunnery was mortally wounded in the chest.

Meaney charged forward to give that soldier his last rites. Japanese bullets riddled his left arm and chest, and but for the fact that an identity disc deflected one round, he would have died. Two or three other rankers were cut down, and with that the whole movement became paralyzed or "pinned down," as the saying goes.

Colonel Kelley was hugging earth. Next to him were Lieutenant Colonel Jimmy Roosevelt and Colonel Clark "Nick" Ruffner, later a four-star general and army commander. All three of these men have displayed high courage under fire, but for the moment they were spellbound by the situation.

Colonel G. J. Conroy, the regimental commander, convinced that the flank was being held in check by a solitary sniper, came forward on the run. Ruffner and Roosevelt tried to shout him down. He wouldn't listen. Getting almost to Meaney, he was hit by a hail of bullets. Roosevelt and Ruffner started to crawl toward his body. Kelley yelled at them. "Don't do it! He's dead!"

Somebody yelled for Giltner. He came forward and knelt next to the boy that Meaney had been trying to help. A machine gun burst hit between his knees and exploded gravel and coral splinters into his face. Giltner jumped up and shook his fist toward heaven. "Goddamn that Jap!"

Everyone laughed. In that second, all of the tension miraculously evaporated and the line started moving again.

Later aboard ship I said to Giltner: "You were wonderful. That was real Silver Star stuff. But why, when the clutch came, did you curse?"

Joe said very soberly, "I wasn't cursing. That was the most fervent prayer I ever uttered in my life."

Chapter 8
The Double Mission

Thanks to my own big mouth my primary mission in the Pacific was to search for some new system of battle reporting that would clear away all of the confusions of the fire fight. Nothing I had read about combat in World War I that purported to be history had ever satisfied me as to either its accuracy or completeness, and I had repeatedly expressed to Kemper and Taylor my conviction that there must be a better way.

Yet I had no theory about it and not the glimmering of an idea about how to start my quest.

However, in operations out of Oahu, any attached General Staff officer was given a secondary mission in case his primary mission did not pan out. General Smith had given me the chore of trying to increase our capture of Japanese prisoners, which promised to be no more difficult than Captain Ahab's hunt for the white whale.

It was pikestaff plain that I could do neither one thing nor the other without going ashore, and the sooner the better. Making the start did not come easy. No trial of the war gave me greater dread than that first descent down a cargo net in the dark under light pack and carrying a carbine. Unlike the troops, I had had no practice. I hadn't even seen a cargo net. The Higgins boats were bobbing up and down on a five-foot swell. If anyone stepped on my fingers going down, or I misjudged the displacement, I was a goner.

I touched down on Red Beach 1 after the second wave, and stayed just long enough to get my olive twills soaking wet and to note that the Japanese were making only a token defense of that end of the island. Then I returned to the *Calvert* and spent the morning checking the ship-to-shore movement of cargo.

At high noon another battalion, the 2d, under Lieutenant Colonel John F. McDonough, landed at Yellow Beach on the lagoon side of the island and just short of the enemy citadel, a fortified area about 200 yards deep, extending from lagoon to ocean, complete with tank traps, log-walled en-trenchments, and bunkers. I went along. We dropped from the ramps into chest-deep water. Some machine-gun fire was coming at us from a pier called On Chong's wharf, well off to our left flank, and we were getting head-on sniper fire from the palms directly ahead, though not much. The battalion's mission was to cut straight across the island and wait for the battalion that was driving inland from Red Beach 1, a very simple plan.

Well behind the skirmish line when I hit shore, I made it just in time to see one rifle company falling back through the palms. The sniper fire had intensified. These men were just about to back into the open where a wide sand road ran parallel to the shore. That would make them fat targets. I yelled: "Halt!" and then: "Go flat!" They did. Troops under fire will respond to anyone if the order is loud, clear, and sensible.

When their officers got this company going again, I followed along for about a hundred yards into the bush. There, after just a few stumbling steps, I fell apart. My senses reeled. I was hit by such weakness that I dropped my carbine and could not unbuckle my belt, but that was not the worst of it. Within seconds my nerve had gone completely and I shook all over from fear.

I lay flat under a pandanus tree, telling myself: "It's combat fatigue. You've been kidding yourself. You are too old for the wars." Being unable to walk, and scarcely able to think, I decided to stay where I was, wait for a stretcher-bearer to come along and get me back to the *Calvert,* where I would stay. For possibly ten minutes I waited.

Before any aid man came my way, a rifleman stopped and stared at me. Then he took a bottle of pills from his jacket pocket and downed a couple of them.

I asked weakly, "What you got?"

"Salt."

"Gimme some. Nothing can make me feel worse than I do."

He gave me the bottle, saying he had another. I washed down eleven salt tablets with the lukewarm water from my canteen as fast as I could swallow. Within the next ten minutes my nerve and strength were fully restored, and I was never again troubled; yet that lesson had to be learned the hard way. No one had ever told me that one consequence of dehydration is cowardice in its most abject form.

Throughout the rest of that afternoon I moved with the battalion in the attack, questioning officers, squad leaders, privates, and even a few navy files with the ship fire control party. Nothing I heard helped me a bit. Not only were these people extremely vague about what they had seen and what the unit had done; much that they reported was clearly hallucinatory. I spent that night on the *Calvert.* Two of my roommates were already dead, and I don't believe in running extra risk.

Early next morning on shore I resumed my search for the new system, though with no better results. Out of such individual interrogations as I made came mainly froth and foam, and I could be certain only of what I saw. Some of that was highly enlightening.

The fight was still going on, though the citadel had been stormed and taken and our troops were advancing beyond it. General Ralph Smith had come ashore and had set up his command post in a tent halfway between Red Beach 1 and Yellow Beach, where the corps commander, Major General Holland M. Smith of the marines, continued to harass him.

We three sat there together batting at mosquitoes while Holland Smith nagged at Ralph. Suddenly, there was a crackling of rifle fire, close in and on three sides. An excited assistant S-3 came running our way, shouting: "Snipers! They've got us surrounded!"

Ralph Smith picked up his field phone and told the regiment to have a couple of rifle companies prepare to sweep our way from either direction.

Holland Smith picked up his carbine and stalked into the bush. He was gone for about five minutes, and then returned, rubbing his hands. "Well, I took care of those bastards."

It was about as ridiculous a grandstand play as I have ever seen by a general officer, which is saying a lot. The sniping continued for about twenty minutes following his boast.

Then he turned on Ralph Smith. "Get your troops going; there's not another goddamned Jap left on this island."

Ralph Smith said: "General, that plain isn't so."

Right then I decided that I would take a very special interest in Holland M. Smith. He was clearly a bully, something of a sadist and, I guessed, tactically a chowderhead.

By late afternoon at least eighty Gilbertese who had been in Jap country the day before had passed to within our lines. Some came from far up the island, among them the chief. General Smith gave them welcome, told them how happy the Americans were to liberate them, and offered them every assistance.

At around 1700 we saw some of them acting itchy and looking in the direction away from us. Then the chief explained that he would have to lead some of his people back. They hadn't brought their mosquito netting out, and facing the Japanese was preferable to coping bare-handed with Makin mosquitoes.

That night, due to freak circumstances, I got penned on the island. Rear Admiral R. Kelly Turner, aboard the battleship *Pennsylvania,* was in overall command of our part of the invasion. Through error, late in the day, he ordered the abandonment of Red Beach 1, which, though unsatisfactory due to roughness, was still essential if the tonnage was to keep coming. The *Pennsylvania* had pulled its hook and was preparing to put to sea. We couldn't raise Turner on the radio; so Colonel Farris and I jumped into a patrol boat, overtook the *Pennsylvania* while she was barely underway, persuaded Turner the order should be rescinded, and then turned back to the island.

That put us at Red Beach 1 exactly at twilight. To move into the bush without guide or guard with night coming on fast was unthinkable. There was no choice but to dig a foxhole apiece about halfway up the beach. Not having eaten all day, we went supperless, though that was a small thing. I had a head netting, wore gloves, and had closed my twills to my wrists with an elastic. Still, the mosquitoes worked their way inside my clothing and let me have it through the night. Maybe I owe them something for not letting me sleep.

A sentry walked a post about thirty yards long, back and forth along the shingle, about thirty feet away, between my foxhole and the edge of the bush. In direct line with me, but fifteen feet closer to the water, three supply handlers slept flattened on the beach. Some time after midnight, one of these men sat up and cried out, possibly in his sleep. The sentry shot him dead. The other men jumped up. They were both shot dead. The bullets were not more than a foot above my head. I did not say a word or move a muscle except to crouch lower in my foxhole. Had I moved, I would have been shot. Here was stark panic fear, and there was no sensible way to contend with it except to await the sentry's relief in dead quiet.

There was much of this at Makin. When next day General Smith spoke to me about it, I told him that trigger-happiness and over-strained nerves were just part of the price we paid. Our largest problem was to get soldiers to fire. To publish strictures against loose fire would be moving in the wrong direction. Very few of the options in combat are pleasant.

At the same time I told General Smith that my primary mission wasn't working out, that if there was any better way to cover combat the secret still eluded me, and that I was moving on to my secondary mission (the capture of more Japanese) that same morning. It seemed a little late even for that. All of the main enemy works in the heavily populated end of the island were in our hands. Such enemy soldiers as still lived had faded back into the bush and the sights and sounds of resistance had almost died out. Most of us, however, had the uneasy feeling that the gathering calm was wholly deceptive.

Already the quieting and deepening of the rear area was giving Smith some charming administrative problems. The Gilbertese women wore grass skirts with nothing above the waist. Though the topless show as a whole didn't wow troops, one of the younger women, whom we nicknamed Makin Mary, was not only handsome but spectacularly stacked. The boys drooled as they followed her about. So doing, they had discovered early that morning that Mary and four of her pals repaired shortly after dawn to a secret fresh-water pool well hidden in the bush where they laved in the nude. The word went out and in minutes a mob of these hairy apes had collected along the bank, chattering and laughing.

Shortly after that, the old chief was at Smith's command post, protesting the indignity.

Smith was with him all the way. He would get out an order at once. Every approach to the pool would be covered by a guard. Not one Peeping Tom would ever again violate the sanctuary.

"You don't understand," said the chief, "it's all right for them to look, but the girls don't want them to laugh."

Dear Makin Mary. I wrote some light verses about her which were made into a troop song that is still sung at vets' reunions.

That morning I joined the 3rd Battalion of the 165th under Lieutenant Colonel Joe Hart. Its mission was to advance to the far tip of Makin Island via the one dirt road next to the lagoon shore. The battalion would not beat the bush to round up Japanese, but if it made contact anywhere, it would engage—that is, provided I couldn't talk the enemy into quitting. With me went a jeep-mounted public address horn and one Nisei interpreter, Corporal Kubo.

We marched through the afternoon and covered only three miles. That distance at the equator under a full sun is just short of killing. At the end we were simply stumbling through the sand. When we bivouacked at sundown and went into battalion perimeter, men were too exhausted to eat, and the officers didn't bother to inspect our defense lines to make sure that the heavy weapons were set properly so that their fire bands would interlock. In fact, not one thing was done correctly. None of us dug in. We couldn't dig. Even had the loose soil not been laced with thick sub-surface roots, we were too far spent. I shunted two battered palm logs close together and lay down between them. This was to be my only cover if we became engaged. I remember telling myself before I dozed off that if I had to die for failure to dig, then it was time to die.

The story of all that followed is told in my *Battle At Best* and in the official army history. It came to be known as "The Fight on Sake Night." The battalion had come to rest less than a hundred yards west of a cluster of shacks we called Bight Village. Still closer to us on the other side, though we did not know it, was the one large body of Japanese left on Makin Island, and they were already crazed with liquor before we came up. As the perimeter quieted, we caught the sing-song of voices and even the gurgling of the sake as it was poured from the bottles. Later it was estimated that about 170 of them shared the cocktail party.

Then, with the dark, they came on in a series of wild charges that lasted the night. Eleven times they hit and each time our forward line was bloodied and lost some weapons. Two of our guys were run through with Samurai swords. The position finally dangled on only one machine gun that held the center. Hour after hour the melee continued. When dawn came the heat against our front was still so intense that it took two tanks and one rifle platoon to cover the pull-back of the one gunner who had saved the battalion. Suddenly everything quieted.

As we resumed the march to the end of the island, I said to Joe Hart: "If I can find out what happened to us last night, I'll know the way to clear up confusion in battle."

Joe said: "I agree; I haven't any notion what my own troops did."

When we reached the tip of Makin just before noon, I sent for the standout machine gunner and his lieutenant. Their stories clashed head-on. I collected all survivors from the platoon, and questioning them as a group, made them start at the beginning—that is, when they moved into the position. Piece by piece we put it together. The story of the night's experience came clear as crystal. It was like completing the picture of a jigsaw puzzle. At last I knew that, quite by accident, I had found what I had sailed west seeking.

Just about then Hart told me that his telephone lines to the rear had been cut, which meant there had to be more enemy about. Being the only attached officer present, I volunteered to go back and bring up more troops. That was nearly my final mistake.

With me in the jeep were Corporal Kubo and the driver. One mile along the sand road we were hit by a drenching rain, and within seconds thereafter, we moved into ambush. The remaining Japs on the island had set up a fire line just off the road where the shrubbery and trees ended so that they were within less than 25 yards of us as we came bucketing into their trap. The ambush was strung out over about 150 yards, and it was fire all the way with nothing saving us but the downpour and their bad aim.

I fired wildly with the pistol and yelled: "Let 'er buck!"

Kubo, from the back seat, cried out: "I'm hit!"

I reached back, grabbed him, and yelled to the driver: "Gun it! Everything you've got!"

He had been doing half speed because, with the wet sand, the jeep was slithering all over the road and he was afraid of ditching.

The vehicle jumped forward and in only a few seconds we were out of the ambush.

I called to Kubo: "Where are you hit?"

The Nisei came out of it with a grin. "I'm all right. Nothing happened. I just wanted to make him move faster."

In less than thirty seconds after that, we met, coming west along the road, two rifle companies from Lieutenant Colonel "Black" McDonough's battalion. I showed them how to deploy along the beach and where to set their boundaries so that they could make a sweep from both ends and box the ambushers. Forty-three Japs were eliminated in that final pocketing.

During the ride along the enemy fire front, there had been no time for fear. It was all too swiftly done and too wildly exciting. During the few minutes of preoccupation with the fighting problem, the nerves held steady. I got back to Kubo and the driver. There were thirteen bullet holes in the jeep. By the time we finished counting them we were shaking like aspens in the breeze.

Of many lucky days in my life, that one tops all. Within the same hour had come the discovery of a new reporting system and then the deadfall that should have ended my roamings. And I had not been made to pay. The main part of my life's work came of the events of that day.

By the time I got back to headquarters, General Smith had already fired off his famous message, perhaps the briefest of all communiqués: "Makin taken." Some troops were already heading for the transports. The fleet put to sea every night for cruising to lessen the danger from submarines. Though I was steamed up and ready for an ocean voyage, my first sight of the *Calvert* was dismaying.

Now unloaded, she loomed up like a side of Gibraltar, and, with my load, I had to climb that cargo net rising from a bouncing sea. I felt queasy just from the sight of it. I wasn't wrong. My strength wasn't equal to the strain. I couldn't get over the rail. A seaman reached down, grabbed me by the shoulders, and pulled. I lay there on the deck gasping like a fish out of water. Just as I was about to rise again another gob came along paging me: "Orders for you, Colonel Marshall. You are to report to General Smith aboard the *Leonard Wood*." Do that damned thing all over again? The experience of crawling up that second cargo net must have been too painful; all of it has washed from my memory. Right there I earned ten Medals of Honor although General Smith simply wished to talk over the campaign with me.

We zigzagged back and forth across the equator maybe a hundred times that night. A tropical cruise on a serene sea is good for the soul of man at any time, though there is no other spiritual uplift to match that of coming directly from battle to comfort, a hot shower, good food, gentle weather, and secure living all at one bound.

We seemed so very safe that night. We were strong, we were many, and the convoy stretched for miles. I stayed on deck late to thrill to the spectacle and got back to the rail at dawn next morning for the same reason.

Smoking my pipe, I stood there idly looking at a Kaiser-built baby carrier maybe half a mile off our port bow. Two destroyers left her side and moved suddenly farther out, at right angles to our course. The carrier was still in my gaze. One second she was there solid and untroubled. The next, she was only a sheet of flame shooting skyward, smoke billowing, and a few moments later my ear caught the report.

Such was the wreck of the *U.S.S. Liscome Bay*. By my watch, she went down in less than four minutes, though navy records say a little longer. Of more than 900 men aboard her, only 100 and a few odd got away. We on the *Leonard Wood* picked up most of the survivors, since we were closest to them. One Jap submarine had decoyed the two destroyers by firing a flare well out from the line the convoy was taking. When the carrier became exposed, the Jap slipped in and put two tinfish into the *Liscome's* side. One blew the magazine.

Some of the men we picked up had been too badly burned to survive. We buried them at sea. All of the postbattle happiness was gone as we steamed back to Pearl. The survivors sat in the wardroom day after day, shocked men who would respond to a question if asked but were otherwise lost in their brooding. They stared into space. Games were not for them. They would not even communicate with one another. It was my first and only experience with group shock.

When I think back to those hours and that voyage and what they meant to me, the only words that seem to fit are those at the close of Donn Byrne's *Messer Marco Polo:* "Ah, well, if it's go, it's go . . . I'll say goodbye for the present . . . and . . . Oh, my God Almighty."

––––––––––––––––––––– ★ –––––––––––––––––––––

Before settling down to work in Hawaii I called on Major General Charles H. Corlett, commanding the 7th Division, to tell him what I had observed of Holland Smith at Makin and to air my conviction that Smith was determined to make trouble for any army general who came under him. Corlett heard me through without shifting one facial muscle. Then he thanked me coldly, from which I judged that the message hadn't gotten through. I was never more wrong.

My days were filled with the mass interviewing of the companies that had fought at Makin, which gave me my first on-the-job training with the technique I had acquired at the tip of the island. In the evenings I pondered the other problem—how to soften the Japanese. Though well aware that there had to be a psychological key to the riddle, I realized that all of our G-2 wizards had missed it thus far. Then a feeble light flickered and I began dimly to see that everything we were doing was probably wrong. My administrative chief at the time was Colonel Fielder, the theater intelligence chief. Our relations were still on a rather formal plane.

What I put to Fielder was that we were making the mistake of using the sort of Japanese phrases spoken by a person conditioned by our own culture. We had the words but we were not singing the right tune. I sketched a hypothetical situation to make my point. We were on a Pacific island in command of Americans, totally surrounded by Japanese. We knew we could not hold out much longer. Then a Japanese voice came over the air saying to us: "You Americans big damn fools. We kill you. You quit now. We give you nice girls and show good time." That sort of talk would have no more impact than the ravings of Tokyo Rose, but if the voice said: "I am speaking to the American commander and his troops. You have fought hard but you are now through and we know it. If you surrender now, we will treat you with the honors of war. If not, we will have to kill you," that message would strike home. Still, in the field we were putting out the equivalent of the first message and missing the spirit of the second altogether. It was time to change.

Fielder asked: "What do you propose to do about it?"

I told him that I'd like to form a council of older advisers from among the Issei on Oahu and get them together with the division G-2s to work out a new set of ideas and different phrases.

Fielder said: "I'm against it. There would be too many risks in such a council."

Since he didn't forbid it outright, I went ahead, first calling on Baron Goto, director of the extension department of the University of Hawaii. Together, we chose eight other Issei for the council. From that time on the council and the division intelligence chiefs met twice weekly at one of the teahouses, and in brainstorming sessions that lasted until past midnight worked over all kinds of proposals. From them we got the three basic ideas that gained us the breakthrough.

• Promise they would never be returned to Japan.
• Promise that if they became POWs, we would give them a nice ride to the United States.
• Threaten that if they did not come out we would gas them to death.

To our American ears these proposals at first seemed ridiculous, but when we understood the Issei line of reasoning, the logic was clear enough. The Japanese soldier who voluntarily surrendered would lose all honor and couldn't face his country. The average Japanese has a strong desire to visit America. As for the last proposition, it was Goto who reasoned that, to the mind of the average Japanese soldier, death in a form that is completely mystifying to him must have a special horror.

In the battle of Kwajalein, these were the ideas that we used on the last day when we had so many of the enemy penned in air raid bunkers. We took 167 prisoners in voluntary surrender. I personally witnessed Japs who were already wounded to the point of death come crawling from the bunkers when we threatened to gas them. The number may not sound impressive, but it was the largest catch in twenty-seven months of war. Here was real psychological warfare, and we were all so thrilled by the achievement that I got together with Generals Smith and Arnold and some of their advisers to discuss such moves on a grand scale. From Washington the Office of War Information (OWI) sent a specialist to work with us in the early stages of the planning.

Here was the prospect. Going into the Marshalls to hit Kwajalein and Roi-Namur, the fleet had bypassed island groups like Wotje, Jaluit, and Maleolap that were heavily garrisoned by the Japanese. The tide of war just flowed on and around them. We dreamed about getting voluntary surrenders from these marooned garrisons and of using the fact of mass surrender to propagate fear and weakness wherever we dealt with the enemy in the field. Becoming a ground swell, it could crack Japan.

The plan was elementary. We would rig a yacht to do the offshore broadcasting. On off days, against Wotje for instance, the language expert would give the garrison the business in much the same way that we had worked at Kwajalein. The pitch would be heavy with glittering promises, offered on condition that the garrison ran up the white flag. Every quiet day's pitch would end with a threat that would be carried out: "You surrender now or we bomb you tomorrow." Only a couple of bombers would go the first time. Then, after one day's remission, if there was still no surrender, we would hit with four. The attack would continue to build up on that scale. We were confident it would get results.

Unfortunately, after the OWI man got with us and our enthusiasms had begun to banish all doubt, we piled up on the rocks. The personnel problem became the insuperable obstacle. Every crack Japanese language expert available to the United States who was also an expert in enemy military psychology was already in a top priority job with the army, navy, or OWI and could not be released. Such an undertaking simply could not be confided to the judgment of our halftrained Nissei interpreters. Though we kept trying, the combined support of General Richardson and Admiral Nimitz could not get us the right kind of brains.

It might have made some difference in the long run. What impressed me during the Pacific War was the paucity of our human resources in the face of such problems, the lack of imagination in people in high places, and our total failure to take the proper measure of the enemy in the psychological sense. We fought the whole war according to the fundamental assumption, which was absolutely wrong, that the masses of civilian Japan were as unified, adamant, and fanatic as the males in fighting suits. We never regarded them as emotionally vulnerable. In short, we were blind to the nature of the enemy, and we did not try to learn better as we went along. Whether that should be laid to Pearl Harbor or to protean ignorance, I am not prepared to say. The fact is that we fought the war head down in the hardest possible way and at excessive cost to both sides.

Mail from Kemper had promised me a relief, but since none had arrived, I asked for permission to accompany the 7th Division and was made a member of the club. The ordeal of troops at Kwajalein is told in *Island Victory,* and I have also done essays on the fighting there. Though most of my field work was done on Kwajalein proper or Burton Island, I slept every night in a foxhole on Carlton Island without blankets or other cover except some palm fronds and leaves that I had woven together overhead in an idle attempt to buff off the rain. The third night the roof was sheared away by a shard of flying metal as large as a man's head. About eighty yards from me a 155-mm howitzer, while shelling the main island, had blown up from a faulty fuse, and part of the casing had come my way. Six men had been killed. The whole battery position was threatened by fire, and the gunners had formed a daisy chain extending from the lagoon in a fight to save it. I got down there, observed the action, and later wrote the paper citing the battery for group heroism.

Also on that day some of our infantry on the big island had overrun the Japanese paymaster's office right in the middle of the fire fight. In one of the grandest jests ever staged by American fighting men, these playfellows held up the action, outposted their position, then filed to the boodle building to draw their pay in yen. The show was staged with mock ceremony, each man having to sign on the line for yen received. In the end, something hilariously funny was to come of that.

Kwajalein was the most stinking piece of real estate I have ever smelled in war. The island was virtually matted with rotting flesh and drying blood. By the end of the fourth day the stench was so unbearable that we were trying to mask it out with towels and handkerchiefs. When at last the order came to mount ship again, that horrible smell stayed with us three miles out into the lagoon.

That sunset return to a state of relative decency remains an imperishable memory. We were all so happy to get clean deck timber under our feet. I was returning with General Corlett, his staff, and a large part of the 7th Division aboard the *President Harrison.* As men climbed up the cargo nets we stood at the rails and cheered every arrival. Then came the last soldier, a rifle sergeant. He reached the very top. The rope broke in his hands, he pitched backward into the sea and we never saw him again. A shriek of agony went up from every man watching. We had been with death for days and here at the very last was the most terrible shock of all.

Corlett sent for me next morning. He had a story that he wished to make of record. He had taken seriously what I had told him about Holland Smith. Two days later General Smith had called to talk over the operation. He quickly began ridiculing Ralph Smith. Corlett arose and said: "Don't you dare ever talk about me that way," and Holland Smith stomped out.

When shortly afterward Holland Smith was promoted to Lieutenant General, the marine returned to the attack. "Corlett, you were insubordinate to me the other day."

Corlett arose. "I'll say the same thing again," and repeated what he had said. Again, Holland Smith turned on his heel. Then, when the order came out, Corlett learned that Holland Smith was on the command ship, *Rocky Mount,* with the admiral, whereas, he, Corlett had been put on another transport. On the advice of his staff, Corlett had made a sticking point of it; either he would go on the *Rocky Mount,* or he would ask to be relieved. He got his way.

Then, two days before we reached Kwajalein, Smith came to him and asked when Corlett proposed to go ashore. Corlett said he didn't know, then asked: "Why is it important?" Smith said he would go ashore at the same time. Corlett said: "I don't want you ashore until the fighting is done. This is my battle. You may put some staff officers ashore as observers. If I find they have tried to issue any orders, I'll have them arrested."

To his surprise, Smith gave him no argument.

On the morning the battle ended, Smith came ashore on Kwajalein. Immediately, he called a press conference. Corlett came up behind him to hear Smith telling the newsmen that the infantrymen had done a poor job on Kwajalein compared to the fight of the marines at Roi-Namur. That was too much for Corlett. He broke in to inform the correspondents that the corps commander didn't know anything about either battle since he had been kept aboard ship the whole time.

Corlett concluded in his talk with me: "And so I think that he will probably prefer some kind of charges against me."

Instead of that, Holland Smith put Corlett in for the navy's Distinguished Service Medal, which he duly received.

Having been at dead center of these several episodes, however, and still feeling some pique about that ambush at Makin two days after the great "Howling Mad" had declared that every Jap was gone, I made out a full report on my observations of Holland Smith that was handed to the War Department several months prior to the Smith vs. Smith blowup at Saipan.

On Kwajalein Island, during the last two days of the battle, I had undertaken as loathsome a mission as any soldier is likely to know in war. Covering a seven-acre stretch at the tip of the boomerang-shaped battlefield and another five-acre area right next to our fire line, I examined the enemy dead, body by body, to determine what had killed them. Some were obviously victims of artillery fire, their flesh strewn all over. Other fairly whole corpses lay near a crater hardly larger than a wash basin. They had been killed by mortars. The few bodies that stayed whole could be charged off to bullet fire, whether small arms or machine gun. That was about as close as one could come to an analysis without taking account of how many Japanese had perished from the preliminary bombardment, or from being satchel-charged while in an air raid shelter. The estimate that I forwarded to higher headquarters was that 73 percent of the enemy killed in the open had been eliminated by artillery and mortar fire and 27 percent from all other causes.

Then I added a footnote on the effects of the preliminary bombardment by the naval guns and aviation and the air corps bombers, and here I felt quite sure of my ground. At Kwajalein, uniquely, the Marshallese had shared the air raid bunkers used by the Japanese and scattered the length of the island. The natives had gone to ground together with the soldiers the moment the bombardment started and stayed covered until it lifted. Subsequently, as our forces advanced up the island with fire, the Marshallese had to take risks and accept losses while trying to escape to our lines; yet, at the end of the campaign, the overall native losses in dead and wounded was only 3.5 percent of the island's indigenous population. Hence it had to follow that Japanese losses to the preliminary bombardment could hardly have been in excess of 3.5 percent, the natives and the soldiers having shared common cover.

When Admiral Chester Nimitz came ashore on Kwajalein the morning after the fight ended, a correspondent asked him how many of the Japanese, by his estimate, were destroyed by the preliminary bombardment. Without batting an eye, Nimitz replied: "At least 20 percent." This bit is offered only as an enlightening example of how far wrong a distinguished sailorman can go when he is speaking off the cuff out of enthusiasm and isn't in touch with the facts.

After polishing off Kwajalein, our expedition did not immediately sail east to Pearl. We sailed west to give a heavy working over with the big guns and navy bombers to the island of Truk, which in the early stages of the war had profited from an overblown reputation as an impregnable island fortress.

When that shellacking was completed soon after midday, we hove about and sailed east again and within an hour were getting over ship's radio a glowing account of our latest achievement direct from the land of the free. Instead of the broadcast making everyone happy, it turned the ship's company into a gaggle of gripers. What the hell, the broadcaster didn't even know the name of the target island we had just hit. What the hell, his pronunciation was all wrong. What the hell, why didn't he ask us? We're the boys that ought to know. To superinduce greater cheer all around, I typed some lines and posted them on the ship's bulletin board:

> I hear Gram Swing say we hit Truke
> As if it rhymes with fluke or Luke.

> The boys who hit it call it Truck
> As if it rhymes with Buck or Luck.

> But as for my opinion, look,
> Does anybody give a Fook?

The *President Harrison* docked at Honolulu in early morning. General Richardson and staff awaited us on the wharf below amid a motley, jampacked crowd of stevedores, rubbernecks, and cheerleaders. Right then was when the Kwajalein paymaster's yen were put to work. Some screwball had the bright idea of floating his enemy bank notes down like so much confetti on the crowd below, just for kicks. Quickly things began to happen and we all followed suit. What a rain; yen, yen, yen out of heaven! Richardson and staff were knocked flat in the rush and trampled. Seven characters walked off the dock and into the drink while overextending to grab the paper. Finally the harbor police had to be called to break up a small riot.

In this way welcome home became idiot's delight. It was a joke good for too few years—only until we philanthropists learned that we had tossed away real money, good for buying trinkets aplenty in postbellum Japan. Had the stuff looked green we might have been wiser.

A large part of my field work was done during the return voyage to Oahu. We held company assemblies on the open deck every day. By the time we saw land I had sufficient proof that the new method could be applied as readily to the actions of one whole division in battle as to the fighting of one platoon. The rest of the story was wrapped up ashore with the new division commander, General Archibald V. Arnold, backing my work all the way. I owe more than I can say to this sturdy gunner. There was no finer division commander in the war.

Within a few days, the three officers who were to take over from me showed up. They had been there all the time, lost in a replacement camp. With them came a note from Kemper saying that the two younger men probably wouldn't work out, but the captain was so outstanding that he would offset their shortcomings. The two tentative discards were Edmund Love, subsequently author of *Subways Are for Sleeping* and a dozen other books, and James McGregor Burns, the budding political scientist and biographer. They deployed like heroes and proved to be geniuses in disguise. The captain, I shortly learned, didn't know how to talk to ranks and spoke patronizingly to higher commanders. I had to ship him back to the zone of interior (ZI). He later became president of a great state university.

The word had already come that I would be hauled out and sent to ETO in time for Normandy. I didn't like it; we had a going concern in the Pacific and I wanted no more troubleshooting. The generals unanimously bucked the transfer for much the same reasons. We had a system that was repairing mistakes in operations as we moved along, such things as loading tables, landing arrangements, firepower dispositions, and infantry-armor collaboration. We had learned, for instance, that the Japanese soldier wasn't the shifty, versatile fighter we had thought all along. He was stereotyped; his patterns of development and movement in relation to weather conditions were constantly repeated. Since we were getting his number, it seemed better to stay with it. At Kwajalein, we had tried lights in night defense in the sector of the 32nd Infantry Regiment and the navy flares had worked wonders. I was supplying the data and sitting on the board that made the tactical and logistical adjustments, many of them quite radical.

The reasons for carrying on seemed good. The War Department decided its reasons for the shift were better. So I was away. Just prior to my going a small ceremony was held and I was pinned with the first Infantry Combat Badge awarded in the United States Army. I still prize it more highly than any other award I have ever received.

By choice I went by ship to San Francisco and spent the voyage chipping the paint of the old Swedish bucket I was riding, just for exercise and to steady my nerves. At journey's end I was informed that I had chipped the paint the wrong way. Sorry about that.

Johnny Kemper was waiting for me in the national capital with his usual warm smile, an *abrazo,* and a small chore. Within the next ten days I was to write a 50,000-word monograph on the Battle of Kwajalein. It would be used as a pamphlet for distribution in Europe to convince the high commanders that we really did have a new system of covering combat operations.

It was not too much to ask. All of the data were in my hands and I compose very rapidly; so the new product that became the book *Island Victory* was hatched in the prescribed period, though making it a public book was not my doing.

Toward the end, I had become reconciled to my fate and was ready enough to turn to a new horizon, but I was still griping. The Pacific had proved to be my dish. We were doing well there.

John was not only patient with me. He was putting the carrot before the nose of the donkey. He said: "You go and we will make you a full colonel."

I said to him: "John, say that and you're in trouble. I have never asked for a promotion in my life. I never will. But when it's promised me to encourage risk-taking, it had better be delivered."

On that note we parted. Johnny had promised, and I had threatened. We were close friends. We would always remain so. But it wasn't all for the sake of good clean fun. Military people understand this better than businessmen. There is a stronger sense of honor and of binding obligation.

★

Cleared for Europe, we took off. One hour out of Goose Bay, Labrador, we lost an engine over the Atlantic and had to make a limping return to base. I was again the senior officer aboard. Having cleared away at half-past midnight, we touched down at 0320 and were told that another aircraft would be ready to shove off at 0600.

Here was a pressing problem demanding command decision. I said to the others: "There's not enough time for sleep and there's too much time to be wasted in small talk. We all have bottles. Let's do some serious drinking and see how these fly boys handle the problem."

We did. And the fly boys didn't do anything except siphon us aboard. We slept on the floor, with some of our jokers sprawled on those nasty side-facing canvas seats next the hull, until the pilot sortied to shake us and tell us that we were descending into Prestwick. We had missed nothing. The crew hadn't seen the Atlantic, either, so complete was the cloud cover.

There is no more commendable way to ride from one theater of war to another. All mean anticipation, along with nagging retrospection, becomes lost. As I reflect on this, one of my more sterling command decisions, I would still not only recommend but urge this procedure.

On the other hand, for a lightning recovery, there is nothing to be recommended that is more swiftly sobering than going on a lecture tour in England. Elsewhere around the globe, one audience is very much like another. Be they Nationalist Chinese, Israelis, Canadians, or the international mix at NATO Staff College, I have found that one may tell the same stale stories and belabor the same well-worn points with little or no variation in the crowd reaction. The responses—laughter or applause, if such there be, or looks of disbelief, which are almost invariably too frequent—are those of people doing what comes naturally.

But not in England. Each crowd reacts according to its particular discipline and the impact on the speaker may be absolutely devastating, especially if he is confronted by a sea of deadpan expressions for more than an hour.

Soon after getting to the other side, I was called to London to make eleven talks in three days to "selected British audiences." That happened because I was the first General Staff officer to deploy in that direction who had witnessed our big strikes in the Central Pacific. The idea came to Ambassador John Winant that describing to Englishmen the magnitude of these operations might stir their hearts of oak.

My first talk was at H.M.S. *King Alfred*, where eleven hundred naval ratings were to step up to officership on the following day. For one hour I faced a gallery in white, utterly immobile. I rolled it out, so many battle wagons, carriers in unbelievable numbers, armadas stretching out over six miles, the count of ships approaching five hundred. Not one face cracked an expression, not one hand stirred. While I rattled on about our magnificence afloat, I sunk minute by minute.

As I took my seat feeling utterly miserable, they arose and poured it out in a yell that sounded like "Bzoom! Bzoom! Bzoom!" The blasting continued five minutes. The admiral arose. "Young gentlemen, I am delighted that you have accorded your speaker such rapt attention. My proudest wish for you is that, when you leave here tomorrow, you will serve in the Far East where it may be your fortune to associate with the greatest fighting organization the world has ever known. I refer to the United States Navy."

Bewildering is the word for it.

At Essex House I had a break. I was introduced at exactly noon, and as I arose, we all heard a buzz bomb coming in and knew from the sound that we were at ground zero. My audience hit the deck. Standing there in uniform, I dared not. The bomb landed on the other side of our block and destroyed a police station. Our building shook terribly though no glass was broken in the chamber where we were collected. Never had I dealt with a more responsive audience. They cheered so hard I decided they must have been a bit tiddley before they arrived.

My last port of call was Brendan Bracken's war information group, some sixty or so persons. Once again, everybody played the Great Stone Face. Nothing startled them, nothing seemed to please them. Five feet in front of me sat a small Buddha-like figure with a visage wholly inflexible. He gave me the willies. I told myself that I would alter that map before I was through or give up speaking altogether. For one hour I gave it the hard college try. The bullet head didn't stir; the eyes hardly blinked. Score, zero.

When I sat down, there was a wee smattering of applause, perhaps thirty or forty hands giving it the once over lightly. At that point the chairman arose and said: "I would inform our distinguished speakah of the day that at a meeting of the British press, it is more than a bit unusual to evoke cheeyahs."

Cheeyahs? Cheers? I knew the gent was putting me on.

They formed around me in a tight circle and began asking questions. Suddenly that circle parted as if hit by a battering ram. There stood the little bullet-headed man, his hand out. We shook. He said: "I must congrat-u-late"—booming every syllable—"you—as a speakuh, as a soldyuh—and finally—as a mon." Then, lowering his head, he banged right through the crowd again.

The experience was so flabbergasting I forgot to ask anyone his name. By accident, twenty-five years later I was told by a Canadian who had attended the meeting. It was the old Beaver himself, Lord Beaverbrook.

Next day, a Sunday, I visited my old friend J. F. C. Fuller at his country place in Limpsfield, Surrey. The buzz bombs chugged along directly above his house on their way to London, as accurately as if they used it as an aiming stake. One came along about every twenty minutes. I guessed the elevation to be 700–800 feet above our heads. Fuller was squatting in his strawberry patch, and I joined him in the picking. As the put-put-put of the bomb sounded above us, not even bothering to glance skyward, he gestured that way with one thumb.

"Marshall, I want you to think about that weapon for a few minutes," he said. "A better missile than that will come along soon, a true rocket. Then before this war is ended we will see the employment of bombs with atomic warheads. These two weapons will be married later. We will have rockets with such warheads that can hit a target thousands of miles distant. The whole strategic outlook will be transformed for all time to come."

Here was letter-perfect prophecy, and I know of no more dramatic example of Fuller's wisdom and soaring imagination. He had been thinking in these same terms for years. In 1928, he had written a tract, *The Influence of the Constant Tactical Factor in the Development of War,* that in general terms spoke of these same terrible wonders to come. Within a few weeks of our strawberry patch seance, London was hit by the first V-2, the progenitor of the intercontinental ballistic missile (ICBM). While he talked that day, I made notes. Then, at war's end, I was invited to address a mass meeting of 82nd and 101st Division officers at Auxerre, France, on the subject of the future of war. I built that lecture wholly around Fuller's prophecy. The thinking was all his, and I won undue credit for being a mystic.

Lieutenant General Sir Giffard Martel joined us at the home that Sunday afternoon. Head of the British Military Mission to Moscow, he had returned to England for a brief holiday. Fuller's right bower in the original British tank corps, Martel, alone among the allied chiefs of mission at Moscow, had bullied the Soviets into giving him freedom to visit their forces up front.

Martel talked along rather quietly. He was convinced, he said, that the Russians made their battle forces off-limits to the allied observers because they didn't want it known that they were so badly impoverished, so lacking in heavy weapons. Their armored divisions, for example, on average, fielded fewer than a hundred tanks. He kept talking about the shortages.

Then suddenly Martel changed tone. "Don't misunderstand," he said, "the Russians do have one secret weapon. The average Red Army soldier is incredibly brave. Even when the fight seems hopeless, he is more ready to die for his country than our soldier or your soldier. Maybe in the end that is the weapon that counts most."

Sonia Fuller, Boney's beloved, told us that the tea was ready. The strawberries picked that morning had been overlaid with clotted cream. Delicious. We heard another buzz bomb overhead, chugging on its way to target. Fantastic. Boney and Sir Giffard kept talking while I listened. Brilliant.

Though that is about all I recall from the rarest June day I knew during the war, I made an entry in my notebook:

Lesson No. 1 from Fuller: "To anticipate strategy, imagine."

Lesson No. 2 from Martel: "Men, not weapons, will shape the future, so stick with the fundamentals."

Chapter 9
Regulars and Reserves

$\mathbf{A}$s a reservist serving in wartime, my duties in both world wars and in Korea were of such a nature that ninety percent of the time, when it came to command problems in which I needed the help of higher levels, I found myself dealing with regulars. That satisfied me. Most of the time, the American civilian turned soldier, whether he comes up the National Guard ladder or gets his commission direct from civilian life because of some special qualification, is a wobbly staff officer. He tends to play politics and is more intent on ingratiating himself with his superiors than with exerting his influence to strengthen organization. He fears to oppose higher authority lest he be disciplined for getting out of line.

This weakness in my fellow reservists has always baffled and disappointed me. Why shouldn't the civilian officer be a stronger contender than the regular when they are on an equal footing, provided that he truly knows the ways of the service and is morally fit for a commission? After all, he has no career to lose. If in consequence of protest, when he senses that things are going wrong, he is suddenly out of favor, draws a reprimand, or is denied promotion, such a temporary reverse should not ruin him. His life, after all, belongs primarily with his family and the job to which he will return on discarding his soldier suit. Nothing that the service may do to him, unless he has broken the law or is guilty of unbecoming conduct, can jeopardize his major stake in the future. Yet despite that fundamental consideration, the average reserve officer is afraid to stick his neck out.

Here I am talking not so much about commanders in the combat line as reservists on staff duty or in higher headquarters. Being directly responsible for the lives and welfare of other men does seem to make a difference. A reservist commanding a rifle battalion in wartime is not likely to play chicken in his dealings with higher authority if he is convinced that his unit is being neglected or wrongfully employed. Put the same man in a rear headquarters, and though he sees slackness and ineptitude on every hand, he will rarely take a hard line in pressing those who are above him to redress the situation.

I am aware of Justice Holmes's statement that no general proposition is worth a damn, including this one. Ray McLain, who came from the National Guard of Oklahoma, was as high minded a flag officer as I ever knew, a superb strategist and tactician, whose moral and mental integrity remained complete after he rose to high place in the Pentagon hierarchy. Floyd Parks also came up through the National Guard. Furthermore, the regular officer corps has its full quota of misfits. It takes a war to separate the men from the boys. To many serving officers, the army is simply a better 'ole. They do duty routinely in peace time and develop a keen eye for a secure spot where they will have minimum problems and maximum comfort.

Though some so-called line officers are in this category, their wearing of the crossed rifles or cannon is a masquerade; they are not interested in combat, and if they think of it at all, they are caught between chill and sweat. They have no intention of ever going into battle. Should the accident of assignment force them to do so, they invariably fall apart and are relieved for cause, provided they live long enough. This type of officer usually knows regulations to the letter. To his mind, they are as inviolable as the tables from Mount Sinai were intended to be. Being what he is, he cannot understand that regulations are nothing more than a general guidance to conduct, written to protect and advise the soldier, but never intended to fetter him and circumscribe his action when great daring and initiative are required in coping with some unprecedented problem.

Colonel Ganoe, my new chief when I reported for duty in Europe, was not this kind of violet. Still, he did not really understand the army, though he had been around it more than forty years and was celebrated as the author of the only book relating its history from the Revolution to the present. Bill loved the army with unflagging devotion. He was quite willing to die for it. He was thoroughly familiar with the customs and traditions of the service, and could describe in minute detail the soldier of 1812 or the march into Mexico. He had been Douglas MacArthur's adjutant at West Point and had for him a devotion amounting to reverence, but he knew very little about war. He had never been in combat, and his ignorance of the basic nature of troops was simply appalling. That, however, is not what I mean when I say he didn't understand the army. The responsibilities of a commander were Greek to him in that he could not anticipate problems, and he had not the vaguest idea of how to exert his influence when serving on the General Staff, being blind alike to his possibilities and his limits. Maybe that requires a certain instinct. Administratively, he barely got by through leaning on Mr. Fitzgibbon, the chief warrant officer, but since Fitzgibbon was forever advising him what he couldn't do, rather than what he could get away with, having no knowledge himself of the philosophy of regulations, the whole operation was not unlike a squad which can't get off the pivot. When Ganoe was not poring over papers that shouldn't have been initiated in the first place, he was spending his time attending teas and tattoos in the name of cultivating friendlier relations with our British ally, which is a commendable object but gets no books written. Still, with it all, I loved the old man and love him still. There was something so childishly sweet about him, and besides, it was a shame that unkind fate had frustrated him. He should have made his living playing Shakespeare.

All of this preface is relevant to the course I followed upon arriving in England on my trouble shooting mission at the time of the Normandy invasion. My old associate in organizing the Historical Division, Colonel Charley Taylor, met me at the airport that Sunday morning to feed me his tale of woe before I dealt with Ganoe. It came forth—and this I did not know before—that both he and Major Hugh M. Cole had been sent to the theater some months earlier to get Ganoe's project back on the rails before Operation Overlord began rolling.

Had they succeeded, I would have been let alone to enjoy the comforts of the war in the Pacific, where I had the active goodwill of all higher commanders, which is better than cakes and ale. But Ganoe had boxed them in by cordially proposing that all of his correspondence with the War Department should be read by them, provided they also communicated through him. Since in any case he could require them to do the latter, his offer to let them see what he was writing sounded like sheer generosity; so they agreed. Thereby they lost the chance to correct the operation. They could not be caustic and critical in what they wrote to the people in Washington; yet nothing but pressure from the War Department was likely to move Ganoe. However wise the advice from a subordinate, it cannot influence the action of a chief who is satisfied with his position and determined to keep his responsibilities limited. Nothing but fear of being relieved, or apprehension of an entanglement with higher authority, has remedial effect.

There was little prospect of this, in the European Theater. The higher commands simply did not give a damn about the historical operation and tolerated it only to appease Secretary Stimson. This was true from first to last, or nearly so. There was never one inspection of our shop to determine whether work was being done, and if it served the object. After I became chief, absolutely no one from topside ever made such an inquiry. Because— uniquely among all of the forces in the theater—I was able to report month after month that my people were free of venereal disease and I had no court-martial cases, it was taken for granted that we knew our business and were efficient. This is the army, Mr. Jones.

Ganoe was waiting in the damp office in Grosvenor Square that morning and greeted me like a long-lost nephew. After the effusions were over, with Taylor present and listening hard, we came to grips almost immediately. The chief explained his neat arrangement with my fellow missionaries concerning correspondence, then asked: "And of course, Slam, you will agree to the same arrangement?"

In my approach to the task in Europe, this was the one moment solemn above all others, and I well understood it.

I told the colonel I wouldn't do it, that I was sent there by Washington to make the historical operation work.

"I expect to go to Normandy. Where I find our work being neglected, and can determine the cause, I will write directly to the War Department, but I will send you an information copy of my complaint. Your correspondence with Washington is your private affair. Should you object to this procedure that I now propose, I'll take a plane immediately, return to the ZI, and report that I can do nothing."

He thought that over for a moment, then agreed because, he said, he thought I could be trusted. Thereafter I had no doubt that I could get the good colonel to go my way gradually, the main question being whether I had enough time to get his system (or lack of it) overhauled and still cover the war.

That same day he wrote out his instructions covering my mission in Normandy, which I quote verbatim and in their entirety: "You are to go to the forward zone and glean such information as may be of use to our historical teams. But you are to give no directions or orders, and you are to exercise no command authority whatsoever." Since these phrases are next to meaningless, they might have been a stopper. Instead, I found the card good for a chuckle. I already realized that, as an attached staff officer, such impact as I might have on the effectiveness of our field operations would come either through the influence of my example, or not at all. The dutiful men might respond to me, if they were at a loss for guidance. The goldbricks and scrimshankers would have no reason to change their ways because they knew I could not harm them. That still made the odds fair enough.

We embarked for France a few days later. Colonel Taylor was with me on that unforgettable one-night passage. Aboard were members of the First Army Staff. They insisted on a poker game in the wardroom, and like most soldiers enroute to a landing on a disputed beachhead, they bet well but not too wisely. My luck ran higher than a Bay of Biscay tide. By the dawn's early light, when we stood offshore, I was $1,733 to the good, and my playmates were broke, both in pocketbook and spirit. It was time to forget poker for the duration or until I traveled with another convoy.

One Higgins boat was already alongside, waiting for passengers. Members of First Army Staff were at the rail looking down at it, very doubtfully. There seemed no reason to hesitate. The day was bright, the sea reasonably calm. The displacement as the craft rose and dropped with the swell was not more than four feet, but my friends were contemplating descent by cargo net for the first time in their lives. I had done it seven times in the Pacific under more trying conditions. That makes a whale of a difference. I reckoned that all they needed was the influence of a strong example, and I dropped on down, fully loaded, to greet the coxswain. It was a bad guess. Though we waited half an hour, not one person followed. We shoved off, and I had the satisfaction of making a one-man landing on Utah Beach. The staff didn't budge until three hours later when a lighter came alongside the transport. I am not sure that the cargo net buffaloed them; possibly it was ostracism consequent to the poker game.

When Taylor caught up, we jeeped into Montebourg. There is a roundabout in the center of the town with five roads radiating from it like so many spokes from a wheel. As we bucketed into this circle, an MP directing traffic busily waved us down one of these exits.

I yelled to the driver: "Hold everything! That guy doesn't know where we're trying to go."

I walked back to the MP. "Now, you waved us on; where do you think you're sending us?"

"I don't know, sir."

"Which way does that road lead?"

"I have no idea, sir."

"Where do any of these five roads go?"

"I can't tell you, sir."

"How long have you been directing traffic here?"

"Two hours, sir."

"And you've been waving everybody along, without finding where they want to go, or knowing how to direct them there?"

"Yes sir."

"But why, man, why?"

"Because the lieutenant sitting over there on the curb told me only to take this post and keep traffic moving."

I strolled over to the lieutenant. "Why did you post that man there to route vehicles without informing him where the roads lead?"

"Because I don't know either, sir."

This was not the dumbest MP nor the most stupid lieutenant that I met in France. Somehow the expedition managed to find its way across France and ultimately take the right road home again, but from that moment forward, I was a skeptic praying for miracles.

These anecdotes should make clear that I did not land with the first wave on Omaha Beach or share the grandeur and misery of D-Day with the invading Americans. Even if Ambassador Winant had not cut out special work for me which kept me tied to England for four extra days, whether I wished it or not, I would not have rushed to the port and boarded a boat. My orders were cut for June 10, 1944. In the Pacific I had learned by trying it three times that a combat historian can get nothing effective done in the hour of landing amid the chaos of a littered beachhead. He but risks his life to no avail. His rule of action must ever be to push for the opportunity to deal with troops at the earliest moment when they will respond. That excludes the clinching hour when they are under flat trajectory fire, scattered and scared to death.

The combat historian's mind should be wholly free of preconceptions. What goes on, and not what was supposed to happen, should command his undivided attention. I didn't know the plan for Operation Overlord, and I had flatly refused to be briefed on it. Ganoe's young officers, on the other hand, were all thoroughly "bigoted," the term used to mean they were in on the big secret. That was another of their handicaps. The few who made any real effort had been flopping about like chickens with their heads chopped off, looking for deviations from plan instead of trying to take note of how operations had developed.

This was utterly futile: one might as well try to cover an earthquake by ascertaining what public utilities have become unhinged. As quickly as possible, I stopped all that and published an instruction that thereafter historical officers should not be briefed in advance on any unfolding plan. I wanted them to go in green; it kept their minds open and sharpened their appreciation of the realities.

I was not thinking of such things that afternoon. Taylor and I made it to a chateau which was serving as a temporary headquarters. At once I sent out word that I wanted the commander of First Army's historical team to come to me immediately; maybe two hours later he arrived, fit as a fiddle and breathing normally. After mess, we talked until late into the night. I wanted to know what he had covered from the landings of the 16th and 116th Infantry Regiments at Omaha Beach. He had done nothing.

"Why not?"

"Because they are still fighting in the lines."

"But don't you understand that we have to work with them anyway?"

"Well, there are too many companies in two regiments. With my few men, I couldn't possibly spread that far."

"Can't you see that you don't need to think in those terms? You don't have to think about regiments as a whole. I'll bet you a sawbuck that along either of those regimental fronts not more than five or six companies had pivotal performances. The greater number simply ciphered out. Your first job is to determine where the pressure was and how it was overcome. Then concentrate on these particular companies. That's how you proceed. You study the movement chart and then limit yourself. And you must do these things at once."

I then asked him if there was any part of the expedition that he and his team would not attempt to cover, due to his lack of resources. He said: "We're not planning to work over the U.S. airborne divisions: the troops are too scattered in the drop, and it's impossible to determine what happened."

At that point, we made our deal and shook hands on it. We would arise at 0630 next morning. He would head immediately for the 1st Infantry Division and do the work which I had laid out for him. I would go to the 101st Airborne Division at Carentan and would stay with the paratroopers and glider regiments until we had their story in full.

That was one of the coldest nights I ever knew. I had brought no blankets from England. There were no spares at the headquarters, and the chateau had no heat. The temperature was around freezing. With the aid of matches, I scrounged around in the chateau's attic until I found two large fabrics. In the darkness I spread and rolled into them until I was swathed like an Egyptian mummy, but they didn't cut the chill. By the dawn's early light, I was up and taking a first good look at my bedclothes: I had slept in two of the most beautiful Gobelin tapestries I have ever seen. These I folded neatly and left for some other rascal to liberate.

One rule of action I have observed scrupulously since my first day as a soldier: pick up no souvenirs, do no looting. This is not for the sake of honesty but in the interests of self-preservation. Excess weight kills more men in the field than enemy bullets.

Taylor and I waited until 0800 for our drinking companion of the night before to show his face. Then I went hunting, found him snoring in the sack, and yanked him out.

He asked: "What's the matter?"

"You agreed to start for the 1st Division at 0630, and I said I'd take the 101st."

He yawned in my face. "Oh, I thought that was just the alcohol talking."

I wanted to beat him over the head.

Good old Charley Taylor went with me to Carentan and spent that first day standing by. There was a reason. On our ride from England he had voiced his doubt about the validity of the standard operating procedures (SOP), especially the group critique, which I had pressed on the Historical Division during my tour in the Pacific. His skepticism was unavoidable. As a thorough scholar and Harvard professor steeped in historical method, he just couldn't believe that the process could be that simple. When I countered that it worked because it was simple, he objected that, if it were that good, someone would have discovered it earlier, to which I replied that the same could be said about any new thing under the sun. "You come with me one day," I said, "and if, after watching me do the work, you then feel any doubt about the validity of the method, we can renew the discussion."

My old colleague became a convert to the new idea that day. Thereafter Colonel Taylor went on to apply it more widely and effectively than the several younger professional historians we had with us, primary proof that he had more aptitude for his life's work.

In other ways, we got off to an auspicious start in Europe. Major General Maxwell D. Taylor, commanding the division, threw the door wide open and gave us full backing. It was my first meeting with that great soldier though our paths would cross many times through the years to come.

The first regiment with which I dealt was the 502nd Parachute, which had just come under the command of Lieutenant Colonel John H. Michaelis. Here was another remarkable coincidence; his father had been my father's close friend, the first army officer I ever knew. There were no better soldiers in Europe than the Five-O-Deuce. They stayed responsive through six hours of questioning. In fact, at first meeting I was so impressed with these "Screaming Eagles" that I then made the resolve to be with this outfit and make it my home afield whenever it was committed to battle. At the end of the road, when I at last hung up my soldier suit, I had seen more action with it than any other except the 32nd of the 7th Infantry Division, which was my mother in three wars.

In that first session I learned that to cover airborne operations I would have to reverse the working method that I had used with line regiments in the Pacific. Conventional infantry moves from order to diffusion during combat. Airborne troops begin with diffusion—the vertical drop—and move toward collection.

The problem with the airborne is one of following through on hundreds of threads—individual acts—and weaving them into a fabric. As is explained in *Night Drop,* during the process I discovered certain principles applying to airborne operations that the sky soldiers had not themselves yet recognized.

Carentan had been an extremely complicated action. Two of the 502nd's battalions had become so intermingled in the attack on the German entrenched position at Pommeranque Farm, the key to capture of the city, that to reconstruct the action it was necessary to critique the two formed as a whole and to continue the questioning of the formation through five days.

By far the largest group critique ever held, it proved to be hardly less manageable than interviewing a platoon. The most intricate jigsaw problem that I coped with in Europe, it was still a break for me in that everything thereafter was made to seem comparatively easy.

When I first met one battalion commander, Bob Cole, a West Pointer from San Antonio, he was already in for the Medal of Honor for having led the bayonet charge on Pommeranque Farm. The other, Pat Cassidy, as a reservist, had been decorated with the Distinguished Service Cross by General Omar N. Bradley on D-Day. (As I write, Pat is a lieutenant general, RA.) These two became my roommates.

Cole kept ragging Cassidy unmercifully for having won a "quota" medal and also kidded him for having brought his battalion to the fight at the farm after Cole's people had already won the day. Pat kept his temper and tried to laugh off the raillery, but it was not sweet to hear.

When finally I had finished putting the Normandy mosaic together, however, the picture showed clearly that Cassidy and his battalion had outperformed every other U.S. outfit of like size on D-Day. Further, the proof was there that Cassidy and his men had intervened just in time to keep Carentan from being lost by Cole's battalion. Ultimately I put these findings to Cassidy in an official letter that became a factor in his decision to follow a military career.

Once he saw the evidence, Cole accepted the verdict like a sportsman, and the heavy kidding stopped. Having long brooded over him, I would not have my feelings misunderstood at this point. He was my friend and I cherished his company. His breeziness was an antidote to small cares. Still, he was a strange, sad case, and for this reason is the story told.

One day, not long after Carentan, he blasted one of his captains in front of me with every vile name he could cough up. When the man was gone, I said: "You know, Bob, if you talked to me that way, I'd probably shoot you."

"You might, but he wouldn't."

"That's not the point. You shouldn't talk to anybody that way."

"I've got to. Don't you understand that?"

"Why?"

"Goddamn it, because I'm afraid."

"Afraid? You handle a battalion the way a man should lead a platoon—right up front. If you'd use sense, you'd have as much chance to survive the war as I have."

"That's not the problem. Every night I have nightmares that I have failed my men in some way; so I've made up my mind. Our next time out, I'm going to take a bullet, and get it over."

"Bob, you're crazy."

"You said it, I'm crazy."

He kept his word on the next time out. What a mournful waste! Bugged as he was, Bob outwardly seemed to have everything that a combat leader needed, and his soldiers adored him.

★

Eleven days of straight plugging afield, then the 101st and 82nd Divisions were outlifted to England to prepare for another drop, and I perforce went with them to continue the Normandy study. Most of the interviewing of General Matthew B. Ridgway's great division was done around Sherwood Forest. Meeting him was the beginning of one of my life's most rewarding friendships. Few soldiers in our history have had greater depth than he and he gave his own tone to whatever he commanded. I thought him worth following off the edge of the earth.

By July 1, I had completed the airborne, and then two pieces of business took me to London. The first was a call on Lieutenant General John C. H. Lee, who really ran the theatre. I had never met him and had been warned by individuals who should have known better that he was quite formidable.

The talk was brief. I explained to him that I had been called from the Pacific on a trouble shooting job, that I saw no chance to pull it off without his support, and I wished to be sure of his backing when I needed help.

A most surprised expression came over his face. Pointing to my ribbons, he said: "Old man, I respect your service. I'm looking at the battle stars. But if you had none, I would still go the limit for a soldier who talks as you do. You may call on me any time."

Cliff Lee, later so cruelly maligned by Robert Ruark when the latter was serving as a postwar correspondent in Italy, was better than his word. Repeatedly, he came to my help, once when I was bucking Eisenhower himself on an order that he had thoughtlessly given which, had I yielded, would have gutted my operation.

My other mission in London was to make certain that Ganoe did not flush any more good men down the drain of the First Army detachment until we could get it plugged. Three newly arrived combat historians, Captain Dick Shappell and Lieutenants John Westover and Fred Hadsel, had come to me at Nottingham. At the Pentagon they had taken our training course, much of which I had written, but they were as mystified as ever about how to do the work. I had them in the field with me for five days while I worked over units of the 82nd Division. Watching, they got the idea almost at once. Nothing else works half as well as on-the-job training.

When the story on the 29th's Omaha Beach ordeal was wrapped up, Westover and I took off on the most giddy adventure of my military life, and of his, also.

Chapter 10
When Papa Took Paris

From this war there is one story above others dear to my heart, and I have never before written a line about it—the loony liberation of Paris.

There are reasons for this restraint: a promise once made; the unimportance of trying to be earnest about that which is ludicrous; the vanity of the hope that fact may ever overtake fiction; and the blight of the passing years on faded notes.

Then there is another thing—like a sweet dream, yesterday's rose, or last month's pay, the event was gone before one could grasp it. From first to last it was as fantastic as Uncle Tom done by the late Cecil B. De Mille.

When the smoke cleared on the night of the liberation, nine of us dined at the Hotel Ritz. Officially we were the only uniformed Americans in Paris. That knowledge made us more giddy than did the flow of champagne. There was food fit for the gods and service beyond price, but the head waiter made one ghastly blunder.

He slapped a Vichy tax on the bill. Straightaway, we arose as one man and told him: "Millions to defend France, thousands to honor your fare, but not one sou in tribute to Vichy."

He retired in confusion, crying "It's the law!" and clutching a $100 tip. It was our finest and final victory of the evening. Then we did a round-robin signing of menu cards for the benefit of posterity. Among my souvenirs is the paper bearing the signatures of Colonel David K. E. Bruce, Brigadier General Edwin L. Sibert, Ernest Hemingway, Commander Lester Armour, USNR, G. W. Graveson, Captain Paul F. Sapiebra, Captain John G. Westover, and J. F. Haskell. Above the signatures is the caption: "We think we took Paris."

But we agreed on something else. Hemingway said it. "None of us will ever write a line about these last twenty-four hours in delirium. Whoever tries it is a chump." On that pledge, we solemnly shook hands, raised our glasses, broke up, and redeployed.

Still, there had been a few touches which kept the show earthbound, encouraging the thought that we were not sleepwalking. For our column, the advance ended at the top of Avenue Foch in midafternoon. By then Paris was almost as free of gunfire as a modern Fourth of July picnic. I walked on a hundred yards to get a front view of the Arc de Triomphe. At least 6,000 cheering Parisians thronged the Etoile. As I gazed upward, one last tank shell, out of nowhere, hit the outer edge of the stone pillar fifteen feet up. There was no chance to judge the effect on the crowd. The square was absolutely empty before the echo died; the human tide simply evaporated. Not even a gendarme remained to cover the Eternal Flame.

Then I looked down the Champs Elysées, hoping for a sign in keeping with the splendor of the hour. It was there all right, a great canvas ten feet deep, moored to the top stories of the buildings which faced the arch and dominating the broad avenue. It read: "Hart, Shaffner & Marx Welcomes You," the final blessing on a great day. Next morning's promise was even brighter. By then a French antiaircraft gunner from a battery which had set up next to the arch had shot the sign down.

The Etoile, as all who visit Paris know, is like a bull's-eye, the great avenues radiating like spokes from a wheel hub. The last street, as one approaches the arch, rue de Presbourg, makes a circle around the Etoile.

Our final burst of sound and fury in the freeing of Paris occurred along this roundabout. Save for cheering and the popping of champagne corks, the end of the drive along Avenue Foch had been quiet. At the circular street, the head of the column split, and the French armor and halftracks deployed around it in both directions in a pincers movement perfectly designed to envelop the Unknown Soldier, had there been any resistance around him. Curious about the next move, I parked the jeep in front of No. 1 Avenue Foch and walked forward.

That was a mistake. Before I had passed two doors on Presbourg, the street was a gut of automatic and cannon fire which swept in both directions. The scars from that blast are still to be seen on the Presbourg walls. Some of it was random shooting aimed at nothing in particular, but several of the vehicles plainly were concentrating their fire on an apartment building opposite No. 1 Avenue Foch.

There was nothing to do but sink back into the nearest window embrasure, suck in my guts, and hope for the best. Through the shot and shell came the girl from Bilbao who figures in this story. She carried a carbine. She said: "I saw the weapon and knew that either you or John [Westover] was unarmed; so I came looking." What a woman! I pulled her up into the embrasure, and we stood there perfectly helpless.

This mad shooting went on for thirteen minutes. When it died, Paris began the return to normalcy which has lasted until now. I went looking for the French major commanding the forward tanks, simply to ask him: "What in hell are you doing?"

He said: "We're tranquilizing that enemy-held building."

"What enemy?"

His reply was positively fierce. "It is defended by the Japanese. We saw them at the window."

No answer was possible. It would have been as pointless to tell him that he was nutty as to accuse his troops of shooting up Paris real estate to enjoy an illusion of valor. But there was some argument for quitting his battalion at that moment and sitting on the curb.

The show was over. The tanks were moving on to a bivouac in another part of the city. The apartments lining the avenue were now spilling forth Frenchmen laden with pâtés, cold bottles, and frozen grapes. The jeep had taken two bullets from this last round of foolishness, one getting the windshield and the other a tire.

We drank. We ate. We glowed. And there was at least one bit of entertainment. Along the curb opposite, three Frenchmen and one woman suddenly ganged up on one female, rode her down into the street, and were ready to apply scissors to her locks. It was too much for Sergeant Red Pelkey, Hemingway's driver. He was over there in a bound, kicking the hell out of the three men and shouting at the top of his voice: "Leave her alone, goddamn you, you're all collaborationists!"

Amid such diversions, we were still sitting on the curb one hour later when we saw a small Oriental peering from the doorway of the bullet-riddled building across the street. He scuttled through the garden and collapsed just inside the gate. We walked to him. He was bleeding from a bullet crease in the shoulder but was more frightened than hurt.

I asked him: "Who are you?"

"Tonkinese—laundryman."

"What were you doing in the building?"

"Washing clothes."

"You looked from the building when the tanks went by?"

"Yes, I looked out to cheer parade."

So there it was. The major had been right, in a way. We put a first-aid pack on the little man. Unwittingly, he had been a hero of sorts—the last simulated spark of resistance to the Resistance.

Other scenes in this melodrama were no less mad. It is the only argument for beginning at the beginning, knowing that one will not be believed anyway.

★

Maybe Hannibal in front of Rome had as much good, clean fun, but I am inclined to doubt it. He had gone there on purpose and that rules him out. I set it down as an almost inviolable principle that the truly good things which happen to you in war come by accident, like manna out of heaven, rather than because any earthly authority ordered or planned it that way.

Certainly, it was true of my connection with the liberating column. I didn't belong with the expedition, and I had no intention of assigning myself to it for kicks. That's a fool's errand. The law of gravity determined the matter. I simply fell in and in the end couldn't get out.

I had been with two U.S. airborne divisions, the 82nd and 101st, in southern England, completing my mission of determining what had happened to them in the Normandy drop. When I left them, they were already assembled in "The Bottoms," poised for a second jump into France. There was reason enough to accompany them since the show was certain to be a good one.

There was an even more compelling argument for rejoining the First U.S. Army in the breakout, since I hadn't completed the account of the 1st Infantry Division's landing at Omaha Beach. The Big Red One* had been put through the meat grinder; it was necessary to find out how and why it had happened. On leaving my airborne friends, I promised that I would link up with their drop as promptly as possible and then headed across the Channel, looking for whatever sector was held down by the 16th Infantry Regiment.

Now that was where Lady Luck began to take hold. The 16th Regiment was in line, but its slice of the front was quiet, and it was obvious that my work could be completed quickly. On joining the regiment, I happened to mention my other commitment with the airborne divisions to the regimental commander. There followed one week of debriefing his troops on the earlier operation. On the seventh day, at 0900, I completed my notes and dismissed the last formation. It was time to thank the CO for his help.

Before I could open my mouth, he said: "I've got news for you. A flash just came in over the radio. Paris has just been liberated. Also, there has been an American air drop across the Seine. I suppose you want to hit the road."

We didn't take time to say goodbye. Westover, my man Friday, was already heading for the jeep. We took off in a cloud of dust. We didn't stop anywhere to check the reliability of this operational information. A good man had said it and we believed it; the thing was just as simple as that. That is how it happens in war. Natural impulse is ever the enemy of normal caution. The less fortunate die because of it. The hard facts were that there had been no air drop, and Paris was still far from being liberated, but we had to learn these things through trial-and-error while luck ran a footrace with folly.

---

*Respectful army nickname for the 1st Infantry Division, gained from the appearance of its shoulder patch.

As the jeep chugged through a dozen or so liberated villages and snorted through the streets of Chartres, all sights and sounds were consistent with the morning's news. The ways were thronged with milling, enthusiastic crowds, buoyant as if on holiday. The highways were nigh choked with military transport, pushing slowly eastward as if drawn by a magnet. There were no MPs in sight, and seemingly no control points anywhere.

At the outskirts of Chartres, a gentleman farmer flagged us down.

He said: "You have a funny army."

I said: "No funnier than any other army, but why do you think so?"

"Because it isn't allowed to drink milk."

"The hell it isn't; it drinks more milk than whisky."

"You're wrong. I brought out enough milk cans to take care of two battalions passing through. The first company was crazy about it. Then up came a major who told me your troops were not allowed to drink milk; so I hauled the rest of it back to the farm."

He was very sad. I wanted to console him. I said, "You see, old chap, we have in our country a purifying process. Our troops can't drink milk unless it's pasteurized."

At that point, he fairly wailed. "Why didn't they tell me? Pasteur was my grandfather. And you tell me how to purify milk?"

We had no way of knowing that before this show was over, we would have to conclude that the great scientist had pasteurized quite a tribe of Frenchmen.

At high noon we came to Rambouillet. We raced through without pausing for lunch or gas. In fact, we hadn't even noted the name. Six or seven miles past that fair city lies a small village named Buc. We got within a quarter mile of it and approached a wooded hill around which the road twists into the village.

I yelled to Westover: "Stop the jeep!"

He braked, then yelled back: "What's the matter, got the wind up?"

"You're damned right. Did you ever hear anything as silent as this? Not a sound anywhere along the road, and there isn't any wire laid along the road. Turn around and barrel. We're in enemy country."

That was what we did. Two miles to our rear, we bumped into a battalion of French armor setting up a roadblock at a main intersection. I asked the commander: "Why are you going into position here?"

"This is the front."

"Why don't you go on to Buc? There's a nice wooded hill just this side of it from where you can cover a spread of country."

"That's the point. There are fifteen Tiger tanks on that hill partway dug in. We have spotted them from the air. Why fight them if you can turn them? I don't think we'll take that road to Paris. Nobody goes to Buc."

"We went to Buc—or almost."

In a field echeloned slightly to the rear of the French tankers was an American unit—an antiair battery, one of Twelfth Army Group's stray chickens.

Well, they ought to know something. We sauntered over and I asked the skipper: "What are you doing here?"

"Doing here?" As he echoed the words he sounded as if he wanted to have a good cry. "I don't even know where I am. I decided to wait till somebody tells me."

"Sounds very sensible." Knowing no light was to be had from this quarter, we walked back to the roadblock crew. While we were still talking to them, a jeep, mad with power, came racing into the crossroads from the direction of Versailles. It had to stop because of the block. In it were two French civilians and a man in green twill who identified himself as Colonel Williams of the Office of Strategic Services (OSS).

They had come from a rendezvous in St. Cloud, outside Paris, with a group of Maquis who led the Paris resistance. Williams recounted the conversations and got finally to the raw meat. "It's all wrong about the city being liberated. This morning another five thousand SS arrived and joined the garrison. They intend to fight for it."

This wasn't quite the afternoon for jumping a jeep across the Seine. One illusion had gone bang, though faith in the report of an American air drop near Paris still persisted.

Westover and I doubled back to Rambouillet with the idea of getting a cold bottle and victuals while pondering what to do next. On the edge of town we saw a Fighting French motor park and turned in with the sole object of putting the jeep under guard while we engaged in a beer or two. It proved to be the headquarters of the French 2nd Armored Division, which had beaten us to Rambouillet by an hour or so. We learned this when a colonel embraced me and introduced himself as General Leclerc's G-2.

He asked: "Where have you come from?"

Stretching things a bit, I said: "From Buc."

"Impossible!" he replied. "No one has been to Buc."

I told him all that I had heard from his own people and ours—the presence of the enemy tanks at Buc, the position of his roadblock, the news from Williams that Paris was far from liberated.

The colonel's eye gleamed. He said, "I must take you to Leclerc. You must tell him all. This is major intelligence."

"My dear colonel, you could get on a bicycle, ride down that road for about an hour, and learn everything I have told you. You won't find Colonel Williams, though. He headed south, looking for a bath. He says he is very dirty."

"My friend, this is more than we have heard all day. You would be surprised at the distance separating my desk from what I need to know."

Though in the telling the incident seems absurd, the grain of comfort is that in the doing it seemed tenfold sillier. Thus dragooned, we met Leclerc, who even in his fly-ridden tent looked and acted like a miniature Mars. Of this dedicated and courageous fighter for France, killed in a peacetime air crash in the Sahara, many hands have written, and my experiences with him were so brief that nothing worthwhile can be added.

What stays in my memory is as vague as the impression of a Cheshire cat minus the grin. The figure was trim and dressed as if for a skirmish. The face was abnormally pink, the eye steely cold, and the mustache clipped close to vanishing. While I talked, he stood rigid, not even flexing a facial muscle. Well, no, that is not quite correct.

As I reached the point of saying, ". . . and according to Williams there are five thousand newly arrived SS in the city who will fight for it," for the first time Leclerc relaxed.

Putting his hand on my arm, he smiled radiantly and pointed an index finger toward heaven. "Have no fear! I, Leclerc, shall smash them!"

It was a wonderful pitch, and quite suddenly I came awake to it. The colonel had introduced me as historian of the United States Army. Leclerc was talking for the benefit of Clio, the Muse of History.

I got out my little notebook, and I wrote down his immortal words, which are here reported for the first time. On several occasions during the advance, I saw and talked to Leclerc again. His assured presence was an antidote to the contagion of fear, and he smashed the enemies of France at every opportunity.

That was the end of the conversation. Suffice to add that the urge to drop pearls for harvesting by future generations is not peculiar to Frenchmen or limited to their generals. The trouble is that few have the inspired brevity to match Major General Ralph Smith's gem of an official message when he reported the conquest of his assigned island in the Gilberts: "Makin taken."

In the heart of Rambouillet was an ancient hotel, delightfully shaded. There Ernest Hemingway had held forth during the preceding several days while the town was being defended by a group of French partisans (FFI). Colonel David K. E. Bruce of the OSS, later U.S. ambassador to the Court of St. James, was with him. Together, they supervised the irregular operations around Rambouillet, while American units maneuvered in the general neighborhood but did not close on Rambouillet. Many tall tales have been written about Force Hemingway. The real story is good enough. As a war writer, Hemingway spun fantastic romance out of common yarn, but he had the courage of a saladang, and he was uncommonly good at managing guerrillas.

That afternoon he was away from the hotel. Its surrounding apple orchard swarmed with bees darting at the honeysuckle, and big-name war correspondents attacking the apples. There was enough talent in that plot to cover Armageddon.

Ernie Pyle was there, a bit unsteady, a little teary. It was our last conversation. No, he wasn't going for Paris, the hell with Paris. He said: "I'm leaving here to go home. I can't take it any longer. I have seen too many dead. I wasn't born for this part. It haunts me. I'll never go to war again. I'll never let anyone send me. I'll quit the business first."

A great little guy—but hardly clairvoyant.

What I did not know when I talked to General Leclerc and found him ignorant of his situation was that he had been on the road most of that day with his division, barreling from Argentan, which is a hellish long haul for armor.

To jump from the small picture in the Rambouillet apple orchard to the grand design ordered from on high is appropriate to the liberating operation. It had no continuity, and its reckonings were made, as a submariner would say, by guess and by God.

There was in Paris one M. Gallois, leader of an especially aggressive resistance group. In mid-August his forces had started pushing the Germans around, driving them from building to building by fire. The situation became so acute that the Germans asked for a truce, starting the night of August 20 and continuing until noon on August 25. The fact was that General Von Cholitz, their commander, did not have his heart in the defense and was stalling for a break, which would relieve him of his embarrassment without scuttling his honor.

Because of the truce, M. Gallois jumped the gun, taking it for granted that the job was done, and Paris was delivered. That was how the rumor floated out of a semi-solid foundation. Like Revere, Gallois mounted his horse and rode to carry the word, heading for General Patton's Third Army.

From its headquarters, he was passed by Colonel La Belle, the liaison officer, to the Twelfth Army Group's command post. The G-2, Brigadier General Edwin L. Sibert, took what Gallois had told him and went by plane to carry the story to Generals Eisenhower and Bradley, who were at that hour conferring.

On getting the news, Bradley said to Eisenhower: "Let's send the French 2nd Armored in." That is how the decision was made, according to Sibert, the eyewitness, and that is how it was done.

Being at Argentan, at least three days' hard driving from the target city, Leclerc's force was not in the most favorable position to move up swiftly and close the gap created by the Third Army's bypassing of the Paris area. The vacuum around Rambouillet, which Hemingway's bulk had partly plugged, was a happenstance of the wait while Leclerc came up.

General Omar N. Bradley, for all his native shrewdness and hard practicality as an operator, is at heart a sentimentalist. Months before, while in

Africa, he had promised that if he could have his way, when the hour came to free Paris, Frenchmen would do it. He perhaps did not anticipate that it would be his responsibility to call the shots. Still, he remembered.

However, if the high command shared in full the supreme optimism of M. Gallois, it still left very little to chance. The jury-rigged plan which developed around the main idea of passing the laurel to Leclerc's division was framed with due caution. Its parts made Leclerc's advance a major reconnaissance in force, rather than a road march, designed to test whether the Germans intended to stand and fight before backing away.

Leclerc got his orders at Argentan on a Tuesday afternoon. His division was to move to the northwest rim of Paris and demonstrate there. The clear purpose was to threaten and abort the garrison under Von Cholitz if possible, rather than to engage it. In the subsequent move, still not entering Paris, the French armor was to make a great wheel around to the southwest of the city, then force an entry in the neighborhood of Sèvres. In so doing, it should snare most of the game.

The U.S. 4th Infantry Division was then a few miles southwest of Lonjumeau and much closer to Paris. The plan proposed for it was a kind of backstop role, to move but not to fight, to hang its clothes on a hickory limb but not go near the water. Major General Barton's mission was supposed to be complete when his command "seized high ground south of Paris," there to shout yoo-hoo at the Eiffel Tower across magnificent distance.

The 4th Infantry got its orders on the afternoon of August 23, by which time Leclerc was already closing on Rambouillet, so that the two divisions were approximately equidistant from the heart of Paris. The timing was perfect. From the topside view, it must have looked as if everything was set.

Nothing intervened to spoil the script except its own unsuitability. The architects had thought of the liberation as a normal military operation rather than as a what's-it for which the TV people have since coined the label "a spectacular." The plan simply frustrated the desire of the French to fight for their capital even more than it miscalculated the readiness of Germans to give them the opportunity.

Leclerc's assigned mission fell apart when he got word of the substantial force of German armor covering the road at Buc. He might have brushed off this block by bringing up the artillery or calling for an air strike. Now there was a palpable reason for changing direction, declining the oblique maneuver to the northwest, and by wheeling farther south, insuring that he would have to take his division directly into the city. In a very real sense, by momentarily risking the appearance that he was avoiding a fight, Leclerc was gambling that he would get a real one.

However, the change altered the whole frame of operations, whether because high command got an exaggerated impression of German strength or became dubious when Leclerc took the direct approach. On the next day, the U.S. 4th Infantry Division was ordered to go directly into Paris instead of cooling on the outside. Everybody loves a race, and so it happened that the division's spearhead—one battalion of the 12th Infantry Regiment— got to Notre Dame at noon on the big day just as Leclerc was crossing the Seine. History doesn't say so, but history is often wrong.

When in field operations a man jellies on the pivot, wondering what to do next, anything moving in what seems to be the right direction pulls like a magnet. That is how we happened to join General Leclerc's column headed for Paris. Busy man, he had neglected to invite us. Otherwise, he had been most courteous, but this was not his manner toward all men on that day. According to the legend which blooms larger every time any magazine writer dwells on Hemingway and war, he got to Leclerc and told him how to fight his battle and where to expect resistance. There's no doubt that the contact was made, but as to what came of it, Hemingway should be the best witness. He wrote: "We advanced in some state toward the general. His greeting—unprintable—will live in my ears forever. 'Buzz off, you un-speakables,' the gallant general said in effect in something above a whisper. Colonel Bruce, the resistance king, and your armored-operations correspondent hastily withdrew."

In the free-for-all situation, we had no orders. In late evening, we still dallied in the Hotel du Grand Veneur in Rambouillet, having almost given up the idea of joining the air drop across the Seine because the Germans obstinately blocked the road. Four tanks and ten halftracks passed the veranda, French-manned and headed east. Westover said: "Maybe they're going to bull through to Paris. Maybe that story about the roadblock at Buc is bunk. Maybe we ought to get going." With no more thought than that, we mounted the jeep and trailed after. The attachment was made ad hoc and was not thereafter questioned. The blue card which I carried entitling me to move anywhere I pleased in the theatre stayed in my pocket.

It was a short turn with no encores. The column veered south from the road we had traveled earlier and after a half-dozen miles pulled up in a wood southwest of Cernay-la-Ville. It was the division bivouac. In the forest of Fighting French, one almost missed the trees. Enough light remained to pitch the pup tent. That night nothing happened except steady rain and the arrival of an unsteady American major. He was from the staff of the U.S. V Corps but had somehow lost it. His tone was like a child deserted by mama.

Westover said to him: "The hell with V Corps. This show is headed for Paris. Come along, and you'll have the time of your life. If you're already lost, two days more won't hurt. Besides, the boss knows General Gerow and he'll square it for you."

The major said a few noble words about duty, then settled down, sleep-ing under his own jeep. When we were awakened at dawn by hundreds of Frenchmen booming like bitterns throughout the wood, he was all enthusi-asm. How could one avoid it? All around us were warriors scuttling about with the eccentric motion of waterbugs, pounding their chests and scream-ing *"En avant!"* Lasting all of ten minutes, that cry pulled us right out of our sacks, and when at last everyone grew hoarse, we en-avanted.

By breakfast time we were already into Cernay-la-Ville, the first town liberated along the Paris road. It was nice timing. Dear ladies, young and old, came running from their homes with platters of fried eggs, rolls, and coffee. I remember it as a little holiday of generous tears and laughter, unmarred by the crude words of one young punker: "Happy to see you. Give me one pack cigarettes for my papa. We have waited long."

At Cernay, Westover guided the jeep around the main body of the armor, and we joined the advance guard as it marked time on a hillside beyond the village. Again we marched. Chevreuse was already behind us, and the advance guard, made up of a few jeeps and four halftracks, was approaching the airport at Toussus-le-Noble when we heard the artillery speak for the first time. It was a novel situation. The column stopped in a defile where the road twisted through and over a narrow valley as steep-sided as a ravine. We could neither back away nor deploy. Off to our left we counted twenty-three muffled explosions. To me they signified nothing con-sequential.

I said: "They're going out."

Westover said: "Wrong, boss, they're coming in. There's something up ahead of us."

I knew he had to be right about it. Over forty years my hearing, though acute to most else, has never been attuned to the pitch of artillery shell. I'm tone deaf to explosions, though I don't know why. Westover knew the sounds like a maestro knows his scale. He had been a forward observer in Italy before I got him. Even in his sleep his subconscious told him the difference between outgoing and incoming noise. With our own guns pounding next to his ear, he snored happily on, but one incoming round bursting anywhere near would bring him awake. It was a joy to have him around.

Behind us, at some distance, a few French guns countered perfunctorily. Then we lurched on. Nothing ahead had been reconnoitered, but when *en avant* is the watchword, prudence has no virtue. By the time the advance guard topped the rise, we had company. The lead battalion, a motorized unit riding trucks and attended by armor, had closed the interval and was right on our heels. The one road cut straight through the center of the airport. The lead of the column was riding virtually bumper to bumper as we drove along this causeway. We got midway. The passage was still a defile. On either side of us, the fields (which had been an airport), where they were not bomb-cratered, were an impassable morass. Either go ahead or stall—there was no other choice.

It was stall, but not by choice. From directly in front of us, on a beeline, and not more than 1,100 yards away, an artillery piece suddenly spoke German. The whizzbang effect said it was an 88-m. Then ditto, ditto, ditto.

Our little tinclad van was rolling directly into the teeth of an enemy battery. From rightward of the battery somewhere a 105-mm also opened fire, and from left of it a heavy machine gun spat and sputtered.

These latter items were small change, but the fire from the 88s was a fast strike down the middle. The truck three lengths ahead of us was hit dead on. Then a jeep thirty paces to the rear got smacked.

It wasn't the right time to get out. We'd already made it. I had jumped to the slope of a drainage ditch which paralleled the road. Being more agile, Westover had vaulted it and was in a bomb crater beyond. As for the major from V Corps, he had jackknifed beautifully straight into the muck of the ditch bottom. He arose looking like a refugee from a sewer. He said: "I've been thinking it over. It was wrong of me to come along. I must return to my duty." He turned his jeep around and somehow managed to swing out past the stalled armor. We never saw him again, but he was a love while we had him.

No one has ever managed to diagnose the emotions of fish in a barrel. It could have been that bad but only momentarily. The shelling continued, but the German battery was getting nervous, and its stuff began going wild. Westover was much more comfortable in his bomb crater than I was, flattened on the bank of the roadside ditch. Since the battery was aiming straight down the road and the ditch ran parallel to it, clear to the guns, its bank offered only that relative mental peace which an infantryman knows when he tries to hide behind a one-inch sapling under shellfire, rather than sit, no more exposed, absolutely in the open. Not how things are but how they seem makes the difference between a tight clutch on the straw of security and a surrender to despair. Westover was happy enough in his muddy crater, but I knew we were not going to stay there; his horselaugh in my direction rang too loudly.

Forward along the road 150 yards, and that much closer to the battery, was a ruined building, partly wrecked by earlier air bombings and now smoking from a hit by the battery. Its stone walls still stood and beckoned. There lay sanctuary from the spite of the enemy, and even more from his noise. My aversion to that particular dual-purpose gun dates from 1918 when we called such artillery "Austrian 88s." The whizzbang impact on the senses even in that day made 88-mm fire seem as personally aimed as the derringer bullet that shot Mr. Lincoln. Except for a one-pounder, nothing is more demoralizing.

I yelled to Westover: "See that building? That's where we're going. Get moving!" As we slogged along, the battery fire seemed to be drifting off, as if the frightened gunners were reprieving the stalled column just when they had it dead to rights.

Nothing in life is stranger than the way in which a new association of ideas may quite suddenly change one's emotions toward a particular object, thought, or strain of music, and fix them steadfastly for all time. Until the war I had abominated Debussy's "Clair de Lune." It had been the theme song of the soap opera "Mary Marlin," or one like it, and like all gems in a huckster setting, had been well tarnished.

Not knowing it, I was at the point of change as we drew near the wrecked building. Its immediate setting and some brightness in the decor bespoke that it had been a cafe. One shell from the battery had knocked the sign from above the door some minutes earlier. We turned it over. It said "Clair de Lune." In the years since, I have loved this piece of music steadily and passionately. There was a charmed hour within the strong walls of that old cafe. Inside was what reporters describe as a shambles. Part of the wall was blown in. The furniture was all either smashed or overturned. Empty bottles, cruets, and shattered china littered the floor. The air hung heavy with the mingled aromas of horse manure and stale beer.

While we looked and poked about, hopeful of finding a name brand to be plucked from the burning, from under the overturned bar came the low-throated chuckle of a woman. There was something very pleasant about it, as if she were laughing at us, not because we looked funny but because that was the best way to greet another human.

We turned the bar upright and she stood. It is enough to say how she looked on first sight since she did not change later. She was small and slight and much too ill clad and dirty to be described as a gracious figure. Her dark face was marred by conspicuously bucked teeth. The eyes were brown almost to blackness. Tangled hair hung stringily halfway to her waist. Her gown looked like a cut-down Mother Hubbard, once black, faded to gray, and frequently slept in. Such was Elena and she was just eighteen. No unkempt damsel ever wore a warmer or less embarrassed smile. I will give Elena that, adding also that her courage made her seem beautiful during the two days we knew her.

The reason for these rough-hewn details is that the great American novelist was later to picture her as a gorgeously bewitching siren who held every man of the column in the hollow of her classic hand. Also, he made of her a profound philosopher, spouting great words about noble causes, whereas I have known few women who have had such an appalling gift of reticence. That was for *Collier's,* but it was also for the birds. Elena was, as I have set her forth, simple and unbeautiful. Hemingway hadn't yet stumbled into this scene, but he was on his way in search of a friendly wall. Outside, the stalled armor was still taking a pasting from the battery. It was good to be inside.

Elena's first words were: "What is American opinion of Marshal Pétain?" So help me—that was what she said, even before she had tugged at a stocking or straightened her dress. A most unusual woman, though the strangeness of her mental processes was not more startling than the irregularity of her speech. A light dawned. Since her French conjugation was almost as abominable as my own, she too must be a stranger.

I said in Spanish: "You are not French?" (We never got around to saying how Pétain rated back home.) She grinned proudly and replied: "I'm from Bilbao. I came here to fight with the resistance. My man is FFI. He's somewhere out in front of this column."

As she said it, Hemingway came through the door. We had last talked at Key West in 1936, but it could have been the day before. Like Elena, Ernest wasn't saying any onstage words for history. As if the sun would also rise, or there might be death in the afternoon, depending on the answer, he yelled: "Marshall, for God's sake, have you got a drink?"

The answer was no.

"We've ransacked this place," I said. "We don't have; we have not."

Westover spoke. "Boss, there's a fifth of Scotch in your pack back in the jeep. You put it there three weeks ago and forgot it."

"Okay, bigmouth, for having such a good memory you can walk back through that fire and get it." He did.

One of the minor surprises of war is the great thirst of any group of fugitives from the law of averages. With Elena helping on the Scotch—I had just introduced her to Hemingway—that bottle was a dead soldier within twenty minutes. So by then were quite a few members of the German battery, the French artillery having at last gotten the range.

That isn't how the story came out in *Collier's*. Here's how Ernest saw it: "I took evasive action and waded down the road to a bar. Numerous guerrillas were seated in it, singing happily and passing the time of day with a lovely Spanish girl from Bilbao whom I had last met at Cognieres. This girl had been following wars and preceding troops since she was fifteen, and she and the guerrillas were paying no attention to the *accrochage* at all. A guerrilla chief named C asked me to have a drink of his excellent white wine." Ah, there's romance, and isn't it fun to be a pack of guerrillas once in a lifetime? Who'd have thought it?

Too late for him, early enough for us, we were joined by a remarkable character with the nom de guerre of "Mouton," leader of the local FFI. His real name was Michel Pasteur. This particular descendant of the great scientist was about thirty-five, tall and spare, with flaming red hair and sky-blue eyes. He had the stride, carriage, and dress of a hog drover. Beyond his courage, Mouton's overawing asset was his silence. He had maximized the art of making himself understood by means of variously intoning a grunt. It wasn't his fault exactly that in the Hemingway stories about the liberating of Paris, Mouton became the reincarnated Demosthenes. Somebody had to put words in his mouth, or they'd never have made it.

Mouton grunted, belched, and pointed left. We took it to mean that we were to prowl outward through the ruined hangars toward the German machine gun to see if it was still in action. By then we were all feeling hardy as lions. Hemingway said: "If we get in any trouble, I will take care of you," which gave Westover such a giggle that he almost split his Silver Star ribbon. Such cracks were a habit with Ernest, due to his owning the copyright on war. There were other reasons why he was called Papa, but this one was good enough.

The German battery was still firing feebly, and with the occasional rounds from the 88s was mixed some supporting stuff from one automatic gun and a few rifles.

Out of this unique situation came the weirdest order of attack that I have ever seen in any military operation. We advanced with jeeps in line first, followed by trucks in line, followed by halftracks, followed by tanks. In the emergency there was no other way to thin out the formation. As the unarmored vehicles began to spread over the open fields, the halftracks and tanks, gripping on solid ground, would swing out and around, pinching in toward the battery from both sides.

From where we rode, the prospect could be faced cheerfully. We were the next to the last jeep with the advance guard. The road ahead, at the point where the extension would begin, was shaded by a straight line of Lombardy poplars all the way to the battery and slightly inside of it. When the other jeeps deployed, we could hold the road and hug the line of the trees. It was a very satisfactory bumper guard now that the battery was dying.

Silly as it sounds, the thing went off well. We were within 500 yards of the guns when the finish came. The tanks and halftracks completed their sweep, firing like crazy. No flag was waved. No shout was heard. Suddenly we saw twenty or thirty men come out of the nest and stagger across the open field toward us, hands in air. Only one man couldn't, because one hand and arm had been shot away. Still, he reeled along. Others were bleeding from chest, head, shoulder, or legs.

No one minded or paid the slightest heed. They were walking emptily into nothingness, and we were again back to the road with everyone straining toward Paris. Some must have continued this march macabre until they bled to death. I have seen few uglier sights in combat.

Because of the slough, the knocked-over hangars at the air field, and the wreckage of the two B-17s, we didn't get very far very fast. Finally the way was wholly blocked. It was then that Hemingway said: "I think we ought to patrol all the way if you're up to it." Mouton grunted. Again Westover laughed. Together, we shagged back to Clair de Lune, and there was no further mention of patrolling.

It was all so like Papa. He would still have tried to amble forward had anyone picked up his idea; that he might have been shot for his pains was immaterial. He loved soldiering, with reservations. Being in an armed camp exhilarated him, and he had a natural way with the military. The excitement and danger of battle were his meat and drink, just as the unremitting obligation to carry on was his poison.

To put it more accurately, he loved playing at soldier on the grand scale, with shooting irons; yet in him it was not a juvenile attitude. I truly believe he played at it because he enjoyed the game more than because he was interested in studying men under high pressure. There was this difference in view between us. I have always looked at war as a matter-of-fact business, requiring the rejection of every unnecessary risk and the facing of any danger along the path of duty. A man fully aware of his genius can afford more than that.

There was sudden motion at the front of the column. No signal came to us at the wrecked cafe, but it was in the air that we were about to move again.

Hemingway said: "What about the girl?"

"Well, what about her?"

"She can't be left here. The countryside remains in German hands. The column is only mopping up a highway. Leave her here and she may be killed or captured."

That was how we came to welcome Elena aboard the jeep, and why it happened that a Spanish girl held high the first American flag that went into Paris. I was not under General Leclerc's orders, he didn't dare bounce me, and no one else felt safe to lift her. We suddenly acquired a traveling companion, and Hemingway made a first sighting of a love theme for another story about men in war.

The column was still in a defile, made so by the quagmire on both sides of the road where an air field once had been. In the van of the column were jeeps and trucks. Perhaps 500 yards forward of the first vehicle, the earth flanking the road became solid. There we could fan out and deploy in line.

That sudden decision to pick up Elena and take her to Paris, made as lightly as one plucks a kitten from a puddle, had unlimited romantic consequences, not at the moment foreseeable.

Elena was the innocent catalyst rather than the prime mover. We lacked a spare helmet or knitted cap, the jeep was topless, and with her long tresses floating in the breeze as we buzzed along, there was no way to disguise her. For that day of razzle-dazzle fire and movement, she was a conspicuous heroine, the lone woman in a column of armored Frenchmen.

As night fell, the men obviously thought of other things than war. By the time a late moon found us bivouacked in the gutters opposite the Renault plant on the wrong side of the Seine, there was not a tank, halftrack, or truck in the column but bloomed with women. Each frowning turret looked like a beauty-parlor ad, and the squealing within and around the hulls did not come of grit in the bogie wheels. Leclerc's mobile division had suddenly doubled in size while losing half of its fighting power, which is a modern miracle. Higher officers tried to do something about it. Men pointed to the river as if to say "Go jump!"

There were other attachments than Elena, less embarrassing but not more mysterious. At Toussus-le-Noble, a number of U.S. correspondents got up to the advance guard. I remember few names and faces, but I think Jack Belden, Beaver Thompson, and Ken Crawford were in this sortie. Leclerc just didn't like newsmen, though he loved historians. One of his staff colonels tried to give these heroes the bum's rush, shouting that they lacked orders.

I said: "Turn them over to me. I'll be responsible."

The colonel protested. "But you have no troops!" and when I said, "But that will give me some," he more or less folded.

However, he got in one parting shot. "You will report on them regularly!" which was wonderful, inasmuch as I never saw any of them again, except Hemingway. He stayed close. The others wandered off, looking for this or that, and some got the heave-ho from the French as soon as they passed from sight.

Memory's a witch. Thinking back, I would have sworn that the German battery at Toussus was overwhelmed in a breeze with no loss to our side, but thumbing through my faded notes I find this entry: "As we advance, one French halftrack, turning into the battery, is hit dead on. Ahead of me an overloaded weasel takes a direct hit from a shell. Our losses, six killed and eleven wounded." Possibly someone paused to give first aid, but I do not remember it. The pell-mell nature of the advance produced a kind of hypnosis which dulled the mind to sights and sensations.

We churned on to Jouy-en-Josas. There the column blocked and stopped as the van started uphill through the main street. We were hard by the railway station, and for five minutes the wait was joyous. Out poured the townsfolk, their arms loaded with cold bottles of champagne. Mothers lifted babies to be kissed, only to be crowded out by the younger beauties of the place who had the same general idea. Old soldiers, who looked like relics of the Franco-Prussian War, lined the sidewalks, standing at stiff salute.

Then the music started. The Germans had a heavy mortar battery in a nearby chateau and behind it two field guns. They had the right notion but lacked the range. A few rounds hit the town church. Others landed on a wooded knoll immediately to our backs, without visible effect except to increase the flow of bubbly. Three French tanks charged the battery position; one was knocked out, the others finished the action.

We moved up to the main street and again halted. Twenty-one German prisoners, several of them wounded, all of them captured in the fight around the chateau, were brought back to be paraded single file down the main street of Jouy-en-Josas. About sixty Frenchmen of the advance guard formed facing each other within the street, holding aloft their rifles, mess gear, or any hard object that was swingable. As the Germans entered this gauntlet, they cracked down hard, aiming at the heads of the passing men. The Germans didn't try to run. They marched. Except where they reeled or fell from a blow, they took it heads up, eyes to the front, saying not a word, uttering no cry. They emerged from it looking as if they had been torn by wild beasts. There was wretched and unforgettable depravity in this scene, redeemed only by the bearing of a few helpless young men who knew how to walk seemingly without fear. To have tried to intervene would have been bolder than any act I saw along the road to Paris.

We were in motion again, and shortly we made a sharp turn onto a main avenue three kilometers east of Versailles. The road ahead was a mass of greenery, its surface blocked by a half-mile-long line of felled sycamore trees. At the far end was a conspicuous block formed by two overturned trucks banked with rocks and timber.

The leading French tanks moved uncertainly into this stuff and shunted away the first half of it, while we idled in the jeep. Four hundred yards off to our left was a dense copse covering an area the shape and size of a city block. Suddenly a man came running out of it, screaming in the wind.

I asked Elena: "What's he saying?"

"There's a German antiaircraft battery in that wood, three guns altogether, and they're ready to open fire."

So with the way partly cleared, we sped ahead, looking for the commander of the forward tank battalion to tell him he was about to be smacked broadside. We made it—or almost.

Through Elena, I told him. Nothing had yet happened. With every second counting, he still might have gotten his tanks around. At least he listened respectfully. Then he answered: "I know all about it; we've already taken care of that battery."

Never was an overconfident statement more beautifully punctured. It came like this—Boom! Boom! Boom!—right on our rear. At 400 yards point-blank the Germans couldn't miss. Behind us there was loud screaming. One vehicle on the pivot exploded. Another burst into flame. Said the French Major: "So now we know."

So much for the legend that intelligence supplied by Hemingway, with an assist from his two adjutants, Mouton and David Bruce, enabled Leclerc and troops to slip through to Paris, skirting the nodules of resistance. Nothing nastier could be said of them; not one sign of applied intelligence distinguished the operation. We careened through the countryside as witlessly as a convoy of boob bandits trying to shake off the law.

During this and the succeeding scenes, our great and gentle friend, Papa, was close beside us, right to the finish. Blessed be his memory, and hallowed his reputation for fighting gumption. They should not be sullied with canards such as this, quoted from one American magazine:

"Behind Papa's jeep wheezed the long line of Renault sedans, taxis, jalopies, and trucks, all of them crammed with Task Force Hemingway's fighters, now numbering more than 200. 'We'll tag along with Leclerc as far as Buc,' Papa said, 'then near Versailles where our information shows we will be slowed down by resistance, we'll swing around and come into Paris by a back road one of our bike boys found. The chief of staff didn't think the road was quick enough, but I do.' Just as Hemingway anticipated, Leclerc was temporarily pinned down along the south bank of the Seine by a small group of determined Nazis left behind by the retreating Germans. When Leclerc finally overwhelmed the resistance, his advance patrols moved into Paris. The Germans had deserted the city. As Leclerc entered he noticed a large sign hanging from the door of a cathedral: 'Property of Ernest Hemingway.' "

Well, glory and hallelujah. Papa stayed with us, then and later, never breaking away toward Versailles. His only attachment was Sergeant Red Pelkey, his jeep driver. Leclerc's boys acted like nitwits, but if they were slowed anywhere by resistance, it came from the mademoiselles, not the krauts. Papa deserves more credit than he has been given; he was not one to force his talents beyond their natural limits.

Our final lurch, after the column swung past Orly Field and then, turning leftward, entered the solidly built-up area south of the Seine, took twenty-four hours. Through the whole ride we were as perverse as possible. We tore madly along when reason whispered that we should proceed with care. We stalled insensibly whenever the way seemed wide open. It was less a fighting operation than a carnival on wheels. Take what happened after the German battery, concealed in the copse just off our flank, ripped the column broadside. Rather quickly, tank fire killed that battery, yet we did not turn back to see how much damage had been done to the people behind us. On the run forward, the jeep had pulled up between two medium tanks. In the shuffling which attended the exchange of fires, the tank behind us moved forward a few yards. It became impossible to turn. Then both tanks resumed the advance, and we went along between them willy-nilly rather than be run down. This proved embarrassing. A half mile forward our route turned left, at which point we headed straight toward the Seine.

Right at the junction, with piled explosives only twenty feet from the road we must take, was a block-long German ammunition dump. The stacked shells were already blowing sky-high, and even at a distance, the smoke, blast, and flame seemed like an inferno. For that, we could thank the killed-off German battery. With a final round or two it had fired the dump just before being knocked out of action. In so doing, it had blocked the road, or to put it more precisely, that was what we supposed for the moment.

The lead tanks came to the intersection. There was not even a pause for a close-up view of the danger. They wheeled left and advanced in file right across the face of the exploding dump. Metal showered the roadway, and the heat was like a blast from molten slag.

For the people within the tanks the risks were trivial. They had battened their hatches, and the plate was thick enough to withstand the hot fragments. They did not take it on the run as they should have done; they snailed along at about six miles per hour.

I yelled: "We can't make that run."

"We've got to," Westover yelled back, "or the tanks will crush us. They're not stopping for anything."

That's how it was. The jeep-borne people spliced into the tank column were held feet-to-the-fire by their own friends. That Mazeppa ride lasted not more than forty or fifty seconds by the clock, but the clock lied. There was no protection against either the flying metal or the infernal heat. The best one could do was cover his face with his arms, double up into as small a target as possible—and hope for the best.

Being on the outside, the jeep drivers had a little more insulation, but being drivers, they had to sit more or less erect to keep the vehicle on the road. Everything evened up, and nobody had it very good. Those were moments to be remembered. As here described, the thing may sound worse than in fact it was but no more ridiculous than it then seemed. Or is that really accurate? Was the folly of it given even a passing thought? In the swift transition attending a sudden danger, there is not even time for fear to down the first surge of wild excitement. That is also true of running into ambush in the jungle. The shaking comes later.

We pulled out of it whole-skinned. One shard had smashed through the hood of the jeep. Another had smacked the metal panel next to the jump seat, missing Elena's bottom by inches. The quarter-ton still perked. It was hellishly hot, and we were horribly thirsty.

There was not far to go. Where the dump ended, the metropolitan city began. We were soon among houses and stores and banking both sides of that broad lovely avenue were the people—and what a people!

They had waited four years for this parade, and they were ready with the *vin d'honneur* and much more. There were again the old guard standing at salute, wearing faded kepis and fresh-shined medals, young mothers rushing out with infants to be kissed, more beautiful blondes and brunettes (and some not so lovely), platoons of urchins screaming and frantically raising their hands in the V-signal, old gammers showing their petticoats when they raised their skirts to weep, and everywhere, men and women, shouting, laughing, crying, and embracing one another in ecstatic delirium.

It was about then that Westover pulled a folded star-spangled flag from his pack, mounted it on a pup-tent pole, and gave it to Elena to hold high. That small gesture of pure patriotism was the great mistake. Right then the unattached females along the march route began climbing into Leclerc's tanks and halftracks to stay. Elena had challenged them. It was time to strike a blow for France—and they didn't have any flags.

There was no way to refuse that mass of mad humanity. There were countless stops and starts by the column. Repeatedly, the people surged onto the avenue and stood solid until the armor ground to a halt. When they rushed the vehicles, it was not to pour champagne, cognac, and calvados; they dumped the bottles whole, the champagne chilled, the hard stuff still uncorked. When the jeep at last reached the bank of the Seine, like coals to Newcastle, it was carrying sixty-seven bottles of champagne on a run into Paris. To cap the climax, we gave it back to other Frenchmen. Like I say, everyone was a little cuckoo.

Papa Hemingway was still with us, and very busy, not instructing the FFI scouts, advising Leclerc, or bending the elbow. Like a happy tourist, he was snapping pictures of everyone and anything in sight.

That night we bivouacked on the broad avenue, a hundred yards short of the Pont de Sèvres, directly across the Seine from the Renault plant. From the Longchamps race track, the German artillery tried to bring the column under fire, but the closest shells hit high on the ridge running off in the direction of Versailles. Through the night our tank destroyers returned the fire from positions along the river bank. At midnight a flight of German bombers came over and dropped a few eggs. The explosions were hardly audible above the tumult in the street.

All morning long the column idled impatiently, but we couldn't cross the bridge before we came to it. The generals behaved like union men honoring the noon whistle. At exactly 1200 on August 25, 1944, we cranked up and rolled across the Seine at Pont de Sèvres. Except for occasional out-of-bounds rounds plunked into the scenery by the German batteries at the Longchamps course, there was nothing to remind us that the advance was a military action and not a pictorial parade into pandemonium.

"You Were There," the TV program that tried to reconstruct historical events, some years ago dramatized the loony liberation. It signally failed to recapture anything even vaguely familiar. Mass delirium and military moonshine, while rapturous to the participant, are much too elusive for art.

Scouts and heralds, with trumpets and dodgers, must have been sent forward to muster the crowd, for Paris was already alerted to the entry and had cast off its chains, though formally the Germans still held the city. For the first mile or so of march, the wild, high carnival of the prior afternoon was repeated, except that the crush had thickened and was less controllable.

Place-St-Cloud is the first roundabout beyond the Sèvres bridge. As the jeep turned into its spacious circle, suddenly the column blocked solid. We could not see why. The clamor had ceased. The central garden of the circle was utterly deserted as was its outer rim, which is built up solid with apartment houses. That one moment was pregnant with silence, made more awesome because there was no explaining it.

Then two things happened at once. A volley of rifle fire erupted directly behind us, and an artillery shell out of nowhere struck and felled a chestnut tree on the parkway so that it fell as a screen between the jeep and the nearest apartment building, thirty yards to our right. In those few seconds while the tree was settling, the tanks and cars ahead of us emptied, and the people (including Hemingway) ran for the buildings on the far side of the circle. Such was the effect of the surprise fire. We couldn't follow the stampede. All of the rifle fire was coming from the building just back of the jeep and the fallen tree. Westover crawled to one end of the tree so that he could cover the windows with his carbine. Elena stayed in the center. My part was to watch the other end lest someone from the lower story (which we couldn't see because of the tree) tried to push through the foliage toward us.

Punctuated by random rifle fire, this interlude lasted not more than five minutes. Then there was a roar and rattle from the direction we had come. Six French halftracks followed by five tanks raced into the circle, turned inside the stalled column, and continued round and round the circle with their machine guns wide open, blazing at the building we were facing. That fire grazed just above the jeep and stripped every twig and leaf from the upper part of the fallen tree. During the ten or so minutes that the French armor played merry-go-round, honoring our sector as if it alone contained the brass ring, no fewer than 5,000 bullets zipped directly above our heads or buzzed past our bottoms. It was not a choice spot to be stranded. There was nothing to do but hug the gutter and curb. Westover sang "I'll See You Again" through his teeth, which was always his habit when the wind was slightly up, a sign that he was thinking of home and Eloise. The Spanish girl said: *"Tengo mucho miedo,"* and laughed like hell to prove it. She was worth any ten duchesses in such moments. We knew great fear and high excitement exquisitely mixed, for it was touch-and-go whether we'd come out of it. The shooting stopped when there was nothing left to fire. We were whole-skinned and not yet shaking. The whole thing was stark mad, and the escape of our party was due purely to luck and not to the quality of French marksmanship. We had heard any number of bullets zing as they bounced off pavement and curb. Still, the jeep was untouched.

The tanks rumbled off. The place quieted. We heard a man yelling from a great distance. Then we saw him, and the sight was more whimsical than all else. He was on the third floor balcony of the apartment building across the circle, and he was hunched far over as he scuttled along. "Looks like Lon Chaney haunting Notre Dame," said Westover. The man had his hands cupped, and though he shouted in French the words barely cut through the wind, but we knew the voice. It was Papa again.

"What's he saying?" This to Elena.

She answered: "There are Germans in the building behind us. We have to get out. The French are bringing in artillery to blow the place down."

We got out. Elena went first, taking those eighty yards like a startled doe. We followed at twenty-second intervals, with Westover coming last so that he could cover the windows against snipers during the getaway. Not one hostile round dignified the extrication. When we made the portal on the far side, there was Hemingway with his carbine at shoulder, laying down the covering barrage. That was a big building, and he could hardly have missed it. The French artillery duly arrived and did its sterling stuff. Whether there were ever any Germans in the apartment or the fire had come from a few rascals trying to make whoopee was never proved to the satisfaction of the trio closest to the scene. In any case, if the situation was as painted, it would have been better handled by a half-squad armed with a dozen hand grenades—but that would have been poor theater.

Soon after the column had its last hurrah at the head of Avenue Foch, we said goodbye to Elena. A French major came down the line screaming, "Get these————women out of the vehicles." That had to be resisted, since the honor of a very gentle person was concerned, so the major was told off, loudly, profanely.

From behind me, a voice roared. "You tell 'em, Marshall. Since when hasn't a soldier the right to company in his sleeping bag? That's the way I won————," but the name was lost in the roar of approval from the crowd. Papa's wisecrack got to her, where the major had failed. Without a word she slipped away to seek her lover, and we never saw her again.

From the Etoile, John and I drove the short run to Hotel Claridge. We were tired. The desk clerk refused us a room though the hotel clearly was untenanted. We demanded to see the manager, and when he came forth, our money was on the counter.

He said: "There are no rooms. This hotel is reserved for the German Army."

I said: "You've got just five seconds to get it unreserved. This is the American Army moving in." We got the rooms and quickly learned the reason for the attempted stall. Each bathroom bore a neat sign bidding warm welcome to German officers. The embarrassed host wanted time to remove them.

The story was told at the clambake in the Ritz that night. Jack Ritz commented drolly, "What could you expect? Hotel men have no country.

They're the only true internationalists." Here is the probable basis of the greatly embroidered legend about Hemingway's liberating the Ritz. Wrong hotel. Wrong cast. I know Jack was waiting there with Dunhill pipes as souvenirs for each of us when we made the Ritz lobby, slightly ahead of Papa.

Until the last dog was left unhung, the grand event had these overtones of *opéra bouffe*. Von Cholitz, the enemy commander, had his headquarters in Hotel Meurice, that monument to the rococo. In early evening a tank went by the Meurice, fired one round at an ancient chevy parked alongside, and set it afire. That was enough boom-boom to save Von Cholitz's honor. He and twenty of his staff officers came running from the hotel, hands in air. Von Cholitz, with his boys stringing along, was taken to Montparnasse where Leclerc told him to surrender the twenty spots where Germans still held out. Captain Paul Sapiebra, USA, wrote out twenty copies of a surrender order, and Von Cholitz signed them. The twenty staff officers were then loaded in twenty jeeps and speeded to twenty points of resistance. That no more ended the sniping than did the next morning's sun tranquilize the throb of the hangover, but it was the formal ending to the German occupation and the story.

Chapter 11
Taking Over

Westover and I at last were able to shove north from Paris. We had tired of the whoopee, and we had work to do. We were in the lines at Brest with the 29th Division from September 4 to 18, 1944, researching both the Omaha landing and the Brittany campaign. Practically all of our work there was done under fire, and we proved finally that troops will respond readily to exhaustive interrogation irrespective of stress.

By the end of the campaign, Westover and I had completed our task, having covered between us every combat unit that had hit Normandy on D-Day. The big thrill at battle's end is doubled by the knowledge that one's own work is done. Still, the campaign had been wearing. That part of Brittany is a crazy quilt of hedgerows and tortuously twisted sunken roads. All of this mazelike battlefield was badly posted, and one could not move behind the natural cover in any direction and stay certain of his bearings for long.

When the siege ended with the storming of Fort Montbarrey, built under Napoleon, everyone expected the reward of at least a day or two of relief from official duties. To lie in a fat meadow and soak up the sun or sit on a seawall and watch the surf while the gulls played hopscotch on the floating mines—ah, these were the things worth doing. Brest itself was to be avoided like the plague. The city I had known so well in the Great War had been systematically gutted by the Germans. Homes and stores unscathed by bomb and shell had been either dynamited or torched, then booby-trapped, while the port facility, for which so many American lives had been spent, was in irreparable ruin.

Our serene anticipation of a recess was soured by a note from General Charles Gerhardt requiring all unit commanders and staff officers to report for a briefing at his command post. The spot wasn't bad. Charley had chosen the best for himself, a palatial chateau overlooking the sea. We collected at its rear in a natural grass-covered amphitheater. The puzzled

119

audience was scattered around the sides of this velvety hollow. Down at the bottom was a huddle of riflemen, not more than a dozen. Facing them, a few paces distant, stood Gerhardt attended by one staff officer. The setting, the tableau, was supremely mystifying.

Then my friend Gerhardt opened his mouth, and the air became vibrant. Charley has a two-pitch nasal twang, the effect of which is not unlike an old-fashioned ticktack perfectly in key. The words were no less startling.

"Gentlemen," he said, "you will remember that in the action on Hill 130 we lost a rifle company to the enemy. After that, in talking to some of our German prisoners, I have learned that the reason we were beaten is that in the middle of the fight our men quit firing to hunt for enemy souvenirs. Now we have liberated the survivors of that company. I have them here. I intend that the G-2 will question them in front of you so that nothing of this kind will ever happen in the 29th Division again."

While he spoke, I was watching the knot of riflemen. They were seething. Several tried to rise. A big sergeant sat in the front row. He either waved them down or grabbed their arms and pulled. When Gerhardt stopped, the sergeant arose and, giving his name, asked, "Sir, do I have the general's permission to speak?" Somewhat taken aback, Gerhardt nodded.

The sergeant began. "Sir, you see here all that is left of that company. You have spoken ill of it. They were the best men I have ever known. It is true that the men you see here were captured on Hill 130, and that we and the men who will not come back lost that fight.

"Just why we lost, I cannot tell you. We were in the center. We reached our objective. We intended to hold it, but the chance to do so was taken away from us. According to the orders, two other companies were supposed to support us on the left and right. They never got up there. We fought all alone. Why they failed us, I was never told and it is not my business. It should be of interest to high command.

"After we gained the hill the enemy threw a box barrage around us. There was no longer any choice as to retreating. We couldn't fall back; so we fought on until our last round of ammunition was spent. It was then that I surrendered these men.

"Now something has been said about our ceasing fire to pick up souvenirs. It is true there was one such incident. I am the guilty man. I'll give you the circumstances. Sergeant Jackson was shot under the heart and was dying at about the same moment that my M-1 was shot out of my hands. Being unarmed, I reached down and grabbed the Luger pistol he had in his hand. With it, I continued to fire until the last round. True, a Luger pistol is a souvenir. Jackson had liberated it at St. Lô. So blame me, but do it knowing that I am more proud that I fought with these men on that day than that I am a member of the 29th Division."

That man gave me as high a moment as I have ever had in the army. We all wanted to cheer. No one dared. Put in as embarrassing a spot as ever harried a general, Gerhardt recovered splendidly.

He saluted the sergeant, then said loudly, "Gentlemen, the British have a phrase for it; I have had it. May I add that I am prouder that I belong to an army where an enlisted man can talk like that than that I command the 29th Division? You are dismissed."

★

I had forced Ganoe to move his shop to the continent after getting word from his secretary, Joan MacMaster, that he had taken a vote of all personnel, military and civilian, as to whether the operation should deploy or stay put in London. He panicked when I warned him that putting such a decision to his people was so unseemly as to put his job in jeopardy, so he had best hotfoot it to France.

Still, I was getting no information from him as to where and when he had moved or anything else. After doubling back to Normandy, we learned that Ganoe had set up in Paris, and we turned the jeep about. I found him rocking at ease in the Majestic Hotel, the ETOUSA Headquarters, and told him that Westover and I were leaving at once to cover the Market Garden attack (sometimes called the Arnhem show) in Holland.

He said: "I forbid you. Kemper writes that you are taking too many chances. You're to be saved for the CBI."

I told him that as I sized things up, China-Burma-India was out. The Holland show had to be covered, and I was going.

He took it amiably.

Then I added: "And I want the chief of the First Army detachment relieved right now and Dick Shappell put in his place."

He said: "Well, Slam, we have to talk to him about that." The man under discussion was idling in an adjoining room. Ganoe came out of a huddle with him to tell me, "He says this is just a fight between the War Department clique and our group. What about it?"

The other man had followed him in. I said: "I don't expect to hear any army officer raise such a question. He's failed on the job. I want him relieved. He can come with me to Holland if he wishes and I'll give him a chance to restore himself."

He did come with me to Holland. His work, though he tried hard, proved mediocre because he could not distinguish between the important and the trivial. He drifted from job to job and swore ever after that I had ruined him in the army.

We were six weeks on that front, the island north of the Waal and south of the Neder Rijn, and all of that time we were working with troops of the 82nd and 101st Divisions. More artillery and mortar ammunition was being shot off by both sides to no good purpose than on any front I saw during World War II. If one were tucked up in a house just under the dike of the Neder Rijn, one could be very cozy. Most of the time the stuff screamed harmlessly overhead.

With two of my intimates, Colonels Harry W. O. Kinnard and Julian Ewell, I loafed one night at Ewell's command post, a house right next the Neder Rijn dike. All that noise overhead is somewhat conducive to drinking. We were well at it when Harry popped off. "Slam, you have the best job over here. You can go where you want when you want."

"It has its drawbacks. Think of the end product. Most military history is bunk, nonsense. There isn't much satisfaction."

"Give me an example."

I went on. "Take the Old Guard at Waterloo. The French commander, Chambrun, didn't say, 'The Old Guard dies but it never surrenders'; he said, '*merde.*'

Harry wanted to know what *merde* meant, so I helped him with his vocabulary, and when he asked for my sources, I gave them, adding that there was a monument to Chambrun on the Waterloo field where the naughty word is inscribed. He was so intrigued that when we left that front he detoured over a weekend to visit the monument. Now it was Harry who, as Operations Officer of the 101st, several weeks later persuaded Tony McAuliffe that it was highly proper to put "Nuts!" in a military message. One need not dig deep to locate the genesis of that inspiration.

By the time we were through with Holland, Colonel John M. Kemper, my real boss out of the Pentagon, was in France with blood in his eye. He had come with authority from Stimson and Marshall to pressure top command into relieving Ganoe and had already discussed the problem with the bosses of the theater. Then he came to ask for my support.

I gave him an outright turndown, and for one hour we had a knock-down-drag-out row. My point was that it is folly to relieve anyone unless what follows is certain to be an improvement, and Kemper had no plan. Furthermore, if Ganoe were summarily relieved, his old friends in the theater, many in high places, would be offended, irrespective of the cause.

John finally cooled and asked what I proposed.

I said that, if made Ganoe's deputy, I could work it out. John objected that as certainly as I was put directly under Ganoe's authority, he would find a way to fence me in.

I said: "John, you've been my boss for almost two years. Have you found any way to fence me in?"

On that argument, the discussion ended and we shook hands. I would not go to CBI. I would stay with ETO, which was really the make-or-break theater for the historical operation in World War II. It was good to know that I was done with my tinware peddling for a time and could talk a tougher language than gentle persuasion. Ganoe was altogether agreeable. He knew there was no other practical solution. All higher authority saw it the same way. The absurd part is that the same move had been possible at any time since D-Day. The people in power had simply procrastinated, and we had wasted six months.

By this time I was getting very windy. I knew I had been pushing my luck, and with some show of dignity I could at last leave combat work to the kids. Being deputy would require constant attention to detail. Ganoe's mind seemed to be befogged through most of the day, and he could not be trusted with decisions. A way had to be found to keep the figure there while taking over the power. That was worked out in discussions between us over the first two days, and his thinking was so hazy that he did not realize that he had yielded all authority over the operation.

I took two initial steps, first to inspect everything in our establishment, to make sure we were foolproof and to get it going my way. Then I published a brief order to the people, in three parts: "(1) There will be no excuse for deviating from the rules of military courtesy and proper dress. (2) You will be given important work to do, you will be held to it, and I will do it with you. (3) If you don't know how to fire a weapon, report to the exec for training, for you will be going where you need one."

Ganoe called me in and gently protested. I didn't understand modern youth. I was following what I learned in 1918. I had forgotten that our soldiers were American civilians in uniform. I was upsetting his system.

I reminded him that I had been brought in as deputy because his system had failed. I said that, as I read history, human nature had changed very little throughout recorded time. Man's main drive still derived from self-interest. Even so, I couldn't expect to get the best results out of any specialist unless I had due respect for him first in his role as a military person. If I didn't respect it, certainly he would not, and he would be inclined to slough off all down the line. That was my theory of command, and if he had objections, I wished to hear them.

Ganoe said: "You have ordered an officers' call for every Saturday morning. I wait until I have something important to announce, then I get all of the people together."

I answered: "My officers are one group; my NCOs are another. They may be treated as one on social occasions, not otherwise. If I haven't something of value to say to my officers at least once a week, then someone should take over from me."

It must have been the right treatment. Within one week, while Kemper looked on, we had the organization out of the woods and moving to the high ground. I gave main attention to my noncoms and at first did little with the officers. My time in ranks had fixed my belief that, if I can get my NCOs to move fast, the officers will either have to get going or they will be overrun.

In taking over a downed outfit in war time, when it has failed due to tepid or ill-advised leadership, one has no choice but to move fast and make drastic changes, not worrying about the normal percentage of mistakes that attends multiple decision making under a forced draft. There is no substitute for the shock treatment. Nothing else will generate the initial momentum. The people already there, who have felt relatively secure in their jobs, will at first resent it, and some will try to resist the new, rough hand over them. Some may even conspire to thwart it, but they must be made to feel it—and swiftly. While one must respect the dignity of man at his labor, that principle itself has to be suspended when the work itself is mainly waste motion and valueless. As to the object that the administrator must keep in mind, I like the words of James Dewey Watson: "The aim is to get enough bright people around you that most decisions can be made with their concurrence, and so, when the decision is made, you don't have to fight with them."

The trouble with Ganoe's headquarters' organization was that it had become hardened into cells. There was no control or direction from the center and hence no unifying influence. Each section was a small fiefdom.

All but one of the sections was immediately stripped of authority. Only the War Artists Group was kept in status quo, for it was well led. Its members were directed, however, that henceforth they would paint only battlefields and battle scenes, and no more pictures of French waifs, cafes, and cathedrals. That change of direction initially rubbed a few of the artists raw, though as they got with the new idea they changed their views.

I was beginning to plug ahead when two events, one earth-shaking, the other personal, changed the whole problem dimensionally and forestalled further stage-by-stage planning.

• Hitler launched his surprise offensive into the Ardennes.

• From my invalid wife, Ives, in Palm Beach came a cable that she must undergo major surgery and another message from her doctor that it was her wish that I not return for the operation and that he advised against it. Knowing her courage, her desire to give her soldier all the support possible, I could honor her only by staying on course.

I was almost morbidly aware in those hours that this was a crisis and our whole fortune in the ETO was in balance. We had already failed or done second-grade work in following through on planned operations that should have been easily covered. Now, if we could do a nigh faultless job on a surprise enemy offensive that already promised to be the largest battle of our war, all past transgressions would be forgiven. It was a fairly large order.

Major General Royall Lord, Lee's chief of staff, had, for no good reason, forbidden Ganoe entry to the war room in the Majestic. I sent Lord a memo saying, "Request free use of the war room and need it right now." He folded and I got the pass. On the second night of the battle, Kemper and I pored over the situation maps for six hours, estimating what the Germans were doing and how far they would get with it. Our snap calculations ultimately proved almost unerringly accurate. Some reassignments had to be made that night. Based on our chance-guess calculations, I began to redistribute the combat historians in and near the battle zone.

A telephone call came from the Operations Division at SHAEF: "To keep our records straight we need to give this operation a name right now," to which I replied: "Just call it the Battle of the Ardennes." The caller finally agreed.

My resolve not to go into battle again was shattered by what was happening to Ives. Her ordeal was scheduled for December 30. The interlude of waiting was sheer torment. Westover had already been committed at Bastogne, along with 2nd Lieutenant Joe Weber, with instructions to cover armored and tank destroyer operations only. I had promised to join them and take on the coverage of infantry operations so, after the corridor was cut to the encircled 101st garrison by the 4th Armored Division's task force under Creighton Abrams, I went there. Under fire for the next nineteen days with the 101st and 17th Airborne Divisions around Bastogne and at Houffalize, I felt no sweat and clean forgot that I had worried about my number in early December. Ives and Ives only was on my mind. The saying that man can hurt only in one place at a time applies not more to the flesh than to the emotions. I became, in short, like the GI who said he had volunteered for infantry after driving a school bus until his nerves gave out. Bastogne was in that sense a therapy. I decided I would keep covering combat operations as much as possible until war's end.

My lone companion on the jeep ride to Bastogne was a strange driver from the motor pool, Pfc. Joseph Nardello. Joe was short, swart, and made attractive only by a toothy grin suggesting amiability. At Bouillon on the way east we parked to go for a full-spread meal, champagne, and cognac. When he lunged for the check, I told him he knew things were not done that way in the army, and he replied that "the gent with the most dough has the right to buy," whereon he pulled out a bankroll big enough to choke a crocodile. I told him to have his fun.

When we hit the road again, I asked him how much money he had in the roll, and he replied twenty-seven grand.

"Black market?"

"No, from the States—call it the trucking business with certain rackets mixed in."

He had been in the army three years. When asked why he didn't wear stripes, he said that he had two brothers with commissions and he could buy them both out.

I said: "Maybe they have something you haven't—character."

"What can you sell that for?"

"That's the point; it's not for sale."

Joe was with me every day at Bastogne. In this, his first experience under fire, he would grunt as if hit between wind and water every time a shell exploded anywhere near us; yet he gave of himself with the improvidence of the good child. His courage was as unfaltering as his good cheer, and at last, for valor above the call, I put him in for the Silver Star.

The day before he was to be decorated, some six weeks later, he called at my office in Paris. Whereas he had always kidded me unmercifully when we were forward, this time he was deadly serious. "Been thinking about that character stuff—what you said to me—now getting that medal—it does make me a little different, don't it?" I nodded. Somehow up there in the Ardennes fog and snow, Joe, then in his midthirties, had divined the secret of life. He had made peace with himself.

★

Our people made an unqualified success of covering the Battle of the Bulge. Sixteen of the headquarters crowd, including five war artists, were deployed into the fire zone to fill gaps. The second costliest fight in American history, it is also the campaign most completely documented, and in the end we had to reconstruct the German side of the story, also. After going over all of the field work, I put Captain Robert E. Merriam in charge of a special Ardennes section at the headquarters because, among many valiants, he had performed outstandingly. Bob later ran for mayor of Chicago and then became special assistant to President Eisenhower.

At Bastogne we did not feel ourselves extremely challenged or even heavily burdened. Our working conditions could be described as ideal, viewed in retrospect. Beset as we were by blizzard, drifts higher than my head, and bitter cold, ringed in by enemy artillery that pounded us night and day, we still had the total cooperation of command and troops wherever we moved. That was what counted.

There was something dreadfully spooky about that artillery. Placed as we were at the center of a very narrow salient, we had to be drawing fire from the high ground at our front and both flanks, but time and again it seemed to be coming from our direct rear also. Patrols went forth seeking ghost batteries that had infiltrated the corridor. Of course, they were never found. It was all illusion.

Even so, the guns that were real enough could range in exactly on any large target in the town. The division command post was located in a large stone building called the Belgian Barracks. On one thunderous afternoon, while we sweated like beavers in the basement, the upper stories of that structure were ventilated by 316 shell hits. That was when Lieutenant Colonel Sid Davis, the signal officer, went to General Taylor and said: "We must move the CP now. I have only one telephone line left to the outside."

Taylor nodded, then asked quietly, "What are the last several messages over that line?"

Davis answered: "They're all from the regiments. A big squawk. The troops want to know when we're going to divide up all that cognac we took over from Eighth Corps."

On another afternoon, I jeeped along with Colonels Kinnard and Ewell to visit the 501st Regiment's outpost lines. Ewell was proud of his men and wanted me to see how soldierly they were.

The driver made a wrong turn, and instead of heading for Marvie, got on the road to Wardin. Since Wardin was held by the Germans, that wasn't very nice. When suddenly a long burst from a .50 machine gun swept just above our heads, we were all better advised.

In the next second, we dipped down into a swale, out of the gun's line of sight.

I wasn't saying or thinking anything.

Ewell spoke in his normal slow drawl. "'Pears to me, son, you're on the wrong road. Suggest you turn and barrel the other way."

We made it to Marvie.

Leaving the jeep, the three of us walked forward to Ewell's most advanced position east of the town. A youthful paratrooper was walking post, covered only by the bank of a very thick hedge. As we came up he neither halted us nor saluted.

He asked: "What are you, a bunch of sightseers?"

Kinnard said: "Yeah, sightseers."

I asked him: "Soldier, where is the German front line?"

He waved his arm toward the Longvilly road, which ran along a hill about half a mile away.

"Somewhere out there, I think."

I tried again.

"Look son, you see that head moving along behind that stone wall and something bobbing behind it that looks like a stick? [The wall was about a hundred yards away.] Don't you realize that is a German walking sentry the same as you?"

The boy said: "Don't shit me, mister, I know the score."

Ewell hadn't said one word.

We walked away.

I said: "Some troops you got, Julian."

Harry said: "Some troops."

Ewell growled: "Yeah, some troops."

Incongruous is the word for much that happened at Bastogne. Take my own situation. With my own small gang—the officers already mentioned; Nardello, the driver; Olin Dowes, the war artist; and Lieutenant Ace Hudson, the air coordinator for the defense of Bastogne—I had set up housekeeping arrangements independent of the 101st Division.

We took as a billet the upper story of a rock-walled Belgian farmhouse at the hamlet of Sibret about one and a half miles from the center of Bastogne. The incongruity is that the nest we chose was only about 600 yards from the nearest Germans with no American support in men and weapons between us and the enemy, and the nearest friendly help was far, far away in Bastogne proper.

There were two arguments for that calculated risk. I figured we needed to be together at night so that each day's work could be planned by the group in such a way as to prevent overlapping, and I was certain the Germans were in no shape to raid toward us. I also imagined that the German artillery was more likely to disregard us, we being so far removed from dead center.

Though most of these guesses worked out, one morning I popped out of our billet just as a shell exploded on the road. A Belgian woman who lived in the next farmhouse was walking the road with her two small children. The blast killed the kids and tore off her left arm. We rushed her to an aid station.

Twenty-two years later, while touring Western Europe with my brother, I again saw Sibret because the Volkswagen was out of gas, and my old billet had become a filling station. While the tank was being filled, a one-armed, terribly stooped and white-haired old woman—once beautiful—emerged from the place next door. Seeing her was like getting a full-armed blow next the heart. The irony of it. I, the wholly legitimate target in war, had escaped hurt and continued living in the world of action. She, the innocent, had stayed captive all the while, not only to her stone walls but to her memories.

The big blizzard in the Ardennes blew up about one week after the New Year began. We in the Sibret billet were accustomed to gathering for a meal about dark and then redeploying to various points to resume interviewing.

One night the storm stopped me. I tested the drifts, the depth of snow over the road, and after due regard for how the white stuff was falling, said to the others: "No work tonight: The jeeps wouldn't make it."

We turned to arguing, what about, I don't remember, and it is unimportant. Soldiers always argue.

Thirty minutes later there was a knock at the door. Entered Major Dick Shappell, chief of the First Army's historical section and one of my protégés. His face and uniform were frosted with snow and dripping water like melting icicles. I knew that his proper post was at whatever point First Army headquarters had settled after fleeing Spa.

I said: "Dick, what in hell are you doing here on such a night?"

"I came over to check on you and the others to see if you are doing your work all the way and to ask if you need help. After all, you are in *my* army area, and I am responsible for the coverage of this fight."

That sort of left me gaping.

Someone yelled: "Have a drink, Dick."

"Not tonight. Some other time. I still have places to go."

The check was made. We briefed him on everything that we had done up until then and what we planned for the time ahead. This editor-on-leave from the *Flint Journal* saluted not too formally, said goodbye, and returned to the blizzard.

I relate the story not simply to emphasize what military officership is supposed to require from any man who accepts commission, but as an example of Clio's stern demands on the individual who would serve her properly. History is not an embroidered tale spun long after, nor is it, as Macaulay wrote, "an instruction . . . received by the imagination as well as by the reason." Essentially, it is what occurred at the time, what was to be seen, heard, and sensed, so that the record may be as accurate and complete as possible. Despite Macaulay's sneer to the contrary, history is an old almanac. Its interpretation for better or worse is another problem, sometimes within the scope of the historian.

----------------------------- ★ -----------------------------

The 101st Division did not depart Bastogne heads up and tails over the dashboard as portrayed in the movie *Battleground*, based on one of my books. It exited tails down, too much being asked of it. Following its departure from the Bastogne salient and the breakup of my small crew of retainers, I went alone with Task Force Stubbs, out of the 17th Airborne Division, to Houffalize, to observe the action by which the Bulge was sealed off and the Battle of the Ardennes ended.

Colonel Stubbs that first evening placed his command post in the barn of a Belgian farm. There were many geese about, and they honked stentoriously as if in protest against an invasion. Stubbs with his exec and I talked along for an hour or so about the operation.

Then because I had to go I had to go.

Stubbs cautioned me.

"The slit trench is just around the corner of the barn. You turn left. The trench is down the slope. Be careful. That hill is icy. You wouldn't believe how slick it is. A few of our heroes have already taken the warning too carelessly. You could do the same."

Stubbs was wrong about that. I believed him absolutely. My care was exquisite. I inched along to the top of that slope. Dan'l Boone was less stealthy sneaking up on the b'ar.

Then my feet shot from under me. I careened like a toboggan down that iced glacis on my rear end and for all of forty feet to land, bottom down, square in the middle of the slit trench. It couldn't have happened to a more deserving citizen.

With not one person on hand to observe for the benefit of the records, I pulled myself out of that fell pit, covered all over from head to foot, covered all over with sweet violets, sweeter than roses. Bringing off my fumigation became one of the major problems for the heroes who had sealed off the Bulge.

Still, as the battle ended, I was jubilant, or at least more so than smelly. I knew that my guys had made it. The score was as if someone had hit a sack-clearing homer in the last of the ninth to win the ball game. From there on out, no one would be able to stop us. We were in, and I was happy that I could so report to my chief.

What I did not realize as the battle ended was that I was heading into something far more unpleasant. From Houffalize, the view seemed clear enough; I could see the light at the end of the tunnel. Returned to Paris, I was chilled by the murk within it.

In my absence, Colonel Ganoe had gone off the deep end. Assuming that he had the authority, he had issued orders bodily transferring several men from the Ninth to the First Army and from the Fifteenth to the Third. Not only were these moves—these shufflings—basically senseless, but the men were directly under the army commanders, and we lacked the power to transfer them. I had to spend several days appeasing the staffs of two of the affronted army commanders.

That made the bind unbearable. I had too little time to waste repairing crockery that the chief capriciously broke. I went to General Lee and told him that Ganoe had to be relieved. Lee, who was aware of the problem, passed the unpleasant task of breaking the news to Ganoe to his G-1, Colonel Franey.

Twenty minutes after Ganoe was called to Franey's office, I was asked to follow him there.

The two men sat there grim-faced.

Lee had failed to tell Franey that I had instituted the proceeding, which was his mistake. Franey was simply trying to be fair to Ganoe.

He said: "Colonel Marshall, I called Colonel Ganoe here to tell him that we feel he is not doing his work properly and must be replaced. He says that is not true. He said his deputy will say that he is doing his work. He demanded that you be brought here to support him."

There Franey let the subject dangle. My throat did not feel uncomfortably dry. Ganoe was my friend; I neither coveted his job nor wished to hurt him. The way Franey put it left me no choice.

I said: "I have always held that when asked such a question, my duty as a soldier is to tell the truth. Well, then, Colonel Ganoe is not doing his work. There's something wrong with him physically. For two hours every morning his mind is clear. Then he becomes irresponsible. I have begged him to go to hospital for a checkup. He will not listen to me."

They said nothing.

I continued: "There's another thing. He has a professional disease. He's afraid of higher command. He'll walk around the block rather than encounter one of his superiors. In consequence, our operation gets no support from anyone, here or elsewhere. It is totally neglected. I would not stand what he takes for one minute. Either I would be given what is needed to put the program over, or I would turn in my suit."

Ganoe murmured: "I'll plead guilty. It's like Slam says. I am afraid."

Franey was toying with a pencil, seemingly worried about what to say next.

Then he came up with it: "I think we all understand you here, Colonel Marshall. You'll get everything you request from now on."

He paused briefly. "But what are we to do about this problem?"

I said that I thought asking me what the command should do about the relief of my superior was a little bit unusual within the military.

Franey countered that the circumstances were also unusual.

I proposed a formula.

Ganoe would report to hospital the next morning and not again set foot in the shop until war's end. If, as a point of honor, he wished to have his name on the rolls as head of the operation until victory day, that would be all right with me, since the work, not the title, was the all-important thing. On V-E Day, he would be automatically relieved.

To Franey's question, Ganoe replied that the arrangement was to his satisfaction.

Ganoe went to hospital next morning. Almost immediately, it was discovered that he was suffering from an advanced case of diabetes. The best effect of the relief was that his life was extended for another seventeen years, in which time he wrote a quite charming novel, revised his *History of the United States Army,* and did a fulsome monograph about his god, Mac-Arthur.

Chapter 12
The Big Picture

The conclusion of the Battle of the Bulge coupled with Ganoe's departure near the end of January gave me my first breathing spell in which to review my problems in single-minded detachment.

My main goal was to have a history of ETO operations that would stand the test of time and critical examination by the actors, but directing the input was no task for me. I lacked the breadth and scholarly approach. Taking the long view of what we had to do, these were put down as the essential steps:

• Procure a deputy who would complement me, take charge of training, and provide the technical direction.

• Win entrée and cooperation at the Supreme Headquarters, thus far off limits to our people.

• Initiate across-the-board exchange of historical information with our Allies while the war was still in progress.

• Consolidate my headquarters, which was spread over three widely separated buildings in the heart of Paris.

• Find more combat historians somewhere.

• Insure keeping the operation intact for at least one year after war's end.

These things done, we would come to rest on high ground. They were in no sense interlocking problems. Each was many faceted; they would be solved only by taking them up one at a time in person. That is how they must be presented here.

Hugh M. Cole was an ineluctable choice as deputy, the only man in the theater possessed of the professional competence. We had no fondness for one another. At a party in the Lancaster I had asked him whether he would be available. He said he believed our show was doomed to failure, that he would prefer transfer to the Pacific, but that, if ordered, he would comply. The trick lay in talking General Patton out of one of his staff jewels.

Proceeding to Luxembourg City, I put the question to the immortal Georgie and his chief of staff, General Hap Gay, an old friend. I also asked for Cole's executive, Major Delos Dayton, and Sergeant Gordon Harrison, a topflight writer. To tempt Patton, I could promise nothing better than that, if the division achieved nothing else, the book on Patton's campaign in Lorraine would be published first on the list. We would also replace the three men. It was strictly an appeal to his vanity, and to my astonishment, it worked.

I said: "But I must get Cole as a lieutenant colonel."

Gay objected. "We promote no one out of turn in the Third Army."

"What the hell, Hap. You can promote him one second and put him on orders to me two minutes later. That's not promoting a man out of turn. I can't put a major over lieutenant colonels, and it will take me ninety days to get him bumped up."

Gay reluctantly agreed. As I made ready to depart, he said: "Don't send us any Jewish officers as replacements."

Two days later Cole was transferred to me in the grade of major. I called Gay immediately. He turned mad as a hornet. "God damn it, Slam, I won't argue with you about the promotion of a major in the middle of a battle."

"I'll argue with you any time when you don't keep your word to me."

He slammed the phone. Another voice came on the line to say, "Slam, it wasn't Hap's fault." The phone clicked off again. I had recognized the voice.

I knew Patton had done it, and I thought I knew why. Patton was a large hater, and the apple-polishers on his staff went along with his hates. He hated the Supreme Command, the First Army, the Jews, and above all, the British. Before transfer, Cole had applied for Georgie's approval of his marriage to Joan MacMaster, a British girl; otherwise he would have to go through another ninety-day wait at my headquarters. That was enough to rip it. I thought Patton's smallness was nauseating.

I went to Lee's G-1, Franey, told him the story, and said: "I think this is a bad way to run a railroad in wartime."

Franey agreed and supported me in a call to Colonel Gregory, the G-1 of Twelfth Army Group. Gregory listened sympathetically, and while I held the phone, he went in and talked to General Bradley. Bradley called Patton at once and told him to cut the foolishness, rescind the order, promote Cole, and then transfer him to me. Thereafter Patton did not hold it against me that I had called his hand.

There was one more pitch. After going over our rolls, I sent him the three ablest Jewish officers on my staff. Each was a whizz kid. Gay called me. "I thought I told you no Jewish officers."

"Okay, Hap, send me a memo saying Patton doesn't like them because they're Jewish, and I'll pull them back."

A muffled explosion came over the phone. Five weeks later I moved these men into other assignments, feeling they had had enough exposure in the wrong direction. Years later I told them why it had been done.

Once Cole came to the job I breathed more easily, and we began to make hay. Our friendship ripened thereafter.

The relocation problem was the real pushover. I sent scouts out to look for the most suitable building in Paris already in army hands. It was at 87 Avenue Foch, the present site of the Canadian Embassy. A mansion built for one of the Dolly Sisters, the den of the Gestapo during the German occupation, it was being used by a brigadier heading the Theater Artillery Section, who had only 23 people rattling round in a property that would house my 152.

I preempted his place by, in effect, blackmailing him. I told him that, when called before Congress to explain why my operation had failed, I would blame him for not yielding at a critical time. The brigadier was polite, urbane, and even offered me a beer, but at first brushed the bid aside. Two hours later he called to say he had changed his mind, and all at once our operation was in clover. That gunner was one of the finest gentlemen I ever met in service, and his magnanimity helped me tremendously. Also, we were grateful for the gold-plated doorknobs and the alabaster tubs once used by the Dollys. Our thoughts while bathing might have been more blissful, more romantic, but for the more recent ablutions of the Gestapo. A pity, that.

I was at this time dictating the longest monograph I ever put to a stenographer. She was Sergeant Eva Spencer of Rapid City, South Dakota, the most diligent and cheerful woman I ever knew in service. This paper was ultimately published as the book *Bastogne: The First Eight Days.* Even the appendices, including documentation for practically every sentence, were dictated during the twelve days that we composed the monograph.

There was a double reason for handling the manuscript in this manner. The folderol, clutter, and footnoting that scholars believe essential to any work in history has always irritated me. Its messiness distracts the reader. Still, I wished to do one work demonstrating that any neophyte could turn the trick. More to the point, the monograph, which quite by accident became a public book, was written solely to make the right impression on one man. The problem of winning acceptance at Supreme Headquarters was one step nearer solution.

But *cherchez la femme*, and I turn back the clock. Almost from the day of my arrival in Detroit in 1927 I had known Dee Furey, still a single woman and the publisher of a sports magazine. A striking blonde, she was extremely attractive to men and proportionately disliked by women in the horsey set. She married and divorced Charles Mott, the vice-president of

General Motors, today in his nineties and celebrated for his philanthropies. Next she married and divorced Lewis Bredin, a steeplechaser and foxhunting man.

Neither of us could ever strike the slightest spark in one another, but we were friends and were drawn together in many strange ways. It was not simply that we worked together a number of times in judging horse shows. She was the only woman in whom I confided before I married Ives; she was with me when I shopped for the ring, and that night she drove me to the train. When her marital difficulties came to crisis, she would call me, and we would talk things over. Later she tired of Detroit, moved east, and became boon companion to Elizabeth Arden. I lost track of her. We still had yet to learn that we were born on the same day within an hour of one another.

Then when I flew back from Normandy during the buzz bomb period, I met her in London while walking on Park Lane. She was there doing her bit, broadcasting overseas for the BBC. Born in Java, she spoke Dutch fluently. She invited me to a cocktail party that afternoon at her apartment in the Park Lane Hotel.

Over martinis at her place I first met Edward Murrow. He was moody, rancorous, somewhat jumpy from the V-1s, and positive that anyone who styled himself a military critic must be a phony.

The heartiest character at the party was Brigadier General Oscar Solbert, chief of Special Services in the theater, a vice-president of Eastman Kodak on loan to the army. He told me that his personal relationships with Eisenhower and Bedell Smith were the closest possible. During the next two days I cultivated him. Before parting in London he volunteered to become my bridge to the Supreme Headquarters.

At the time I completed the Bastogne monograph, we both had apartments in the George V in Paris. We got together frequently in his quarters, with Anna Rosenberg making it a threesome. Her son, a Signal Corps lieutenant detailed as her special aide, mixed the drinks. I passed the monograph to Solbert, asking that he hand it to Bedell Smith and importune him to read it.

One week later a note came from Smith: "Have read your paper. You know your work. There are a few notes that I might add to round out the picture. When you find time to work with us, let me know."

There it was, all wrapped up, sealed, and delivered, and I decided to let it rest for a while. The big headquarters was loaded with problems and so was our shop.

The search for additional personnel took a most unlikely turn. Upstanding replacement officers were almost impossible to procure except for the combat line. When at last the dam broke, or at least spilled something our way, it was because the waters of the theater had become clogged with human wreckage.

These were the ETO's combat fatigue officers. They were passed to me fifty or sixty at a time like worn parts moving out of a factory on a conveyor belt. Most of them were trucked to Paris from Liège. My part was to look them over, giving a few minutes to each man, to see whether there were any that we could salvage. No recollection from World War II now gives me such a feeling of repugnance. I felt ashamed, not because we had a certain percentage of men who couldn't stand the ordeal, but because our system was so blind that it insisted on running these poor chaps through the mill all over again. Any person of common sense and reasonable compassion, after dealing with a representative hundred of these cases, must have concluded that at least sixty of them should have been returned home immediately and discharged honorably, in decency to the man and out of respect for the uniform.

Whether the Medical Corps could have done so at its discretion, I do not know. But if we were so hard up for men that we had to do these things, and so ignorant of human nature that we regarded it as a duty serving some useful purpose, then we were closer to the verge of manpower bankruptcy during the war than has been officially confessed.

The men came into my office one at a time for the interview. I looked each subject over. His chin was up, though usually his eye had the look that you see in a dog that has been kicked and expects to be kicked again. The first duty was to talk to the man in a friendly way about his calling in civilian life, his family, and how long he had been in hospital. He began to unburden himself. He wanted to feel like a man. He knew there was useful work somewhere that he could do. He was proud of his folks, and they were proud of him. He didn't want to let them down. There must be redemption somewhere.

I have heard men go through this routine who were obviously so nervously ill that the strain of speech shattered their last reserves. Their teeth would begin to chatter, and they would lapse into silence like a child suddenly abashed. If these men were fakes, they were the finest actors in the world, and any one of them could have made a prime career in Hollywood. I don't think they were fakes, though naturally, when the subject was this kind of derelict, there was no point in continuing the discussion. I remember a young preacher from Kentucky who had gone into the artillery, become a forward observer, and then flunked out as one of the worst shock cases. He cried like a baby when I told him I couldn't use him. The look of final defeat on his face reminded me of Warne, the British parson in Benstead's novel, *Retreat*, who spent the rest of his life cursing his God because shellfire had convinced him that he was not quite a man.

Then there were other types who talked rationally and confidently up to the point when I mentioned artillery fire and asked whether they could take it, provided the job called for it. Their faces would undergo a swift change of expression. Some of them fell apart emotionally at the question. I have often wondered whether that was because they were afraid of recollection or fearful that I might cut them. Others returned an answer as clear as daylight: "Sir, I have tried it and know that it is too much for me. I failed it once and would probably fail again. I can't tell you why it gets me. God knows I wish it didn't." More times than not the man went on to say that he would gladly take on a job with any other kind of danger, such as being an air courier in transoceanic service or working in a contagious ward.

Such was the material from which the high command expected me to pick my replacements. Altogether, I tried thirteen of them—the few promising grains of parched wheat in a bushel basket of chaff. They served well and faithfully, and every one saw his job through to the end. When it became possible for them to return home on points, they volunteered to extend until their work was finished. Some I kept permanently at the rear. Others I sent to the front for brief periods of duty as part of the therapy. Enabling them to discover more or less for themselves that they could stand within sound of the guns and suffer no ill effect was like a tonic. They returned with a fresh spring in the step and a new light in the eye.

Out of the breadth of his experience in war, General Patton concluded that all such crackups (shell-shock cases we called them in World War I) are simply malingerers to be straightened out by a kick in the rump. Before ever becoming a soldier, I was aware that we are not all made of the same stuff, and after putting on the uniform I did not expect to hold all men to my standard under stress. I came to believe, from the screening of these men, that some built-in physical weakness, not understood by medicine, accounted for the majority of failures. Some human systems cannot stand intense sunlight. Others are hypersensitive to pollen. It is hardly a wild speculation that there are bodies not built to stand the clamor and concussion of battle. So saying is not to imply that the human race is better off because of these exceptions.

★

Bringing off all-around collaboration with, and between, our Allies in the exchange of historical information, if not the knottiest problem, was by far the stickiest. It had more heads than Medusa had snakes, and I had no official club with which to whack any of them. Further, in what I was about to do, I was far off limits. I was not then chief theater historian, under the flag of the supreme commander, with responsibility to assist the historical work of our Allies, also. That title and purview were given me after V-E day.

The problem would not wait till then. The first move had to be initiated before the fighting ended. All battle documents—those of our friends, as well as our own—are classified, usually secret. Under law, they cannot be passed around to an ally. We were having many joint operations, with the British, French, and Canadians. We needed their information, and they needed ours, if the story was ever to be complete. If I waited until the fighting ended to begin the exchange, some stickler higher up would cite regulations and block the *alliance cordiale*. But if I took the bull by the horns while the big wheels were concentrating on the fight, in all probability no one would ever call me for doing it, and if by the end of war we had the exchange in full swing, momentum would carry it along, with no one thinking to ask, "How did all of this get started?"

With the Canadians, it was apple pie and ice cream. Their system was much like ours, and their excellent historian, Colonel C. P. Stacey, and I saw eye-to-eye that an ounce of practicality in a given moment must ultimately outweigh a ton of policy guidance. The start with them was like a shot in the arm.

The French were willing enough. In talks with Generals Juin and Koenig, there was full agreement that we should begin the exchange. The trouble was that their historians were antiquarians still pondering 1870 and the Great War. Our trading had to be done little by little.

The big dragon was in the Twenty-first Army Group. We had no contact whatever with Field Marshal Sir Bernard L. Montgomery's headquarters and no light on how to bring one off. Unlike many of my compatriots, I take no dim view of that figure. In my book, he is a great commander, and I personally have a true liking for him, but he is not the most modestly receptive celebrity in our time.

I flew to London to talk with Brigadier Harry E. Latham, chief historian of the War Office. He listened to my sad tale, then said: "Marshall, we don't know how to deal with a bloke like Monty. We put fifteen historians ashore with him in Normandy, and he proceeded to boot them from the theater. Now what would you do with such a fellow?"

I shook my head. Latham went on. "I have an idea. Should you return to Paris and write the War Office, doing it in the name of the supreme commander, requesting that Monty's headquarters cooperate, you might get what you want."

Though I was willing to try anything, that notion seemed ludicrous. Latham then explained that, while Monty didn't hesitate to nettle and frustrate the War Office, his code required total respect for chain of command. I returned to Avenue Foch and wrote the letter, certain it was a waste of time.

One week later a full colonel in British battle dress entered my office, gave me an awesome salute, and said: "Colonel A. E. Warhurst reporting, sir." It came out like warhorse, and he looked like one. I asked what I could do for him.

"Sir, I'm here from the field marshal's headquarters to see what he can do for you."

Along with Warhurst had come Major Douglas Draycott, a London lawyer in civilian life. Discussion with both men made it clear that Draycott was by far the shrewder of the two; so, keeping Warhurst as a hostage, I sent Draycott back to the Twenty-first Army Group with a statement of how we would like to have things go. He was back in a few days with the compact signed.

Draycott said: "I sat with Monty and De Guingand [Montgomery's chief of staff] in his tent talking the matter over for about an hour. Twice the field marshal got red in the face, and I thought he was going to boot me out, but he didn't. Really a nice chap, you know."

So we kept sailing along, with Warhurst and Draycott with us for quarters and rations while doing their liaison work. They added tone to the mess.

Spring came early that year to find us a happy shop, getting everything we wished from the high command, attracting new talent from the oddest places as the word spread that we were making a score, and, above all, staying on top of every assignment.

Along the front the detachment chiefs no longer had difficulty getting their men to stay with the fight. From the headquarters we deployed more and more men forward to assist them *ad hoc*. The war artists were discovering to their delight, though it should not have surprised them, that every pivotal battleground was a picturesque landscape, worthy of their brushes. Two of the stalwarts, Sergeants Olin Dows and Manuel Bromberg, came out of the war well decorated for heroic conduct.

When the Remagen Bridge was captured, two field historians and two artists were on the scene within twelve hours. The artists painted the bridge while troops were still crossing it. That work completed, they moved to the far side. Then the bridge collapsed and, facing about, they painted the ruin. Opposite me in my study as I write are two bottles, specially labeled, sent me by special courier that day. The legend reads: "These are two of the twelve known bottles of wine brought from the town of Remagen a few hours before the bridge collapsed. These come from the cellars one hundred yards from the east end of the Ludendorff Bridge and are believed to be all that remains of the wine that shortened the war—by two days or two months—that left one bridge still standing when all should have been destroyed. This is the wine that the Germans drank a little too much—or not enough. On February 17 there were thousands of these bottles; on March 17 a few hundred. Now there are twelve full bottles, a lot of empties, a lot of broken glass, and some pools and puddles of wine in the cellar at Remagen. This has been the best wine of all."

That classic bit is signed by "Lieutenant Bernard Arnst and Sergeant Harrison Standley, Exporters." Had I known earlier that these two Rembrandts were that poetic and bubbly, I would have taken their pallets away and made them reporters.

★

By April operations were going so smoothly that I could break away to move frontward again. My companion was Captain Bob Merriam. The race for Berlin was on, and we sought a piece of the action. Scanning the map, it seemed clear enough that the spearpoint of General Ray McLain's XIX Corps, then approaching the Elbe, had the inside track on the run to the Nazi capital. We plowed through the U.S. Ninth Army from rear to front until we hooked up with its farthest eastern element. We were with it when the first firm bridgehead was thrown across the Elbe at Barby below Magdeburg by the 331st Infantry Regiment. We were still with it when the halt order came from Eisenhower that stopped our lunge eastward.

Not one person present felt cheated on that day. All were more than willing to halt in place. The corps was sprawled out, embattled along both flanks and front, and resistance against the bridgehead mounted steadily. I believed that the Russians were certain to beat us to Berlin, and the best XIX Corps might do would have been to put a few patrols into the western outskirts of the city. Once the halt order came, Merriam and I started north to join Major General Alex Bolling's 84th Division.

Our route was the highway paralleling the Elbe on the west bank. The day was glorious, the sky perfectly clear, the air just crisp enough. We rolled through Magdeburg, the most shattered city I ever saw in war. Everything was down. Humans crawled in and out of basement warrens that were all but buried under the masses of wreckage. They humped along bent over, scurrying like rodents through a city dump. The day quickly lost all charm. When one repeatedly sees human misery en masse, there is no pity, only revulsion that such things have to be. Cry for them, cry for everyone, cry for me.

We sped out of there, as fast as Merriam could gun the jeep, and bucketed north. Five miles along or maybe ten our odyssey came to an abrupt end. Trees and hedges bordering the highway had obscured our view, and too late we saw that we had entered into a deployment of troops coming from across the Elbe. The left flank was moving up the bank and about to hook across our rear. The right flank, in column, was plainly in view, and they wore the wrong uniform. I yelled: "Bob, turn about!" He was already turning at such speed that he almost ditched the vehicle, and we shot out of there. This was the last gasp of the Hermann Goering Division, marking the fourth time that I had blundered into enemy country in Europe. Horseshoes, just horseshoes lined with rabbits' feet, all the way.

Soon after the fighting ended a party of about thirty of the nation's leading publishers, editors, and writers arrived in the theater on a sightseeing tour. The main object was to get them to inspect Dachau and Buchenwald. General Eisenhower hoped that in this way some of the shock felt by our forces when they first overran the Nazi atrocity mills would be transmitted to the home front.

It was a somewhat vain expectation. When at the close of their tour the gentlemen of the press were banqueted by about thirty of us from the high command, they seemed to be far more interested in a number of other things. The horrors of the camps were hardly mentioned during the cocktail hour or later when the oratory flowed.

Stanley High of the *Saturday Evening Post* was the first speaker. His message was that a miracle had recently taken place in San Francisco. The United Nations had been born, thereby insuring perpetual peace on earth, thank heaven. The army speaker who followed High simply seconded the notion. There were loud cheers. Amon Carter of the *Fort Worth Star-Telegram* then came on strong with a pitch for universal military training. We had to get it at once, he said, or nothing that we had won during the war would long endure. The army speaker who followed Carter very courteously concurred with his comments every syllable of the way. More cheers.

My turn came. I said that, since every press man present thought of me as an army officer, and everyone on the General Staff regarded me as a journalist, I didn't have to follow anyone's line. In fact, I disagreed with all that had been said. The UN was not going to save the world or insure peace; universal military training would not secure the American birthright and we were not going to get it, anyway.

The main problem was right next us, where we sat in Paris. Just over the frontier was a land in chaos, and for that matter, France wasn't in very good shape, either. To the east of Germany was a great power, one of the victors in the war, bent on exploiting that chaos to its own political ends. Yet we, in this same hour, were approving Soviet dismantling of the German industrial plant, such of it as remained, and the shipment of same into the USSR. I said that, until our policy began to take account of the absolute necessity of reconstructing that part of Germany which could still be aligned with the West, it would contribute only to the ultimate communization of Europe. That talk was as well received as a cockroach in the spaghetti.

When I sat down there were no cheers, though that did not surprise me. Colonel Joe Starnes of Military Government, a former congressman from Alabama, had teamed with me to try to persuade Eisenhower, Clay, Bedell Smith, and other influential soldiers to counsel Washington against the course we were pursuing. We worked all summer and we got nowhere. Big men are sometimes just that blind.

Chapter 13
Some Shadow Boxing

Victory Day in Europe, which meant joy to the world or a fair piece thereof, fell on us like a curse. Most of the theater went on half time or less, except those members of the staff who were far overburdened with the uncharted problems of redeployment. We kept our people on a full seven-day schedule, and the lights burned well into the night.

There was some grumbling. We tried to still it by setting 0930 as the start of the workday, which meant that our characters could have a night on the town and still sleep it off before reporting. That worked for a while.

Colonel Charles E. Beauchamp, with General Lee's blessing, left it to us to decide how all historical personnel in the theater should be reassigned or disposed. We could recall the best ones from the army field detachments, either to flesh out the strong team that we were preparing to redeploy to the Pacific, or to fit into jobs in the central operation. The deadheads, provided they had points enough, could be sent to a forwarding camp for return to the United States.

It was the points system that threatened to put us on the rocks. Everyone was going along with it, Eisenhower, the General Staff, Secretary Stimson, and my opposite number in the War Department, Colonel Al Clarke, who had replaced Kemper. The need for long-term retention, if the historical program was to serve any purpose, was totally disregarded by the very Washingtonians who should have fought to safeguard it. The more we strove and strengthened in the workshop on Avenue Foch, the more agitated Cole and I became that it was all for nothing, because we would be washed out elsewhere. I needled Clarke time and again, only to get rebuffed.

Clarke and I had not hit it off well, which was mainly my fault. Clarke is the salt of the earth, and I cherish our long friendship, but we did not know one another then. He kept prodding me for monthly reports, as he did other chiefs in the theater. I refused pointblank, telling him that we did not have time to write long screeds for his comfort and that eventually our work must speak for itself.

Weighted by the dilemma, I wrote a long letter to an old friend, Senator Homer Ferguson, asking him to convey the sense of it personally to Judge Patterson, undersecretary of the army. The import was that, unless the Pentagon changed its attitude and took measures to conserve our operation, it would be a total failure.

My assistant exec, Captain Harry Salisbury, had been private secretary to one senator from Missouri. I called him in, showed him the letter, and told him: "Harry, I cannot tell you to write a letter to the President of the United States, but if you wish to let him know what we're sweating out, it will be all right with me." Salisbury went ahead.

Hardly were these letters in the mail when there was published in the theater a directive from Washington that thereafter communications from overseas to the Pentagon on problems of redeployment, and policy pertaining thereto, would be restricted to theater commanders.

I went at once to Major General Harold E. "Pinky" Bull and said to him: "If I comply with that directive, my operation is dead."

Pinky, who was sitting in as acting chief of staff for Bedell Smith, took it with a grin and gave me a classic reply. "Well, Marshall, I can't authorize you to disregard a War Department directive. I can only assure you that, if you do, you will get into no trouble with anyone in this theater."

Next day Cole and I put in for trans-Atlantic conversations with Clarke and his administrative superior, Major General Clayton Bissell, G-2 of the army. I had met Bissell and disliked him cordially. Within a few hours, we were seated at the scrambling machine in the big headquarters, listening to the Donald Duck voices from the Pentagon and telling them what we thought.

It was a slanging match from the opening bell and got worse through the hour. We told them they were letting the show down and that, unless they moved, the operation would go bankrupt. Bissell wanted to know how many of our peple would apply for long-term work in Washington, provided he could set up Civil Service jobs. I told him not one damned man, that I would advise all hands to shy away from an establishment so weakly managed. We went on from bad to worse. The ring-off came when I told Bissell, "All you're proposing to do is pump more air into a dead horse and that's senseless," to which he replied, "You have said one word too many."

That implied threat ringing in our ears, we crossed the street to the nearest bistro. Doc said: "Confinement to quarters—maybe?"

"Maybe. Or relief and a quick ride home."

"Then we might as well get plastered now."

"Good idea."

We weren't laughing, but as we sat to table, Joan MacMaster, who had monitored the conversations, said: "I get sick and tired of you two guys.

You're always talking shop." Suddenly things seemed funny again.

Two days later I had a telephone call from General Bull. "I have a cable here from Secretary Stimson. It may interest you. It says, 'If we allow officers to stay on as volunteers, provided they have essential work to do, and approve the discharge of enlisted personnel having points to come home, and their retention overseas as civilian employees with civil service rating, provided they are willing, will this satisfy your mad historian?'"

"General, that's just what the doctor ordered."

Bull went on. "There's just one catch. If they apply it to you, it will go for everybody."

"Wonderful. It may save some other poor beggar."

So far as I know, this was the only brake applied to the mad scramble and bail-out that was called redeployment in World War II. Thereafter our operation stayed on firm ground.

Immediately after, Eisenhower tried to lower the boom. At a cocktail party he had promised our Avenue Foch building to the Canadians for use as their embassy. It was done as casually as that, with no consideration of what it would do to us. I couldn't let it go. Right at that time we were consolidating and reorganizing with the sections coming in from the field. To move would have set us back irreparably.

The bad news arrived with Lieutenant Colonel Donovan Yuell, from the staff of Lieutenant General Tom Larkin; he was sitting in for John C. H. Lee, who had returned to the United States to get married.

Yuell came to show us new quarters—three buildings in the palace grounds at Versailles—into which he had been directed to move us the next day. Doc Cole and I went with him to inspect the premises. They were ill lighted, ratty, and otherwise wholly unsuitable, as we pointed out.

When we got back to Avenue Foch, Yuell again raised the question: "Will you comply with General Larkin's order?"

I answered no.

Yuell drew off and said to Cole: "That goddamned prima donna," which Doc promptly reported to me.

I said to Yuell: "Say that out loud to my face and I'll prefer charges against you at once."

He apologized, then returned and told Larkin that our shop had best be left alone. I thought the thing would cool off.

Doc and Joan got married (General Lee had turned his quarters over to them for the reception and dinner) and then went to the Riviera for their honeymoon.

On Saturday morning, twelve large vans from the Seine Base Section drew up in front of our place. They had come to move us lock, stock, and barrel, and there were plenty of barrels. The boys liked beer.

A quartermaster captain was in charge of the convoy. I asked him how many men were with him, and he said thirty.

I said: "I have 150 men inside those walls. I have told them that if your men enter, they are to be pitched into the street. Now wouldn't it be wiser to turn that convoy around?"

He agreed.

General "Ples" Rogers commanded Seine Base. I called him and told him what I had done. He said he didn't blame me, that he thought the order was intolerable.

He said: "Why don't you call General Lee and ask for help?"

The idea shocked me. Lee was in California with his bride. It would be most inappropriate, all of which I pointed out.

Ples said: "You've got it all wrong. He will do anything for you. He has told me so."

I called the Old Man. Cliff Lee answered as if I were doing him a favor of some kind. He cabled Larkin not to move me until I said I was ready to move, and Larkin, who was simply trying to keep Eisenhower's feathers smoothed, was happy enough to pull off. I both knew and respected Larkin. He was a gentleman soldier. I have tried only to tell here why Lee has a very special place in my heart.

Reluctantly, I had decided that Major Shappell would lead the team to the Pacific, and his ablest officers would go with him.

Cole was with me when I gave him the news. He did not demur, but his physical reaction spoke for itself. He had expected to go home. Cole suggested we take a break and get down to details in half an hour.

Doc was bothered about the decision. Shappell had gone all out in his combat work, and he had a family. Major Hatch of the Ninth Army detachment was a bachelor, a capable administrator, and had seen less fighting. In fair play, wasn't it more sensible to send Hatch to the Pacific? Having spent a year there, I didn't think the stakes were that major, but when Cole spoke, I listened.

We got with Dick again and I told him that we had reconsidered. Hatch would go in his place. We hadn't counted on his reaction. He stood and he glared. He said, "No sir, not on your life. Most of that team will be formed of my officers. Where they go, I go." No other words than these better epitomize the born leader, the man who draws others to him because he is drawn by them.

I said: "By the way, Dick, you'll get to no war in the Pacific. You'll have several weeks' leave in the ZI. By then the fight against Japan will be finished, so you'll be demobbed before any of us here."

"Do you really mean that, sir?"

"You can count on it."

Dick went forth, bet $500 among his teammates that they would never redeploy from the United States—and collected! Knowing when to bet toward morale-boosting, while at the same time making a pot with the losers feeling no pain, is also the mark of a good leader.

Thirty-two days after the first attempt to shunt us into nowhere, I called General Lee's exec and told him that we were ready to move, provided that we were offered a building that was suited to our needs. General Bissell meanwhile had arrived in the theater and was nosing about in a highly official manner.

The spot chosen was the Chateau Hennemont at Saint Germaine-en-Laye, an estate of the Maharajah of Indore, or some other such prince. It lay twenty or so miles from Paris, a great stone pile that had been smutted so that it rose sootlike to the sky, which mistaken try at camouflage gained for it the wondrous nickname bestowed by my imaginative crew. It was ever after *The Black Bastard.*

The stone-walled estate included about 500 acres of forest. Next to the main gate and forward of the chateau proper were stone lodgings with more than enough beds to house all of our enlisted people, and manses on the banks of the nearby river had been tabbed for the officers and married couples.

Further, from that hour forward, we were strictly on our own. We would be a self-sufficient military unit, responsible for our own messing, transportation, and all else except hospital care. We could operate in cold detachment from the rest of the army. That is, almost.

I recall those first days of early summer in 1945, and I glow. There was beauty all around us, and it was ours to enjoy as we pleased, for at first we were wondrously cut off from the disorder and stress of the rest of the theater. The estate was rolling country, and a clear-running brook bisected it diagonally. The sun was burning bright, and the deep shade under the great oaks and walnuts was sweetly restful during the hour-long break that followed the noon meal. Troops loafed about, playing cards or catching a few winks under the trees. Others strolled the grassy meadow by the brook. There being about twenty young French women working for us as clerks and typists at Hennemont, couples paired off to roam to the far corners of our private domain, no doubt the better to commune with nature in her loveliest forms. So blissful was our bounty as to leave no room for small taboos. Live it up, live it up—and we did. The whole thing was intoxicating.

Our idyllic situation at Hennemont was much too good to last untroubled when elsewhere in the theater redeployment was blighting all operations. The morning came when we discovered only by its absence that we no longer had any U.S. motor transportation. The unit to which our drivers belonged had pulled stakes overnight to head for a base port and home, and not one word of warning had been given Chateau Hennemont. We hired five Paris taxicabs to stay permanently on station. Those heaps must have seen action under Gallieni in the First Battle of the Marne, and judging by the look of the cabbies, they still had their original drivers, though somehow they got us over the roads.

Then the military police guard detail attached to us vanished homeward bound and without warning.

Delos Dayton, my customarily calm and collected exec, viewed it as a crisis that would scuttle our housekeeping arrangements by bringing about the removal of our German POW attendants. He was about to call higher headquarters when I stopped him. I said: "That's the last thing to do. Very likely everyone up top has forgotten that the prisoners are here. These Germans have no place to go. They're living high, so we will keep them without any guard. Escapes are unlikely, but if any of them take off, then what? It won't be our fault. We didn't remove the MPs. So long as we do the most reasonable thing in any circumstance, we can always defend our ground."

Nothing came of it. The prisoners stayed, all the happier that the guard was gone. Their reaction was so very, very German.

The day the second atom bomb fell, I was lunching with Bedell Smith at the Ritz. He gave me the news. The flash had just hit the big headquarters.

I voiced my surprise about the event at Hiroshima, for I had known nothing about the Manhattan Project. Smith said: "We were in on the secret. Eisenhower and I had to know about it. Berlin was to have been the target for that first bomb."

At my George V apartment were about four cases of booze, a reservoir collected out of rations. The bottles were loaded in the taxi. By two in the afternoon I was back at Hennemont. A memo went to all hands to knock off work for the day. The officers would assemble at their club, the NCOs going to their own club. The liquor was divided down the middle.

Nothing about that second bomb had been heard at Hennemont, and I did not tell them. I gave a short talk to the assembly. "I will be leaving in three hours for Berlin to be gone five days. Before I return the war will end. I won't be here with you, so I say let's celebrate now—and do it hard." They were wholly bewildered by my certainty, and it didn't hurt their thirst one bit.

★

The memory plays funny tricks in old age. One thing ties into another. An experience shapes up in the mind by thinking on certain words or smells or a strain of music. Recollection then jumps from episode to episode.

For example, as I dwell upon that first visit to Germany's shattered capital, the thoughts that pop up are of art, avarice, and medals, and over all is the reek of urine. Out of this jumble I move to the question of why I identify these thoughts with that experience and how one event connects with another as the mind weaves a fabric out of things past.

There should be far more in these papers on the subject of art, for our section of painters included men with national reputations and superb talents. Impressing me above all else is the recollection that the one artist whose work was praised above all others by the ten men in the section was little Harry Dix, and in civilian life he had been the least successful. Being as ignorant of art as was the public that could not appreciate Dix, I will stay with anecdotes.

That first morning in Berlin I visited the wrecked Reichschancellory. Perhaps fifty feet from the rubbled wall in a flagstoned courtyard was a bronze figure of justice that had come through the bombing unscathed. It was still unapproachable. Surrounding it was a puddle of urine and piled up feces, the collective gesture of Red Army soldiery toward Hitler's justice. Some had even climbed the figure to pee on its upper portions, a feat not more gymnastic than repellant.

The great central hall of the building was open to the sky. Its vaulted walls had been a repository for German military decorations. Americans would have pocketed them for souvenirs. The lower orders of Iron Crosses had been dumped on the floor. There were thousands of them. The Russians had first stomped on them, then given them the same treatment as the figure in the courtyard.

The American holding in Berlin at that time was in two widely separated sectors. Late that night, driving from one to the other, the sergeant handling my jeep made several wrong turns, and we found ourselves in the Russian-held and heavily forested Grüncwald, where we wandered around for most of an hour trying to find our way out. I took out my .45 and told the driver that if anyone tried to stop us, I would fire, and he would try to keep going. Afraid? Naturally, and with good reason, but fear is like a suit of clothes: you get into the habit of wearing it. Days earlier one of my lieutenants had been kidnapped by two Red Army soldiers while east of the Elbe. They drove him more than thirty miles into Russian country, and when they stopped to relieve themselves, he shot them both dead with a .22 pistol that he carried in his hip pocket. Then he walked back.

Later, when I discussed these things at our officers' mess, two Britishers were in the group. They were RAF pilots from a nearby squadron who were attached to us for rations. That is how art enters into the story. What I had said led them, after some weeks, to take me into their confidence. They were men of Colditz, the no-breakout camp where the Nazis penned the most incorrigible Allied POWs. While captive, they had laid their plan, which they proceeded to execute upon liberation. They made for the nearest British air base and hijacked an observation plane, then flew for Berlin, accepting the full risk of a landing there while the Russians were still grappling for the city. They were in civilian clothes, and they spoke excellent German. They carried sidearms and several blocks of TNT.

The first night they blasted their way into an art museum and "liberated" six old masters. For a lark, by early morning light they visited the Reichschancellory and found it deserted. In the same messy hall where I later stood, before one Russian had put foot there, they saw a dial in a wall, knew it was a safe, and blew it. Inside were fourteen of the highest German decoration, each centered with a large diamond. No part of their plan, it was quite a windfall. Then they returned to the ship as swiftly as possible, and flew for Allied country and back to England.

"We have the stuff stashed there," one of them said lightly. "Our fortunes are made if we can just wait long enough. The question is when can we safely put it on the market."

I had no advice to give them, playing fence for art objects not being my line.

So far in these papers I have said little about our work other than that directly connected with the writing of history. There was much more, prior to V-E Day and later. Whereas in the Central Pacific I had been one of the three-man committee that directly revised our procedures, tactical and logistical, on the basis of battlefield research, in Europe this service was performed vicariously.

The Senior Observers Board was present in the theater and was charged to advise the War Department on such changes as seemed justified by what troops were experiencing. Composed of older field grade officers, the board simply could not gather the data on fighting operations; the game was too strenuous for them. Our much younger battlers had the hang of it; so they harvested the information, we passed it along to the SOBs (this elision is pure unhappy coincidence), and they wigwagged Washington on what they divined from our field reports.

Their chairman was Colonel Wayne Archer, in whose honor a monument should be raised at Fort Benning. No soldier was ever more devoted to the U.S. infantry. Wayne and I would get together by night for long talks at the George V. At these bourbon renewal programs, he would give me long lectures about foot fighting. It was my duty to write it all down. I would say, "Yes, Wayne," and would make promises on which we would shake hands, Boy Scout's honor. I didn't take them very seriously. Finally, Archer crowded me into a corner and forced me to write *Men Against Fire*.

Then there was duty on the Theater Awards Board. I was the holdover member through three successive five-man boards. Coupled with that burlesque, field experience in World War II, Korea, and Vietnam made me better schooled in the ironies of the decorations system than any American at any time. In postwar years I wrote numerous articles raising questions about the inequities, several of them for *Collier's*.

The first ETO board, chaired by the inspector general of the theater, stayed honest, made so by a majority of three, of which he was not one. The second board was more inclined to study the politics of the case than to base the verdict on an honest judgment of the citation and narrative. I had Doc Cole sit in my place.

The third board was utterly corrupt. Its decisions were moved by a desire to make Brownie points with all superiors. I blew my stack when it approved a Silver Star for a major general, chief of service, who had cited himself with no supporting witnesses. He had never been within five miles of the front. Both Doc and I boycotted meetings and left the bestowal of medals to a four-man plunderbund.

My work for Eisenhower in disposing of unit citations was strictly personal and wholly unrelated to the seat on the Awards Board, yet some of the ultimate consequences were almost as frivolous as anything contrived by that august body. Colonel John Ames, another retread from the Big Red One, spoke for G-1 at the Frankfurt headquarters. He was a delightful associate, and while I never quite understood how he got into the act, he was doubtless equally at a loss with respect to me. Together, we were the big I Ams, the factotums, and at least one of our problems called for the wisdom of Mr. Anthony.

The French had pushed to our army a quota of ten Croix de Guerre to be awarded to divisions. The Belgians had proffered six. Every U.S. division that had fought in France had recommended itself for the honor. So had every U.S. division that had fought and bled for Belgium in the Battle of the Bulge, including one that had merely launched one patrol onto Belgium soil. There was simply no way to take care of all of our heroes.

John and I got together one Saturday morning to square the circle. I said: "John, you know this is all fiddlesticks. Out of the pack we can choose, say, fifteen divisions that did great work fighting for France and as many that starred in the fighting in Belgium, but as for choosing between them, bah! We would be kidding ourselves; so let's look at the options. We can use the Chinese system. Write the numbers on a paper, roll it up, stick a pin through, and there we have it. Or we can take the best ones and put their numbers in a hat. You pick one. Then I pick one. What's it to be?"

"I prefer the hat method. It has more style."

That's how we did it, and thus were the great honors bestowed. In years that followed, I ran into hundreds of veterans and active servers from these proud divisions that wear the scarlet-and-green cordon. In cafes, buvets,

NCO clubs, and dives, at such out of the way places as Nikko, Guam, Taiwan, and Adana, I have listened to their boasts about the immortal outfit. They know they are in a class apart and superior to other soldiers. The cord says so. I bite my lip and do not enter into the argument.

I wondered then and wonder now. Who is to say? What difference does it make? At what point does illusion become reality? Does it truly matter? Does anyone care?

The C.C. Marshall family, 1902.

In battle dress on Western Front, October 1918.

At Brest, France, 1919.

With Jack Dempsey making up the sports page, 1926.

War correspondent, Mexico, 1923.

Author and his chief, W.S. Gilmore, *Detroit News*, 1927.

The 1936 fishing trip. Ives Marshall standing with Hemingway. Seated, Hemingway's son, "The Mexican Mouse," Hemingway's sister, and Harry Sylvester. Photo by the author.

Holding a critique on combat, Brest, France, September 1944. We were under fire at the time.

At No. 1 Avenue Foch, the evening of 25 August 1944 as we ended the liberation of Paris.
Photo by Ernest Hemingway.

General Ralph Smith at Makin.

Decorating Captain Westover
with the Silver Star,
March 1945.

Chateau Hennemont, St. Germaine.
My HQ, summer 1945.

On departing 7th Division front, Korea, June 1953.

The first Sinai Campaign, 1956.

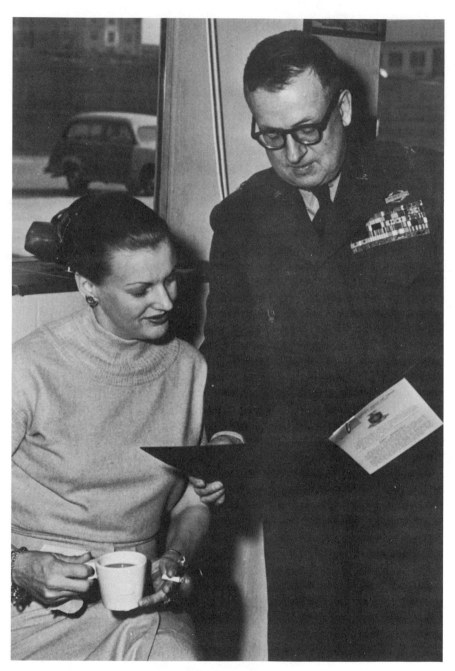

Cate and SLAM at Fort Sill, Oklahoma, 1958.

At extreme left, holding critique in a blocking position at the time of Pork Chop Hill, April 1963.

With Generals Art Trudeau, left, and Darryl Daniel, right, Korea, April 1963.

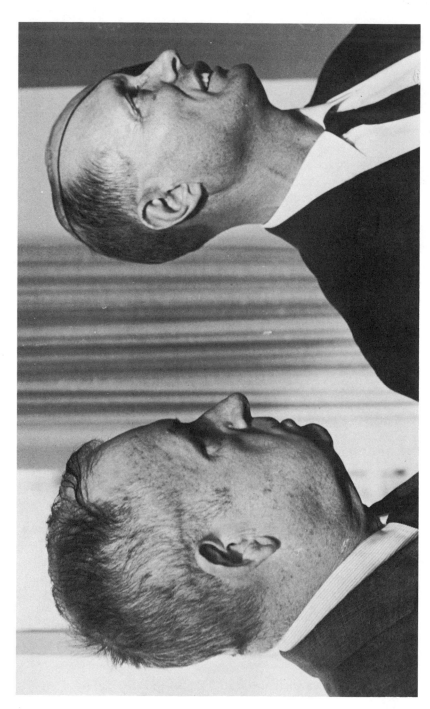

With Moshe Dayan in Detroit, 1966.

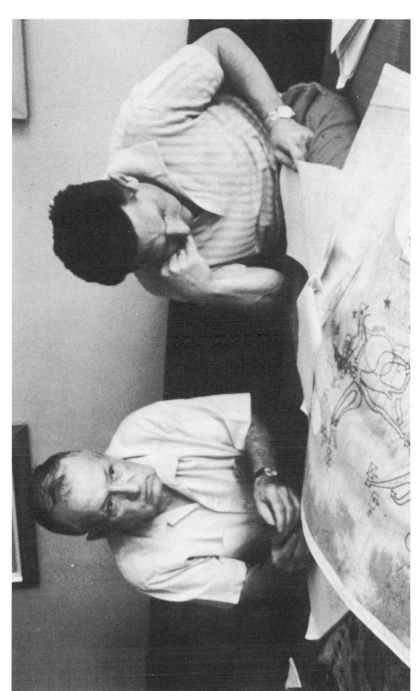

With General Rab Yariv, G2 of Israel, working over the Six Day War.

With General Keith Ware, Vietnam, 1968. Ware was killed two weeks later.

With Dr. Christian Barnard and General Mark W. Clark, Capetown, April 1969.

Chapter 14
Camping with the Germans

For months my head had buzzed with the idea that I had to find a way to enfold the German high commanders and their main staff officers in our operation, or else we would never know more than half of what had happened to our forces from Normandy on. The Germans would never do their history. We had captured most of the records, but the records were not enough. We needed to know the reasons for decisions, and we could only get them from the live witnesses. Failing that, our story would show only one side of the hill.

Doc Cole flatly opposed me on this; it was our one big disagreement. He accepted the reasoning and the theory. His objection was on the purely practical grounds that our work force was already overextended, and I was proposing that we practically double our research effort.

Doc was not alone. The War Department was against it. So was the Supreme Headquarters. There was hardly a person around who did not believe I was jumping off the deep end. The explanation of all this negativeness is elementary. Resistance to the thing that has never been tried before is human. However, as I weighed the odds, I reckoned they were about even. There is no joy like that of bucking the whole crowd while believing that the thing that must be done is doable.

Thinking mainly of how I could make the breakthrough, I concluded that there was no way except by means of a tour de force amounting to trickery. My first step was to fly to Britain just after V-E Day to talk things over with Marshal von Rundstedt. I wanted him to answer one main question: Could I count on the cooperation of the German commanders? I found von Rundstedt fuming because his name had been given to Hitler's mad try at the Ardennes, but he was otherwise cordial and helpful. He said the question was too far out of his field for me to stake anything on his judgment. Then he advised me to talk to General Walter Warlimont, the operations chief of the big staff. If Warlimont said it would work, I could depend on it.

I flew to Germany at once and talked to Warlimont in prison camp. He was all enthusiasm. "Oberst Marshall, I am so certain it will work that I would volunteer right now for your operation if you would have me."

My problem lay primarily in General Lee's headquarters, because the prison camps were administered therefrom under the provost marshal general. However, in the long run I would have to win the full support of Eisenhower's staff because his G-2 had direct responsibility for all dealings with the German higher commanders. Either headquarters therefore was in position to roadblock me.

Every fortnight General Lee regularly called a day-long conference of his chief subordinates. The assembly included all base commanders, service chiefs, and members of his staff. At these deliberations the average attendant used his reporting time to boast about how nicely things were going. I found it a handy platform from which to lament that we were not doing better and to suggest where our progress required stronger support from the command. This was wholly unorthodox and irregular since it shortcut staff channels, as oftentimes I could get a decision on the spot. Having gotten away with it month after month, I saw no reason to stop. Shortly after I had conferred with the two German generals about the project, I laid it before all of the big wheels at the biweekly parley. When I told them about Warlimont volunteering to work with me, the room rocked with laughter. That was their answer; I was being ridiculous.

In the interim, Dr. George Schuster of Hunter College arrived in Paris on a government mission. He was to deal with the ranking Nazis then held prisoner in Nuremberg and write a report on the economic aspects of Hitler's attempt to take over Europe. Among his aides on the junket was my old chief, Colonel Kemper. Instead of giving Schuster the VIP treatment, both of the big headquarters all but ignored him. That was not their fault; they were busy, and no one in his party pressed hard for him. I undertook to entertain him and clear the road for his mission. He was most appreciative. Then several days before he was to head for Germany, I asked his permission to attach one of my staff officers piggyback to his group so that he might test the receptiveness of the ranking military prisoners. Schuster was quite willing.

When I named Major Kenneth Hechler to the task, Hechler bucked like a bay steer. He wanted no such duty; he was aching only to return to the United States. Being told that he would do it and like it, he still went forth grumbling, little realizing that the mission would become virtually the cornerstone of his distinguished career.

Once in it, he did yeoman service. All the enthusiasm with which he had applied himself to combat work visibly returned. He had bucked only because he was tired. After three weeks in the field, during which he had exhaustively interviewed Goering, Keitel, Jodl, Doenitz, and others charged with war crimes, he returned with his briefcase bulging with papers proving that the Germans were receptive and would respond.

There was still the problem of winning all concerned to my point of view, since logic and documentary evidence had little to do with it. While Hechler was away, I had sent a team of my own to prowl the POW camps. It was formed of two captains and a sergeant interpreter skilled at interrogation. Their assignment was to explore in detail the conditions we had fixed on the enemy high commanders in the camps and report back to me. No sanction was asked of anyone before this step was taken. The team was told it would have to use its own wits to get in and out of the camps. I hadn't the slightest notion what my men would find.

At just about the time they were completing their survey, we were making the move from Avenue Foch to Chateau Hennemont. Our new home with its strong walls and ample quarters appeared ideal for the expansion then in planning. We could mount our own guard, and we would be in a relatively remote countryside, safe from prying eyes.

Once we were set at Hennemont, I arranged a rendezvous with Hechler at Frankfurt. There I told him that I wanted him to get Generals Fritz Bayerlein, Heinrich von Luttwitz, and Heinz Kokott, and Colonel Meinhard von Lauchert out of the POW compound at Oberursel and bring them to me at the I. G. Farben building for one day of interrogation. These were the main commanders who had opposed us at Bastogne. When Hechler returned with the four Germans in tow, I told him to reserve five air spaces, fly the whole party back to Paris that evening, and from there taxi our guests to Hennemont. Bayerlein, who spoke good English, listened wide eyed to these instructions.

"We can't do it, sir," said Hechler. "That would be kidnaping."

Maybe it was in a sense, I told him, but that would be my doing, so he was off the hook. All he had to do was obey an order. There was full reason to believe we could get away with it. At least three weeks would pass before the Oberursel authorities would learn where the men had gone. By that time I would have worked them over, and we would have the pilot model for the more elaborate German studies that would follow.

Ken was still mighty dubious. My plane to Paris took off earlier than his, and I was in my office just at the supper hour when he arrived with the four prisoners.

He wanted to know what messing arrangements should be made for the Germans. I told him that we had no time or spare personnel with which to set up a special facility, and he should therefore escort them to our officers' mess and have them dine with our staff. When he objected that our people wouldn't stand for it, I answered that they would have no choice in the matter.

Some minutes later when I went to dinner, I found my officers still loafing at the tables, with Hechler and the Germans standing uncertainly in the vestibule. This was nonsense. The time was past for clearing the mess, and our officers well knew it; so I moved the four Germans on in. I could hear a great buzzing at the other tables.

An hour later Cole came to warn me that we had heavy trouble. Some of the smaller fry in the officer circle were raising hell about Nazis in uniform being imposed on their mess.

I asked: "So what are the boys going to do, Doc, stage a revolution? I doubt it. Tonight they think they have to strike an attitude. By tomorrow noon they will be fascinated a bit by this extraordinary situation. By tomorrow at dinner they will be falling over one another at the opportunity to deal directly with the German brass. We don't have to worry about our people. Human nature will bring them around. Just worry about the story being leaked to the *Stars & Stripes.* Some of the fellow travelers on that staff would blow up a big scandal, and that would kill us. Make sure that the guard keeps all reporters out of Hennemont. If we can do that, we're safe."

Any risk that has to be run must be worth taking. The thing worked out exactly as forecast. We had no trouble of any kind. Within a few days our fellows had swung so wholly over to the idea that, when I set about collecting tobacco, candy, and other luxury items from them to spread among the prisoners, there was ample for the need. This bounty was not in the interests of coddling anyone. I knew that, if we were to win the working cooperation of the Germans, they had to be given special consideration.

Within the next several days I was hard at it, working with the four Germans on the Bastogne pilot study. My reason for beginning with them and with that particular battle was that I knew the operation from the American view far better than any other. As to what our forces had done, my research was already so complete that at every point I could check the accuracy of the enemy commanders' statements as I related cause to effect, and the imprints were so clear in my memory that I could do it without notes.

Bayerlein, who had served under Rommel before commanding Panzer Lehr Division, was the spark plug in the group. A terrierlike individual, then age fifty, he fairly vibrated when he spoke. His contempt for von Luttwitz, who as corps commander in the attack on Bastogne had been his superior, was my first tipoff that in a POW situation, rank, even among Germans, no longer had the privilege of imposing its view. Thus, by getting staff officers grouped with their commanders as we went along, we would elicit corrective and more dependable information. When von Luttwitz rambled in his conversation, Bayerlein would wave a hand in his face and snarl, "Not important! Not important!" And when the somewhat paunchy Junker tried to strike a pompous pose (he still wore a monocle), Bayerlein would turn him livid by howling, "Nuts! Nuts!" It was Luttwitz who at Bastogne had received Tony McAuliffe's four-letter reply heard round the world. Bayerlein believed that von Luttwitz had made the worst fumbles at Bastogne, though the record showed that Bayerlein's individual actions and estimates had cost the corps some of its finest opportunities. About those mistakes, and the mistakes of all others, he was brutally frank. They became almost a mania with him. When confronted with his own gross blunders, he would put his head back and laugh with abandon. At times he seemed more than a little bit unhinged, but still thoroughly likeable.

While the pilot model proved satisfactory, at the same time, Bastogne had been a rather small affair. The test run would therefore be meaningless unless we got the break that would enable us to apply the same process to all operations in the European Theater and go on from that to interrogate the Germans about their war with the Soviets.

The break came with the return to Hennemont of the team I had sent out to inspect the POW camps. After reading their report I felt ready for the calculated risk. At the next full dress conference of the General Staff, I made my pitch about the need for picking the brains of the German General Staff.

There followed the longest wait of the day. The chief of staff turned about to speak softly with General Lee. With that exception, there wasn't a whisper in the room during the prolonged two-way conversation.

Then quick as a wink the tension lifted as the chief looked up to say to me, "I agree with you completely. I take it that you already have your formula. Bring it to me tomorrow morning and I will act."

Victory! I knew that the outcome was another expression of Cliff Lee's confidence in my judgment. Still, my faith had been shaky. When I resumed my seat I was trembling like a leaf, too unstrung to relish the moment that should have been so satisfying.

Two days later the order was published, and we had the authority to proceed. Nothing was more certain than that the order would not clear the path wholly. Other bureaucratic opposition would arise if only because we were attempting something unprecedented.

It came soon enough. The G-2 office at the higher headquarters tried to block us in detail, taking the attitude that we were invaders of its private preserve. When I protested the interference to the executive officer of that shop, he said: "We have no time to waste on foolish operations."

The insult did it.

I went directly to General Bull, who was again sitting in for Bedell Smith as chief of staff. I pointed out to him that we were getting straight-out opposition instead of compliance with an order. General Bull was very good at flattening insuperable obstacles one-quarter inch high. He removed the executive officer and thereafter, thanks to Bull, we had clear sailing.

Within the next week another thirty German generals were taken out of the Oberursel POW enclosure to become billeted at Chateau Hennemont, thereby taxing our facilities. We set up another historical shop, with private quarters to house another twenty generals, at dead center of the Oberursel camp.

While that may sound like a large jar of kraut, it was only the first mouthful. Ultimately, more than 250 enemy field marshals and generals moved in and out of our shop to participate in the exercise. Smiling Al Kesselring proved to be one of the most prodigious workers. Other main contributors were Von Rundstedt, Blumentritt, Speidel, and Zimmermann.

When research on the war in the west was at last complete, a new direction was taken to concentrate on those high commanders who had served mainly on the eastern front so that we might learn all possible about the fighting methods of the Red Army.

As I have already mentioned, we lost our MP detachment at Hennemont so that it might go home. At that point various adjustments had to be made, among them that some of my younger NCO historians had to return to quasi-soldiering again. There was no other way to guard the premises and keep all property secure.

Due to this sudden disarrangement, I had had no time personally to inspect the conditions under which the German generals were being housed, though they continued to dine at our officers' mess. Then at last I got to it on a Sunday afternoon. I found the Germans billeted in a small barrackslike building enclosed by a barbed-wire barricade within the grounds about a city block from the chateau proper.

Three of our armed guards were walking sentry around the compound. I immediately dismissed the guards, telling them to turn in their rifles to the officer of the day and let him know that there would be no more of this nonsense.

The day was brightly sunlit, yet when I walked into the barracks I found the Germans all under the roof, either playing cards or loafing in their bunks.

I asked: "Why are you in here instead of enjoying the fresh air?"

Their spokesman said: "Oberst Marshall, when you walk that small compound, you feel like a caged animal. When we are out of sight of the guards we enjoy the illusion that we are free men."

"There are no guards out there. The barbed wire is down. Walk wherever you please over the estate, but be sure to return in time for the evening meal, or you may go hungry."

He looked at me, his jaw dropped, and he bolted for the door. The others followed him as if they had been shot from a gun. Almost before I got the words out of my mouth, they had been swallowed by the forest. Never have I seen such a scamper by older men. We saw not one of them again until dinner, which is some measure of how greatly a fairly brief imprisonment had made these men crave the open spaces. Though we continued to give them as much liberty as the estate afforded, not one ever tried to make a break or move off limits.

As I saw them in the months we worked together, the Germans fell roughly into three classes—the enlightened professionals who bent to their work with a will because it interested them, the apple-polishers who sought to curry favor with Cole and me, and the unreformed diehards still embittered over the loss of the war. Within a short time of coming to us even the more recalcitrant SS characters had softened, and so did Major Buchs, who had been Hitler's personal adjutant.

I saw none of them thereafter until 1965, when in Johannesburg, I ran into Major General F. W. von Mellenthin, the author of *Panzer Battles*. His is a distinguished book, the material for which he cribbed from our files while a prisoner. I wondered at the time why we were getting so little work from such a clever fellow.

By 1965 Mellenthin had become head of Lufthansa for all of Africa and personally owned one of its large feeder lines. He read in the press that I was in the city and invited me to a large party where the other guests were his fellow expatriate Germans. Due to a traffic tieup, he got home from the office five minutes after I had arrived and met the company.

Mellenthin came striding across the room and stuck out his hand.

"Ah yes, General Marshall. It seems the last time we met, I was your house guest."

Chapter 15
Records and Archives

One day in Frankfurt, Bedell Smith called me in. After we had cleared the atmosphere, he told me, "I have been offered the embassy at Moscow."

"That strikes me as an odd choice."

He grinned. "You're right, but I want the job."

"Why?"

"I've never been able to make any kind of a stake in my life, and I think that at that post I should be able to save as much as $15,000 a year."

I was still puzzled over why he had sent for me. "What does this have to do with me?"

"I need money now, at least ten thousand or so for outfitting, formal clothing, that sort of thing."

"If I only had it, I'd write a check."

Again the Beedle laughed. "I'd bet you wouldn't," he went on, "and that's not the idea. The *Saturday Evening Post* has offered me sixty thousand for six articles on Eisenhower's six great decisions. With that I can get started."

I jumped to another false conclusion. I said, "General, I simply have no time for ghost-writing."

"That's all taken care of. The *Post* is giving me a ghost, but the command stuff is much too thin, as you have already discovered."

"Then what?"

"I am wondering if your command stuff out of the research with the German generals has gone far enough that some of it can be put back-to-back with our material to round out the series."

"I think there's enough already in the files."

"Will you let me have it?"

There was a long pause. Whereas he might have ordered me to turn over the papers, his gentlemanly approach raised a nagging doubt. On the minus

161

side, if I let him scoop official material for private gain, the boys, Hechler chief among them, would rightfully take offense. The work was theirs, not mine; the deal was hardly fair.

I said: "General, I'll have to think this one over. Give me one night."

We met next morning. I said: "You can have the German papers for this one use, provided I can have access to that archive over there," and I pointed to the large walnut cabinet containing his and Eisenhower's personal papers and the most precious documents in the Theater, the conference notes, and the like.

He fairly exploded. "Hell, Marshall, you have it. You know you can go into that cabinet any time."

"That's not what I'm talking about. I mean access from now on, whatever happens. I don't want those papers locked out in the same way Pershing did it."

"You know I'll need time to give you an answer on that one." What he meant was that he'd have to talk it over with the big man.

That night General Eisenhower sent for me to discuss the problem. I pointed out that the papers would be used within utterly discreet limits, and I said that if he would go that far, he would be setting an example above and beyond that of any great commander or public figure in the past, the majority of whom, like Winston Churchill, exploited the records for personal gain.

He said: "I believe you're right. Let me think on it for a while."

Next morning the answer came from Bedell. The deal was on.

The sequel came the following May, 1946. I was about to leave for the uncertainties of civilian life. Smith, marking time in the Pentagon, was loading up for Moscow. A story in the *Washington Post* said that the secret ETO command archive was locked tight in the bowels of the Pentagon with a major detailed to see that it would stay that way. Colonel Al Clarke, the chief of military history, was wringing his hands and crying that the game was up.

Never having told him of the deal with Smith, I wrote out a paper to be signed by the Beedle, which authorized me or my agent to make use of the archive when needed. When I tossed it to Al, he wailed. "Smith will never sign it."

We bet twenty dollars.

Bedell looked up when I entered, glanced at the paper and signed without saying a word.

He asked: "Anything else?"

I said: "It still strikes me as a peculiar choice."

"Get the hell out of here."

The six articles in the *Post* went over so well that they were made into a book, which added to Smith's pile.

———————————————————————★———————————————————————

The Sunday that General Patton had his fatal motor accident while enroute for some bird shooting, General Frank Ross and I had scheduled ourselves for the same sort of outing. We were living weekends at a manse not far from Frankfurt in the same general area. In midmorning Frank went outside to sniff the weather, came back, and reported, "Only a fool would go bird shooting on a day like this. Visibility about thirty feet. Leave us sit by the fire and have a highball."

Instead we had a redball—Frank's version of a Bloody Mary. He was entitled to that change in nomenclature. Frank had dreamed up and operated the still famous Red Ball Express.

Patton's untimely death superinduced a helpful change in our affairs. He had been bounced out of command of the Third Army, by order of Secretary Stimson, into the presidency of the General Board that was analyzing the strategy of the theater. The vacant chair was taken over by Lieutenant General Leonard Gerow, who had commanded the skeletonized Fifteenth Army. While the board was based on Bad Nauheim, we possessed the essential records at Chateau Hennemont in St. Germaine.

For more than a month the central committee of the General Board, chaired by Major General Royall Lord, Lee's former chief of staff, became attached to us for quarters and rations. On the night they reported in, Lord asked me what arrangements I had set up for messing his galaxy of generals.

I said: "No special arrangement. I have none for myself. I prefer to move into any chair that's handy. That way I keep contact with my younger officers. Why don't you try it for a month?"

The generals were quite willing. They mingled with the kids and with the German brasshats and came to relish it more and more. On the last night Lord was in my office taking leave, and we were polishing off one for the road.

He said: "I can't understand it. We've had a wonderful month. Your people are right on top of their jobs. They find what we want, and they get it quickly. They're courteous and wear the uniform well. They're a happy bunch. Yet everywhere else this army is in collapse. How do you do it?"

I said: "General, it's easy. We've done it by ignoring every memo you put out on how to maintain morale among troops."

Lord laughed and raised his glass. "Touché, old man."

Right after that I went to see Gerow and put it to him. He was now through with the records. If he would state the fact in writing and add that he recommended immediate return of the records to the ZI, I could proceed. Then there would be no later risk of anyone tampering with the archive.

Gerow said that he didn't have the authority.

I told him that I thought he could take the authority and no one would question it. It would be a favor to me and a service to the army.

He grinned and did it.

With that small piece of paper, we proceeded, asking leave of no one else. My next move was to see Frank Ross.

I told my old friend that I wanted to have immediate gangway for about forty-six tons of paper, all of it classified. That would call for a special train to Le Havre, or whatever port, under full guard, absolute security at sea, and probably in excess of 7,000 square feet of ship space, depending upon stowage. The documents were all in wooden filing cases, which would have to be pallet-loaded for safe handling. We would supply an escort party, but there would have to be additional guards.

Frank exploded. "Just another goddamned logistical problem!" Then shifting gears instantly, he added, "Slam, your mountain of paper is practically on its way to the ZI this minute."

The one other trick was to free Corporal Cal Vogts to ride home with the archive. Though there would be other officer-historians in the escort party, he was the one man who knew the records best. Cal didn't have enough points by more than half to qualify for return to the ZI, and only the theater commander was authorized to make exceptions. By chance another amigo of my earlier years, Colonel Wally Barnes, was acting for General Joe MacNarney in such matters. He signed the release instanter.

There is no other moral to this story than that there are several ways to skin cats—always provided you have friends at court.

By the end of 1945 all that I wanted to get out of the army was myself. Work had become drudgery. From the day I had quit the Pentagon to head for the Pacific until I packed to ship from Europe, I had not taken one day's leave or made one detour in the interest of seeing new scenery. I had become so tired of one subject—Operation Overlord and the war in Europe—that for seventeen years thereafter I would not attempt any in-depth writing on that theme. Thus it came about that my field notes for the book *Night Drop* lay fallow for almost two decades though my research on the airborne invasion of Normandy was complete before I shook the sands of the Cotentin from my boots for the last time.

The time came when the work load could be shifted to Doc Cole's aching back, and we knew our mission in ETO was an assured success. We knew further that our division had set a standard which would make possible an objective official history for the war as a whole. Operational blunders would be included as well as the great strokes of genius; tragedy would be in proper balance with triumph.

While that was the kind of history that General Eisenhower had told me he wanted, it was really General Bradley who validated the idea. Colonel

Charles Taylor had completed his study of the Omaha beachhead by the early winter of 1944. The work was incisive and critical, and command mistakes were not deleted or played down. I hand-carried the manuscript to General Bradley and made this request: "Will you please instruct the reviewers that it may be questioned as to fact but not as to interpretation?" He passed it along to the staff of First Army with exactly that instruction, and the manuscript was returned to us within five days, unchanged. His approval of that pilot model was a long leap forward.

Though the record was satisfying, the score was short of perfect. At the end we knew that two main questions would go forever unanswered because they were mysteries beyond solution. Otherwise we were without blanks or significant blemishes.

What was the strategic object in the staging of Operation Market Garden, the airborne invasion of Holland? There is no saying. Under questioning, General Eisenhower told me one thing, Marshal Montgomery another, this many months after the Arnhem fight. When the commitment was made, they had discussed it person to person, made no record of what they said, or of the ultimate intention, and thereafter had not confided in their chief advisers. Subsequently, memories had become befogged; the result was an irreconcilable conflict in their statements to me.

Why was the Falaise pocket not closed? Again, there was no saying. General Gerow in one conversation told me that he thought he had made the critical error, but couldn't be sure. It had to do with the arrival of a Canadian unit within the lines of his corps, his mistaken assumption about what it signified, and his oral communication to someone else in higher command. Try as he would, he could not remember, so we were obliged to leave the question dangling.

Today there are more than a few books that will tell you exactly why the Falaise Gap came to be and will define precisely the intent of the high command when Holland was invaded by the airborne. One may only smile wryly at this assertiveness, this zeal to tidy up everything, this assumption that the historian in his easy chair may shed fresh light on the thoughts of minds that were themselves muddled.

--------------------★--------------------

It comes as a bit of a shock at this late date to discover that I cannot remember by what means I returned to the United States, whether by sea or air or donkey, what base or port I departed, and where I first touched down on the blessed soil.

Our house contains only one souvenir from my extended junket in Europe, a prize to remember and use in just the proper way.

In Hitler's Eagle's Nest there was a large circular conference table that is pictured in Albert Speer's memoirs. The cover thereof, owned by Hitler, was a large and heavily tufted chenille spread, eight feet in diameter and weighing seventeen pounds. Around that cloth Hitler and his playmates had their fun and games.

Upon capturing Eagle's Nest, troopers of the 327th Glider Regiment presented this treasure to their colonel, Clarence "Bud" Harper. Bud got tired of lugging it about and gave it to me, though he later said I should have been less ready to snap at it.

While rummaging in our attic one day, Cate found the fabric and had it dyed turquoise blue, thereby eliminating the several tobacco stains. The relic has since seen service by day as the spread on the king-size bunk in our master bedroom.

By night, that historic tapestry is folded onto the chaise longue where it makes a most becoming nest for our Cairn terrier, Pepper. The pup always sleeps well at night, but being a very serious beastie, doesn't seem to get the joke.

———————————————★———————————————

Between the time of my separation from military service in May, 1946, and the outbreak of the Korean police action in June, 1950, I was called up for military duty forty-seven times, the tours ranging in length from forty-eight hours to six months.

Neither quite a soldier nor better than half of a civilian, I was at least getting ahead as a quick-change artist. Very few of these summonses arose from the work of the Historical Division of the Army. Even had I so elected, I couldn't have taken employment with the history shop. My education was too scant to warrant a living wage under civil service, and I had rejected any notion of staying in the army despite my natural inclination. Ives's invalidism and the costs of nursing made that impossible, then and later.

My indecision as to what course to follow ended with a telephone call from W. Steele Gilmore, my old chief and faithful friend on the *Detroit News*. Overnight, things had gone haywire at the office. Two of my former editorial writing colleagues had been packed off to hospital for major plumbing repairs. Doc Gilmore said that, if I would return to close the gap temporarily, I could thereafter keep up my lines with the armed services, traveling where I chose, and thereby keeping the paper informed on military affairs.

My oral contract with Gilmore pulled me back to the *News* and Doc kept the bargain all the way, graciously and generously. I was given freedom to work as a military critic.

The first call taking me away from the *News* came from General Ray McLain, then army chief of information, who wanted me to return to Washington to write policy for Omar Bradley. Gilmore made the decision easy for me by saying, "You must be the judge of whether any call to military duty is sufficiently urgent."

I dug in at the Pentagon and remained on duty in McLain's office for various staff papers on national policy ... policy that led to NATO, the Berlin air lift, and Tito's problems with the Soviets. In between I was back at my Detroit post.

Chapter 16
Eisenhower: Sidelights

In early 1948, my editor, Doc Gilmore, sent me to Washington to see Eisenhower and to get from him, if possible, some explanation of his enigmatic attitude toward the presidential race. He would neither jump in nor declare himself out, which Gilmore and other staunch Republicans thought most unreasonable. By then Eisenhower was well tired of the chief of staff's berth; the army was in decline and moreover the position did not truly suit him.

There was no difficulty about getting the interview, and he made no effort to fence around or evade direct questions. He said he had no real party leanings or decided political views and that he could as gracefully affiliate with the party in power as with the GOP. His failure to declare himself one way or the other, he added, was anything but equivocal. These were his words: "Should I say flatly that I will not run, that might bring MacArthur into the race. I intend to prevent that, if possible."

I did not ask him why he felt that way. I already knew the story, having had it from Thomas Jefferson Davis, MacArthur's longtime aide. Eisenhower's break with MacArthur in 1936 had come over politics. Eisenhower was backing Mr. Roosevelt and betting heavily upon him. In a careless moment he advised his chief to take the long end of some of the three-to-one money that was being offered in Manila. MacArthur, who hated Roosevelt, turned on Eisenhower and for five minutes reviled him for wagering on such a despicable character. Ike, a man with tremendous self-pride, was not one to take insult. Next day he told MacArthur that he wanted to be relieved—perhaps the wisest decision of his lifetime.

During our interview and later, Eisenhower seemed very tired. It was as if he were struggling to summon the right words.

After Bedell Smith returned from his tour as ambassador in Moscow, he gave me the forty letters that had been exchanged between himself as emissary to the Soviets and Eisenhower as president of Columbia University. That happened because I had intended, with their permission, to write a study of their command relationships in World War II, a project that was jettisoned when Smith died before I was half finished. The letters revealed little or nothing new to me about the Beedle. He was his normal self in his loyalty and devotion to his former chief and his concern for the country in the light of what he had learned about the Russians.

Reading, I recalled being with Smith at dinner in Frankfurt the night he and Ike returned from their official visit to Moscow. There had been an incident in Red Square just prior to the review as Eisenhower stood with Stalin. The dictator had pointed to thousands of small children massed around the square. He said: "Look at them!"

Ike replied: "They look strong and healthy."

Stalin said: "That isn't what I mean. Notice their posture. We train them to be soldiers from babyhood. You don't. That's one mistake you are making."

Then Smith added: "It chilled Ike through and through. I have never seen him more depressed."

Eisenhower had himself told me about his shock at a conversation with Marshal Zhukov, who was twitting him about the elaborate technology developed by the U.S. Army for the clearing of minefields. "We find it simpler," said Zhukov, "to march troops over them and take our losses."

If such incidents shook Eisenhower at the time, he had forgotten them two years later, as I learned from questioning. As to his share in the exchange of letters, he dealt at length with things trivial and abstract more than with great issues and affairs. He wrote about his worries over his health, how his golf game was going, of orchids that had come his way, and his attitude toward national politics, all of it in a strangely naive and immature way. From the early summer of 1945 on, he had not seemed to have a tight grip on himself. Throwing off cares rather than attending to tasks seemed to preoccupy him. All along I had been wondering what had happened to him, and I wonder still.

On his final day as chief of staff in 1948, we members of the Army Historical Commission were his guests at lunch in the Pentagon. By his choice, that was his last official act. He was in a mellower mood than usual. After the meal he began discoursing on his love for history, above all, Civil War history, and out of that, one particular field, Gettysburg.

"I will never be able to understand," he said, "why Lee let the battle get away from him. He did, you know, by not taking a firm line with General Longstreet."

While my own feeling is that his point was irrelevant as to the prospects on the Gettysburg field at that hour, I answered him by saying, "I don't see the mystery. Lee acted that way because he was General Lee."

Ike said: "Slam, I don't follow you."

I replied that it seemed to me that Lee was performing in character. He was incapable of taking a hard line with a subordinate. It was against his nature. Therefore, he could not meet the requirements of that particular field. Longstreet tested and found the chink in the armor. And Lee had other weaknesses. One must not start by assuming there is such a person as the perfect general. I begin, as I told Ike, with the proposition that, being mortal, all commanders are flawed.

"What are my flaws?" Ike asked.

"Let's hold that for another session."

Everyone was laughing. All had been said in the name of good, clean fun, more in banter than in earnest. He was enjoying himself, and we had warmed to him.

Well before that, I had seen enough of him to be aware that the public image was so brightly burnished that the dazzle blinded most eyes to his few character defects. Still, they were there. He was as intensely proud as he was ambitious, and he blazed with anger at what he thought to be an unfair attack upon his reputation, or the failure of a friend or subordinate to defend him to the limit when any such attack took place. Since I incline that way myself, and his treatment of me was ever gracious, I do not say these things critically. The difference was that he expected more of human nature than I do, so he was much too easily wounded, and some of his tirades went beyond reasonable limits.

Ralph Ingersoll's book, *Top Secret,* put Ike in a towering rage. This was while he was still chief of staff. His fury was less because Ingersoll had written cheaply of him and had slighted his dignity than because he had disparaged Ike the better to extoll Omar N. Bradley. The latter had neither lifted a finger to stop him (which would have been impossible) nor raised his voice in protest. While I thought that *Top Secret* was a sloppy book and felt that Ingersoll's comments on SHAEF were crudely vulgar, I commented: "You're expecting too much of General Bradley. After all, he's head of the VA right now. He'd not only have to step out of character but commit a gratuitous folly to denounce Ingersoll at this point."

Ike simply would not be appeased. The more I protested, the angrier he became—at both Ingersoll and Bradley. I would not oversimplify the matter. Eisenhower and Bradley had been more than amicable before the Bulge. Then, soon after the battle started, Ike took the left flank of the Twelfth Army Group (the troops on the North Shoulder) away from Bradley and put them temporarily under Field Marshal Montgomery, with repercussions that continue until this day. Ike's decision was made because communications with the left flank had been cut. Beyond doubt, the decision was right. However, Bradley felt outraged, and word of his deep resentment inevitably got to Ike.

Thereafter, the personal staffs of these two celebrated commanders did their best to exacerbate the friction, each circulating rumors that would needle the other and in general behaving like family spoil-sports. I thought they were shameful and told some of them so. The bickering was still growing strong when Ike went to Paris in 1950 as SCAPE while Bradley ran the Pentagon roost as chairman of the Joint Chiefs of Staff. Monty was then Ike's deputy and the appearance of Bradley's book (one of the best World War II memoirs) was used to tweak him and reopen old wounds. The high pride, or call it egotism, of the big chiefs I could understand. At times it may be obnoxious, but one learns to live with it.

When I visited Paris in the midsummer of 1951 with the object of briefing the SHAPE General Staff on weapons effects in Korea, General Eisenhower was on a visit in Heidelberg, and so my dealings were primarily with his chief of staff, my old friend General Al Gruenther. The lecture was in early morning, and had I not been slightly hungover, I would have been wholly thrown by one of Al's actions just prior to the introduction. General Stan Michelson, one of my companions on the tour, was holding forth on the platform, projecting Nike Zeus and that wonder to come, the antiballistic missile, which was then only a dream, later to become one of the hottest of political issues.

With only two minutes remaining to Michelson, Gruenther passed me a note that read: "Slam, talk to them about allied relationships in Korea; that would be useful in our situation."

It was a subject to which I had not given a moment's thought, and also another fast curve from Al Gruenther. Had I not, since my twenties, been accustomed to that kind of pitch from him, it might have decked me. As it happened, the suddenness of it gave me a flash inspiration. This headquarters seemed stuffy. It probably hadn't heard one off-color story in soldier language since it was formed. Maybe that would be the way to cut through the murk. I started by saying that we had such allied harmony in Korea that it was even reflected in the rough humor of the theater.

An American and an Aussie sat on a railway embankment outside Pusan.

Along came a goods train.

"Do you know what we'd do with such dinky boxcars if we had them in the United States?" asked the Yank.

"Sure," said the Aussie, "you'd either eat it or you'd———it. That's all you bloody Yanks are good for."

My bunt in the right direction almost broke up the ball game. Then I continued in a serious vein.

• In World War I, we learned nothing of one another. We didn't try. We simply ridiculed anything an ally did that wasn't our way of doing it.

• In World War II, we made a great stride forward. The several General Staffs got to know one another and learned to work together efficiently.

• In Korea, we had become a band of brothers, each concerned to understand the other's problem and assist in its solution.

The extemporization was not a simple workout of wind and wit or a parade of generalizations but a serious attempt to document the subject and evaluate the progress made through three wars. I should have spared myself that gallant try, for I am certain none of it sunk in.

After the meeting, Gruenther led me into his own sanctum sanctorum, where we had our first private conversation in several years. In its course I was briefed on the great secret undertaking at the SHAPE diggings that was expected, in due course, to change nothing less than the folkways of Europe. Until our talk I had heard nothing of the European Defense Community (EDC), and in this I was no more innocent than all of my fellow scientists and scribes and the masses of my countrymen.

Once Gruenther had unfolded the grand plan, it did not strike me that the brains I had been with that morning were likely to succeed where Napoleon had failed. The idea for EDC had germinated in Ike's fertile imagination, and a staff section under Brigadier General John H. Michaelis was actively in charge of its midwifery and incubation. Mike's name appears frequently in these papers; he keeps bobbing up in my life. While at that time I was aware that he had some impressive credentials, I knew of none that suggested he was qualified to play Metternich.

The atmosphere then prevailing at SHAPE seemed hardly conducive to the carrying forward of a vast and original enterprise. Ike was already dreaming of the presidency although he was still unwilling to admit it publicly. Granted that his presence and personality might carry weight in the chancelleries and bend a few European statesmen in the desired direction, a man thinking primarily of the White House could not devote his main attention to the problem of fundamentally reforming the politics of another continent. It is not given to mortals to look east and west without turning. While these several factors gave me doubts, the climate in the SHAPE offices gave me more since little feeling of urgency pervaded the headquarters. The boss man was away visiting much of the time while Gruenther, a brilliant chief of staff, was fully occupied regulating and harmonizing his multinational organization. SHAPE was still largely a facade with far too little power afield to be an impressive shield and safeguard.

I voiced my misgivings to my old friend Al Gruenther: was it proper for this headquarters to concern itself with a grand political design? Would western Europe, especially France, be receptive?

The chief replied that intellectually he had the same doubts but his faith told him that EDC must succeed.

I commented that throughout my military life, when my intellect pointed in one direction and my faith in another, I had found it best to keep plodding along the path of common sense.

We had enjoyed since our twenties a heavy kidding friendship. The infectious Gruenther laugh came louder than usual when he replied, "When you get deadly serious, I don't know whether to feel amused or alarmed."

A year later General Eisenhower returned to the United States to seek the presidency. One of his first stops in the preconvention stage of campaign was Detroit. By this time he had forgotten what he had written to Bedell Smith three years earlier: "Nathan Hale did not want to serve as a spy; still he did it for the sake of the country. In that same spirit I would accept the presidency if it was a clearly manifest duty. It could be such only if there was an overwhelming public demand and no opposition. I cannot imagine any such condition arising."

Indeed, it had not arisen, though he was clearly on his way. We talked together in the Detroit Veterans' Building, where his meeting was to be held. By that time SHAPE's secret was out, and the prospects for EDC were being widely discussed editorially at home and abroad. Inevitably, our conversation swung to that subject. I asked him what he thought of the outlook.

"Excellent! It will go over. Why, only one week ago I talked to the French Academy about it. I said to them, 'Gentlemen, just think the thing through. In our time we have moved mountains, harnessed tides, and brought the atom under control. The reform we are now attempting requires only changing the thoughts of men.' "

That one really jarred me. I asked, "General, didn't anyone in the academy remind you that that is the most difficult trick of all?"

Just then a press photographer snapped our picture. No reply came forth. I think he felt I had been rude.

I did not see him again until he returned to Detroit for his final campaign speech prior to election. His right-hand adviser, Major General "Slick" Persons, whom I knew well, invited me to a political huddle at the Hotel Statler.

Slick's first words to me were a confession. He laid on the line the information never made public that he personally was responsible for the decision taken by Eisenhower to say nothing in defense of his friend, General George C. Marshall, while making the hustings in Senator McCarthy's territory. Against his better judgment, Ike had refrained at Persons' insistence. Slick said: "I convinced him that this has nothing to do with the military. We are in a political war. Nothing counts but votes."

Then his face brightened as he continued: "We now have a big idea, something that we believe will swing the election. That's what I wish to talk over with you. I have proposed that in his speech at Olympia tomorrow night, he will make a pledge, 'I will go to Korea!' I think it will sweep the country. What is your view?"

"Slick, he has the election won anyway—hands down. He'll do little good for troops over there, and he can't end the war. It will rock along until the Communists decide to blow the whistle. You are just making a gesture. But what about Europe and EDC? Nothing less than his touch at this time is apt to win the necessary support in France."

"That will have to wait until later. Now we're thinking only of what will win the most votes."

"Fair enough, then, the idea will ring bells."

Things worked out as we all know. Ike made the pledge, won the election, and shortly flew for the theater of war. In retrospect, I cannot say that this was one of his major mistakes. The European Defense Community would not have worked out anyway. As for his latter-day claim that he bluffed the Communists into a truce by secretly brandishing the atom bomb, that is as lacking in substance as was his hope for EDC.

Chapter 17
Korea: An Oblique View

Carl Sandburg was in rarest form on the night of Memorial Day 1950 as to his wit, his minstrelsy, and his thirst for bourbon.

For four hours three of us sat in the basement of my home in Detroit singing and yakking, the other visitor being one no less dear to me, Ted Davison, the English poet who was one of my staff officers in World War II. Carl had been twanging at the guitar all evening. Ted has a joyous tenor.

At precisely midnight, Carl dropped the nonsense and arose. Puffing on a cheroot, with eyes closed, he stood as if demanding attention. It was a wonderful act, and he got what he wanted.

When the voice came it was loud and shrill. "I hear war drums! I smell powder! This nation will be at war within thirty days!"

Wholly startled because of his air of prophecy, I said: "Sit down, Carl. You are slightly pie-eyed."

"Mark what I say! It will be Korea." Then he sat down.

In less than thirty days, we were in it, which merely proves that a poet can be more prescient than all of the diplomats and intelligence agents serving a country.

On the night South Korea was hit, I called my brother, Burton, who was then on the Policy Planning Staff of the State Department. I told him: "Do what you can to keep us out of it. This is a bottomless pit. The North Koreans will be far tougher than anyone in Washington is prepared to believe." My brother believed me and did what he could. I also called a top figure on the Joint Chiefs of Staff and was told that I was needlessly alarmed; North Korea was not militarily formidable.

There were alternative ways of dealing with the crisis, but these were not even considered. Beyond doubt the United States committed itself to that war under the mistaken impression that limited resistance would make the Communists back off.

Ten days later I was in Washington going over notes that ultimately became the paper "U.S. Strategy 1950" under the signature of General

Omar N. Bradley. On that visit I learned that Defense Secretary Louis Johnson had severed all communication between the Pentagon and the State Department except for one liaison officer, which stricture came of his view that all hands in Foggy Bottom were pinkos and not to be trusted. That fact came out when I talked to Bradley about the need to program for operations beyond the thirty-eighth parallel and suggested a plan that would extend operations only so far as the waist of North Korea. He replied that, according to the press, our chief policy makers had forbidden any planning for operations in the north.

To my mind it was appalling that with the nation at war there could be no across-the-board conversations between the top figures of State and the military. I pressed Bradley to have another go at Secretary Johnson on this matter. Two days later I got a wire from Colonel Ted Clifton that he had tried and failed.

I spent the next several weeks at home writing and broadcasting about the new show and feeling wholly dejected. When the nation is at war and I am functioning only as a sideliner, I have nightmares.

Several weeks after the Inchon Landing the report came that the first Chinese Communist volunteers had appeared on the Korean front. Nine men had voluntarily come over the hill and surrendered. Beyond doubt they were all agents who had been given that specific mission to generate mystification.

Simultaneously, I received a wire from Major General Pinky Ward, chief historian of the army, saying that the department was asking me to ship for Korea immediately to take charge of historical operations there. This meant that I would also have to recover five months of backlog. Both my wife and my civilian chief, W. S. Gilmore, agreed that I should go.

I immediately called eleven members of my old staff in Europe, asking each if he were ready for such a call. Obviously, I would not have time to train new people. All were willing to cut and travel. I then wired Ward that I would go provided that seven of the eleven officers were given orders with me and that the list included one field officer. Only one such was on the list, Roland Ruppenthal, who had been my chief of logistics in Europe. To my amazement, within forty-eight hours I heard from Ward that the whole thing was off.

I went to Washington to learn why. Ward said: "You specified that one field officer go with you. Under department rulings we can send reservists to Korea but not in field grade."

I exploded. "Well, then, how in hell can you send me?"

"You're a very special case."

"So all you have to do is make Rupe a special case."

"If we make too many special cases, we wear out our welcome with the high command."

I said that that didn't make sense to me. Pinky laughed thinly, then admitted that in the department they had concluded that the Korean thing would be over in two or three weeks.

I said to him: "General Ward, you here at the department must be out of your minds. This war is just getting started, and if you don't get with it, you're unpardonable." Then I walked out.

Two days later Dr. Ellis Johnson called me to say that Operations Research Office (ORO) was sending a reinforcement to Korea and wanted me as the infantry operations analyst of the Eighth Army. The same arguments applied as before; so the decision was already made for me. Moreover, the slot provided a prime chance to be of direct service to the army.

For some days ORO had trouble getting my name cleared. Johnson later told me why. The FBI had learned that in 1948 I was the General Staff officer who wrote the initial paper urging that for strategic reasons we consider giving some kind of aid to Yugoslavia to keep the break between Tito and the Cominform from being resolved in a takeover by the Moscow crowd. Consequently, the FBI suspected me of pro-Communist leanings, an utter absurdity when profiled against the fact that what I had recommended had later become national policy. The logjam was finally broken when General Tony McAuliffe went to J. Edgar Hoover in person to voice his anger at this official folly.

The orders came and the rendezvous was set for me to join my colleagues in San Francisco. That was done because I had previously engaged to lecture at the Leavenworth Command and General Staff School enroute. Taking the train, I hit Chicago by night amid an ice storm. There were no cabs at Michigan Central station, and with my fifty-two pounds of baggage (the limit I regard as optimum for operating overseas) I started walking for Michigan Boulevard to get a taxi for LaSalle Street station.

My feet slipped on the ice. I landed heavily on my back and dislocated a vertebra. Just then a cab came along. The train to St. Louis crashed another train on a siding somewhere in Illinois, and we were stalled for four hours. By morning I was in agony. In St. Louis I used the telephone in the army recruiting office at the Post Office building to call Leavenworth and tell the executive that he would have to have an osteopath waiting for me at the Kansas City depot if there was to be any lecture. He said Roger.

Leaving the recruiters, I went to the john. That part of me was still working all right. Between the toilet and the hall there was a full step displacement. Not noting it when I entered, I missed it on exit and dropped like a boom, landing on my back. I went down cursing and came up singing hallelujah. That second jolt had ironed out the kink.

Here again was unbelievable luck, and I continued west feeling light as a feather and thankful for the omen. My Leavenworth talk was on the subject of combat leadership. After the lecture and following the coffee break, I was drawn aside by the commandant, Major General Horace McBride, and his staff. They wanted to discuss what lay ahead in Korea.

McBride believed there would be no war with Red China. At worst, it would be a screening effort, a bluff.

I said: "General, Red China is a great power. Now, what possible gain could there be for such a nation, conscious of its own prestige, to simply play at the game of intervention?"

"You are saying you feel certain that they will come full length?"

"I have no doubt—and they will wait until we are overextended."

They were left wholly unconvinced. Their optimism struck me as one of the oddest aberrations of the period.

We made Tokyo on Thanksgiving morning. Major General Charles Willoughby greeted me like a long lost brother. His chief historian, Dr. Gordon Prange, also gave me three cheers. Willoughby thought I had come over to take on the Eighth Army historical task, and I learned for the first time that he had initiated the request that Ward had passed along to me as a Department of the Army idea.

Two days later I saw Sir Charles at his histrionic best. In the interim the Communist Chinese had crashed the front of the Eighth Army along the Chongchon River. That morning that much-maligned G-2 mounted the platform in the MacArthur war room to do his briefing on the "new war."

He said: "Gentlemen, now for the big picture. We have to my left here an army, our friendlies. We have there, far to the right, a corps, also friendlies. There is a twenty-six-mile gap between, and no communications. The enemy is pouring through. You must grant that this is a highly original situation in war, and what to do is a bit of a headache."

Immediately after, I flew for Seoul. Some of our party, half military, half civilian scientist, went along. It had been understood all along that I would be working pretty much on my own.

I had barged north to contact what was left of the 2nd Infantry Division after the worst of all clobbers at Kunuri. We met north of Pyongyang. I had realized without being told that my primary mission was fundamentally changed. Instead of concentrating primarily on our tactics, that part of the search would be almost incidental to getting the measure of the Red Chinese as a fighting body so that I could report on their use of weapons, manner of deployment, rate of advance, signal system, and so forth. In the head of each U.S. rifleman who had faced them were bits and pieces of vital information which he probably thought unimportant. Once these fragments were extracted and fitted together like a mosaic we would have something.

This was my task in working from one tactical unit to another as we continued the fallback toward Yongdonpo. Today I look back and salute those old friends. To be among them made every day good. Theirs was a beaten, battered division, almost drained of flesh and blood, its rifle companies cut to fifteen or twenty men per unit. They understood the enormity of their misfortune, yet the few who survived glorified it by their spirit.

It happened time and again. I would finish a critique. Then some tattered sergeant (the division had lost all of its supply and possessions except some of the weapons) would arise and say, "One question, Colonel. What's wrong with the United States? We can beat those bastards. Why don't they turn us around? Have people up top lost their nerve?" In times when jests are few, and light seems to be fading, I remember those men and feel a bit better.

Most of what I learned during the retreat has been published in *The River and the Gauntlet, The Critique of Tactics and Weapons in Korea,* and some other official documents. My aim in this writing is more to account for myself than to decant lines from old battles. I was well into the job by the evening we went into bivouac at Panmunjom. My billet was a Korean flimsy, and the burner under my bunk on the matted floor lathered my belly with sweat while my feet froze.

Next morning at the general's mess there occurred one of the strangest scenes in my military life. We were having our porridge when Brigadier General Sladen Bradley, the division ADC, entered.

He rapped for order, then began speaking. "Gentlemen, I have just learned that General Keiser is being relieved as commander of the division. I want that command. I deserve it. Now, each one of you must know something to do that will help me. What have you to suggest?"

Colonel Epley, the chief of staff, coughed and replied softly, "General, that problem isn't quite in my line."

Colonel Bud Messinger, who sat next, said: "I'll have to pass, also."

Bradley pointed to me. "Colonel Marshall, how about you?"

There was no way to worm out of it. "I'll remind you what Bruce Clarke said at St. Vith when things brightened on the second day and General Jones thought of resuming a command he had yielded to Clarke. His words were 'Make up your mind, but remember, no one is likely to come out of this with much honor.' That goes for here, too, General Bradley."

So ended the breakfast table council. Bradley was himself bounced out that afternoon, which cold-douched at least that one ambition. By then Major General Laurence B. ("Dutch") Keiser had returned from a quick trip to Seoul and had sent for me to come to his van and discuss the scenario.

He had received an early-morning message from the Eighth Army command post in Seoul advising him that he was ill with pneumonia and must report to hospital in Tokyo. Dutch got the message; he understood that he was to be made the goat for MacArthur's blunders that had brought on the disaster in the north. He would not take that lying down, and so he rode for Seoul.

When Dutch walked in on Major General Lev Allen, the Eighth

Army's chief of staff, Allen bridled, saying, "What in hell are you doing here? You're ill with pneumonia."

"You can see for yourself I don't have pneumonia so cut out the bunk."

"But are you going to comply with the order?"

"Yes, because it is an order, but I don't want you to kid around with me." Then Dutch turned toward the exit.

Allen called after him: "By the way, General Walker says he will take care of you with a job around this headquarters."

Dutch turned back to say, "You tell General Walker to shove his job up his ass."

This is the scene as he described it to me that evening. He wanted it in the record. I took his temperature; he had none. Though I have seen many generals in this most humiliating of all situations, none held his head higher than Keiser. He voiced no pity for himself. He said simply, "I did the best I could. They're wrong and they know it, so my mind is at ease."

I knew I could not spend much time at my task; the need for the information was too urgent. The body of the army was still engaged in the long retreat, and no meaningful decisions were being made by any one at the top. But for the emergency, I would have insisted on first debriefing the 25th Infantry Division, which had also been badly mauled north of the Chongchon. By the time our column was moving into the outskirts of Yongdonpo, where it would refit and refill, twelve days had elapsed. I had completed about two-thirds of the research on the 2nd Division's operations around Kunuri, and I judged I had best risk projecting my general conclusions from this relatively small sampling.

That night I reported to General Walker and staff on what I had learned about the battle in the north—the performance of the 2nd Division and the tactics and methodology of the Communist Chinese. Colonel (later Major General) Bob Fergusson, the Army's combat G-2, introduced me to the others.

The critique and questioning concluded, I sat all night pounding out the tactical stuff. It was rushed from my mill to a duplicator. By daylight we had it in bundles aboard trucks speeding north to our embattled forces. Due to a fluke and the help of heaven, the stuff stood the test of subsequent events, and so I earned my pay.

I had closed my talk the night before with these words: "I can find no fault in the 2nd Division or its commander, General Keiser. The army should be proud of them."

Walker came to me immediately. "I want you to go before the press tomorrow morning and say the same things, except for the classified information."

"Does that include what I said about Keiser and about how well the few integrated units fought?"

"Those things especially."

I didn't talk to the press gallery; I gave it hell. I said it had been writing irresponsible copy about a bugout army based on rumors and spook stuff from malingerers. I reminded them that the Eighth Army was in retreat, with our national affairs in crisis, and that an American wasn't divested of all moral responsibility to his nation just because he held a news job. I said: "Now, I can account for 2nd Division. I'll tell you what you need to know. If you want to argue, get up and do it now, but if you haven't any argument to make, for God's sake quit writing stories aimed to doom your country and its cause."

Afterward Fergusson and I had coffee with two of the sterling veterans, Hal Boyle and Leif Erickson. Hal said: "It's the young punks that do this. We try to stop them; they simply blow you down. But I think you've cooled them."

As Fergusson and I walked back to the headquarters, an orderly rushed up to him with a message: The United Press correspondent had just put in the clear the order of battle of the retreating Eighth Army, which meant that the enemy would have it in an hour or less.

I invaded General Walker's private cubbyhole to talk about that one. "You know, it reminds me of Tannenberg. That's how the stupid Russians lost the battle, by putting their movements in the clear. We are playing Rennenkampf and Samsonov all over. Now, if I commanded an army, and a correspondent did that to me, I would throw his ass in the clink and it would rot there until war's end."

Walker, who was at his imperturbable best in those most trying days of his life, answered quite gravely. "Marshall, I rather think you would. Should I do so, MacArthur would relieve me." I knew he was not really greatly concerned about that. He had braved the lightning.

On November 30 or thereabouts, after the well-known commodity had hit the electric fan in both the Eighth Army and the U.S. X Corps, Mac-Arthur called both Walker and General Ned Almond of X Corps to a conference in Japan and gave them the word from on high. Then he asked: "Have you anything to recommend?"

Walker answered: "Yes. Put one general in command of all forces in Korea, and I don't care who it is, but just *one*." Walton Walker was the old faithful, order-taking type commander who rebelled too late at the principle he had followed slavishly: obey the boss, whatever. He had moved with his army from south of the Chongchon against his better judgment. His army had paid dearly for the one big lesson he got shortly before his death, but at least and at last he had learned.

On the day after my Seoul press conference, what I had said made headlines in the United States. The copy mainly covered two subjects. First, that the 2nd Division, contrary to reports, had performed valorously in the north, and next, that the integrated companies of the 9th Infantry Regiment had fought as well as any such units ever in national history. Most newspapers gave more attention to what had been said about the performance of the black soldier than to the corrective analysis of the Eighth Army's action as a whole, which did not surprise me. Newspapers have an allergy in common with government; they seem to strangulate when forced to eat their own words.

On the following morning there came from MacArthur in the Dai-ichi building an official reprimand for having talked publicly when, as a person, I was classified. I had never had an official call-down of record, the stupidity of the message annoyed me, and I was curious. I said to my boss, Colonel John Dabney, the G-3 of the Eighth Army: "I'd like to fly to Tokyo tomorrow and have it out with those lunkheads." John, who was one of the most reasonable of men, said: "You go, and God bless you."

Lieutenant General Doyle Hickey, who was sitting in for General Ned Almond as MacArthur's chief of staff, was one of the better figures in the army of this century—good soldier, great gentleman. He opened the talk by saying, "Believe me, Marshall, I'm very sorry about all this, but as the message made clear, you were granting an interview on your own responsibility."

I told him that he couldn't be more wrong. I did nothing on my own. When I operate under an army commander in the field and he asks me to do anything, that is tantamount to an order. I then have to decide whether the order is proper, though that's a personal problem. I had no doubt as to what Walker had asked of me.

Hickey answered: "Marshall, we had no idea that General Walker requested you to take the action. If that is true, the reprimand will be at once stricken."

I thanked him, commenting, "Why wasn't some effort made to find out? I am curious about why the message was sent in the first place. What went wrong?"

"What you gave out in the interview is counter to the policy of the Department of the Army, which makes the guidelines for this headquarters."

I found that rather enigmatic, and told him I didn't really see what he was driving at.

"It's what you say about the Negro soldier. Here we do not recognize that there is any such thing as a Negro soldier or a white soldier. They are all simply soldiers serving in the uniform of their country, and we treat them all alike."

In that moment he reminded me of Will Rogers who had a tall gag, the punch line of which was "There is no north nor south; we're all one today."

"General Hickey, that's absurd. We have black regiments and battalions in Korea. We have solidly white units. The blacks aren't doing very well. The whites are good soldiers, but their lines are too thin. They could use more good bayonets."

"I understand that, but this headquarters is not supposed to differentiate. That's the army line. We cannot raise issues that have to do with separation or integration. That is forbidden."

"Are you speaking of the army policy statement by General Bradley somewhat more than a year ago? That's the one in which he spoke on the race question. If so, you are dead wrong. The clear implication is that the army will move any time that social reform may be undertaken for the army's own good. We have now just such an opportunity."

"How can you be so sure of what was intended?"

"Because I wrote the statement."

"We will both withdraw the reprimand and make an official apology."

"Thanks, but I won't need it."

About thirty minutes after I had returned to the windowless cubbyhole that served me as a temporary office in the Dai-ichi building, I was waited upon by a colonel who almost kissed my foot. Headquarters had just heard from the Voice of America. It wanted my statement of the Negro soldier and the fighting of the integrated units expanded to 4,500 words. Could I do it? By midafternoon the dispatch was completed. It then went upstairs for review by the staff wiseacres.

At 1800 three colonels arrived. Attached to my paper was a staff study that ran twice as long as my copy. The chairman said: "We have corrected your statement, and we hope you will go along with it." I reached for the staff study. Everywhere I had written "Negro," "white," or "integrated," they had struck the offending word.

I said: "You have two choices. Send it as I wrote it, or wastebasket it, but I will not agree to this command stultifying itself. Why do you think the Voice of America wants this statement?"

There were more huddles in the Dai-ichi that night. The lights burned late. The mill of the Gods ground slowly, but by midnight they had made the great decision to send forward the story as I had written it. Echoes of the altercation got back to the Pentagon, and it was due solely to this circumstance that, when I returned to the United States in April, I found myself in the strange position of being the ball carrier in the cause of integration.

On December 16 I flew back to Seoul. Though the mood of the population in that hour could be measured by a stranger only as he witnessed the pitiful flight of half-clad children and ancients streaming south to the Han River through snowdrifts (the roads were clogged with military vehicles), the emotional strain on Americans was all too apparent. Naturally it varied from man to man, as the Red Chinese drew closer by the hour. The faint-hearted thought only of how to get away; the resolute were concerned with how to stand their ground despite all difficulty. Oddly, these disparate strains caused little friction in the command. General Walker was not disposed to clutch tight to those persons who sought to bail out. At the time I doubted the wisdom of his attitude, though in retrospect I believe he was right. It does no good to harass the weak when what is needed is that strong men will feel as one in a time of great emergency.

On the same day that I briefed the correspondents, I had repaired briefly to that ghettolike, gray-walled barracks where both the newsmen and the ORO scientists held forth. The newsmen were keeping their nerve far better than my other colleagues, who were supposed to measure all problems in mathematical terms. One exception was Dr. Ellis Johnson; he was rock steady. After dealing with some of his staff, I said to him, "Ellis, you better make air reservations and move the whole group back to Tokyo. These men are too windy to do their work. They're just in the way." He acted on that advice. Johnson stayed on briefly. Later that day we went to army headquarters. I found the light colonel who headed the army's historical section directing his people in the packing of all records and equipment. I protested, saying, "Why are you going to Japan when the most important period of your work lies just ahead?" No answer came. He looked at me as if I were slightly mad.

On my return from Tokyo, I found that nothing had changed for the better in forty-eight hours. The flux and the bugging out by the frailer headquarters types continued. The Eighth Army was falling back from Line Red to Line Blue. No decision had been made on high to stand anywhere. Here were procrastination and blue funk inconceivable.

Again I went to Colonel Dabney. I said, "John, I've read this bunk about Seoul being in an undefendable position, and I've heard it from people on this staff since I came. What in hell are they talking about? I'd like to have this army and get an order to defend this city. We're set up for it. I'd put the armor out on the left flank to cover the line of the Han, which is the only weakness. Then I'd dispose infantry and guns to the high ground. We ought to be able to hold here till hell freezes over. Why can't we get a decision?"

"I agree," Dabney replied. "Seoul can be held, and we should have guts enough to make the stand. The worry is that the position is a cul de sac. If we lose a main battle here we can't get the army out."

"Have you thought about preparing to stage a Dunkirk out of Inchon as a last resort? That calls for getting a quick survey of fishing boat resources in Japan."

"No, we haven't, but if we can't get a decision of any kind, no plan is worth a damn. I suggest you talk to the chief of staff."

I wanted a witness, so Dr. Johnson went with me. What followed is beyond explaining. I had known General Allen in Europe as a resolute soldier. Suddenly something had happened to him. My every argument was brushed off.

"Colonel Marshall, you don't get the situation. This expedition is defeated. It will be driven off the peninsula. If we get anyone out alive, that will be fortunate."

"If you're right, then I don't get the situation, because I don't believe it. If that is your estimate, have you put it to anyone in the ZI? Certainly if that is the sense of the command, then high authority back home should be advised."

"No, we are just soldiers, and we must stay here and take what comes, die in our tracks if necessary."

He was becoming a little too melodramatic for my blood and besides, I hoped, by trying again, to shake him out of it. The idea came to me that being a little rude might work.

"Well, if you can't communicate, I can. I can double-talk a message to Washington that would get your estimate across. I wouldn't agree with it. I think we can defend and hold right here."

Allen shook his head sorrowfully, saying, "Colonel Marshall, I forbid it. That would be quite unmilitary."

So ended the conversation. As we walked out I said: "Oh shit!"

Johnson, who had backed me all the way with Dabney and Allen, flew to Tokyo within the next few hours. He had already alerted his staff there to do the survey of Japanese fishing craft. Soon after he arrived at the Dai-ichi I got a message from him on what we had code-named "Operation Sampan." The report said there were more than five thousand boats of the right draft and troop-lift capacity. It was enough to evacuate the army. Though we continued to hope, that proved to be just one more wasted effort. No one in high authority over U.S. military operations was in those days willing to commit himself boldly by word or act. It was a total abdication of responsibility that might have been resolved only if General Matthew B. Ridgway had come earlier to the scene. It was clear, at least to me, that the Red Chinese were slowing down and would be short of fighting supply and energy well before they reached Seoul.

For the next ten days my work was cut out for me. I got back to the 2nd Division at Yongdonpo on a mission far more important than my analyst's task. That beaten-up outfit was temporarily leaderless. The artillery brigadier, Loyal M. Haynes, had nominally taken command, but apart from the gunners, he had no real communion with the people. He was a decent and very reserved soldier, and while he saw what had to be done, his terrible experience in coming through the gauntlet south of Kunuri had so aged him that he could not extend himself. His hair seemed to have been turned white in a single night.

The problem was this: We had to take the tattered remnant that had survived the battle in the north, and with raw replacements from the States, flesh out a battle-worthy division of 12,000 men within twelve days. The artillery replacements had received refresher training only in infantry arms. The rifle replacements had been given nothing. This was America, Land of the Free, doing things on the cheap.

To replace Keiser, the Army Department had ordered Major General Bob McClure on from the Marianas where he had been serving as governor. On the day he arrived, and before I saw him, Colonel Collier, deputy chief of staff under Walker at Seoul, had come to Yongdonpo. I met him briefly and renewed an acquaintance from ETO days. Then he talked to McClure in private, and all I know of that conversation is what McClure told me. Collier told him: "Colonel Marshall has the confidence of the army commander. He knows a great deal about how to reconstitute forces out of a demoralizing situation. You should trust him."

Collier said nothing of this to me. He was far overstating my abilities, but the effect on McClure was astounding. Some hours later he called me to his van. Not drunk, he was well on his way. He said right out that the new orders were a terrible shock to his nervous system, that he had never expected to lead troops in battle again, and that for the time he was not up to it. He went on. "I can only brace myself by hitting the bottle. I'll be doing a lot of drinking, so you go ahead. Program whatever you wish. When something calls for my appearance, give me fair warning and I'll get in shape, but don't expect too much. On the other hand, don't worry about me. This is just a phase. I'll come out of it."

While sympathizing with his problem and admiring his frankness, I admit I felt that a soldier's duty requires the same kind of candor with higher authority when any general feels himself not equal to the task. Rebuilding the division was a more complex problem than commanding it in battle. Even so, through that difficult period I enjoyed my relations with Bob McClure.

It will be understood that the details of receiving and sorting out men, distributing material, and programming such basic training as the brief time permitted were worked out by the competent officers and commanders who had survived the battle in the North. My mission was to give the rebuilt division a sound moral foundation, to see that new soldiers got a feeling of belonging, and to restore to companies and batteries a sense of unity and combat sufficiency.

In consultation with General Haynes, I had already worked out the method at his request, and we were already hard at it when McClure came along. The program was elementary. I already knew what each unit had done on the Chongchon and in coming through the gauntlet. We gathered together the replacements with the old hands. Then we went back over the score, pointing out in detail what the unit and the division as a whole had been through.

Toward the close, I would say something like this: "That was the worst ordeal ever given an American division. It survived only because the men who came through are the most rugged fighters that have ever served in this uniform. Yes, you are getting an extraordinary number of replacements, some of whom haven't seen combat for years, and others never. From what you've heard today, you must know you are in good hands. And I get it from the leaders that we are filling with soldiers just as steady as any the division lost. That's all it takes."

Sure, all of it sounds corny. Still, it worked. After each presentation we had a prolonged question period dealing not with the past but with the future and concentrating on technical problems of interest to troops. One regimental commander, Colonel (later Major General) George Peploe of the 38th had been rather holding out against me. I couldn't blame him; we were meeting for the first time. He was a professional and I an amateur dabbling in what he thought was his specialty. Also, he was suffering from flu. At just the right moment Brigadier General George Stewart arrived to become the new ADC. We had been friends since ETO days, and he knew Peploe. He cleared the atmosphere between us, and from thereon I had Peploe's full support.

My use of McClure was quite eccentric. He stayed in his van day after day and did not get out to the troops. Every night I arranged for a special group of outstanding leaders to dine with him at the general's mess. Sometimes it would be sergeants who had starred in the battle in the North, on other nights captains or battalion commanders. There would be a reception and cocktails, with the feed following. A few hours before the formation, I would go to McClure and tell him it was time for a brace. He would shower and take a few pills. Usually when he appeared he would be shining, with no sign of wooziness.

On the night when the battalion leaders came, he was something less than his best. I had briefed him on the performance of each one of these soldiers. When I introduced him to Jim Skeldon (later Major General), McClure gave him a bear hug and said: "You old son of a bitch, they tell me you're quite a fighter."

Jim shook him off, straightened, and glared. "Sir, when you call me that you better have a smile on your face." McClure smiled.

When shortly thereafter, on schedule, the division left Yongdonpo for a new battlefield, McClure had himself very much in hand.

On the day that General Walker was killed—it was Christmas Eve— my jeep was just a quarter mile behind him. The road was a glare of ice, and we had been creeping along at ten mph, and even so, trembling. He passed us doing forty, and the hurry cost him his life, but that accident also did something for night defense. Knowing him and loving him, I was perhaps happier to see General Matthew B. Ridgway arrive than anyone in Korea. His routine greeting was "Slam, do you have anything that will help me right now?" Almost at once he asked me to take on single handed the task of writing a plan for the use of the illuminated front in Korea, specifying what material would be needed, how the various items should be distributed and equated for operational use, what tactical situations would call for their employment, and so forth.

The manual had to be done by-guess-and-by-God. I was shocked to discover that, after almost a half century of battle experience with pyrotechnics, the army had no doctrine for their use, no training guide, no catalog, nothing. The subject had been overlooked by everyone, which is not unusual. As I worked into the planning, I saw that the problem was inherently logistical, since an illuminating round kills no one, and if the caisson or the mortar party is carrying too many flares, the fight will be lost. On main questions, such as at what distance our searchlights might safely operate against an enemy front fixed with heavy machine guns and mortars, I perforce dealt from the seat of my pants, there being no guidance in print. I estimated a thousand yards, which figure was sustained during all subsequent operations in Korea. No target is more difficult to bracket than a searchlight; the beam itself confuses calculation.

Working in the dark and aware of my limitations, I sought help wherever I could find it. About artificial moonlight I knew very little, having never fought with a unit that employed it. We needed the information quickly. The 24th Infantry Regiment was in line holding a peninsula to the west of Seoul, and our three searchlights (that's all we had in Korea) might be a tonic to the morale of the soldiers in night defense. That season was strangely free of heavy cloud formations, but we were getting snow nightly. Would light bounce off snow as it did from cloud and bathe no man's land in a mellow glow? There was no one to say, but we tried it, found that it worked, and the soldiers were comforted. Still, we needed to know far more than that. I cabled my old friend, B. H. Liddell-Hart, in England, who rallied around him General Hobart and other experts in artificial moonlight. They sent the guidance and data tables we needed by special courier. I also sought help from the MacArthur staff, though nothing came back.

At that same turn of the year insult was added to injury. General Willoughby, MacArthur's G-2, held a press conference. I learned about it from the newspapers. His object was to boast to the boys that the high command knew all about the Communist Chinese fighting system and hence knew how to defeat it. He then stated in the clear how they were armed, how they used or mishandled their weapons, how they formed for the attack, their tactical method in squeezing out a position, what their signals meant, and so on. What I was reading was exactly what I had written in early December, the same guidance that had been sent forward to troops under a classified heading.

Very likely by that time some Chinese had captured the paper and the enemy already knew that we knew; yet one can't be sure of that. Here was Willoughby saying the words that invited the other camp to shift radically from what had become stereotyped. We were putting it in the clear to the Red Chinese: "You are no damned good with hand grenades, though you think you are, but on the other hand the way you push your machine guns to the fore raises hell with us." Had I published my own paper for public reading, it would have been a court-martial offense, but merely to get favorable publicity for the brains in the Dai-ichi Building, Willoughby made the same release with impunity. I wanted to spit in his messkit.

From the very beginning I had objected to the Eighth Army's use of company-size perimeters in night defense, calling it tactical lunacy and an outright throwaway of human lives. It shook me that higher commanders made no attempt to stop it, and that junior commanders accepted it without protest.

Now follow the reasoning. We simply could not man a flankless front for lack of troops. Stretched thin as we were from sea to sea, we could be penetrated almost anywhere, even should the front again become stabilized. There was no way to stop it. As long as we used company perimeters, the Communists could attack any ridge we held, apply pressure by fire, and take over the ground in four hours just by draining the defenders of ammunition. On the other hand, if we used battalion perimeters as a minimum, even though the enemy numbers in the attack should be trebled, the defense could hold out from three to four days without running its weapons dry. Also, morale would rise radically with the use of larger defensive circles. The whole, in brief, is vastly more than the sum of the parts.

This is not to imply that all else in the small picture was roses. Our minor tactics were deplorable; it was as if junior leaders had thrown the book away. Outposting was being done at ten to fifteen yards; one might as well dispense with that type of outpost. On the march, the point was often at about that same interval—ten to fifteen yards—from the main body, which made it of no value. Company leaders had forgotten how to employ smoke, and when I talked to them, saying that we must come to the fullest possible employment of lights in night defense, they grimly protested. "That would be fatal. It would give the position away." Yet many of these officers had served in the line in World War II. I came to see in those days what I had not understood before—that one should never underrate the speed with which an officer body can put aside the most valid lessons out of personal experience in war.

Bugging me more than anything else was the perimeter question. Much talk had superinduced no action. In an effort to get some leverage, I took a new line with Colonel Dabney. On the east coast, the navy had at last completed the evacuation of the much-battered U.S. X Corps from Won-san. The marines were to assemble around Masan in the South. I said to the boss man: "I am certain that, had the 1st Marine Division been using company perimeters, it would have been destroyed at the reservoir." The fact is that at Seoul we knew nothing of what had happened to the independent corps, except that it had been driven back to the sea. John asked: "Well, why don't you go and find out?"

The army looked at this proposal with some trepidation. An army figure scouting out marine secrets? It had never been done. Letters of introduction had to be prepared for me from MacArthur and Walker.

While I waited, there was another conference. Dr. Johnson had flown back from Tokyo. The question raised by the bevy of brains to which I was to supply answer was this: Where are the Red Chinese to be found during daylight? Our reconnaissance planes had found no trace of them. Air photos revealed nothing. In my first briefing to Walker and staff, I had pointed out emphatically that we were dealing with a maneuver mass and not an entrenched enemy, and had proved my point. That stirred the second question in their minds, and they pressed for an answer.

I said: "Just think a minute. There are no mine shafts in the area and no forests or other natural cover. They can only be one place; they must hide in the villages."

Someone objected: "But that's impossible. These are great masses of men. The villages are small. Our rekkys never see troops around the villages."

"You are thinking with a western mind. Think now of a Korean hut, twenty by twelve. We could put two squads or maybe a platoon in there somewhat uncomfortably. What of the Chinese? Standing them up all day, packing them in like sardines, they could make it satisfactory cover for a company plus. One small hamlet could conceal two battalions."

They accepted the argument. Dabney asked: "Will you write this out in a staff paper and recommend using heavy bombers against the villages?"

"No, I could be wrong. If so, I could get a lot of innocent Koreans killed."

Dr. Johnson broke in. "Slam, you have always said it is elementary logic that if all other possibilities must be excluded, then the hypothesis is bound to be valid."

"Correct!"

"Now you are rejecting your own principle."

"Ellis, not at all. This should be a command decision. Don't ask me to take over for the commander."

"Would you object if we write it out and sign your name?"

"If you choose to commit forgery, that's your problem." On that happy note the conference disbanded.

Chapter 18
Korean Finale

I threw away the letters from the high commanders before flying for Pusan to get to Masan. Shaefer, my stenotypist, was still with me and doubling as jeep driver. When I reported to marine Major General Oliver Smith at Masan, that happy warrior said just the right words to assure me that his regimental commanders would cooperate fully. In this way I became the only army type ever to serve as operations analyst with the marine corps. Most of that routine was straight operational research—getting data on the Chosan operation—if only to prove that small perimeters were a form of suicide. Those field papers were finally turned over to Robert Leckie for use in his history of the campaign.

My lot at Masan was brightened by the company I kept. Marines are more my kind than army, as I had long been aware. The comradeship in the regimental mess during the cocktail hour had a glow and inspiration that banished small care. When we sang, men pulled out all stops. Ragging and pulling the leg of the commanding officer was done with impunity in this hour only. Everyone participated all out, and I guess that was the difference.

In the field work I got everything I wanted. When some weeks later my report of the operation was published, General Oliver Smith sent a message to the Eighth Army: "We will settle for that." By night I saw much of Colonel (later Lieutenant, General) Al Bowser, the G-3; it was the beginning of a lasting friendship. I shared a billet in a Korean hut with four members of the staff. Otherwise occupied by a middle-aged Korean woman and her fourteen-year-old son, the hut was on a small ridge half a mile from the division command post and as far from the main supply route. Unlike army divisions, the 1st Marine Division wisely had almost doubled its staff for the Korean venture. The difference told. Every army "G" was badly overworked. The marine staff had the reserves to withstand exhaustion under utmost pressure.

193

All of it was much too good to last. One evening the division was abruptly ordered to saddle up for an immediate move to Pohang to clear the countryside of guerrillas. I got the news while elbow-bending with Colonel (later Lieutenant General) Chesty Puller in his tent.

Chesty had a grouse to air. "That man Ridgway came here today to tell us that he is going to turn this army around and make it fight. Does he think marines don't know how to fight?"

I said: "Chesty, you take it easy and you'll get the measure of this man. Generals don't come any better."

Just then a captain barged in on us. He seemed agitated. He said to Chesty: "Colonel, I got the word, formed the company, and told the men about the move. One sergeant stepped out and said: 'Sir, we'll go because we're marines, but what are we fighting for? The United States? How can any country be as chicken-shit as it is acting now?' I didn't know how to answer him. What would you have said?"

Chesty replied: "Son, I couldn't answer that one, but I'll say this. Until the time comes when someone up top—at Taegu, Tokyo, or Washington—can make up his mind, don't let one of your men volunteer for one god-damned thing."

Chesty added, in an aside to me: "I never thought I'd live to say that."

It seemed time for another drink. When I got back to my billet, telephone and power lines had been removed, along with nearly all supply. One friend was standing by with a jeep to lift me out. I explained that I didn't dare go to Pohang. The temperature had suddenly dropped to ten below zero to begin the coldest spell of that winter. Shaefer, my driver, had disappeared. I had a bad cold and was running a fever. The 1st Marine Division rolled, leaving me stranded.

Some time after midnight my chest told me I had pneumonia. There were no options. If I went outside, the cold would likely prove fatal. The Koreans, wholly sympathetic, mournful faced and almost tearful, didn't know what to do, and I couldn't tell them. I vaguely felt that the best chance was for me to sweat it out in my sleeping bag and have the boy pour fruit juices into me as long as I was able to beckon.

The trial lasted about a week. The third or fourth day I became delirious, for how long I don't know. Finally the fever broke, as did the weather. With the boy and his mother supporting me on either side, I was able to flag a truck and get to the base hospital in Pusan. The major-doctor looked me over. "Colonel, you have pneumonia."

"Sorry doctor, but I *had* pneumonia." Even so, he kept me flat in bed for one more week.

Up again, I made for Taegu with nothing but my ears hurting.

Eighth Army Staff still had no idea where our recovery might begin, if there was to be one, or what would likely happen next. They were not being cagey. Ridgway was far forward with the divisions, pepping and prepping them, and had little converse with the chaps at Taegu. They were becoming miffed by his neglect of them. I studied the war room map, trying to read Matt Ridgway's mind. The 25th Division had just beaten back into Suwon after backing off some miles to the south. There were three armored battalions around the city, and Lieutenant General "Shrimp" Milburn had set up his I Corps flag there. I flew north, all but convinced that Ridgway must attack out of Suwon toward the line of the Han, a gambit favored by the two paralleling highways from city to river, set just right to let our tank forces exploit with utmost advantage. Once we became solid along the nigh bank of the Han, we could work the squeeze against the Red Chinese in Seoul. So went the deductive reasoning.

During luncheon at the I Corps command post, Brigadier General Milo van Brunt asked me, "Aren't you a friend of Michaelis?" and I replied that I had known him a long time. Van Brunt continued. "Then you better take my jeep and go see him. His command post is only about half a mile from here. He'll be returning to the ZI any day now."

But for the jeep, I would never have made it. The whole area south of the Han had become a sea of boot-deep gumbo due to the melting snows. That February was abnormally mild, and every day we basked in bright sunshine. Still, the mud raised hell with operations.

Mike was in his billet. He said: "What in hell are you doing here?"

"Catching a street car. The fact is that I came to congratulate you about going home."

"You're crazy. Who ever said any such thing to you?"

"Never mind. I got it straight."

"What do you think this is all about?"

"My hunch is you're going to get your star."

"I can't believe it. I can think of at least six of my friends who deserve it more than I do."

To end that part of the conversation, I said, "So can I, but don't let that stop you."

He invited me to unpack and move in with him, which I did. All evening long he was fidgety, reaching for the telephone to call the Eighth Army and ask what his change in station was all about. I restrained him, admonishing that, if goodies were coming, a gentleman took them quietly and thankfully, which was never Mike's way.

At about 2300 we tucked in. Everyone in that headquarters was sleeping next to his weapon. The night before, the Red Chinese had run a platoon-strength patrol into Suwon via the rock-walled canal that wended through the city. Wholly undetected, the patrol had knocked off the Korean national police barracks across the street from Mike's billet, killing eleven policemen. The wrecked building was about forty feet from our cots.

My carbine was against the wall next to my pillow. About an hour after we went to bed, I was wakened from deep sleep by a terrible clatter in the darkened room. I thought the door had been crashed. I grabbed the carbine and was about to shoot. Then, coming out of my foggy mindedness from the sudden awakening, I switched on the light. Mike was sprawled on the floor. He had overturned a table in going for the telephone. I yelled: "Damn it, Mike, don't you get it that I damn near killed you?" Mike was contrite. We both realized that I would never have been able to explain it.

Next day we got down to business. Decisions had been made. The forces of I Corps would attack north, Mike's 27th ("Wolfhound") Regiment being the cutting edge, along with two armored task forces, Bartlett and Dolvin, so named after their commanders.

Mike and I together worked out the tactics for that operation, which was code-named Punch, and it was beyond compare the most successful American show during the Korean war. Our side lost 356 men killed and wounded, and we counted 5,037 dead Communists on the battlefield.

Having dealt with the two situations, one south of Kunuri, the other north of Koto-ri, in which U.S. columns had been ambushed from both flanks by Red Chinese holding the high ground, my part of it was to assign command responsibility during joint operations between armor and infantry in such a way that no foul-up of that kind would again occur. Mike's part was more subtle and had a touch of genius. He had dreamed up an idea never used before or after. The two armored task forces would move shuttle fashion. Task Force Bartlett would advance through the day on the western axis, Task Force Dolvin paralleling it on the east. The armor would fire in support of infantry and at targets of opportunity, but in late afternoon both columns would be withdrawn to Suwon for bivouac. This would be done four days running. In effect, each day we would win the field and then give it back, thereby continuing to suck the Chinese back onto the same killing ground.

During this same time, Hill 440, the great hill mass north of Suwon and between the two highways—the dominant terrain feature—would be attacked directly, and as we won ground there, we would hold it.

The general plan worked to perfection. I kept moving from flank to flank in a bubble-nose chopper. Mike stayed up with troops. We saw one another at the billet only late at night. He kept telling me about the charming people he knew in Yokohama, and I responded with information about how his companies were fighting, which I knew better than he did. I was also up on the operations of the 35th Infantry Regiment, which was going at the hill mass in the center. The details of this story are in the classified work *Hill 440,* which is still kept under official wraps only because I had written in an unkindly manner about the Turkish Brigade, which had the best press of any force in Korea, little of it earned.

One of Lieutenant Colonel William Kelleher's battalions of the 35th won the crown of Hill 440, the decisive ground. The company that topped the crest had held it two days and nights under attack, going that time without food and water; these men were phenomenal stalwarts. I flew up to see them once on the high ground, and I was with them again when they descended. Of 123 men, 92 were frostbite cases. That was "Easy Company" under Lieutenant Leroy H. Glunt. They had undergone great privation and had received little support; yet to my surprise not one soldier was grousing or malcontent. They were infinitely proud that together they had withstood such rigor. They kept saying to me, "We're pretty good, aren't we, colonel?"

Before Glunt and his men had ever attacked straight up the ridge, one of Michaelis's companies had been hard used in an attempt to assault up the ridge fingers from the west. That was in the 3rd Battalion under Lieutenant Richard W. Keys, a first-rate commander. I was with Dick Keys that morning at his combat command post on a subridge just under 440. A French correspondent had just been killed by a sniper while taking a look from the subridge's crest a few feet above our bunker. It was his first view of any front; I had tried vainly to restrain him. Then the company got in motion, approaching the big hill via a blind draw about 400 yards to our left. Within five minutes we got the word over radio: "We're stopped by mortars. Eleven men KIA."

I said: "Hell, Dick, that's impossible. I saw that draw yesterday. It's a perfectly safe approach. Let's go see."

We went at a run. The dead were there all right. Instead of staying in defilade by hugging the slope to the right of the draw, the column had moved via the path in the center, this with the Red Chinese looking right down on them from the crown of 440. It's an old story, all too typical of Americans in combat. As General Bill Dean has written, even our best troops get careless unless fire is beating directly against them.

By jeep, Michaelis and I started back to Suwon and got as far as the first crossroads just off the high ground. There we found confusion unlimited, vehicles stacked up in four directions. One truck had careened off at the intersection, gone into the ditch, and blocked everything. Trucks loaded with fighting supply couldn't get up; ambulances were stalled coming off the hill. The mud was just too deep to permit swinging off the road. Already more than forty vehicles were stalled, and the truckers were doing nothing about it.

I said to Mike: "Bring up two companies of riflemen or anyone else to repair these roads. I'll try to clear the jam." He went afoot.

Not since World War I had I undertaken any sort of engineering job, and at first it looked as if I had bitten off more than I could chew. The truck that had caused the block was lodged between two trees. They had to come down, or we couldn't get started. In all those vehicles there was not one axe or saw and there were only three ropes. I sent scouts out to round up tools from the nearby Korean farmers. They returned shortly, bringing the farmers also, and the Koreans felled the trees. With the three ropes, using the power of other vehicles, we then winched the truck back onto the road.

By the end of an hour, when we were beginning to clear, Mike was back with two rifle companies. There were any number of abandoned farm houses in the vicinity. We put the riflemen to work razing their dwellings so that we could use the tile from the roofs and other hard materials to stiffen the surface of the two roads which were almost as mucky as the surrounding fields.

Though by evening I knew I had earned my pay, that was not the end of it. Four days of observing the inordinate strain on troops at Hill 440 and contending with the conditions of the field had taught me something.

All this time General Ridgway had been at Suwon monitoring the battle. I went to him and we talked. I put it to him that his front was near collapse for lack of pioneering labor and that troops on Hill 440 were taking as much of a beating from the loads they carried as from enemy fire.

I said: "We've got to have a fully organized, quasi-military Korean labor force as an auxiliary to the Eighth Army, which means putting them on our payroll."

Matt asked me: "Slam, what's the formula?"

"One Korean to do cargador or engineering work for every three riflemen we have in line will just about suffice."

He called in Colonel F. Winton, his aide and my friend since Normandy days. "Listen to this. Then call up the people at Taegu and tell them I want it done at once." That was how Ridgway operated in Korea.

Ten days or so later I was at army headquarters and asked Colonel "Keg" Stebbins, its outstanding G-4, whether he was running a staff study on the Korean Service Corps. Keg said: "Hell no. We're recruiting it."

So far as my personal life is concerned, all of these doings reported of Hill 440 are trivial and shaded by one other incident—the bayonet charge by Captain Lewis Millett's Easy Company of the Wolfhounds at Suamni. The story is fully told in *Battle at Best*. Being with Task Force Bartlett that day, I watched the charge from the shelter of a tank about two hundred yards from the base of the hill. It was the deadliest affair of its kind since Cold Harbor. When I critiqued the company on the spot, I could not foresee that my future would pivot around this event, but I was no less certain that Captain Millett deserved the Medal of Honor than that I would get it for him.

The battle over, Michaelis's new orders came on, though they told him little or nothing. He was relieved as commander of the 27th Regiment and would go to Japan for rest and recreation (R & R). There were various ceremonies. At one staff dinner Mike was counseling his people in a fatherly way that they should try for more rest. Turning to his S-2, Major Hawk, he said, "Why, I'll bet a dollar that you've lost twenty pounds since you came with me."

"Right," answered Hawk, "and you've enjoyed every damned bite of it."

While Mike flew south, the 25th Division turned east to relieve the 1st Cavalry Division on another sector. I went along because I had not finished my work on Task Force Dolvin and needed more conversations with Colonel Gilbert Check, the new boss of the Wolfhounds, and with Colonel Tom Dolvin.

The very first night we huddled in Check's command post, a stinking Korean hut with a vile stove that smoked up the place but gave no heat. We had barely begun to talk when in walked a figure well trench-coated and carrying pencil and notebook. He flopped down on the table between us without saying one word. Then he opened up full blast. "I'm a war correspondent from the *San Francisco Chronicle.* Colonel Check, how does it feel to take over a regiment from a famous man like Michaelis?"

Check, having his first go with a newsman, replied, "I don't know what to say. Colonel Marshall, you're a writer, how would you put it?"

"I think the story would be better if he went to the line and asked troops how it feels to be taken over by someone like Check after knowing the touch of Michaelis."

"That would take too long."

"Well, what's your rush?"

"I've been in Korea five days and haven't filed a story."

I asked him if he'd ever been to war before or had any military service or had ever been in any way in close association with the armed forces, to all of which questions he replied no.

"You remind me of my favorite Mae West joke," I told him. "A gal reporter asks to interview her on the subject of motherhood. Mae says, 'Fine, have you ever been a mother?' The gal answers 'no.' Mae says, 'Neither have I. This talk is certainly going to enlighten society.' "

Whether the war correspondent got the point or not, no more questions came. He finished his cigaret, strolled from the hut, and we went on with our business. That boy, however, got the last laugh. He later became a senior writer on the Pacific Coast and, having been made a military expert by his tour in Korea, was given my books to review. Being weak kneed, I didn't sue for libel.

★

Soon I had wrapped up my work with the 25th Division, not to see it again until Vietnam. The first reward was at Taegu, where I got my first bath in five weeks. The dirt was caked on. I tubbed for two hours while a Korean maiden stood by giggling about the color of the water.

Then on to Pusan, the port city immortalized by troops with their own parodied version of Sioux City Sue: "Hail Alma Mater, Oh Pusan U."

From there I flew to Japan. I went for the express purpose of writing the narrative and citation for Lew Millett's Medal of Honor. It pressed on me because in Normandy Michaelis and I together had botched the one best Medal of Honor case that ever came our way. Since I could get no secretarial help at the Dai–ichi building, I sought it from Yokohama Command. Between spells of dictating, I again met Cate, the lanky gal with the delicate air who eventually was to become my wife.

My last month in Korea produced little that would add to this narrative. Ridgway had vitalized the Eighth Army by his own spirit and wisdom. Mine were undistinguished, submarginal tasks. Also, I was somewhat emotionally spent after the December-January crisis.

In the war's worst time, an atomic committee had been formed to work out the problem of how to use the bomb, if the worst eventuated for the expedition. As a member, I had formulated the equations as to its effect on the Communist Chinese infantry mass. I look back gratified that I reported the weapon to be of little value tactically. The statement had been carefully measured, based upon all we knew about the enemy concentrations from the Yalu to the Imjim River.

The military delude themselves about use of the bomb or smaller atomic weapons in the maneuvering of field armies. There is an inveterate disposition to think and reason about the bigger bang as only that, when in fact it is as little related to conventional weapons as was the St. Petersburg mine to a cap pistol. Thus, since 1945 I have written almost exclusively on warfare with the old tools, as we have it and not as it might be, believing that the millennial dawn is nowhere near and that averting the atomic cataclysm must be the main and controlling object in all we do militarily.

Chapter 19
Selected Subjects: From Fear and Fatigue to MacArthur

Work on the General Staff in time of war has one thing in common with journalism: Stay with it long enough, and in time everything will become grist for your mill.

For example, until it happened to me in Korea, I could not have imagined that the time would come when my knowledge of music, acquired in the early years when I believed that I might make my living that way, someday would have a spectacular payoff on the battlefield.

Furthermore, I had no intimation that I was about to launch on my most bizarre piece of field research when in the first week of December, 1950, I joined the U.S. 2nd Infantry Division beyond Pyongyang to stay with it during the retreat south that followed the debacle on the banks of the Chongchon River.

Almost as soon as I started the interrogation of General Dutch Keiser's shattered units, I was impressed with one fact that the division's tactical leaders had somehow missed. In the surprise nighttime attack that had crashed the division's front in the first five hours, a breach that was not thereafter sealed, the Chinese employment of weapons had contributed less to the demoralization of our troops than the enemy's use of musical instruments.

Nothing in their training had prepared the Americans for that weird reality. Out of the dark had come a new and baffling enemy with a bag of tricks seemingly bordering on the supernatural. As the fight began, or even before it started, when the presence of the Communist Chinese maneuver body was still unsuspected, there would come a blaring of trumpets, a piping of shepherd's horns, or the trilling of fifes and flutes. The blowing of bugles would persist throughout the battle. The other musical effects were used not unlike overtures. However used, the instruments were getting to the American nerve, and the troops felt spooked.

Soldier after soldier would say something like this: "They blew taps—our own call—to get at our nerves. We heard it just as we were about to lose the hill. That really shook us." As it finally developed, the notes were not those of taps, though the Communist Chinese call, a signal for local withdrawal to regroup, sounded much like it.

In order to solve the problem and dispel the mystery, I undertook what proved to be one of the most difficult pieces of field research in my military life. My trial was three-pronged.

First, there was the elementary problem of trying to recall the musical scale after the passage of so many years. Getting with rhythm again, and marking the difference between the weight of an eighth, quarter, or half-note does not come easy.

Then there was the cold, and it was bitter. All work had to be done in the open, without gloves, and I couldn't risk freezing my fingers. I would have to pause at intervals for warming.

More frustrating still was the search for the one soldier whose brain had the print of what he had heard.

A sergeant would speak up. "We heard a bugle call, and then they got up and came straight at us."

"That must be the charge," I'd say. "Try to remember the call."

He and the others would concentrate, only to tell me finally that it was no use. They couldn't remember.

Though most of the time I would draw blanks, now and then I would get fragments, and only very rarely a full call, or approximately so. I kept on plugging and at last ran into a gold mine.

An Jong Sup, a Korean soldier serving in the 38th Infantry Regiment, had once been bugler in the Japanese Army. He had both the ear for music and an infallible memory. From him I drew confirmation and amplification of what I had collected—in fact, all that I needed to know.

The group interviews of the first two days had made conclusively clear that, whereas the prebattle use of the flutes and horns was for the purpose of demoralizing the defense, the bugles were being employed for tactical signalling in lieu of radio or other means of control. To begin, I ignored the other instruments and concentrated on the bugles.

By the end of five days, thanks to help from Sup, I had scaled off six calls for the benefit of the Eighth Army and the damnation of the Communist Chinese, this at the slight cost of two frostbitten fingers that soon came around. That completed phase one of the undertaking.

Then followed a canvass of these same units, to which I walked cap-in-hand, making my pitch about as follows: "Some of you have a shepherd's horn, bugle, or flute in your pack. You want it for a souvenir. That's fair enough, but we need these trinkets right now to help save this army. Let me have the instrument, and I'll give you a receipt for it. You'll get it back some time."

Before the first day closed, I had all of the instruments. There was a small and rather crude instrument factory in Seoul. Quickly, it was reproducing the bugles and shepherd's horns, but could do nothing about the flutes, which were unimportant anyhow.

Once the problem had become clearly defined, headquarters recognized the importance of nixing the Chinese music. By the first week of January, 1951, we had buglers with our combat divisions who had been schooled sufficiently in the Chinese calls to use them toward the enemy's confusion. Our first experiments had been run within the 9th Infantry Regiment during night training exercises. From that point on we stripped the element of mystery from the Chinese Communist way of warfare. I took more than average pride in that ploy because I had done it on my own.

★

Over the years I have contributed but two main ideas to the theory and practice of military operations; all else that I have shaped or influenced toward helpful change derived from these two major findings. The series of accidents by which I learned how to dispel the fog from the fire fight are fully described elsewhere. The other discovery is that, throughout all past time, scientists and soldiers have failed to understand the essential nature of fear, or conversely, of courage, with all that it implies as to individual and group effectiveness under ordeal. This biological truth has application far beyond the military.

All that I learned of that subject, finally to reach a positive and radical conclusion when dealing with the panicked and fear-ridden but still mobile units in the Omaha Beach landings in 1944, I should have understood in the early summer of 1918.

My regiment had been hardened to road marching for twenty miles and more under full pack. Yet on a balmy evening, I saw these same strong men make an eleven-mile approach march, moving up to the battle zone for the first time, and arrive in a state bordering on total exhaustion, almost too weary to unbuckle their packs. When one moved up on the Western front it was not the distant rumble of artillery that frayed the nerves, but the incessant pyrotechnics—Very lights, flares, starshells, and rockets that seemed to bespeak unremitting action. The phenomenon became more mystifying still when some weeks later I saw the men shoulder their packs, and marching away from the front, do thirty-two miles in one day, arriving not too beat. All that this indicated to my immature mind was that it is easier to march away from battle than move into it, which truth should hardly puzzle a lance jack.

Yet historians and tacticians do not get it. If they did, there would be less nonsense written on the subject of vigorous pursuit, such as the recurrent criticism of General Meade for allowing the beaten Confederate Army to slip away after Gettysburg. The Union Army was spiritually and physically spent after three days of battle ending in victory. Getting away, the southerners were homeward bound with no need to be urged.

From 1918 until 1944, I did not give another thought to the subject. Then, in February of 1944, following the Kwajalein campaign, Major General Archibald V. Arnold dropped a tactical problem in my lap. He wanted to know why it happened that, in the fighting over the atolls, if troops were checked three times by fire, even though they took no losses from fire and had moved not more than a mile or so, their energy was spent, and they could not again assault on that same day.

As is fully explained in *Men Against Fire,* I was able to recommend a tactical solution to the problem. On being adopted, it enabled us to eliminate or at least alleviate the problem, simply by insuring prompt collection and restoration of group awareness every time that a check occurred. But the mystery continued to haunt me. Why would successive checks by fire deplete all physical energy when there had been no true bodily strain or damage? There was an X factor somewhere in the equation and we were missing it.

Then, after Omaha Beach, as is described in my small book *The Soldier's Load,* I dealt with numerous rifle companies whose battle experience had variously gone the whole gamut from utter defeat and mass panic to preserved order under heavy pressure and distinguished achievement. It was Company M of the 116th Infantry Regiment that finally opened my eyes. This was a strong unit with many large and powerful men. They had escaped seasickness while in the small boats. They had hit the beach thinking themselves still fresh. Then to their dismay they found that burdens that in training they could carry on the run, such as a machine gun mount, had to be painfully dragged across the beach a few feet at a time. Still, Company M had managed to clear all of its loads to the shingle, a unique achievement on that day and place. When at last my field notes were complete, I knew that I had found something.

Fear and fatigue impacted on the body in the same way, draining it of energy. That being true, the overloaded soldier became more susceptible to fear, and the more heavily fear began to oppress him, the less strength he had to sustain his burdens. Overloading plus fear—result, mass panic under fire.

Certain as I felt, I still hesitated to speak, not being a scientist. Then in 1948 I discussed the subject with my friend, Dr. Raymond W. Waggoner, chief of psychiatry at University of Michigan, and a sage in many fields. Ray was at first skeptical of the theory and said that the physical effects of fear and fatigue might seem to be the same, but he believed the rebound from fear would be more rapid. When I stood on the documentation, he called in some of the biologists. They rallied to my side of the discussion, admitting that they had been thinking along these lines for some years but had lacked proof. After hearing them out, Dr. Waggoner warmed to the subject, gave me a private lesson in biochemistry, and imparted the confidence that enabled me to proceed.

Because I am not a scientist, the organic reaction to fear is not a proper part of this statement. My role, in this instance, was simply that of pathfinder, not historian. We found that we were on the right track. After the theory was launched, medical laboratories in several of our great universities took it under study and by varying tests proved it valid. One of them, I now recall, made its findings by examining men undergoing major dental surgery and determining the count of male hormones excreted through the urine before and after. Still later, during the Korean war, one of the research organizations serving the army put scientists into the line to make comparable tests of fighters before and after combat, with results doubly confirming what had already been substantially proved.

The army took seriously what I had written about optimum loading in *The Soldier's Load.* One army board set up its own test apparatus, complete with treadmill, to measure human stress under assorted loads at varying distances. The Quartermaster Climatic Research Laboratory ran other parallel tests and published reports of same, continuing into the late 1950s. These several studies resulted in a reform of all field equipment for the soldier. The army board confirmed the figure (in pounds) that I had stated would give the man in the fighting line a main chance. The opening paragraph of the quartermaster report stated that the research had been stimulated by my independent observations. From that same writing by Dr. Farrington Daniels, Jr., MD, I quote only these words: "It is disturbing to speculate that since 1750 several hundred million men have gone into combat on foot carrying back loads, while during this time probably less than a hundred men carrying loads have been subjected to scientific study."

In Korea, when the scientists were double-checking the laboratory data, I was viewing the same problem off and on in quite another dimension, and going on to a startling tentative conclusion. Here was a unique battlefield. With its ubiquitous high ridges, limited foregrounds, climatic extremes, and short-duration fire fights, Korea gave us the best opportunity to measure combat stress that we will ever know. We took almost no advantage of it.

My field notes convinced me that we needed to take a fresh look at the recovery interval that follows troop exhaustion, whether from fear or from fatigue. Man is much better than we know; his tired mind and body will rebound far faster than we think.

Take one example. After a wearing approach march followed by the digging of foxholes, two rifle companies went into perimeter on adjoining ridges. The two units were equal in strength. The ridges were almost identical. Both units were dog tired. One commander ordered a 100-percent alert. The other put his men in the sacks and left only a few of the stronger NCOs to keep watch. Thirty minutes later the Chinese Communists hit the two companies simultaneously. The company on "alert" was routed and driven from its hill immediately. The other company bounded from its sleeping bags, fought like tigers, and held the position until finally ordered by the battalion to withdraw.

Another incident is described in *The River and the Gauntlet.* One company of the Wolfhound Regiment was flattened when overrun by a Chinese brigade. Fear, more than fire and actual loss, had done it. The unit looked and acted as if utterly spent. The Chinese brigade charged on to take position atop a ridge blocking the route of withdrawal for the regiment. The stricken company, after one hour in the sack, was ordered to take the ridge. Even before the ascent started, every company officer was felled by fire. Without a break the survivors swept the slope and carried the crest.

If these episodes mean what they say, some of our security procedures in the presence of the enemy need to be overhauled. Worn out men cannot fight or think. It is folly to press them beyond endurance when just a little rest will work a miracle of recovery.

There is a collateral proposition that is best illuminated by citations from marine operations. When the 7th Regiment emerged onto the Koto-ri Plateau in November, 1950, it was met with bitter cold and the first sparks of enemy resistance simultaneously. Returning patrols showed all the symptoms of men in intense shock. Pulse rates were frighteningly low. The individuals gibbered, grimaced, stared vaguely, and could not articulate. The puzzled doctors treated them empirically with a heavy shot of grog and bed rest. Eight hours later they were normal.

On the other hand, the remnants of the 7th Infantry Division elements, which the 1st Marine Division brought out over the ice of the Chosan Reservoir in an heroic exploit, had been enveloped and held by the enemy for the greater part of one week. The cold, the privation, and the suffering of these men at the hands of the Communist Chinese had been harsh throughout. It was decided that the men must have 48 to 50 hours total rest. At the end of that time, those who had escaped both frostbite and wounds were returned to normal duty and marched down the mountain from Hagaru-ri with the division column.

There are relatively clear indications that the recovery period is in ratio to the duration of the extraordinary pressure resulting in exhaustion. Appearances are not to be trusted. The unit knocked out by five hours of marching, digging, and fighting may look no less down and dispirited than the unit saved after three days of envelopment and hand-to-hand combat on a hilltop. It does not follow that what the two require for recovery is at all alike. This subject requires far more attention than anyone has given it. There is more to be learned about man under pressure than we yet know.

One trouble is that we are slow to alter our procedures, even after ordeal by fire has shown where they are at fault. This is due to the drag of orthodoxy, which is quite a different thing from tradition. Another difficulty is that the practical lessons that we learn in war and apply under the gun are too often obscured in the pursuit of some other object under the conditions of peacetime training.

One dramatic episode will underscore what I mean. In early November, 1956, I had flown in a navy aircraft via Port Lyautey to Naples. Before enplaning on an El Al Airliner for the Middle East, thereby to join the Israeli Army in the Sinai Desert, I spent a weekend with the U.S. Sixth Fleet off Sicily. On Monday a two-battalion exercise was to occur, an attack by marines on Sardinia, with the navy doing its part. That Sunday morning we gathered on the flagship, and with Admirals Walter F. Boone and Charles R. (Cat) Brown present, the full-dress briefing prior to attack went as smoothly as a Broadway musical in its second year.

At the end Admiral Boone asked: "Any questions, General Marshall?"

"Yes, one question. As I get it, the battalion attacking just after dawn gets in landing craft four miles out. The beach is defended at the waterline by about two companies working heavy mortars and machine guns, along with small arms. Their bunker line is along that low-lying ridge 700 meters inland. The battalion in the attack is to take that bunker line by midmorning. It will then go on to that first high range marked 1,500 meters, where the enemy artillery is based. By sunset these same men are supposed to assemble on the range beyond that one where they meet the other battalion coming up from the west coast. Now, have you told the troops that if this were war they would be doing well if that first line of low ridges were theirs by the end of the day?"

Boone was startled. He said to the two marine commanders: "Is this true?"

They withdrew to consider the question, then returned to answer: "We agree with General Marshall."

Boone asked: "Then why are we doing it this way?"

Someone replied: "Any smaller plan wouldn't give the forces enough of a workout."

"Fair enough," I said, "but you have not answered my question. Have you told troops, staff, and everyone else that the plan is far overextended and unrealistic and that operations would not have that much reach if men were fighting?"

The answer was "No."

I said: "That's the hell of it. No one ever does. Out of such plans and exercises in peacetime, we create our own myths about the potential of our human forces. Then, when war comes again, men who discovered the bitter truth the hard way are all gone. Voilà, we've got to learn all over again."

There is only one way to stop such drifting. Realistic training derives only from the continued study of what has happened in war. The first duty of an officer is to challenge what he feels to be illusory. He is little qualified to do that unless he has experienced combat, for it is only in the field that one begins to understand the nature of main problems and where lie the unresolved questions.

★

The night after I returned from Korea in April, 1951, word came that Secretary of Defense George C. Marshall wished to see me and that I should leave the afternoon clear.

When we settled into our chairs, my first words were: "General, how are you enjoying this job?"

He laughed. "I never had a better time."

Very much surprised, I replied: "I thought you'd wear it like a hair shirt."

Again he chuckled. "You see, I'm having a wonderful time reading pieces by columnists who are accusing me of being senile."

The afternoon's exercise was to prove that there was nothing wrong with his mind; it was on the beam every minute.

He had called me in to discuss the main needs of the army in Korea, in order of priority and exactly as I saw them. Before we got into that, though, he wanted my views on the Negro soldier.

I cited what we had learned, almost accidentally, through the arbitrary use of black troops in the white battalions of the 9th Infantry Regiment just before the big battle in the north. Integration, I concluded, was the only way.

He agreed, adding that he had believed ever since he was a second lieutenant that this was the right answer.

We moved on then to the main business of the day. "First of all," I said, "the Eighth Army needs additional motorization. Its front is near collapse daily for lack of it."

He was reluctant to believe it. In the last week two division commanders from Korea had been in his office and had not said a word about it.

I said that was natural, since each thought it a problem peculiar to his division and due to the division's failure in first-line maintenance. It probably did not occur to either man that the problem was as broad as the army front.

I went on to explain that at Pusan there were several thousand motor trucks held in reserve and idling in a park. The commander of the rear was holding them for a "strategic emergency," thus cushioning his own position while ignoring that the emergency was already present.

Then I added: "That condition suggests that the theater organization is wrong. The Communications Zone should be under Tokyo, rather than subordinate to the army commander."

I was fairly sure of my ground on this, having checked with my old friend, Frank Ross, retired major general and former chief of transportation, European Theater, when I had come through Los Angeles. He had said reorganization was imperative.

Next, I mentioned the acute shortage of pioneer troops and porterage. The lack of serviceable roads, of hand labor for constructing defensive works, and of willing backs and A-frames to get fighting supplies forward, and cramped operations through the winter. I went on. "But I think we can scratch that one. It's a problem on its way to solution." Then I told him about my conversations with General Ridgway at Suwon and of his immediate response—the organization of the Korean Service Corps.

I brought up the third item. "We need rotation and we need it right now."

"We have a complete plan for rotation," General Marshall said. "It will be operational in about two months."

I told the general that we didn't need a perfect plan two months hence; we needed any kind of a jury-rig that could be put into effect immediately. The marines were already rotating, and you couldn't let one small fraction of the army's infantry carry the whole fighting burden. If the soldier sees no way out but death, he becomes totally demoralized.

Marshall asked how I would do it.

I suggested that one way would be according to the number of Purple Heart wounds received in Korea.

Marshall paused, got on the telephone, and called General Bradley to the office. He repeated our conversation.

Bradley was agreeable. He urged that men be pulled out of line and returned home on the basis of combat decorations, to which arrangement I saw no reason to object. Then we moved on to something else, and I did not think to ask about the "complete plan" that was due to become effective later. Had I been told, I would have stated emphatically my opposition to it, since it was militarily unsound for numerous reasons.

Bradley then left.

I went on to the next topic. "The Eighth Army needs a definition of the object. Lacking that, the war seems interminable, and for the combat line that is very hard to endure. We must have some idea of the point at which we would be willing to negotiate our way out. Then why not state it? For instance, I cannot see why the Pentagon is so aroused by what General MacArthur said in Korea several days ago. That's the kind of thing I'm talking about."

There was a prolonged pause. Then Marshall very quietly began to tell me something of the problem. He mentioned rumors of bad feelings between General MacArthur and himself: rivalry, jealousy, that kind of thing. He said he truly admired MacArthur, that he was a great soldier—there was no more inspired officer in our history, none who had won greater distinction in war, or reaped so many deserved honors.

However, they had had trouble with MacArthur in this war, principally because of our allies. Several times, such as after his letter concerning Okinawa and the Nationalist Chinese, our allies came to Marshall, protesting, "Your government does not have this commander under control."

Then we got together with our United Nations allies to agree upon a definition of the object of the war. An information copy was sent to General MacArthur, along with the notation that it was for his reading and suggestion only, and no further use should be made of it. Instead of following that instruction, he flew to Korea and made a public pronouncement on the same subject which in effect reversed the letter and spirit of the memorandum. Staff considered it insubordination beyond question, and further, out in the open. Our allies were furious. They were convinced that this man could not be controlled.

General Marshall paused.

Then he told me that he would have to go to the president the next morning and tell him that he must relieve General MacArthur.

Though he knew I was a newspaperman, General Marshall had not told me to keep what he said in strictest confidence. I knew the biggest story of the season was in my keeping. What to do with it?

I flew back to Detroit that evening, told Gilmore, still my editor at the *News,* that MacArthur was about to be relieved for sufficient cause, though I could not tell him the whole story. I proposed that I be authorized to write a lead editorial urging that MacArthur be relieved, citing only the indiscretion of his letter to Joe Martin. This was done, to the shock of Detroit and the horror of my friends. Also, that evening I wrote a memorandum for my own private files covering the conversations with General Marshall, a sanitized version of which was placed in the files of the *News.* So far as I know, General Marshall confided fully to no other military or semimilitary person on this subject at the time, and there were good reasons why the relief story had to be treated with extreme care, so that it remained thereafter half told.

Bradley, W. Averell Harriman, and Dean Acheson were the other confreres who twice discussed the relief of MacArthur with President Truman. I never got to this subject with Bradley but did talk it over with the other two. They were emphatic that Marshall could not have been the instigator, but to the contrary, defended MacArthur and played devil's advocate at both conferences. I am certain that they also were taken in. It must have been a beautiful plan, well played out.

Such were my last sights and sounds of the soldier I admired above all others, General George Marshall. I never ceased to feel awed by him. No other celebrated figure ever affected me in quite the same way. Though approachable, he possessed a certain native majesty. There was something of the eighteenth century about him, for he had its aversion to too roseate dreams about the possibilities of human progress, and also its profound consciousness of homely worth and simple wisdom. Right in the middle of World War II, he published a memo to the General Staff which opened: "Don't expect too much. There will be no miracles out of which come abiding peace. We must take the peoples of the world as we find them, with their imperfections, their prejudices, and their ambitions, and do the best we can to live with them."

Chapter 20
Noncorrespondent

My motives in going to Korea for a second tour were threefold. My wife, Ives, had died. My whole life would have to be reoriented. I sought first of all some peace of mind and hoped that I could find it on the battlefield. A new editor in chief at the *News* was breathing hard on my neck, and though I might have put up with his pressure indefinitely, I was curious about how it would feel to go along as a war correspondent with U.S. forces.

As matters developed, I was to miss that part of my education the second time out in Korea. It is curiously the case that, while I have worked alternately as a soldier or as a newsman accompanying military forces, I was not to know the luxury of "going along for the ride" with my own army until Lebanon in 1958, and even there I did part-time military duty. That unkind phrase is used deliberately; I never saw the war correspondent as a glamorous figure or one who shared the risks of war. True, a few unlucky ones get killed at it, but certain risks attend almost any mobile profession, and those of the war correspondent are considerably less than the labors of the trucker or the lumberjack.

Having tried both, I say that playing war correspondent with our forces is a sinecure compared to assignment as a foreign correspondent. When an American newsman accompanies our forces in the field, the credit of his home establishment is so fully behind him, and he is accorded such prestige and status by our government, that he can hardly miss. On the other hand, if the same man is assigned abroad to an area with which he is unfamiliar and in a situation where officialdom has no good reason to curry favor with the foreign press, he is altogether on his own. The name of his paper, the size of his city, count for little or nothing.

There is no parallel, furthermore, between the work of a war correspondent and the obligation of the serving soldier. The latter has to stick it and has no choice about the risks he will run. With a very few notable exceptions, our war correspondents will not stay with combat danger long enough to begin to understand the ordeal of troops. They are another variety of sightseer. They flit in and out of the scene, hear a few shells explode, take a quick look at frontal living conditions, ask a few trivial questions of the hometown boys, and then beat it back to secure billets to pound out tear-jerking pieces about the horrors of war. With few exceptions, they will not stay on the job. When I returned to Korea in 1953, however, I hoped to share their lot and come to some better understanding of their viewpoint. It didn't work out.

An old friend, General Mark W. Clark, was the supreme commander in Tokyo, and I had to touch base with him. The liberator of Rome has been dealt with somewhat harshly by a number of ersatz military historians in my time. As the British might say, I fail to associate myself with these sentiments.

Mark Clark's strengths interest me more than the picayune criticisms of him. Mark is an approachable man, dedicated to his country, and intensely loyal to anyone, VIP or plain GI, who has stood with him in trouble. Ambition does not warp his perspective on the fundamental values. He was first and foremost a highly competent soldier, though when he took over Fifth Army in Italy, he was probably a bit green for the high responsibility. It is fair to say, I think, that his mind and scope developed as fast as circumstances availed him. In private conversation he had the charm that derives from original thinking clearly expressed.

I pushed on for Seoul then as rapidly as possible, mainly to talk with General Maxwell D. Taylor, commander of the Eighth Army. During the war in Europe I had had several serious differences with this immaculate and tightly reined soldier. I respected his scholarly mind and high abilities as a tactical leader, and our relations had gradually improved once we came to understand one another better. He remained one of a very few West Pointers in my experience who were a little too militarized for my blood. Further, I questioned his strategic judgment, though John F. Kennedy was to have implicit faith in it.

What I sought of him this time was his overview of the situation of the Eighth Army and the worth of its fortified front. Press correspondents had compared it to the Western Front in World War I, and from my knowledge of the Korean terrain, I couldn't imagine that there was any real similarity. When we got on this subject, Taylor cut short the discussion by saying, "Sam, I'll tell you nothing. Believe me, you have to see it to believe it."

There he left it dangling, whetting my curiosity to a fine edge. Some days later I found out what he meant. The front was a monstrosity: position by position it violated every rule of military engineering and sound tactical procedure. (For details see *Pork Chop Hill*.) Thereafter I went along believing that our army would never contrive anything worse until I saw some of our temporary forward bases in Vietnam.

That night at Taylor's formal mess, two of the other guests were General Pak, the burly Korean chief of staff, and a newly arrived U.S. general, Truman Smith. On meeting over cocktails, Smith said to Pak: "I have met a corps commander named Pak and a division commander named Pak. Are all Korean generals named Pak?"

Pak smiled widely. "Now, tell me again, what is your name?"

"Smith," said the general.

"Ah, yes," grinned Pak, "that's how I heard it the first time."

Taylor and I spent the next three days together, bucketing about in his command ship inspecting Korean training installations. Taylor spent all of his time aloft studying the Korean language. At Taegu we walked in on a class at the Command and General Staff College. The students were working at a problem on a Gettysburg map. Five minutes after we arrived President Syngman Rhee and his wife, the mouselike Austrian, walked in on us. Such was the intensity of the concentration with which the class was following the instructor that not one student looked up or stood up at the president's entry. While we greeted the Rhees and small talk began between us, the class kept right on going.

That same day a message came from General Clark. I was to get to him at Panmunjom at once. I guessed what it meant; I was needed on some military duty.

The background was this: Operation Little Switch, the first exchange of wounded and ill prisoners between the United Nations forces and the Communists was about to begin. Clark's General Staff had drawn up twenty-four special rules to regulate the censorship of what the returned men would say when interviewed. His public relations staff looked askance at the taboo list, certain it would kick up heavy trouble with the press. After my arrival Clark decided it was time to call me in as an arbiter, since years before I had written the *Combined Services Manual on Field Censorship*.

Clark awaited me in a quonset hut perched on a subridge hard by the town. The only other occupant was Lieutenant General William Harrison, our chief negotiator at Panmunjom, one of the brainiest fighting men in our annals and a lay preacher of the Gospel. A more quiet, modest man is not to be found in a soldier suit; yet he could be as hard as nails. Harrison is another of those American flag officers who attain greatness without artifice, flair, or affectation. They are almost invariably the best ones.

I went over the list of proscriptions at once and objected to five of the rules. Clark wanted the reasoning in each case and got it. For example, the staff had ruled that, if a returned POW said anything questioning the good faith of enemy commanders, it should be struck. I said: "The minute this man gets back to us, he's a soldier, not a POW. If he hates the guts of Kim Il Sung and calls him a liar and a cutthroat, that's all to the good, and besides, it's true."

Clark went along with me on all five points and then asked if there was anything else on my mind.

I said: "Yes. What if the whole thing is a stacked deck? Suppose that every returning American is a progressive spouting the Communist line?"

Clark asked what I would do in that case.

"I'd cut out censorship altogether—just let everything go."

Clark wanted to know the reasoning. I said that if this were the situation, there could be no logical cutoff point. It would have to be all or nothing, and we might as well let the country get the full impact of what had happened.

Clark reflected, then agreed, later adding, "The trouble is, I have no one on my staff who can judge such a matter."

"So you want me to represent you on the ramp tomorrow morning?"

He nodded. "How long do you think it would take to judge the pattern?"

I thought that, barring accidents, and provided the POWs began arriving at the ramp by 0700 as scheduled, I ought to have the feel of the situation by high noon; so it was arranged. At 1230 I would call him.

I then advised that, in my opinion, if every returning American was spouting communist doctrine, Clark should at once renounce truce negotiations, for that would be proof of maximum bad faith on the part of the enemy.

Clark thought about that for all of two minutes. Then he said rather quietly, "I'm ready to do that. I will do it—do it on my own—if that's how the thing works out."

At his suggestion, we relaxed. Mark and I had a whiskey and soda. Uncle Billy Harrison ordered coffee. Mark said: "By the way, Slam, I think your fears are groundless. I know now that we're going to get a truce. In the last seventy-two hours the Communists have changed their tune at the table. I don't know why, but the change is there."

Harrison nodded in agreement.

As Clark had put it, every word was big news, the story for which the world had waited through two years of communist stalling. I asked whether I could cable that a truce was coming for certain, not quoting him, but stating it as my view and giving the indications.

"If you wish."

"General, damn your truce. We could have won this war and wrapped it up before now. We didn't even try, and so we will pay and pay and pay. I wouldn't write one word that might suggest I favor what we are doing."

Harrison was slapping his thighs. He said softly, "You tell him, Marshall. I've tried to tell him."

Mark sat there a moment, twiddling with his glass. "That's all very easy for you two to say. I've been given a dirty job to do for our country. Someone must, so I'll do it. When it's over, I'll turn in my suit. I've had all I can take."

We sat there with our thoughts. The Scotch seemed to have lost its flavor suddenly. Presentiments can be greatly saddening.

Early next morning I started my work at the Panmunjom ramp, the entrance and tents of which had been decked out as if for the staging of a small world's fair. Immediately, there was a hassle with some of my fellow correspondents. I was wearing the green brassard with a large "C" that gave me entry anywhere, while their movements were greatly restricted.

The show, that is, the interviewing, was the first big wartime go under television lights. As the POWs came on, and after I had explained to the other newsmen that I was on a special military mission, there was a rush for the main tent. Australians and receptionists representing other small allies had smaller adjoining tents, not unlike those of a circus side show. Lieutenant Colonel Jess Willoughby, one of Clark's public information officers (PIO) interviewed the first three returnees while the lights popped and the cameras clicked. The fourth boy proved to be a Detroiter. Before I could stop him, Willoughby called to me, "Colonel Marshall, you better take over. He's from your city."

No sadder plight ever came my way. The kid proved to be not only terribly debilitated physically, but the first "progressive," talking the Communist line. I went thoroughly into his story. He was from a poverty-stricken home. While in grammar school he had contracted tuberculosis and seemingly recovered. Eventually he was drafted into the army. In his first combat action in Korea he was rushed from behind by two Chinese and pinioned, this while firing his weapon; so here was a soldier trying to do his duty. In prison camp he was again hit by his disease and came near death. In his fevered condition he was attended by a Chinese doctor and became fairly mobile again. The physician, who treated him with great kindness, was also his indoctrinator and had been in attendance right until the hour when he was picked for the ride to Panmunjom.

Was it reasonable to regard this boy as a Benedict Arnold, a traitor to his country, because he had fallen for an alien ideology in such circumstances? I would insist not.

By noontime, after observing several other returnees, I was reasonably sure that I had the pattern and called Clark to tell him. "I don't think we need worry. It is not a lineup of progressives. We will be able to continue the normal, agreed-upon censorship."

"What is it then?"

"They have chosen the men in such way as to get a maximum distribution over the country. We've put thirty-seven POWs through by now. No two of them have come from the same city, and so far they represent twenty-six states. That could hardly be a mathematical accident. What they are trying to do is to superinduce the largest possible emotional spasm over the United States."

Clark accepted the analysis, and all subsequent developments at the ramp served to confirm it.

Next morning I flew for the Yokkokchon Valley where the U.S. 7th Infantry Division was based. It was commanded by my old friend, Major General Arthur Trudeau.

Of these wholly fluke circumstances it came about that I was the only writing man present at the battle of Pork Chop Hill. More than 350 correspondents continued writing sob stories from the Panmunjom ramp approximately fifty-five miles from where the battle action took place during four tense days. Not one of them came near the scene of the fight; none even requested air space. This lack of company was another of fortune's favors to me.

Pork Chop Hill, if not one of the classic fights in American history, was to become one of the most celebrated. Its name would ultimately be linked with the Alamo, Bunker Hill, and Bastogne, among other famous fields. That was less because we won it or that I wrote a book about it than to the fact that over the world Gregory Peck gave it fresh luster in film. To him all hail: he made a factual battle movie, free of hokum.

General Trudeau had another military job for me, bucked down to him by General Taylor, commander of the army. Patrolling by our forces across the Eighth Army front had become wholly undependable after the onset of rotation. Goofing-off was not only fairly common but probably more general than faithfulness to the mission. All higher commanders knew it, but little or nothing was being done about it. Patrol leaders had learned to lie with some proficiency, and it was increasingly difficult to hold them to account.

That was the problem put in my lap. At the same time I was given a military staff, a van, a chopper, and three sergeant assistants to birddog stories for me so that I could meet the requirements of the *Detroit News*. In effect, I was serving Trudeau as an extra ADC, done without pay but with all of the backing I needed.

The problem was not complex. I solved it by relieving all lower commands of their responsibility for the debriefing of patrols that had been engaged in a fight to any extent. The debriefings would all be done thereafter from division level, and I would do them personally to establish the techniques. I was not merely suspicious. I knew that at company and battalion levels there would be covering-up for patrols that had fouled out, and I was also aware that interrogation down below was weak and too easily subverted.

The work had the threefold purpose of demonstrating the weakness in the old hit-or-miss method, substituting a system that could be centrally controlled, and starting a school for the training of people who could extend the system. Had the war lasted, it might have proved more than a novel, local experiment.

I dealt with the patrols as rapidly as I could get to them by jeep or helicopter, starting as soon as the word came through that a patrol had been hit. We did our work in the early morning hours, meaning from around midnight until 0500 or so, before the survivors had been given rest or a chance to clean up. The average debriefing session lasted four hours, and we gathered in whatever bunker was handiest to their point of return in our front lines. As the story of the patrols as well as the account of the Pork Chop Hill battle have appeared in other of my writings, little more than that need be said here.

Most of the work was done by guttering candlelight, my desk being a rude bench or stack of empty jerry cans. It made little difference. I had long since had the knack of writing under any conditions. The data on an average patrol fight would run around 12,000 words.

The men, irrespective of how grievous their losses, were eager to talk things out. Recounting the experience and getting it on record was a kind of emotional purge for them, and they could find untroubled sleep when we finished. None of this surprised me, though it did astonish their own commanders. I had learned in World War II that such work eased their brooding, made them feel that some recognition had come and that not all loss had been waste.

The battle and its aftermath stay with me because out of action I had found what I had been seeking—some peace of mind. Working with Trudeau was likewise a balm and a boon. He was both a general and a whole man. Technically a superb engineer, and so energetic that amid battle he was rebuilding sector by sector the miserable positions he had taken over sixty days earlier, he was also rebuilding men. A division grievously neglected and humiliated under its former commander had become heads up and proud amid ordeal through his human touch.

Trudeau, though an amateur, is as much a virtuoso with the banjo as Captain Eddy Peabody. After the Pork Chop Hill battle, he led the scratch orchestra that we had whipped together. I fitted in as soloist and song leader. After our day's work was done, we toured main positions putting on small shows for the troops needing it most.

Trudeau also set up an R & R center in the division rear area so that line fighters who were wearing thin could be pulled back from the bunkers and given diversion for a week or more without having it counted against leave time. An experiment, it worked beautifully, due to the interest of a general who truly cared about people. I had long been aware that our system is woefully slack in this regard. All psychiatric counsel is too far removed from the pressure zone. Good men get pushed beyond endurance and are broken when just a few days of relief might restore them wholly. The gap between high command knowledge and the roots of this problem has not narrowed appreciably since my recruit days.

All of the field interviewing of the 7th Division and its attachments was done either while the unit was in a blocking position or occupying front line bunkers. During daylight hours the front was fairly somnolent. I spent three nights on Dale, West View, and Arsenal Outposts, which lay between our main trenches and the enemy-held ridges, my mission being the regulation of our supply system. I found that each outpost was stocking at least four times as much ammunition as it would be likely to fire in a full night of engagement, which meant that, if any became overrun, the overload was a gift to the enemy. This condition had been present for months. Trudeau knew nothing about it until he sent me to check, but his regimental commanders should have inspected and corrected the situation.

Dr. David Rioch of Walter Reed Hospital and two light colonels from his staff (all were psychiatrists) had followed me around for two weeks listening in on the group critiques. At the end Rioch came to my van one evening. He said: "We've seen troops open up for you in a way that they never do for us. What's the secret?"

"There isn't any. You begin at the beginning. You work through to the end. You preserve chronology. Your brain has to be able to do that and to think about the missing pieces. Doing that, you can get recall."

Rioch wanted to know if I had learned anything new from the interviews in Yokkokchon Valley. I told him I didn't know yet. Time must be allowed for reflection. It is only through the repetition of the thing not heard or understood before that the brain becomes alerted, freshened by a feeling of possible discovery and extended like a hound after a rabbit. The assimilation is done in the head as the search progresses, and the written record is simply a handy body of proof should my conclusions be challenged.

Doing my daily piece for the *Detroit News* wasn't even a minor worry. Much of what I wrote home dwelt upon the wondrous beauty of the Korean spring, in contrast not so much to the war as to my dismal impressions of that country in 1950–51. "Korea," a British officer had told me before my first visit, "is merely a mountain of dung." So I had found it, and on leaving, hoped that I would never return.

My second time out, nature at her loveliest proved how wrong I had been. From a point in no man's land, our fighting front looked like a rhapsody in pink, so thickly covered were the slopes and saddles with wild plum and chindolea, a shrub somewhat like a rhododendron with large blooms the color of fuchsia. For three weeks this radiant flush relieved the normal monotony of an otherwise drab countryside. Above the pink sea the profiles of the ridge lines also had that temporary look. Instead of a natural, sharp-edged silhouette, it was squared off and cubed with man-made habitations that from 300 feet away looked like the cliff dwellings of Mesa Verde. These were the warming dugouts in the American front line, set not more than thirty feet from the forward rifle pits of the company garrisoning the hill. From grass-green sea in the valley bottom up to blue sky, it was layer on layer of vivid color, the sweetest front that anyone ever smelled.

We fell asleep to the sound of gunfire and awakened to the song of birds. There were larks overhead, and the bright bush fairly throbbed with music in early morning. Two cardinals that I saw preening themselves on the sandbags of an artillery bunker looked no different from the pair that visited my backyard at home. Birdwatchers among the troops had also identified the canary, the brown thrasher, and a first cousin to the Baltimore oriole. Between the areas controlled by the Chinese and the United Nations along the Yokkokchon, no man's land was alive with quail. Much smaller than our bobwhite, they ran strictly in pairs rather than in coveys. Gray doves, somewhat larger than our own, sounded the only mournful note heard along the pine-dressed ridges of the outpost line. As in my youth in France, I saw in middle age in Korea that man needs some danger so that his senses may enjoy to their fullest the wonders of nature.

With beauty all about, there was nothing ideal about the life of the troops. Rifle companies had to spend from twenty-five to thirty days in the line without relief. Their men were tied to one small piece of earth for all that time. During darkness they maintained 75 percent alert on the main line and 100 percent in the outposts. As replacements from the United States were fed into the line, they were given no chance to meet the company as a whole. Until relief came and the company was moved back to an assembly area, the new arrival knew only the three or four men with whom he shared a warming bunker—usually a tight hut of logs and sandbags built above ground on a reverse slope. Through the morning hours, the most gracious time of day, the men tried to catch up on sleep. In the afternoon they cleaned weapons, repaired positions, and stood inspection. At sundown they went on guard again. For utter dreariness the routine was much like any other war, except for the extra issue of silence, isolation, and monotony.

My tour terminated when I completed my military mission. Five days before I was to leave for the United States I happened to express my regret to General Trudeau that, while I had seen a great deal of VT (proximity fuse)* fire during night operations and had been in bunkers twice when it rained down on us, I had never been in just the right position to observe clearly the display as the shell broke above the target and then hit into it. It

---

* A special radio fuze which would automatically burst at the optimum point above the target. The fuze was a highly secret development of World War II, and while in general use in the army, was somewhat of a novelty at this time in the Korean War.

was merely a passing remark with as little behind it as if I had said, "I'm sorry that I have never tasted green cheese."

But my friend thought that I really hankered to see a VT display and would feel unhappy if I did not get it. On the last night the Division Staff and regimental commanders were throwing a small dinner to celebrate getting rid of me. Shortly before cocktails, Trudeau asked, "What do you say about going forward at midnight to see a little artillery shoot?"

I said: "I don't think so, Art. I've been up with patrols three nights in a row, and tomorrow I fly for Seoul at 0800. I better turn in early."

He went to the phone and talked for a few minutes. Then he returned and said: "Suppose we put on the shoot at eleven o'clock tonight?"

Only then did I tumble to the fact that he had planned a special VT demonstration for my benefit. "Ok, let's do it," I said.

Dinner was over by about ten o'clock. That left time for a good cigar before the moment when we had to enjeep and proceed to Observation Point No. 19, which was on the brow of the highest ridge commanding the right flank of the division. The ride through the valley to the main line took up about twenty-five minutes. The night was calm and clear. Quite suddenly more than a few hands decided that watching a laid-on VT shoot was good nocturnal amusement. General O'Meara decided to join us as did Colonel George Van Way, commander of the 32nd Infantry Regiment, and another half dozen officers. Life at the front is normally a great bore, and this was one interesting way to kill a few hours.

What had been planned was still less exciting than an average July 4 fireworks display at the county fair. Six hundred yards forward and down from OP 19, near the center of the Yokkokchon Valley, was a very small ridge named Yoke that one platoon of the 32nd manned as a fortified outpost. Approximately 500 yards beyond Yoke was the Red Chinese–held hill mass called T-Bone. Both positions figured in the planned shoot. According to the arrangements, the show would open with the firing of five illuminating rounds directly above American-held Yoke. With the broad valley thus lighted, there would follow a shoot of twenty-five VT rounds against Chinese-held T-Bone. Maybe three or four minutes of pyrotechnics, and so to bed.

We got to OP 19 exactly three minutes before the appointed hour. There was barely enough time to get binoculars adjusted. The lights came on promptly at eleven.

We looked at the brightened slopes of Yoke, we boggled, we gasped, hardly believing what our eyes told us. There, right at the foot of the little hogback, fully revealed in the magnesium glare, two companies of Red Chinese infantry were just beginning an attack up the slope. So far they had not fired a shot, and Yoke's garrison was still unwarned. The flares had gone off in the precise moment when the attackers began to move upgrade and before they were in position to direct aimed fire against the defensive rampart.

Needless to remark, the planned twenty-five VT rounds never got fired against T-Bone Hill. For all the astonishment to us yokels gaping at Yoke, no time was lost in exploiting the tailor-made situation. Its details could not have been more perfectly shaped toward a complete kill. Because of the practice shoot and the knowledge that Trudeau and O'Meara were both going forward, the entire division artillery was at the alert. Both commanders were already on telephone to the fire direction center, and the rounds intended for T-Bone were diverted to the lower slopes of Yoke. More lights were called for above Yoke, and more and more killing salvos followed the first twenty-five shells. It was like shooting ducks in a gallery; there was never a chance for a Chinese getaway.

One of the more fascinating battle episodes in my experience, that incident had to go unreported; otherwise Trudeau would have been skinned by some congressman for wasting ammunition to entertain a visiting fireman. In years since I have wondered what might have happened to Yoke that night if Trudeau had been parsimonious about artillery shell, or if we had agreed to wait until midnight. It's not more idle to speculate than to believe that the thing had to happen just that way.

★

On my return to the United States I felt satisfied with the job done. Physically, I felt well and vigorous, but I was fitful and restless at home and in the office. I couldn't work. I thought I had become reconciled to Ives's death long since but, as my dear friend, Dr. Ray Waggoner, pointed out when I consulted him, I had not. He prescribed that I get used to the reality by traveling, not working, roaming at will. It worked.

Several months later I married Cate, and a new chapter in life began. I wrote an article on a Korean battle. When the *Detroit News* was closed by a newspaper strike, I expanded the article into a book—*Pork Chop Hill.* My writer's block was gone for good.

Chapter 21
Washington Follies

During most of the Eisenhower administration I sat as the military member of the Defense Department's Special Operations Commission. My six colleagues were social scientists whose patter I could understand now and then by trying extra hard. We supposedly were ranking scientific advisers to the military on psychological warfare, escape and evasion training, and green beret operations. For some reason that now escapes me, I was named a committee of one to deal with escape and evasion, which included lessons learned from our sad experience in the Korean POW compounds.

All sorts of cooks were messing with that broth. Defense Secretary Charles E. Wilson had appointed an all-service panel to determine what standard should be set and whether some kind of corrective training was needed. The panel deadlocked over the question of whether the Spartan requirement of "name, rank, and serial number only" should be upheld, and it was finally dissolved in early 1955.

The air force had already centered its service-wide resistance-to-interrogation training operation at Stead Air Force Base, Nevada. Key members of the faculty were ex-POWs from the Korean camps who had resisted nobly. The heart of their method was to scrap the Spartan code, permit the POW to engage in a game of wits with his tormenters, and teach him how to evade a harmful response to security questions.

At the request of Donald A. Quarles, the secretary of the air force, I made an official inspection of Stead. My classified report to him approved what was being done at Stead as the sound solution for all services and pointed out, among other things, that irrespective of nationality, not more than four percent of military personnel can indefinitely resist some communication with the enemy when held POW. We know from a plethora of statistics that such is the nature of men in general.

I had raised only one main question with the faculty at Stead. The training was too realistic. The pit, the box, and other horrendous fixtures of the Korean camps had been duplicated, and students were subjected to the ordeal briefly.

It seemed to me to be a public relations booby trap. If the press got hold of it, there'd be trouble.

They said the students insisted on it, and they would have to run the risk of exposure. I couldn't contend against that argument.

Well, it blew! *Newsweek* got the story, tipped off by some disgruntled trainee, and puffed it up into a national scandal. Quarles went on a national hookup to defend the position, saying, "I have had that base inspected by an officer in whom I have full confidence, and I will stand on his report."

The interviewers asked for the name of the man.

Quarles said cryptically, "I can't tell you, but he's one of your kind." Then he called me to ask if he could release my name and the report. I was astounded. "Mr. Secretary, by no means. One-third of that paper is highly secret information."

A second committee on the same problem was shortly formed under the nominal chairmanship of Undersecretary of Defense Carter Burgess and the inspirational leadership of General John E. Hull, former supreme commander, Far East.

I was called as the final witness before that group of flag officers on July 5, 1955. Their conclusion was that the Spartan code had proved to be unworkable, and we had to go on to something more practical. The object of our conversation was to elicit from one another additional arguments for what we proposed.

After lunch I was detailed as chairman of a subcommittee, along with General Merritt A. Edson of the marines and Admiral C. A. Lockwood of the navy, to write the Military Code of Conduct. I was the actual penman of the code during the several hours that we worked together, and my main fight with my colleagues was to keep purple phrases out of the composition. I felt it would be more effective if the words marched like a set of general orders. In the end I was almost successful.

At the last minute Carter Burgess stuck his head in the door, picked up the draft and insisted on adding the words, "I will trust in my God and the United States of America."

I protested.

Burgess said: "Don't forget, we must sell this thing to the press and to the pulpit."

Several weeks later it was sold to the White House and made official with the publication of an executive order signed by President Eisenhower.

What came of it then? The army, navy and marine corps turned their backs on what had been directed and resumed training under the Spartan code. In 1962, Defense Secretary Robert S. McNamara, purely for the sake of economy, scrapped Stead Air Force Base, the one sound training operation in support of the code. Just two years later, the Joint Chiefs of Staff completed the sabotage by directing a return to the Spartan code, though under law they have no right to override an Executive Order.

It wasn't that these gentlemen made an honest mistake. McNamara and the chiefs did not even try to understand the problem.

★

In 1955–56, I was a member of an ad hoc Department of Defense panel charged with the unlikely task of analyzing new agents. This sounds as if we were an adjunct of CIA, but far from it! The mission became one of determining the military characteristics of a particular mystery drug then known to some scientists, as yet unheard of by the public, and to our innocent minds, never likely to become a household word or a scourge to the younger generation.

Our study group was chaired by Dr. Harold G. Wolff of New York Hospital, and I was the one military member. My associates were three distinguished psychiatrists and three no less prominent pharmacologists. We were looking at a patented product on which a Swiss drug firm had a monopoly, and our interest was whetted by the fact that the Soviet Union was then buying two-thirds of the world supply.

The British military had already conducted at least one notable experiment along the same lines. When the drug was given to twenty intelligence officers, all but three in the group proved susceptible and spilled official secrets readily. We suspected that the stuff was being used by the Russians in what is loosely called brainwashing.

It was in this way that I got in on the ground floor of LSD, and but for a lack of vision, I might have thereafter superseded Brother Leary. We at least went at the problem with more imagination than the British. We undertook to prove that LSD, when exploded into a vapor, would disarrange a tactical formation and make its members incapable of any cohesive action. My part of the act was to set up the testing exercises. In a way, I was fulfilling the dream of my mentor, J. F. C. Fuller, who years before proposed introducing such a novelty in warfare. Instead of shooting up the landscape, the attackers would loose a cloud that would either put the defenders to sleep or keep them loco long enough to be rounded up and stowed away.

During the six months that we held together, we established beyond doubt that LSD so employed was wholly disorienting to troops, and might be made, in the words of Artemus Ward, a sweet, sweet boon to warfare. We must have performed superbly. In my files is a letter from J. B. Macauley, deputy assistant secretary of defense, thanking our group for its "splendid services" to the military.

I would still ask: "What splendid services?" for the project ended on that note. Within a few years after the filing of the report, our top secret agent had become a drug on the market. Small fry in our town referred to it as acid, and when they spoke of taking a trip, they didn't mean travel. I speculate that thereby LSD was denied any future as a military weapon. It had lost all dignity.

In 1957 I was on another panel, chaired by Marx Leva, formed to advise the U.S. Senate on foreign aid programs. My colleagues were Generals Joe McNarney and Jerry Higgins and Admiral Mick Carney. We met two days out of each week for about two months. Often we talked with such senators as Joe Saltonstall and Dick Russell. It was to learn that, without exception, members of the committee did not want to make foreign aid efficient and faithful to the national purpose. "Just show us how to get rid of it!" they dinned in our ears time and again. And that is about all they would say.

We of the panel were unanimously of the belief that foreign aid should be put on a semipermanent basis. It could then be held accountable by one central control where the formulating and balancing were done. As things were, the programming developed out of the jockeying and tugging of the country teams, most of which regarded their host nations as favored clients. There was no overall review, no system of inspection. That was not really our problem; we were there to write a report pleasing to the senators. They wished us to play Clancy lowering the boom.

On the final day we heard reports from two national research organizations whose experts had been receiving Senate pay for six months, surveying analyses of foreign aid needs and programs. The two reports were in agreement on one main point: the one outstanding and model analysis had been done in Europe for the NATO countries.

I asked: "Was any one person responsible for this work of art?"

The man looked at his paper. "Yes, one Doctor Hugh M. Cole."

At that point we broke up.

Cole was waiting in his car outside the Capitol to take me to lunch.

I asked: "Doc, do you know you're the greatest?"

"Friend, cut out the horseshit."

"It's on the level. You're the one wizard at foreign aid analysis with greater powers than old Hokosa, the wizard, the one great mind we can use as a datum plane."

"What in hell are you talking about?"

I told him the story. It turned out that he had spent less than thirty days on the study while at the same time bringing along two other projects. That is some measure of the care taken in dispensing the wealth of this nation once it is milked from the taxpayer, but people decline to believe that governments can be both stupid and blind.

In the interregnum that followed the 1960 national election, I was named a member of an ad hoc committee, along with Paul Nitze and Dean

Rusk, to advise the incoming president, John F. Kennedy, should any international crisis develop prior to his taking the oath of office.

The committee never met. No alarm was sounded. The interlude was conspicuously free of seeming threat.

But Mr. Kennedy was exploring one small strategic opportunity in that same November. He may have reckoned it to be of such minor import that outside advice would not be needed. It was in that month that he was briefed by Eisenhower's staff about a project then building in the mountains of Guatemala where, under CIA direction, several hundred Cuban refugees were undergoing combat training for possible use against Fidel Castro. The Eisenhower crowd had no plan to throw any such meager force against Cuba in direct invasion. There was only a fuzzed-up general idea about putting them ashore to operate as guerrillas in the Escambray mountains.

So began Mr. Kennedy's first fateful step toward that monumental folly known as the Bay of Pigs. That was when he needed a professional SOB by his side to tell him the notion was lunatic. Since Nitze and Rusk were of the small official group that finally told him to go ahead, they would hardly have qualified, and we would doubtless have fallen out as a committee.

Some months after the debacle, Dick Bissell, who masterminded it for the CIA, asked me, "General, where do you think this thing went wrong?"

"Mr. Bissell, I've been all over it and I can't think of a single thing that you did right."

Out of chronological order and solely because it suits me, there is one other experience out of that decade when I was wallowing in the bureaucracy that may be worth telling.

My time on the Special Operations Panel coincided with what is called the McCarthy Period, an era less remarkable for the obnoxiousness of the person from which it draws its name than for the lack of moral courage in men of high place whose duty was to take him on. As an adviser, when the senator turned on the army, I tried in vain to get its secretary to stand and fight. He wouldn't make a single move.

Many government security officers in that time turned villain and became outright oppressors of individuals requiring clearance. Shortly before Armistice Day, 1954, following a long meeting of the panel, I was told that Secretary Wilson's chief security officer wished to have words with me. I found myself dealing with a soft-eyed whippersnapper of about thirty-four, whose name I have happily forgotten. He got right to business saying, "By the records, you have either made an error or lied about your credentials."

"Go ahead, spell it out."

"In one place you say you went to Texas Mines. Later you say it was Texas Western."

"It's like this. I did go to the Mines, and it became Texas Western. Then that school gave me a high honor. Since then I have put its name in the forms."

In this way the inquisition began. He consulted his notes again and looked up. "How long have you known Charlie Chaplin?"

"I knew him only when I worked with him in my childhood."

"How much correspondence do you have with him?"

"None. He would not even know my name."

Back to the notes again.

Then the question: "Why did Leon Trotsky talk with you more frankly than with other correspondents?"

"You would have to ask Trotsky that question. It was a great break for me as a reporter. I made the most of it."

"Are you a member of the POUM?"

"Of course not. Your question is ridiculous."

He studied the notes for a long time. Then his head bobbed up. "Why were you chairman of Russian war relief in Detroit?"

"For some of the same reasons I was an official of British and Greek war relief. Then there was something added. An emissary came from the State Department with a note saying the organization was needed. Your boss, C. E. Wilson, wouldn't take the job, nor would anyone else in the motor industry. They were afraid of the onus. The messenger turned to me because I was known in the community, and I agreed to serve. Someone had to do it."

"Why did they continue your name as honorary chairman throughout the war?"

"I didn't know they had, but I appreciate the compliment."

"Why did you make the welcoming speech to the new Soviet ambassador when he made Detroit his first call in the early summer of 1946?"

"It was like this. I had just returned to Detroit. The ambassador entered there because the Detroit committee had done better than any other. Dr. Whittaker, the chairman, asked me to make the talk. I would have accepted in any case, but the day before, Dr. Whittaker had made my invalid wife the present of a wheelchair when I couldn't buy one on the market."

He was back at his notes.

"Why did you join the Committee to Free Earl Browder?"

"I have never heard of it."

"Why did you join the American Fifth Column?"

"Again, I have never heard of it. Now, you tell me, where and when am I said to have joined these organizations?"

He looked at his notes before replying, "In Detroit, November, 1942."

"If you had taken the trouble to consult the records, you would have learned that I entered the army long before that and never returned to Detroit."

He came up with the official list of subversive organizations and started to say, "I want you to—"

"Just a minute," I interrupted. "I know that list. I have been over it several times. I have never joined any one of them or any kind of clandestine organization in my life."

The oaf persisted. "I want you to read them off to me one by one and say no or yes to each."

I started, got partway down the list and threw it at him, arose, and started putting on my coat.

"You're not finished!" he squawked.

"Oh yes, I am," I said, "I got as far as the Ku Klux Klan and that was enough. I risked my life fighting that organization before you had quit crapping in your diapers."

He arose, and asked, in the manner of a schoolboy, "You're not mad at me, are you? Won't you shake hands?"

"Why waste our time. No, I'm not mad at you. I'm simply fed up with a system that will stand for anyone like you."

When, hours later, I returned home well after midnight, my wife could see that I was still seething. When I had told her the story, she wanted to know what I proposed doing about it.

"If you agree, I will get off the following telegram right now: 'TAKE EVERY JOB THAT CONNECTS ME WITH GOVERNMENT AND SHOVE UP. I WILL NOT SERVE ONE THAT OPERATES THIS SHAMEFULLY.' "

Cate said: "Go ahead."

The telegram landed on the desk of Wilber M. Brucker, then general consul of the Department of Defense. Brucker called me next morning and offered apologies and support.

★

In the early spring of 1955, Admiral Mick Carney drummed up a global war scare practically single-handed, which is no mean feat for a chief of naval operations, especially when he is not half trying.

As I recall the circumstances, he chanced to remark at a dinner party that he would not be surprised if there were a major explosion around the Formosa Strait within the next thirty days, or something of the sort. Either the several newsmen present took it that the CNO was speaking with all of the advantages of observation enjoyed by Moses on Sinai, or they wilfully became accessories after the non-fact. The dismal forecast boomed into headlines.

None of the noise intimidated my editor, H. V. Wade. If there was going to be a war over Taiwan and the offshore islands, then I had to be on the scene. I told him that in my judgment Carney was more than a little mixed up, that tidally it was the wrong season for invasion, but that since I loved birds' nest soup and fortune cookies, I was quite ready to fly forth and take what came. Wade waved me on my way only because he believed that an admiral couldn't possibly give him a bum steer.

At Taipei I joined approximately thirty freshly arrived American and British correspondents, all scouting the bureaus and boondocks in search of a war that wasn't to be. A more disgruntled and insurgent group of newsmen I had never met. Though no war eventuated, the trip was far from a total loss.

At this time Walter S. Robertson, assistant secretary of state, and Admiral Arthur W. Radford, chairman of the Joint Chiefs of Staff, flew from Washington to Taipei on a much-publicized but highly secret mission. When they left, the press was none the wiser.

Foreign minister George Yew sent for me to talk things over. He told me that the reason for their visit was to advise Chiang that the United States was withdrawing from its commitment to help the Nationalists should the Communist Chinese attack the offshore islands. I made no use of this information then or later, since it seemed unwise. It was through Yew that I first met the generalissimo, and later the vice-president, Chen Cheng, two thoroughly enjoyable and recondite individuals. Chen Cheng, long since dead, was the instigator of land reform on Formosa, from which beginning the island developed as a showcase of inspired agrarianism. Chiang, superannuated only in the number of his years, must have found what Ponce de León sought. Only yesterday (August 25, 1970) I talked with Bill Westmoreland, one week after he had spent an afternoon with the generalissimo. Westy said: "I have never known anyone like him. The brain gets sharper every year."

While in Taipei, I had visited the zoo for the sole purpose of interviewing two and a half tons of elephant. Api was his name. No doubt the last war elephant on earth, Api had made as many campaigns and conquered as much high ground as any of the historic thirty-seven that Hannibal took into Italy in 218 B.C.

I came across Api's story while dining with Lieutenant General Sun Li-Jen. Sun's career was almost as weird as Api's. A graduate of Virginia Military Institute, Sun was probably China's ablest fighting general during World War II. By the time we became friends, he had been kicked upstairs to an office of small influence. Still later, he was put under permanent house arrest, charged with joining a Communist plot against Chiang.

In Sun's living room as we lingered over martinis, I noticed four footstools made of life-sized elephants' feet. In our own living room we have two such curiosities. They never fail us when conversation dulls.

I asked Sun where he got his trophies.

"Belonged to a great female named Paak," my host said. "I captured her."

Then he closed his eyes and unwound the tale. It began in Burma near Naban in June, 1942. Api, Paak, and five other elephants had been taken from Thailand by the Japanese and were being used to outflank roadblocks in rough country.

"Not knowing my division was moving at right angles to the march of the enemy column," said Sun, "we bumped into their rearguard and fought a meeting engagement. We killed very few Japanese, but we captured the seven war elephants."

Through the months of defeat that followed, most of Sun's other animals and vehicles fell prey to the road, weather, and jungle. The seven elephants survived and were used for road transport. When, to the north of Mandalay, Sun at last broke contact with the Japanese to start his retreat into China, he decided that, if Hannibal could put battle elephants over the Alps, then he, Sun, could march them over the Yunnan Hump in the Burma Road.

"It was a hard decision," said Sun, "since it meant that, except for my people who were flown out of Burma, the 38th Division would be slowed to an elephant's pace. My soldiers could march twenty to twenty-five miles a day going upgrade; we had rugged men in those days. Due to its great weight, an elephant is a poor marcher and will break down if given more than six miles a day. So we placed them with the rearguard, and the pace of the column was regulated according to what was best for the elephants."

This drag on the logistics of the retreat over the Hump was more than offset when the division descended into China. Sun's men had exhausted both their strength and food supply during the mountain crossing. There was rice in Yunnan, but Sun didn't care to plunder his own countrymen.

The elephants were screened and set up as a circus. Word was circulated to the villages that the people could see elephants for the first time if they paid with so much rice. The 38th literally ate its way back to Kunming on the food gathered at the elephant show.

By the late summer of 1945 Sun was commander of the New First Chinese Army. He still had his seven elephants and was planning to use them in the assault to drive the Japanese from Canton.

"But by October I had changed my mind and was pondering how to get rid of the beasts," said Sun.

"Then fate intervened. I had arranged a great memorial service for the dead lost by the First Army in Burma and China. Japanese prisoners had been used to build the monument in their honor. I had cast a great bronze eagle eight feet wide from used shell casings.

"At the moment of dedication, my army got on its knees, the men weeping and wailing. As if understanding, my elephants trumpeted in a body for as long as the army remained down. Soldiers are superstitious. My army took it that the beasts had been inspired by heaven. I realized I was stuck with them and that one way or the other I had to arrange for their preservation."

Four were placed in mainland zoos. One soon died. Sun kept Paak and Api for the next three years. Then in the spring of 1949, just two months before Canton fell to the Red Chinese, Sun decided that saving two elephants from Communism was a righteous enterprise. Paak and Api were put aboard an LST and shipped to Taiwan.

Paak, the female, died in 1953 from a parasite that chewed her intestines to bits. Api caught the same disease, and Sun, in his anxiety, turned to the U.S. Embassy for help. Mrs. Karl Rankin, wife of the ambassador, referred Api's case to the director of the Bronx Zoo. Medicine was flown in in time to restore Api to health and when I last saw him, he looked as though he would live on and on remembering everything, as good elephants are ever prone to do.

No major footnote to military history, it still makes a nice little story.

Chapter 22
Toward Israel

The ring of the telephone pulled us out of deep sleep. The time was late October, 1956. Cate and I had gone to Washington to be near the Pentagon and Israel's embassy. The fight in Sinai was well underway. The British and French had made their lunge to wrest the Suez from Nasser's grip, as usual mucking up the show by making the wrong move to begin—fumbling for Port Said instead of jumping brigades into Ismailia.

An excited voice on the far end of the line said: "I had to wake you. World War III is starting."

I knew those tones. It was Harvey Patton, managing editor of the *Detroit News.* I told him I'd poke around, find out what it was all about, and call him.

Immediately I called Colonel Maury Holden, executive to the secretary of the army. Maury had been my roommate in Korea. I told him to dig in fast and call me.

Ten minutes passed and he was back on the line. "Those damned fools on the Joint Chiefs of Staff sent out a warning message to all air bases last night. It reads, literally, 'Don't get caught with your pants down.' So each base commander is interpreting the ambiguity in his own way. Some day the world will explode out of that kind of monkey business."

I rang Patton back and told him to keep his hair on, that a famous warrior of his name had taken a few falls from not understanding that it was the best policy. The news practically ruined Harvey's day. He sounded right peevish about my squelching his Armageddon.

Here I shift into low gear to explain the reasons for my abiding interest in Israel, which for years has been a moving force in the life of my immediate family. Cate and our daughters adore the country, and no part of earth holds greater enchantment for me.

As a child I abhorred antisemitism even as I was mystified by it, probably because my kinsmen on both sides of the family were without racial or religious prejudice. I judged any other boy by what I saw of him, knowing no better rule than that. One of my father's closest friends was a young scholar from Kiev, Henry Grossbart. As a child, I had often heard them talk about the pogroms and debate the why of Jewish persecution down the centuries.

I had thought of the Balfour Declaration as a contract, rather than a vague promise. The idea of a Jewish homeland appealed to me, and I felt indignant when the Allies reneged on that pledge. Also, I was aware that the Arab help to the Allied cause was spectacularly exaggerated by Lawrence and the romantics who wrote of him. The Zionist movement made the more sense to me in that I was schooled in it personally by its most eloquent advocate, Rabbi Stephen Wise, a giant among men.

Yet these sentiments were in no way compelling. Not being a Jew, I felt, thought, and acted as a sideliner. Jewish causes were not my show.

This changed after Dachau. In no way prepared for what I saw there, I felt doubly outraged, horrified that such a thing could happen in my time among people called civilized. Even though I was chief historian of the theater, our government had left us in ignorance about much of the holocaust. My bosses, Generals Eisenhower and Smith, hadn't known. I know that they, as I, felt all the more involved because we had been kept in the dark.

Another catalyst toward my "Israeli connection" came of an altogether chance meeting at the Washington National Airport in the late summer of 1956. I arrived late at night on a flight from Montgomery. While getting my bags, I ran into Major General Tommy Sherburne, USA, my friend of Normandy and Bastogne days. As a colonel, he had taken over the command of the 101st Division artillery from Tony McAuliffe during the famous siege. There was always wonderful warmth and unflaunted courage in Tommy. That night he said: "I have a friend here you need to know."

Thus I met Colonel Katriel Salmon, military attaché in Washington of the embassy of Israel. Black homburg, black suit, tie and shoes, somber of visage, Salmon stood there, looking utterly sinister. What he said in undertones helped not at all. To impress at first meeting was obviously not according to his book of manners.

Next day, out of prolonged conversation at his office, our friendship took root, and he became my bridge to Israel. Dear Katriel. There are so many memories of him. On the day President Kennedy was assassinated (he was by then ambassador to Rumania and our house guest at Dherran Dhoun), when the news came over TV, he wept, though we were dry eyed. His life ended some years later when his car caught fire at the foot of Monte Cassino, and he was consumed by the blaze. That he charmed many women, including my Cate, speaks well of their judgment of male character.

On every trip to Israel I saw Salmon, and he briefed me on Middle East developments that received no attention in our press. His agitation, the steadily increasing concern of a soldier normally reserved, convinced me that crisis was mounting toward explosion. Israel's border troubles, the raids into the kibbutzim, were becoming unbearable provocations.

When the invasion of Sinai was begun with the strikes aimed at El Kuntilla, Abu Agueila, and Themed, I put the *Detroit News* squarely on the side of Israel in editorials and special articles. Most of the papers branded the march a raw aggression. I have no patience with the post-World War II use of that term. It is too smugly hypocritical. Force has its place in the building of a more civilized world. Wholly untimely and unrealistic is the party line in the United Nations, holding that peace may be certified by declaring at will any use of force, other than that of the United Nations, abhorrent and an act of aggression. A state-backed persistent campaign of terror is no less an affront to peace than an overt invasion.

Quickly I got to Washington and, due to Katriel's inside information on the battle of El Arish, I was able to write, twenty-four hours before any of the press services had the news, that Israel had won her decisive victory and the war was all but over. Then came the Franco-British leap at Egypt. I was all for it. I had sized up Gamal Abdel Nasser as being as megalomaniac as was Adolf Hitler, though he was a more clever dissembler. I was bent on getting the United States to leave that play alone, keep hands off, stay cool, let other members sound off if they chose, but say nothing and commit nothing at the United Nations. There are moments in strategy when a negative stand may fix conditions for the better for decades to come, and one small positive action can be ruinous. This was one of those times, and let the Soviet threat of an atomic confrontation be damned. It was as good a time as any to test the reality of Russian coercion and blackmail.

My hours were spent trying to persuade the principals among the military to resolve a Pentagon position that could be passed along to the White House. Secretary Brucker saw it that way. So did main figures in the Navy Department. The block was my friend, General Maxwell D. Taylor, army chief of staff. He said: "Sam, it would be immoral not to intervene."

I said: "I see nothing immoral about this country staying silent in its own interests." But I couldn't budge him. The pietism of the State Department-White House axis would probably have weighted the scales in any case.

Once it became clear that I was spinning my wheels in Washington, I tidied up personal affairs within a few hours so that I could clear for Israel. The time had come for flight. The chants of praise for the White House decision to block Israel and boot our allies in the teeth were getting to my stomach. The main problem was how to get to the Middle East, since Secretary Dulles had barred passage to the war zone for all American nationals. Neither the *News* nor the army could do anything for me. The first rule under such conditions is to move as inconspicuously as possible. I arranged with the U.S. Navy to fly out of New York as far as Naples aboard one of its aircraft. Colonel Salmon sent a message in code to Israel's attaché in Rome.

In Rome, the Israeli embassy was most attentive and courteous, and no less mysterious, though obviously prepared for my arrival. While I was asked for my passport, it was not visa-stamped, and I received no hint of what had been laid on. I was simply to stay put at that base, ask no questions, snooze when I could, and await further directions. At five the following morning I was smuggled aboard an El Al plane by the military attaché, though I had no ticket. Had I been a secret agent, the treatment might have been the same. Such bizarre touches fix themselves in the memory far better than the truly important things.

Though I was then quite unaware of it, I had a large credit banked for me with Zahal, Israel's defense establishment. The army had been organized in 1950. In the same year, two of my books on tactics and combat leading, *Men Against Fire* and *The Mobility of One Man,* had been translated into Hebrew by Uzi Narkis (who later as a brigadier defended Jerusalem in the 1967 war), and published by the army as an integral part of its training and fighting doctrine. The works were pirated—a bill that was later squared—which explains why I did not know. Zahal was quite familiar with my work, record, and background, though I knew nothing of it.

Awaiting me at the Lod airport was a two-man reception committee, arms not exactly open. The tall angular man in the background who simply stood and smiled beatifically, as if amused by the show, was Colonel Dov Sinai, a senior spokesman for Zahal. His co-host, the agitated chatterer up front, was the U.S. Army attaché in Tel Aviv.

He began. "General, what are you doing in Israel?"

"Well, the plane stopped, and I thought it was time to get off."

"Why did you come?"

"To see what I could see."

"Don't you know that you shouldn't be here?"

"No. I can't think of a better place for me."

"Don't you know that you are already in serious trouble for violating an order from the State Department?"

"Not at all. There's no such proscription on my passport, and Mr. Dulles didn't give me the word."

"Are you prepared to take the next plane back?"

I was getting fed to the teeth with this worry wart. "Hell, no. I'll be staying as long as I see fit, and if you want to bet on that, put up some money. Let's get moving. I have work to do."

Dov Sinai was laughing at the exchange fit to bust a gut. The attaché shied off, and Sinai drove me to the Dan Hotel, by which time the flap was over. I talked to the American consul general as soon as I could. He said that as long as I could get a paper stating that I was on a press-authorized mission, the embassy would be relieved of all embarrassment.

Throughout that day my hosts went forward with their arrangements for my travels in the Sinai. Tel Aviv's hotels at that time swarmed with correspondents, mainly British and American, who were either at the scene at war's beginning, or had swiftly moved to it from Europe. The occupied area, the great desert to the southwest into which the brigades had deployed, remained forbidden ground to them, and the no-thoroughfare sign would stay up indefinitely. The Israelis did not trust the foreign press corps, even though it included some first-class, responsible writers such as Pete Lisagor and the Britisher, Kenneth Ames. Too many were writing fakes or pieces slanted to put Israel in a bad light. The only other correspondent besides myself who was given a ticket into Sinai was Robert Henriques, the British novelist. A Jew who had fought for Britain in World War II, Henriques was anti-Israel until he saw it for the first time, at which point he became enraptured.

That day I began to understand that I was meeting a most unusual army. The eye-opening came when I interviewed Colonel Harkavi, Zahal's chief of intelligence. I opened by saying that I would be asking many questions, some touching on too sensitive ground, others that he could answer without attribution, still others that could be handled in the clear; so I would like some guidance.

He replied: "Ask any question. I'll answer it to the best of my ability. I trust your judgment about how to use what I say." Such a response by a G-2 even in one's own army borders on the unique. From Harkavi I couldn't believe it, but he was as good as his word through that session.

After that, I was in conference with the Historical Section of the General Staff. The chief told me that his people were new at the game. Though they had read some of my works, they did not yet understand the group interview technic and thus had not yet moved into Sinai. Would I therefore develop a plan and pattern for them in my work with the brigades and later report such gaps as still needed to be filled?

Remarkable. I was to be given carte blanche in Sinai. I would be able to work over the brigades at the troop level, interviewing where and whom I pleased, following practically the same guidelines as when I worked with the U.S. Army afield. No stranger could have been afforded a more welcome opportunity. I could hardly believe it.

In the lobby of the Dan that evening, still marveling at my good fortune, I was approached by a figure in the badly soiled uniform of an Israeli rifleman. The stranger asked in clearly American accents: "Aren't you Slam Marshall, the military writer?"

"Right, who are you?"

"I'm Leon Uris, the novelist."

"What are you doing in a fighting suit?"

"I came over here to get the background and color for a new book." (The book was *Exodus*.) "I went to work in a kibbutz. It broke my back. I just couldn't take it. The war came along. Anything seemed easier than what I was doing. Joining the army was my way out."

We started at dawn next morning. My escort officer was Lieutenant Colonel Bentz Tehan, who afterward became the secretary of the General Staff and then minister to Ethiopia. It was another great break for me. Bentz is the ideal companion, physically slight, forthcoming but modest, wise in the ways of the military, and utterly tireless. He speaks English with an Oxford brogue and, like most Sabras who are religious Jews, he knows the New Testament more thoroughly than the average American clergyman. Guide, philosopher, and mentor, all in one package.

Just above Beersheba, where the young tree plantations stood hardly ankle-high above the sand wastes, he told the jeep driver to stop. Then he took me for a walk half a mile into the plantation. Since I was straining to get to the brigades and begin work, I was at first a little nettled by the digression. We sat there among the seedlings for a half hour while he described how the land reclaiming programs were going, of what care had to be taken, and of his dreams for the waterless country where we tarried. It was a love story. He sounded like a professional forester and conservationist, yet his calling was that of a warrior. Far from time wasted, the gentleness of Bentz prepared me to understand better the nature of the Israeli Army, which is like none other.

The ranks of the brigades were infused with this same spirit, a deep and exulting pride in the soil of their country and in all that was being done to revivify, wherever water might flow, the land of milk and honey. That came out in the combat critiques of the brigades as I worked them over next to the dunes and spikelike stone ridges of Sinai. They were fully responsive and as sharp at the exercise as any American troops. But as surely as we took a breather, some soldier would ask me some such question as: "Have you seen yet what we are doing with Huleh? You must go to Huleh!"

Our routines were so regulated as to make the most of comfort where it was to be had. Unless the site was too far distant, as was true of Sharm-el-Sheikh, Bentz and I took to the field each morning and made it back to Tel Aviv soon after dark. Long before my years as a "senior citizen," that loathsome term that signifies an American consigned to the scrapheap by our system, I had ceased to hold with the notion of roughing it for its own sake. Camping out, when there is any alternative, strikes me as a primitive urge from which one should recover in youth. As Micawber said, the time comes to take a pause and then fall back. Scorpions in one's sleeping bag are less pleasant the older one grows. Furthermore, the brigades went into bivouac when the sun went down. Lights went out, there was no possibility of doing work, and the desert became a deep freeze. If I were to see much of Israelis, other than soldiers, I had to become a commuter.

Colonel Henriques and I did not work together. As a soldier-novelist, he had one way of going, and as a field analyst newsman, I had another. It just chanced that we never collected our information at any one forward base at the same time. He talked mainly to the commanders, and I was occupied primarily with group-interviewing the assault units. Though these are the lesser reasons, it was inevitable that our conclusions about this army and its combat performance in the Sinai campaign would be far apart. His training was that of a British intelligence officer whereas my specialty was studying the hard grind of operations. Theory and practice are rarely congruent in warfare, and my chief concern was to determine how much Israel's army had closed the gap.

Henriques was bent on "getting out a book about the war just as quickly as possible to be read by as many people as possible." Having in mind an in-depth study, I told him we were not in competition. I did, over coffee one night, suggest the title for his work, and it was by this odd chance that the Sinai campaign came to be known as the Hundred Hour War.

Where we differed fundamentally in our discussions was in his snap judgment that the Israeli Army had lucked its way through to Suez in record time. He would comment: "They make every possible mistake, they go headlong and should fall flat on their faces, yet with them, due to breaks, it works out all right." I told him I felt he had better go slow on that. Both of us were somewhat conditioned by our experience with our own armies. *Toujours l'audace.* Familiar though the phrase is, few armies really meant it or pointed themselves toward taking the supreme risk from the moment of jumpoff. It could be that for the first time we were looking at an army holding steadfast to the controlling idea that the state's survival was staked on such a doctrine, that its every war had to be a short war.

The infrequent observer does tend to judge by the superficial when seeing for the first time the new thing wholly beyond the scope of his experience. Too often we cleave to our own standards. Many of the correspondents were describing the Israeli Army as a motley, undisciplined crowd. Motley was good enough. Certainly they were tousled, bearded, and disheveled. Their field uniforms were dirty and torn. The sentry was to be seen walking his post, bareheaded, rifle balanced behind his neck, which was wrapped round with a bandana to catch the sweat. He munched an apple or sucked an orange while on duty. If his commander approached the post, the sentry addressed him by his nickname and did not bother to salute.

These were the things that shocked western onlookers. The taboos of the armies that they knew were treated with contempt. The familiar forms by which the state of troops was judged elsewhere were nowhere to be seen; so the trivial was mistaken for the important. In sum, as I got to know this army, it was superbly disciplined and wholly unconventional.

In the field, it could pass muster on every fundamental that combat efficiency required. Troops to the last man believed in the sanctity of an order. Obedience was all. Leaders had to lead, meaning that, from battalion level down, the group commander went first. Rifles and other weapons were inspection-proof clean and in working order. Tanks and other vehicles were repaired on the spot by their handlers with no time lost in hauling them rearward.

Israelis are by nature unconventional. Their army reflects the wholesome practicality of the national character. To have burdened it with some of the spit-and-polish flapdoodle of western forces would have dampened its free spirit and wasted the time of troops. As to discipline, the men who shaped that army had not mistaken the shadow for the substance. In the field the army stays relaxed and wary. On parade, it can look as spoony as any on earth.

I first met Moshe Dayan in the cocktail bar at the Dan. He had to put his glass down before we could shake hands. I said to him: "I just read in *Time* magazine that you are a teetotaler," and he replied, "So I am. I just like to sip martinis until I feel a bit dizzy." One of the great captains of this century, he is not less remarkable for his genius as a force leader and tactician than for a reserve of energy that seems boundless.

Later, in his cubicle of an office at Zahal headquarters, we discussed the wisdom of his dictum that in battle the leader must go first. I objected that the cost was too high, that good leaders were too few. He answered that the Sinai campaign had proved its practicality. When I commented that Israel couldn't always count on winning a war in a hundred hours, the subject was left dangling.

Then we got on another point. I thought it absurd that the other military leaders, by order of the government, were kept anonymous and only the chief of staff got mention in the public prints. The reason for this ban was not so much to mystify the enemy as to prevent them from becoming popular heroes which might tend toward the militarizing of the society. In line with this theory, relatively few Israelis are decorated for battle deeds. I told Dayan that I thought the logic wasn't sound, that these were public men and recognition was part of their reward, and that when official censorship went that far it was onerous and counterproductive. I had no intention of writing a book about the Sinai campaign unless I could identify all of the actors by their right names. That didn't move Dayan. Henriques abided by the rule, got out his quickie, and used pseudonyms all the way through. I stayed with the argument for the next two years until at last the block gave way. *Sinai Victory* and *The Edge of the Sword,* the official history of the 1948 war which I edited in the English version, were the first works in which the military of Israel stand clear in the sunlight, full bodied and rightly named. Prior to that, they were spooks, so many phantoms in the background. Once the barrier went down, it stayed. In the 1967 war Israel did what comes naturally. Generals like Yoffe, Gavish, Sharon, and Tal were given their due. Today when an all-around shift in command occurs within Zahal, the names of the principals make news internationally within a few hours. I believe it is better so. The most effective salesmen for Israel are her military leaders.

Between trips afield, I got calls to lecture, first at the Tel Aviv Economic Club, then at the army's Command and General Staff School. In both instances, my subject was the Israeli Army, wherein lay its power and why it had succeeded so phenomenally in the Sinai campaign. The noon luncheon of the club was a joy. There is first a happy hour for cocktails. Wine is served at the table. At the board the guests first arise and toast the president of Israel and then (in my case) the president of the United States. Then came the surprise switch. Instead of the meal being served, the speaker is called on to do his stuff. Result: No one walks out, and appetite keeps the crowd wide awake. Lovely, lovely. Other clubs might try this formula.

David Ben-Gurion sent for me to discuss the same subject. The old lion has one pronounced affectation. He pretends that he knows nothing of the military art, whereas he thinks like a strategist and argues like a tactician.

He said finally, "You call this army good, and because you say it we will have it thinking that it is super. Now, why do you think it is good?"

"Because it is highly professional. Its thought is concentrated on fighting problems and so is its training time. Get two officers together and they talk shop."

He waggled a finger at me. "Ah, General, you forget that it has a great cause."

I shook him off with these words: "And out of history I can point to any number of armies with a great cause that went down the drain because they didn't know how to fight. As for the rest of it, can you prove to me that it is greatness of cause that makes men great, or is it the other way around?"

Ben-Gurion said: "And you give me riddles?"

As Christmas neared, I had been in Israel six weeks and had completed my field notes on the Sinai campaign. It was time to pack and go home. Some interviewing in detail remained undone among units that had fought at the Mitla Pass. That follow-up was left to the Historical Branch of Zahal. My project, however, was far from finished. My study, as I saw it, would describe the battle results as related to what the Israeli Army sought to instill in soldiers out of doctrine and training method. Time had not permitted research in that direction; so there would have to be another trip. Ironically enough, when *Sinai Victory* was at last published, not even the military reviewers took note that the book had this extra dimension, which, as to most book criticism, is par for the course.

I returned to America believing that Israel should get Gaza permanently, not only because the strip was the natural defensive frontier of Palestine on the southwest and the accession would better insure peace in the neighborhood, but because Egypt, which was only in custodial possession, had grievously debauched a trust. Living in squalor on a dole, most of the residents of the Gaza Strip were stateless people, not permitted to enter Egypt. The world little cared and the change in overlordship was not to be.

When, some weeks later, President Eisenhower went on TV to badger Israel into backing away from Gaza, I carefully watched that face that I knew so well. It showed anger. He was obviously provoked that a small cockerel in the Middle East stayed defiant. It was a person-to-person emotion, none of it returned in kind. Ben-Gurion adored him and thought of him as almost godlike, a human incapable of wrong. He told me so. Eisenhower had been so wondrously kind to him when, as representative of the Jewish Agency, the succor of the helpless in the concentration camps was his preoccupation. Out of this passion—his overweening faith in Eisenhower—Ben-Gurion made his decision, and it almost brought down his government.

Most of a year passed. In September, 1957, I wrote Bentz Tehan that I would be coming over to study training. He replied that Dayan was bound for Ghana and South Africa, but that General Yamit, who was sitting in, was prepared to receive me.

I flew to Israel. Yamit turned me over to Colonel Yoffe, who by this time was G-3, or chief of training and operations for the army. Avraham scratched his great bald head when I said we should get on doctrine and forget about training for the moment. So we settled to a discussion of its principles.

The Israeli Army has shaped its beliefs and principles on the fighting game out of theory, native and imported, capitalizing on the best notions wherever they are to be found. The name Marshall came up now and again, the name of Dayan more so, and there were other names.

Since I have written that a military critic is not an innovator but rather a catalyst who brings to focus the thoughts of his associates, claiming credit is not the purpose at hand. Whatever I had put forth that was useful to the Israeli Army I had learned afield in the army. The Israelis simply gave it more concentrated attention because they stick to the fundamentals better than we do.

Next day, with Colonel Yoffe as guide, we explored the southwest coast of the Dead Sea. When I saw that great battlement, Masada, for the first time, I said: "By its look it must have a monumental history!" and Avraham told me of its glory. Since I was too leg-gone to think of climbing it, we continued on to Ein Gedi, that enchanting oasis where David took refuge when he fled from Saul.

We lunched in a sandy-bottomed blind canyon near Masada. The rock walls, rising eight stories high on three sides of us, looked too sheer for scaling. As Avraham snapped the cap from a bottle of cold beer, ten Bedouins, armed with rifles, came over that rim and descended the wall with the speed and agility of mountain goats. My brisket curled. I thought we were trapped. Yoffe kept eating. The Bedouins joined us for lunch. They were some of his people, agents of the Southern Command. Staging that fake ambush was his idea of a jest on the grand scale.

Big stuff. Thrilling day. Yes, but not as big or thrilling as the yesterday when he told me that some of my work had helped Israel, if only a little.

On returning to the United States, I told the leaders of our General Staff once again that we should pay heed to the Israeli Army. It had much to teach us, more probably than we could give it. I ticked off the technics and policies that we should examine—night firing, snap shooting, the use of Class 4 and 5 material (low IQs) within the military, and the field training of field officers in combat decision-making. The suggestion fell on deaf ears. What we don't know can't be taught; since World War II, our military have fallen into the habit of so believing.

It wasn't until the 1967 war that the Pentagon became truly impressed. By 1968 Fort Benning at last got around to experimenting with new training technics in snap firing that the Israelis had been using for a decade.

Chapter 23
On the Run

As a shavetail in Le Mans commanding at Pontelieu Square in 1919, I thought I was hot stuff because I had three dog robbers, one to tend my uniforms and gear, one to keep the tent clean, and the other because he was good at cribbage.

As an eagle colonel in France in 1944, I managed without an orderly because there was plenty of other work for all hands and I had formed the habit of keeping my own boots clean. As a general officer I went without an aide unless one was forced on me. Too late, I learned this was a mistake. Too late, the most brilliant of all aides fell my way.

He was a reservist lieutenant doing a long tour at the Combat Developments Experimentation Center (CDEC) in Monterey, California, when I was assigned there in 1958 on one of my last calls to duty. My mission was to look the establishment over and report where there was room for improvement.

Never, before meeting this dear fellow, had I been smothered with such doglike devotion. He couldn't do enough, but he always tried. The tenderest expression of his love came on the day when together we flew for San Simeon.

The army had a base there. I was to have lunch with the colonel commanding. He was billeted in that dream castle, the palatial love nest that W. R. Hearst had built for Marion Davies. It is a house of renown of which many lines have been written, none more to the point than Dotty Parker's.

> Upon my honor
> I saw a madonna,
> Reposing within a niche,
> Above the door
> Of the favorite whore
> Of the world's worst son of a bitch.

247

We made it just at noon, and I had not yet had time to see the madonna. The colonel rushed me to the main hall. We sank into chairs much too large for the circus fat lady. Our host made ready three beers. Right then the telephone jangled.

My gallant attendant sprang for the instrument and yelled it out: "These are General Marshall's quarters!"

I said: "Son, you have done it. That's the claim to beat all claiming. You have won the Commendation Ribbon."

The colonel looked at both of us as if we were half squirrelly, and he was no doubt right.

Being both new and understaffed, the Army Experimentation Center limited its scientifically directed research into the problem of operational failure and slippage to faults of a technical kind which can be mechanically measured. Yet most old combat hands are aware that usually, in war, behind the story of a machine failure is some lapse in the human material. The field radio goes silent because its operator is too lazy to climb a tree, the machine gun jams because the gunner saw that the belt was fouled and did not clean it, and so on.

At nearby Camp Roberts Captain Ronald R. Dugas, age thirty, had for two years commanded the Aggressor Force, with frequent changes of all personnel. The researchers paid no attention to what he had learned, though he was a gold mine of reliable information due no less to a unique body of experience than to his searching mind.

Dugas had entered the Army in 1946, served five years in the ranks, and won a battlefield commission in Korea in 1951 after nine months at the front as a sergeant first-class. In his two years at Roberts, he had commanded the 'enemy' in thirty-six full-scale field exercises. No American junior officer had ever dealt as extensively with mock battle problems. The brain of this graduate of the school of hard knocks was loaded with new truth about human inertia in military operations, all of which was lying fallow.

We spent two days together. A tall and angular soldier, he had an engaging youthfulness, and he talked straight out. Here I report the most pertinent portions of the interviewing verbatim.

I asked him: "In this size command how many men can you get to know by name and face within thirty days?"

"Two hundred and thirty is the absolute limit."

"What's your system?"

"As each man joins, I talk to him for twenty minutes, telling my policy and what I expect. Then I let him talk to me—if he will. Only 50 percent of our men will open up—usually to discuss a personal problem. If he does that, his identity stays fixed in my mind. It is twice as hard to remember the man who will not give."

"When new officers arrive, how long does it take them to settle in?"

"If the man makes a good impression on his NCOs it will take seven to ten days before he feels emotionally at ease and can do his work well. The support from below has more to do with his working confidence than anything I may say to build him up. If he fails with the NCOs, I have a new problem."

"Do you regard older NCOs as the backbone of the organization?"

"Certainly not. Many times they stay in too long, and looking to retirement, they begin to dog it or become sly and help their officers not a bit. Here I speak of a minority. In any NCO, the right attitude counts far more than combat experience."

"Once an officer has the feel of the unit in a garrison situation, does this adjustment carry over when the unit moves into the field?"

"To the contrary, if he is an able man, it will take him an additional two weeks before he takes firm hold and becomes supported in his decisions. Or to put it another way, after about two runs on battle problems, he is seasoned and able to handle his people efficiently."

"You say you can get to know more than 200 men in one month. How many can you recognize by voice when you hear a cry in the night?"

"Between fifteen and twenty is the absolute limit. For my average officer it would be less than half that number."

"And if you hear the voice on radio or telephone?"

"Just about the same number. That's what kills us in night operations. Even a squad will fall apart because its own voices are unidentifiable."

"What percentage of your men cannot exercise initiative and will fail to act if put in a position where he must do something on his own?"

"At squad level the count is one in four. It works out that way in company after company. That many, in any emergency, would rather do nothing than try."

"How often do operations miscarry because of radio failure due to laziness on the part of the radioman?"

"In my command, never, because I tell them, 'If we fog out because you failed to get to the high ground or climb a tree, I'll kick your tail till it's blue.' And if I didn't give them that word every morning, they would think I don't mean it. You must hammer it in."

"What then is the most frequent cause of miscarriage in a field exercise?"

"The inability of the average American soldier, officer, or enlisted man, to read a map. That's it, just over 70 percent of the time. Our people come from the public schools with no real feeling for maps. Put in uniform, they actively resist map instruction. The army simply doesn't put its program over. We should zero in on the problem and start all over again."

That is all from Captain Dugas, as intelligent an observer and as wise an officer as I ever met at his level. To his summing-up of the points that we covered, out of my longer experience, I would have little to add and nothing to take away. He stated the case. He could offer nothing more at CDEC and was in the process of being separated from the army for having too little formal education. No comment.

★

One night after returning to Detroit, Cate and I were having martinis before dinner. The telephone rang. It was the Department of Defense calling.

The United States had intervened in the civil strife in Lebanon at the request of its president, the man with the sweetly scented name, Camille Chamoun. Would I go over as a correspondent? The Defense Department, according to Martha Holler, was pressing the invitation. I had only the vaguest idea of the turmoil over there, since when I am on military duty, I do not follow the breaking news.

I said: "Will you hold the phone for two minutes?" and turned to Cate, who was biting an olive. She said: "It's up to you." We talked it over quickly. It was 7 P.M. The navy plane was to fly from Washington the next morning, and I had to be at the Pentagon by 8 A.M. to get my credentials and shots. That wasn't the problem. The last plane from Willow Run for Washington would leave at 9 P.M., and the airport was seventy-five minutes from our home, going all out. Could she pack me with everything I would need for three months and drive me to Willow Run on time? With no hesitation, she replied: "You think of the legal details, I'll pack you and we'll make it." Had she objected, I wouldn't have moved a muscle. Routinely, I called my editor to get his approval, and routinely he called the publisher to get his blessing on my freeloading into a war zone to get hot copy for the *News*. After ten minutes, they had come to a decision. Cate had taken fifteen seconds.

The aircraft was buttoning up as I got to the ramp. Time for one kiss.

Cate said: "I'll say a little prayer."

I said: "You say a damned big one."

At the Pentagon early next morning, I touched base with the army's chief of information, my military boss. The chief said: "We have been trying to get in touch with you. We're calling you to duty for the show in Lebanon."

I told him to forget it. I was going over in a civilian suit. "Tell me what you want done and I can do it better that way. A qualified officer will respond; a goof-off won't work out under any conditions." He agreed.

It was my fifty-eighth birthday. The start was grimly, almost delightfully, forbidding. Having arrived after the 8 P.M. curfew, our party was convoyed to its billets among Beirut's seafront hotels with motorized half-platoons of Lebanese infantry covering us fore and aft, their rifles at ready. The city was deathly quiet except for some small arms fire in the distance.

Streets were barricaded and almost deserted. Sandbag pillboxes covered some of the main intersections. Riflemen, most of them dressed in army uniform and some who looked like partisans belonging to the resistance, loafed at the strongpoints or roamed about on patrol. Main streets were dark and most store fronts were heavily shuttered. To anyone who believed what he saw, we were a band of bold adventurers bent on a course that could be justified only by thinking of how good it would feel when we at last got away from it.

I remember one fragment of action epitomizing the melodrama that was Lebanon in the midsummer of 1958. At the U.S. Embassy in Beirut, where our envoy, Robert McClintock, was trying to play global strategist, the cultural attaché was the novelist, David Garth. He had been a fair-haired boy on my staff in the European Theater. One noon, soon after my arrival, I sat in David's office at the rear of the chancellory. We were gazing at a henhouse in the backyard. From it came a muffled bang, a noise no louder than the backfiring of a Honda. The door flew open and a few feathers wafted onto the breeze. Neither one of us stirred from our chairs for a better look. David, who is not exactly steely nerved, said: "Tsk, tsk, nobody here but us chickens." Next day large headlines announced the bombing of the U.S. Embassy in Beirut. The fleabite of mischief that might have done damage to a cockerel or two is a realistic sample of the terror over Lebanon.

Some capsulizing of the situation and the problem of the time may be in order at this point. Violence had broken out in the port of Tripoli in early July and had spread to Beirut and other points. A national election was coming up. Moslem Lebanon wanted no more of Chamoun, the Maronite Christian. The pretext for revolt was that his policies discriminated against Moslems. The truth was much simpler. The opposition was pro-Nasser. It was aiming for a coup with too little of the organization, nerve, and muscle that the all-out revolt requires. In mid-July, the United States had intervened at Chamoun's request. From the U.S. Sixth Fleet, one battalion of marines was landed at Beirut. When we got there, a backup force, one brigade of the 24th Infantry Division, was arriving by air from Germany. These troops became part of the *mise-en-scène.* Rudely encamped on either side of the city, not allowed to move about on patrol or otherwise, they served by standing and waiting in a most unmilitary posture.

When a correspondent moves in cold on this kind of story, he knows from experience that he must first acquaint himself with the cast of characters, moving from there to plot and atmosphere. In this theater of the absurd, it was all simple enough.

There stood Chamoun, one of the walking dead, politically finished, though he seemed not to realize it. By calling for American help, he had become beached in the same hour as the marine landing force. Nothing could restore him. My lasting impression of this sleekly handsome gentleman from one interview, in which not a smile flickered and his hands shook, is that he was taut with fear and too stubborn to recline easily.

Major General Fuad Shehab, the chief of the army, was making himself the man of the hour. He was so devoted to his soldiers that he was fixed on getting Lebanon saved without having one trooper shot. Already he had added something new to procedure in warfare. When one side felt it was being fired on too heavily or too closely, it got almost instant relief by telephoning the other camp. Shehab's supreme talent, as indexed by his command actions and later confirmed when as president he formed his first cabinet, was a general excellence at screwing things up.

Raschid Karami had started the mischief-making at Tripoli. From the start, Shehab had it in his power to snuff him out and make it appear as an unhappy accident. Shehab obviously feared him. The Moslem was a former premier, possessed of an Iagolike cunning, the main stuff of survival in the Middle East. In October, 1969, through more artful dodging, Karami would at last get most of what he had sought in 1958.

However, from Lebanon that summer, owing to the heavy hand of the censor, one could say nothing about the personalities or political futures of the principals, which meant that the real issues could not be put in the clear. So saying is not to speak ill of those bedeviled individuals. Five men were working over the copy of 277 correspondents, a larger mob than was present at any headquarters in either World War. Never had so many written so much about so little.

By the censors' rules, Shehab could not even be mentioned. Any suggestion that it was religious feuding—the pro-Nasser Moslem crowd striking at politically entrenched Christian power—that kept Lebanon convulsed, was blue penciled. To beat the taboos, I twice flew for Adana, Turkey, and once trusted copy to an airline stewardess who was bound for London.

On the other hand, the government left me free to visit, interview, and publicize, even acclaim, any rebel leader in the country, and if I wished to save time, I could ring him on the telephone and get the information. Face-to-face confrontations promised to be the best policy.

I found it convenient to file my dispatches around four in the afternoon, because at that hour the "rebels" invariably fired at the Beirut post office where the censors did their sterling stuff. Hence at that hour the Lebanese and the press gave the vicinity a wide berth, which made it very accessible. There was no real danger from the firing. The boys with the itchy fingers weren't trying to hit or hurt anybody. They were just banging away with their muskets to build up fear, and they were shooting up telephone poles and cornices at such a rate that the cause seemed likely to run dry of ammo.

Nothing seemed stranger than that the tension superinduced by this Fourth of July kind of noise binge could be causing distant tremors in Manhattan or Dubuque. There was no way to classify it. Over an NBC-TV broadcast, John Mecklin of Time, Inc., spoke of it as "politics with arms," John Chancellor called it "battle without bloodshed," and my term was a "sectarian shoot-up." The gunfire crescendoed each night after dark fell. Since no dead bodies manifested themselves dew-covered at dawn, we took it that the shooters were aiming at the Big Dipper, which didn't get hit, either. One couldn't even fall asleep and dream he was at war. The nights were too filled with music, due to the happy crowd of correspondents whooping it up under the stars on the St. George Terrace.

Ah, those feature bits for sidebars, the human interest angle, the personal adventure hair-raiser—such is the grist that keeps a correspondent making deadlines when the theme of what really makes a world crisis begins to wear thin. There was a surfeit of such tangential material in Lebanon, thanks to a resistance that sparkled as many colors as the Kohinoor. Each rebel chief was doing his thing, which may be how that silly expression got started.

The story of my Sunday afternoon with Saeb Salam can now be told. He was the kingfish of all resistors within Beirut, master of a stronghold inside the gates, a challenger close enough to Chamoun's palace that he could have been seen therefrom thumbing his nose without the aid of a spyglass.

An Australian newsman from one of the London bureaus went with me. We could both have been pie-eyed and still have found the place. Any street Arab we stopped and asked was ready to lead on, and if there were no corner signs reading, "This Way to Rebel Headquarters," it was because his PIO had overlooked a trick. The inner redoubt was guarded for several blocks around by Salam's retainers, who wore civies sagging from crossed bandoliers and carried rifles that might possibly have fired despite the grime.

The final block of the approach was protected by two tank traps out in the street and two wire barricades. Neither tank trap could have ditched anything more determined than a wheelbarrow, and the wire barrier might have been sprung with a good yank of one hand. Two armored personnel carriers (APC) might have moved down this road any day and cleaned out the whole nest without ever buttoning up; yet this was the resistance that kept Beirut divided, thereby agitating the affairs of nations.

Salam's citadel worked out as a conventional Arab home on a city street high in the Basta, the hilly section where most Beirut Moslems live. The walls of the central room where the chief held court may have existed, but we couldn't see them because of billowing drapes all around. Other tapestries sagged from the ceiling. At least one picket squad of Salam's armed warriors was formed in a square around the room, backed up against the draperies. It was more power than we had seen enroute to his war room.

As for the big man himself, he sat on an ottoman, spitting out words at the rate of a Gatling gun. Three other correspondents sat there trying to insert a question edgewise. There wasn't a chance. This loquaciously charming and phrase-coining Moslem, then fifty-five years old, looked about as dangerous as a rug dealer. Still, we were looking at a former prime minister who may have known many things, but not how to stop his own chatter.

There the Australian had him one up. Salam got barely started avowing the purity of his aim, his love of liberty, his devotion to the interests of all Lebanese, Moslems and Maronites alike. The Aussie broke in. "I hear you, and I don't believe one damned word you say. You're just a pro-Nasser son of a bitch."

Up came every weapon in the place, and we were instantly covered, the rifles seeming less fearsome than the square of fourteen glaring faces. There was utter silence, the tableau lasting for maybe thirty seconds. That digger brought me to the edge of a nervous breakdown.

Then he laughed and Salam joined in, and the rifles were lowered. Salam passed off the insult with some small sally, and the incident was over. My friend said: "I think we better get out of here." I was sorry to leave—for all of twenty seconds. There is never any telling what an Australian will do next.

A larger mystery than Salam lay far across the highlands. We heard talk of him in the lobby at the St. George—"Kemal Jumblatt, the unreconstructable Druse, the fiercest leader of them all." As the press described him, it was enough to make the hair curl.

Jumblatt was holed up in a remote medieval castle high among the crenelated buttes and waterfalls of the Chouf Hills fifty miles or so to the east of Sidon, where he was decently removed from the news of the world and the turmoil of the capital.

Riding an ancient cab in the hands of a redoubtable Armenian named George, Bill Lawrence of the *New York Times* and I took off one morning to call on this paladin. That journey proved one of the most rewarding experiences of my tour. There is no grander scenery anywhere. It is a countryside of deep gorges, cascades that tumble from the highest of artesian springs, terraced saddles and draws scalloped with rock retention walls to stop erosion, and much spaciousness between the rimrock-crowned ledges.

Where there is water, the mountainsides are green with peach, fig, and pear orchards. The main road is one car wide and mostly unpaved. It hangs dizzily on the side of a cliff and twists through such pleasantly named villages as Homesie and Jazzine.

Enroute to Jumblatt we were stopped and checked ten times at what euphemistically might be termed roadblocks. Each consisted of a solitary rifleman clad in work clothes and turban. Conspicuous were the dum-dum bullets in their crossed bandoliers and the antiquity of their weapons, usually a single shot Mauser or a Krag-Jorgensen. The men were uniformly courteous, smiling and eager to shake hands and accept a cigaret. When I asked to inspect their rifles, they handed them over as if I were doing them an honor. This gentle guerrilla touch was as unique as the appearance of peddlers who bike over these same loop-the-loop roads selling popsicles to Arab small fry in the villages.

We came at last to a blown-out stone bridge. One narrow strip of it, a rock-and-mortar girder not more than two feet wide, still spanned the gorge. The drop-off was about fifty feet. George and his cab could go no farther. On the far side one of Jumblatt's shuttle jeeps was waiting. We crossed over and rode the last dozen miles through the highland orchards to the family castle at the place called Moukhtarah.

A many-storied, Moorish-style building, it stands high among the surrounding lindens and cedars, but its Druse defenders were so poorly armed that a modern rifle squad could have been dropped by helicopter on the bald dome directly to the rear of the castle and taken it within an hour. The Druses had not bothered to outpost the hill. High overhead we could hear American military jets orbiting. Quickly and happily the guards escorted us inside the castle.

The portal gave way to a spacious hall. Painted on the four walls was a great mural of the battle of Lepanto, but what caught and held the eye was an oil painting placed incongruously on one wall so that it partly hid the mural. It was a large portrait of Lassic, no less. Lassie, just outside the war room of the fiercest of the Druse? It didn't seem quite fittin'. Lawrence gave a great snort. But Lassie belonged there, sure enough.

Soon enough we were with Jumblatt, literally face to face with the man in the gray flannel suit. The tailoring was perfect, the white shirt and black crepe tie completing the ensemble. The contrast between this Sorbonne-educated lawyer and his rabble following was nearly absolute. Jumblatt had then just turned forty. Tall and thin almost to the point of emaciation, he was otherwise normal in appearance. His face had the same hooded look about the eyes as Charles de Gaulle's. His voice was quietly modulated, and he spoke without gestures. He was definitely not a fighter, and I doubt that he had ever touched a grenade or machine gun.

While we talked, a lantern-jawed woman of over fifty roamed up and down the room muttering, "How dare they say these things about the Druse? We love everybody. Jesus Christ is our prophet. So is Mohammed. We see good in all things. We don't take sides," over and over like a cracked record. Jumblatt let her ramble. Maybe she was a maiden aunt or an apparition.

That day the fiercest of the Druse, after describing himself as a socialist-pacifist Vedic philosopher, had us almost believing that he was in fact a starry-eyed idealist launched on a Love Everybody Crusade. His list of wants would have stopped Hercules.

He ticked them off—amnesty for everyone, compensation for every casualty and all war damage, constitutional reform so that the people would elect their president, two socialist members in the cabinet, secret ballot reapportionment according to population distribution, selection of judges through the elective process, institution of civil service, and the "purification" of everything in government.

"Above all," he said, "I request, I demand, the immediate withdrawal of American forces."

I demurred. "Such things take time. The election has not been held. Expeditions like this one cannot be lifted out overnight."

"I think I'm a reasonable man. Everything takes time. My program takes time. But I will resist until I get what I want."

When Lawrence and I left him, we still didn't have his number. It took time to reveal that the do-gooder, the holdout reformer, was humbug, a cheap political wheeler dealer and a knavish power seeker. As I write these words, the fiercest Druse is Lebanon's foreign minister, and a few months back he was a party to the deal that sold short the position of the Maronite Christians and gave Nasser another cheap political victory.

Major General Paul D. Adams, USA, another old friend, had arrived to take overall command of the Americans ashore. After my reconnoitering of a rebel camp, I visited with him and his staff to brief them on what I had learned. This was the only time I ever served as first scout for the army. Due to the presence of one first-class army PIO, Lieutenant Colonel Chet Bennett, my other semiofficial task, that of getting some press attention for the paratroop brigade camped in the Choueifat olive grove, became a buggy ride. Together, we worked up a plan, I drew a list of topics that might lure the correspondents, and Chet went to work. Thereafter I continued to scout the rebel territory and report to Adams.

The election was held and went to its seemingly foregone conclusion, with General Shehab overwhelming his opponent, Ramon Edde. Shehab's election, while easing the strain in Lebanon, diverted attention to Jordan. The Middle East watchers were writing that King Hussein, due to a fatal blunder, had only to shake his head to see that his crown was gone. Alarmed at the tremor in Jordan, the little king had called in three thousand paratroopers from Britain to steady the throne. The watchers reasoned that, once the British flew home, Hussein would go out like a light. It seemed a possibility, though Hussein had already survived more death notices than an alley tom.

Israel had to be the best listening post from which to get a sense of whether Jordan was about to pop. It had to be, if only for the reason that I wanted to see my friends in that army once more. There was one other thing: repeated experience had taught me that Zahal intelligence had the pulse beat of the Middle East, whereas western agents did not.

I cabled Bentz Tehan and Avraham Yoffe that I was coming and what subject I would be scouting. They met me at Lod airport and ran me to the hotel. They said something big would be cooking at Tehan's home that evening, and other members of the General Staff would be there, news that whetted my anticipation. I could foresee a full-dress briefing, an estimate of situation, capabilities, intentions, and all the rest of it.

When I got to Bentz's that evening, all of the wives were present, but there were no maps or charts. Bentz flipped on the radio, saying, "You made it just in time. The last round in the Bible question contest is coming on. One finalist is a crippled boy. He's just wonderful. We're all pulling for him. Everyone in Israel is listening."

Bang went the crisis over Jordan. I realized that I was wild-goose hunting. If the Israeli General Staff was concentrating on a Bible contest, then Jordan couldn't be on the verge, and Hussein was not about to take the drop. The Middle East watchers were simply doing some wild guessing. My friends in Israel knew the reality. Next morning I cabled my paper that the Jordan scare was a dud.

From Tel Aviv I booked for home on a KLM plane that would hit Munich and Amsterdam and then hop the Atlantic. Enroute I changed my mind and decided to drop off at Munich to brief our high command at Heidelberg on what I had picked up in Lebanon and Israel. That KLM plane disappeared somewhere over the Atlantic, and the cause of the tragedy remained a mystery thereafter. Cate was given some unnecessary hours of terrible anxiety.

The best days of my life, the rewarding years, rather than the sunset quarter, came of my marriage to Cate. Now seen in retrospect, all the rest of it was a schooling, a kind of prep course for meeting her and falling in with her direction of a household and of me, though she never seemed to lead, such is her magic. This is not to say that our marriage has been a glide. We have known our season of heartbreak, and we have steadied one another.

I have always found it difficult to write of things personal; yet there is no other way to explain oneself or account for one's fortune. The profile takes shape out of the space others grant us. Good and bad, what I am as a person is as much of their making as of mine. If that sounds too simple, I still believe it. Too much has been written of ideals, principles, goals. I am what I am thanks largely to other hands, hearts, and spirits. Fail to speak of what they have done for me, or to me, and there would be nothing left worth recording.

Here I am reminded that, when I was on General Mark W. Clark's staff briefly in the summer of 1951, I wrote a nonconcurrence to a staff paper written by another colonel. It outraged him. He said: "In your objection you have made this a personal issue."

I replied: "You're damned right I have, and if you think there is such a thing as a General Staff process floating about on its own and not influenced by one's humanity, you're out of your mind."

In April, 1961, Cate and I went to Israel, my fourth such visit, her second. The assignment was to cover the Adolf Eichmann trial. We expected to be gone the better part of two months. As usual, our girls waved us off. "Good-bye Mama, good-bye Daddy, have a good time."

I will not write of the Eichmann tribunal. Ten days of listening to the testimony, and I began to part at the seams.

I spent my last afternoon in Jerusalem at UN headquarters on the Mount of Evil Council, an enclave within Jordan territory. There on the east portico, facing the Dead Sea and the River Jordan—as marvelous a sweep of country as is to be seen from any elevation on earth—I sat drinking beer and shooting the breeze with U.S. Marine Corps Colonel Robert W. Rickert, who was deputy to Major General Carl C. Van Horn.

The date was April 18, 1961. While we talked, a secretary came to the portico and handed the marine a teletyped dispatch. He studied it, then tossed it my way. It described the invasion of Cuba by a small amphibious expedition at a place called the Bay of Pigs. The story said that Fidel Castro and the Soviets were openly charging that the strike was backed by the government in Washington.

"Bound to be a mistake there," said the colonel. "Nobody in the United States would be that crazy."

"You're right," I agreed, "nobody, absolutely nobody."

We were at that moment blind optimists, and we should have known better, having seen enough of government by that time.

After a trip to the Congo to report on the civil war for the Senate Foreign Relations Committee, I returned home. That was an uneasy summer for me. Far from bringing any assurance that the administration in Washington, having learned a lesson from its military misadventuring in April, felt properly chastened, the season was heavy with signs that government was preparing to embark on a no less dubious undertaking. There were stirrings afresh about the Communist threat over Indochina and what we further might do to abate it in Vietnam. The president was reacting, too quickly and in just the wrong way, to his chagrin over the Bay of Pigs failure and the rawhiding that Nikita Khrushchev had given him at Vienna. When Mr. Kennedy had talked in March on national TV about the problem in Laos, his oversimplifications were so gross that he lost me. That early, it had seemed plain enough that his administration, though not half organized, was proceeding as if all world problems were subject to the ultimate control of its little group of serious thinkers.

The gloomy assailing doubt, not eased by the Bay of Pigs, intensified when in September, 1961, Defense Secretary McNamara made a speech in

Chicago. His theme was that our military at last had the machines and the know-how to beat down Communist guerrillas. He added that the United States would continue to support South Vietnam until it was done. To my ear, his pronouncement had too much the ring of Montrose's boast that he "nailed his flag to the mast to win or lose it all." I knew that we had nothing decisively different to throw at the Viet Cong. Here was error compounded—a gratuitous commitment that placed in jeopardy the national prestige, a commitment that was based on a tactical assumption that was false. Still, I was a sideliner and not a prime witness to the lack of cohesion in high places.

The secretary was never one of my private enthusiasms. I saw him as a man of brilliant analytical mind, too often lacking in common sense. When his name was first mentioned for public office, I did my limited best to oppose his takeover of the Pentagon and backed Paul Nitze for the top job out of respect for Nitze's unassuming steadiness. I hold unbridled, domineering civilian control of the military to be as grave a menace to our form of society as blatant militarism. The flaw in the McNamara makeup is that he can leave nothing alone and must change, according to his own theories, whatever he touches. That sort of arrogance in high places withers the initiative and chills the spirit of people down the line. Furthermore, McNamara's voice, more than any other in our time, contributed to public mistrust of the military.

Whimsically enough, it was disagreement with my bosses on the subject of McNamara's qualifications that brought about my quitting the *Detroit News* just a few months after his Chicago speech, well before my normal retirement time. His judgment on such a complex problem as Vietnam was hardly deserving of trust by the president or the public, his experience being too narrow, his ambition too great. There are always nets and pits in the foreground to which genius stays blind. The remarkable thing is that, in the hour when we made that fateful turning, there was no hint of the unrelenting, frenzied opposition that came later. Not one respected voice was raised in protest.

Leaving the *News* proved to be the most felicitous decision that anyone else had ever made for me. Thereafter I didn't lift a finger to get the action to come to me. Washington was again doing a double check on American troop behavior in the Korean POW camps and the related question of whether the armed forces had established effective safeguards against a repetition of that dismal performance.

The Special Preparedness Subcommittee of the Senate had going a full-dress inquiry chaired by Senator John Stennis of Mississippi. In the Pentagon, a special commission set up by the secretary of defense, headed by former Undersecretary of the Army Karl L. Bendetsen, was holding hearings on much the same subject.

I was summoned as a witness by both panels. The reason for the call from the Senate was that I would be preceded to the stand by an army psychiatrist whose exaggerated and almost hysterical views of what the Korean record signified had been given national circulation by the John Birch Society and other right-wing groups. A Washington-based group of scientists had prevailed on the subcommittee to call on me to refute him.

During his day on the stand, the psychiatrist proved to be a genius at embellishment, invariably to excess. Then I had my full day, which started promisingly with some hectoring from Senator Strom Thurmond, who had mistakenly assumed that the army had put me on to defend its position. He got off that right quickly.

Wholly different in substance and personal consequence was my appearance before the Bendetsen Commission. Though I couldn't have guessed it, that morning marked the beginning of the long, long trail that wound through the next six years.

A marine colonel, John N. McLaughlin, had preceded me as a witness. Made prisoner by the Chinese during the ambushing of Task Force Drysdale south of the Chosan reservoir on November 29, 1950, McLaughlin had acquitted himself with utmost honor and valor throughout his confinement. He talked to the panel for an hour, and his statement of his experience, like his analysis of the problem, was beyond fault.

When my turn came, I explained that McLaughlin had so clearly stated the views I held in general that for me to dwell on the same subject would waste the panel's time. I added that I would therefore like to put before the panel my views of command responsibility, with some allusions to the special requirements imposed by stress-filled situations, but talking mostly of the standard that must be upheld by the U.S. military.

As I concluded my remarks, Allen Dulles, whom I had not known, leaned across the corner of the table to talk earnestly to Bendetsen. There was a brief recess. Then Bendetsen spoke. "Slam, in a few days we are leaving by special plane to visit and inspect all main military commands in the Pacific, and we will be going as far as Vietnam. We will be checking on indoctrination, code of conduct training, and that sort of thing. We think you ought to go along."

Such was the simple and unpremeditated beginning of my connection with the war in Vietnam. This would, in one way or another, extend over six years and would ultimately result in three tours overseas and the writing of six books and one field manual. To say that I would have gotten into it in any case would be nonsensical. It is an idle exercise to speculate about what might have happened had that which happened not happened.

We were gone for a month. It was too little time. One must settle down for at least that long in any one command to get a real feel of the situation. On this junket, we just scampered and scampered, as if we had set forth to collect random impressions with a butterfly net.

Theodore "Ted" Braun, a big man in the public relations field and another member of the Bendetsen panel, joined us at Los Angeles. We flew to Oahu, bound for Midway, Hongkong and Manila enroute to Saigon. We had two nights at sea aboard the carrier U.S.S. *Hancock* and found that among the crew, as with the forces at Subic Bay, Manila, and Oahu, the navy, as well as the marine corps, was sloughing off code of conduct training, using worthless materials, going through the motions and that was about all. The neglect of that time was never corrected, and an excessive price was to be paid for it six years later by the crew of the U.S.S. *Pueblo.*

Whose fault? We four horsemen had been sent forth at taxpayer expense to study this very problem, among others, and to report to high authority what we found wrong. We did that emphatically, and at least Bendetsen and I had the right kind of professional experience that what we said in warning should have been respected. We did not fail our mission, yet the mission was a failure because those who should have listened would not act. When on our way home we reported to Admiral Felt, CINCPAC, on the conditions in his command which we felt were adverse to morale and the well-being of the services, he rudely shook off Bendetsen, saying that he could not be held responsible for slackness and paltering way down the line.

The neglect of code of conduct training, however, was not the only black spot. In Vietnam, at Nha Trang, Da Nang, and elsewhere, we dealt with U.S. Army service units that had been ashore for almost a month and still had been told nothing about the country to which they had been shipped. Of the military situation in their neighborhood and the enemy threat to their personal safety, they knew mainly that they were not to go more than one-half mile beyond the limits of the built-up area except under armed escort. Worse still, prior to leaving home and on their voyage across the Pacific, they had not been advised of their destination, and when they made shore they still did not know that they were in Vietnam. They knew nothing about the Vietnamese and were making no contacts with them. Having been failed completely, these troops were sadly demoralized; yet at the American Embassy in Saigon, at the same time, every visitor from the States was being given a booklet packed with information about the country.

Before bucketing up and down Vietnam in whatever air carrier chanced to be available, our mission perforce touched all official bases in Saigon and went the full course of briefings, parties, and receptions.

The capital in 1962 was still beautiful, remarkably clean for an Asiatic metropolis, and deceptively tranquil. It was also uncrowded. The one touch of grimness was the garrison points spotted around the city. The Vietnamese units were so heavily wired, sandbagged, and bunkered in that one wondered how they could ever deploy outward. The young women of Saigon made one swiftly forget that ugliness. A beauty parade on cycles, they thronged the city center in their exquisitely draped, gorgeously colored costumes. Nowhere before had I seen such loveliness; yet within three years all of that was gone. Downtown Saigon had become foul, reeking with the press of humanity, and the women had become drab.

We were briefed on the problem and the new tactics by General Paul D. Harkins and his staff. The Vietcong were making themselves very scarce, holding tight to their bases in the jungle, wood copses, and thickets. Finding them was a greater difficulty than routing them out of their nests. Once a fix became fairly certain, an Army of Vietnam (ARVN) unit could be chopper-lifted to an approach path within less than an hour. Those old choppers, American-crewed and as yet unarmed, could carry about sixteen men. Four birds setting down at one time (and seldom was there open space for more than that) could launch two platoons in the attack. One more such serial would make it a full company.

"It's this swift-strike mobility that gives us the advantage of surprise," said the briefing officer.

It sounded good but in fact was too simple to be true.

I said to Harkins: "Paul, it can work fairly well just for a short time. Then, once they get the pattern, they will counter by making themselves obvious. That's when we become suckers for a left hook. They'll ambush the hell out of us."

Harkins said in his usual heavy way: "I know, I know, but maybe we can beat that game for a little while."

The words made it clear enough that we didn't really have any new magic. We were just kidding ourselves about it.

We were staying at the Hotel Caravelle, which exists but to serve mankind and gouge it of the last possible piaster. It is the clip joint par excellence, and no one ever beats the rap there. One evening about fifteen American correspondents (most of whom I had known before in other parts of the globe) and I gathered in the cocktail bar.

That was just about the whole crowd in Saigon at the time, and without exception they had turned sour. They felt bitter toward the army because it would not haul them about as it had done in Korea and elsewhere. Another grievance was that the army would not play footsie with the press on matters that the Diem Government asked be kept confidential. Toward Diem and his whole retinue, the attitude was detestation mounting to hatred.

Diem had crawled back into his shell. Little news was forthcoming from his government, interviews were shut out, rumors were neither confirmed nor denied. This blackout, the consequence of Diem's almost paranoid fear of the press, outraged the newsmen. That evening, as they grabbed my ear with their troubles, they were also exchanging ideas about how to continue the slanderous attack against Diem and Madam Nhu.

I said finally, "Sure, you can bring down a government that way if you try hard enough. But what will you get in its place?"

One of them said brightly: "Old Uncle Ho."

"I guess that's supposed to be a joke, son, but that's exactly what you're bidding for."

I sensed with foreboding the shape of things to come. Our press was becoming hostile to the national undertaking, and unless this could be changed, the odds were against any favorable outcome.

That day Allen Dulles and I flew for Kontum in an ancient crate that rattled in every joint. At Kontum we were for two days guests of Lieutenant Colonel A. J. "Tony" Tencza, the senior U.S. adviser and a former Screaming Eagle. A very gallant fighter, Tony had accompanied his ARVN charges on every combat run. He said to me: "You know, in the field the advisory role is just a polite fiction. Either I participate directly, or they feel I'm letting them down." Yet he had nothing but praise for the average Vietnamese soldier.

We spent one morning together flying directly over the jungle top in a chopper so that I could get some of the feel of the country. A few weeks later Tony and his chopper were shot down while engaging in that same exercise. He was the first American officer to be killed in combat in Vietnam, and it now seems so terribly long ago.

On our return flight to the United States, we detoured via Taipei to look over U.S. forces on the island and to talk with the generalissimo. Chiang Kai-shek was in good form that morning. He has long fascinated me. He has the most luminous face that I have ever seen. Even in repose his features glow as if a gentle light burns within. Dulles and Bendetsen were also in good form. They rattled on at a great rate about their impressions of Vietnam.

Suddenly the generalissimo stopped them in full flight. He said (through the interpreter): "General, I want to know your views."

Thus bidden, I aired my doubts about what we were doing, my feeling that our policymakers were oversimplifying a complex problem, and my skepticism about making the gradual approach to a limited war, whether conventional or irregular.

Chiang saw it the same way. He believed that the Communists would never be beaten if the fighting was confined to the south. He said he would never put any troops there. "Should the United States really go at Hanoi, then I would commit all available forces," he concluded. The implication was that, if the United States did so, Red China would join the war, and that would leave Chiang little or no choice.

Chiang and his government had worked miracles on Taiwan since my extended stay on that island in the spring of 1955. Taipei had become the cleanest capital in the orient, and the other cities, by this time tied together with a modern highway system, all had the well-scrubbed look. The tokens of progress were apparent everywhere, and Taiwan's general air of prosperity was good to see.

When our party stopped off in Honolulu, I attended a luau given by veterans of the 442nd Combat Team, the great Nisei fighting outfit, which I had seen start on its way in 1943. The men were looking to their forthcoming twentieth anniversary and they asked me to invite Eleanor Roosevelt in their name to be their main speaker and guest of honor. When I wrote her, she replied gently that she would have loved to meet with the Japanese Americans but was certain she would never leave her hospital bed. This may have been the first notice to any outsider that she was dying.

For the Pentagon wastebaskets, I wrote a very negative report about our prospects in Vietnam. My main points in objection were tactical—that the bases we were already occupying were not even half secure and therefore would ultimately compromise our advisory position. Bendetsen also wrote a negative report, more on strategic than tactical grounds. My main doubts I also talked over at length with General Lemnitzer and General George Decker, army chief of staff, emphasizing that the hostility of the press corps, while a definite danger, was subject to an in-house correction, if steps were taken immediately. The military chiefs could do nothing about this. Secretary McNamara's office was solely accountable for relations between the press and the U.S. high command in Saigon.

My objections on strategic grounds to the way we were proceeding in Vietnam were stated in two articles, "The Big River," which appeared in *The New Leader* on May 28, 1962, and "An Exposed Flank in South Vietnam," which ran in *The Reporter* on June 7, 1962. The one disagreed with Mr. McNamara for saying that we had achieved adequate force goals in South Vietnam, the other with Attorney General Robert Kennedy for saying, "We will win in South Vietnam." The thrust of the two pieces was that, with the Pathet Lao holding southeast Laos, and with Cambodia a pliable tool of the Communists, trying to mop up the Vietcong in the South with limited forces was akin to stopping a freshet with a dike of sand. It would bring on an inundation from North Vietnam via the two countries to the west. Time and events confirmed this view.

It does one no good to be a doubting dove in an hour of national cheerleading. The hawks of that time were Bobby Kennedy, Sorensen, and Schlesinger, who supported the President's every doing, and Goodwin and the other retainers who wrote books and speeches in praise and in prophecy. But who remembers that now? Who remembers when they changed coats and started blaming the evils of Vietnam on us rampant militarists? The titanically ambitious are not the only great mischief-makers on earth; couple with them the fakers and the second-guessers who cling to their coattails.

Having no mania for commitment, I had no expectation or wish that summer that my first-hand connections with the war in Vietnam would extend beyond that one relatively brief experience.

My last ties with the army were about to be cut, and it seemed fully time. I had been formally retired on August 1, 1960. What a day that had been! *Newsweek* wrote of it: "A ceremony unlike that ever given one of his rank, least of all a civilian soldier." My service had gone the whole distance. Reception in the secretary's office and the pinning of another decoration. After that, a formal luncheon with all the secretaries and the chief of staff and his deputies present. At retreat, an eleven-gun salute and a formal review of the 3rd Infantry Regiment at Fort Meyers with Secretary Brucker reading my retirement orders, as Lyman Lemnitzer stood next him. Who would not prize most those honors that come of the devotion of a few faithful friends?

Thereafter, for two years, the army kept me on a string. I would be called to duty at once if there was a general mobilization. On July 31, 1962, that extension ran out, and I was placed on the retired list, a half year after quitting newspaper work.

When I mothballed my field suits, I was certain it was for the last time, and that was all right with me. On the tour in Vietnam I had been meeting myself as a more than middle-aged man jolly well feeling old, and while I wasn't as crippled as Allen Dulles, it wasn't comforting to hear myself creaking in every joint as I tried to hop in and out of whirlybirds. Also, the long ocean hops on the Pacific run had proved more wearing than in earlier years, and I found myself yearning more plaintively for the feel of earth.

My next move to foreign parts came in February, 1963. It began with a telephone call to my home from President Luis Somoza. Nicaragua was about to stage a national election. Somoza wished to have present at least one newsman from the United States with Latin American experience who would write a fair report on whether the Nicaraguan election was open or rigged. My old friend, Dr. Jose Guerrero, no admirer of the Somozas, had recommended me. If I accepted, I would be given carte blanche to move and do as I pleased and could challenge anything that smelled of irregularity.

I jumped at the chance to see Nicaragua again for the first time since the Sandino Revolution and enjoy a holiday in the sun with all expenses paid. On my arrival at Managua's Grand Hotel in midafternoon of the following day, February 2, to my surprise I found the presidential limousine waiting, and I was promptly bucketed off to the palace.

Luis Somoza was seated in his office with his brother, General Tacho Somoza, then commander of the National Guard, now the chief of state, which mantle is the ultimate family heirloom. The presidency was being loaned on this occasion to a Somoza henchman and stand-in, a dentist, Dr. Schick.

Luis didn't want to talk about the election. He began: "General, I should have let you rest, but I must get something off my mind. It's the Bay of Pigs. I am as guilty of that terrible blunder as is your president. I should have stopped it when I knew it was headed for the rocks. I had the power and the position, but I chickened out. My brother wasn't here to steady me, and I couldn't nerve myself to make the decision."

I said: "I didn't know you had any hand in it." Since he acted like a penitent confessing for the record, I made notes on what he said through an interview lasting over an hour. It seemed at that time an interesting but idle exercise that would lead to little or nothing.

Next morning the only shoot-out of the election—a duel with no blood drawn—took place just under my bay window at the Grand. The fireworks came from the opposition candidate, one Dr. Arguello, a rather silly fellow who handled a pistol as if praying for someone else to relieve him of it. A friendly traffic cop quickly obliged without doing Arguello the honor of escorting him to the jug.

After that flying start, the election proved a big letdown—no bang-bang, no rough stuff at the polls, no visible herding of voters in the main cities that I toured, Managua, Granada, and León, which was all that time allowed. Because Dr. Guerrero was an anti-Somoza "conservador," I took him along as my adjutant. For three days we followed through on the locking of the boxes, their impounding under guard, and the counting of the ballots. Sure, we could have been fooled, but we found nothing to boggle about.

That is not how the story was written by the sixty-and-odd correspondents who had descended on Managua just to cover the election. Some few held to the line, reporting only what they saw or could verify. The majority had been sent forth to hang it on the Somozas, smear the show, and make the dictatorship monstrous. As there was no censoring of the cable at Managua, the dreamed-up pieces about ubiquitous violence and sham election all cleared for home. It made surefire copy, and much of it could be lifted from the columns of the Nicaraguan dailies that were opposed to the Somozas. They were no less free to run cock-and-bull wild as the visitors who covered the national scene without deploying from the Grand cocktail bar.

By the time of my return to Washington, the word had reached the Central Intelligence Agency via one grapevine or another that I had dealt at some length with the two Somozas and they had talked freely about their roles in the Bay of Pigs fiasco. As one absurdity among many, General Somoza had bailed out for Formosa just prior to the event, playing the red herring in a fantasy that the CIA regarded as a "cover plan."

Two CIA agents came calling at my brother's home. They had a proposition: Anything I wished to know about the Bay of Pigs that they could tell me would be traded for such information as I could give them about the attitude of the Somozas toward the United States and particularly the CIA. Were they hostile because of the letdown or would they still cooperate? One might suppose that almost two years later the CIA would long since have divined the answer to a fairly simple question. It was not so. We batted the ball back and forth for about two hours, and though their statements were closely guarded, most of what I told them was reassuring. From them I did learn, however, that to placate the Somozas the United States had given to Nicaragua $16 million in military equipment that was left at Puerto Cabezas when the Cuban venture failed.

Dick Bissell, who had in effect commanded the operation for the CIA and been its most ardent advocate in the decision-making council, was by this time head of the Institute of Defense Analysis. On hearing that his old shop had bent my ear, he sent for me so that we could exchange views on where the planning had been faulty and why the show had flopped so dismally.

With the notebook filling, I went to Admiral Arleigh Burke, who was no longer in government service. He had declined an ambassadorship offered by President Kennedy. Arleigh could only vaguely remember the Bay of Pigs situation, having tried successfully to forget a nightmare. That was not his only difficulty; he had no memoranda. At the final session of the panel appointed to probe the debacle, Attorney General Bobby Kennedy had asked Burke and Allen Dulles to bring all of their notes to the table so that all source data could be double-checked before the report was given to the president. They tabled the memoranda and the president's brother pocketed them with a "thank you" and made his exit, which was the last the gentlemen saw of their papers.

Still, Burke talked as frankly about the detached Jack Horner role of the Joint Chiefs as of his personal trials of soul. The thickening sheaf of notes had become the makings of a book; so I signed a contract with Praeger and Company and was given a tidy advance. Then, after the assassination of President Kennedy, I nixed the contract and returned the money.

Still, the question of how a government could go so far wrong continued to fascinate me. Through the years that followed I extended the interviewing of the principals. Not until 1970, and following his retirement as supreme commander in Europe, did I again broach the subject with General Lemnitzer. Once we had explored it fully, there followed long conversations with General Maxwell D. Taylor, who as chairman of the investigative panel had retained his notes, and with Dean Rusk, whose memory is prodigious. It was startling to discover that at such a late date the former secretary of state and the president's inquisitor remained uninformed about the deep involvement of Nicaragua and the Somozas.

Rusk said: "We will not know the truth until the Kennedy papers are made public in 1990."

I asked: "May we expect it then when the papers are likely to be self-serving?"

Taylor's generally admirable memoir, *Swords and Plowshares,* freshly published as I write, does not come clean on this subject. By implication it shifts the load of blame to the wrong quarter.

From these and other sources comes the body of information which I plan to shape into a critique of an unparalleled governmental fumble. It will not be a book about the shambles on the Zapata beach but simply an assessment of where responsibility rested, how it became possible for so many distinguished men to fail the country so miserably, and how insiders such as Arthur M. Schlesinger, Jr. and Ted Sorensen wrote "true" stories that were lamentably misleading as to the hand of the Eisenhower administration and the Joint Chiefs of Staff in the sorry affair.

Even the name—Bay of Pigs—is wrong. It is not even a correct dictionary translation of Bahia de Coquina. The coquina is a small fish common in those waters. It might better have been called the Bay of Small Fry, though it was one whale of a blunder.

Chapter 24
The Trail to Vietnam

My direct involvement in the war in Vietnam should have begun in early 1964 and would have begun then but for the egoism of the one man who was most to blame for the blundering course of the United States in Southeast Asia, Defense Secretary Robert S. McNamara.

In March, 1964, as McNamara was making his victory forecast, I got a phone call from the Institute for Defense Analysis (IDA) informing me that the Advanced Research Project Agency (ARPA) wanted me to go to Vietnam under IDA's auspices to develop a data basis on combat operations. That means, in essence, studying the fighting problems afield, learning as fully as possible the pattern and rhythm of enemy tactics, and determining the requirements of defensive security. It is done by working with line troops, cramming notebooks with information about what they have experienced in battle, and then sorting out the common denominators. I had spent twenty years at this game, and no other American had worked at it very much. The mission would take a minimum of six months.

Cate was willing that I go. I replied to IDA that I would be prepared to leave within thirty days, provided that I could choose my own team, and provided, further, that I was permitted to write direct to the main commanders in the Pacific to get personal assurance that I would have their backing and that they believed the mission to be necessary. To both of these conditions, IDA readily agreed. I had also pointed out that a main requirement would be direct access to the Army of South Vietnam, since Americans over there had seen very little combat.

For the team, I picked Jim Henry, a scientist with whom I had worked in Korea, mainly because he was already on the staff at IDA. The third man was Dr. John Westover, my military assistant during World War II, by this time a professor at Western Illinois University. John, willing enough, had to take a year's leave from the campus job.

As to the letters of inquiry, Admiral Felt, CINCPAC, replied from Oahu that he wanted me to come on, and would I please stop off in Honolulu to discuss the problem with his staff. General Paul D. Harkins replied that he wasn't sure what could be accomplished, but there was no better way to find out. From Major General Charles Timmes came the clincher. My old friend of Normandy days was the chief adviser to the ARVN. He said he had talked the project over with government officials and with the chiefs of the army. I was wanted and would be given total cooperation. With that assurance in hand, there was no room for doubt that we could succeed with the mission. The army chief of staff, his vice-chief and Lieutenant General Bill Dick, the chief of Research and Development, told me in personal conversations that they would support the team all the way.

We went full speed ahead, bought our field kit and clothing, took our physicals and immunization shots, got our visas, and packed our bags. For me, that month of preparation was costly enough. It necessitated the cancellation of four lecture engagements, one book contract, and two scheduled magazine pieces.

Just forty-eight hours before the team was to rendezvous in San Francisco there came a wire from ARPA: "Higher authority directs you hold for thirty days during determination of whether mission is necessary." Inasmuch as ARPA had initiated the project, and the military chiefs at all levels had cleared and approved, the implications of that hold order were ummistakable. This was Mr. McNamara striking back.

I replied to the wire: "The mission is off. Will not hold for even one day being aware the block comes from Secretary Defense Office."

ARPA wanted to know what the crank-up had cost me. I replied that my losses were of such a character that the military could not possibly compensate for them, though I would have to insist that Westover be given employment for the period covered by his leave from the university. In the end, ARPA insisted that I take payment not only for the out-of-pocket expenses but for the cancelled lectures and magazine pieces. The Pentagon paid high not to send me to Vietnam; so Mr. McNamara also took his bite out of the taxpayer.

Because I landed right side up without bruises, I was the better off for all that had happened. The big man continued publicly to berate the army for not tabulating its field experience when he had sabotaged an enterprise to that end.

However, early in May, 1966, two letters arriving in the same mail popped me over to Vietnam anyway. The first, from John Fisher, editor of *Harper's Magazine,* was an offer for four pieces about the fighting in Vietnam, and there was more than enough to cover expenses. The other was a mad letter from Harry Kinnard, the only one he ever sent me. Two weekly news magazines had implied that one of his brigades had been ambushed during the fighting around Plei Me and, taking their word for it, I had done a column on the theme. "You should know better," Harry chided, "and I want you to come and see how the Cav Div operates."

I settled in with the First Cavalry Division at Camp Radcliff just as the command was being shifted from Kinnard to Major General Jack Norton, another boon companion from Normandy days, and like Harry, a soldier no more gallant than gentle. Kinnard would stay on for several weeks, temporarily commanding the II Corps area with headquarters at Nha Trang. I joined him there, and we flew together, with Harry at the stick of the light plane. Two gunships fly cover for any such gad-about enterprise by flag officers in Vietnam.

On a Saturday we were back in Nha Trang making a parting inspection of the corps' main installations. We came at last to a warehouse area overseen by a colonel I had known years before in the horse cavalry. He led us to the goodies. Here was a galvanized iron structure, without air-conditioning, roomy enough to enclose an LST, stacked with cartons that towered twenty feet above us. The piles were uneven and obviously sagging. The temperature in that building was about 90 degrees. We were looking at a small mountain of candy bars shipped to Vietnam to boost the morale of troops, and all of it was chocolate.

The boxes were dripping. The air was sickeningly sweet with the smell of chocolate.

I asked: "Colonel, what in hell is this all about? That's enough chocolate to last the population of Chicago a year, and troops don't want chocolate in these latitudes in summer."

"I can't tell you. We don't know. I have tried for six months to turn it off. Nothing happens. Every ship entering the harbor brings more chocolate. Let me show you. I now have two hundred tons stacked outside directly under the sun."

He showed me. We ruminated.

I said: "But this thing is dangerous to life and limb. I wouldn't dare move through your warehouse. Some of those piles are about to collapse."

I said to Harry: "It may be the way to end all war. Just make it sound silly. Dream up a headline, 'Hero Killed by Avalanche of Mars Bars.' "

Kinnard grunted. The colonel wasn't laughing. He led us to a stack of small cartons no larger than my writing desk. "You see this? It's what the Congress was raising hell about two months ago and for which Secretary McNamara apologized. We are stockpiling hairspray for the army in Vietnam. That was the beef. Terrible. Terrible. Well, we do have nurses and Red Cross girls over here, you know, and they're entitled to some attention."

The colonel was leaving the next day for return to the United States and retirement from the army. He said he was damned glad of it. He was fed up with Mr. McNamara's computerized logistics. I disagreed with him. I was just fed up with the man.

From that point on, my first hot weather tour in South Vietnam as a correspondent was little different from what would have occurred had I been with the army in the Central Highlands as a field historian with rank. I was in uniform, wearing my star and supplied with a jeep and driver or with a Huey chopper and crew as needed. There was no restriction on my freedom of movement. I could go anywhere that I thought best at the time I chose; Jack Norton or someone else would arrange it.

On any such mission, when I want to get the feel of a war, I have always adhered to one rule: I do all of my field work with one outfit for a minimum of thirty days. It takes me that long to get my ducks in line or work out my own data plane. There are new weapons to be evaluated, new tactics to be studied, and usually, a new vocabulary to be learned. Each new field army loves its own argot above all else.

Once I have done the basic thirty days, I can shift scenery as often as I please, hopping from base to base as the action develops.

I spent the first two days reconning the near countryside in a Huey piloted by General Jack Wright. Within the next six weeks, hardly bothering to stir about unless called, I had three major battles drop into my lap and one classic limited engagement. The battles were in Vinh Thanh Valley (called Operation Crazy Horse), Toumorong (called Hawthorne II), and Trung Luong (called Operation Nathan Hale). The model engagement was Colonel Hank Emerson's attack on North Vietnamese fortifications at Ben Gia Map. These engagements in the Central Highlands were the highlights of the campaigning in South Vietnam through that summer. I had come at just the right time.

All that happened on these fields that I could make known has been written about in some of my other books, such as *Ambush* and *The Fields of Bamboo*. Most of what happened to me personally during the fighting has also been reported, though I have omitted a few details, such as the time I fell into a pongi stake pit off the air strip near Tan Cann and escaped unhurt. The stakes had been there long, had partly rotted away, and they simply tumbled over.

Save for Charley Black of Columbus, Georgia, Operation Crazy Horse was ignored by the press. A gang from Saigon came up to Toumorong for one day and spent several days at Dong Tre during the Trung Luong battle. Our army in Vietnam at that time had no system for recording what happened during battle.

I flew into all parts of the rugged and largely jungle-clad countryside that I wrote about in my books while the heat was on to do my sketching and to develop the scenario. Charley Black frequently went along with me. I make this clear only because, for all of the years since *Island Victory* was written, I have been amused by the reviewers who describe how I draw the tired warriors around me after battle and solicit their stories, as if I had done my work from a swivel chair. Common sense should tell them it would not be possible.

Throughout the Vietnam fighting the common blunder among our line fighters was falling for ambush—getting sucked in. I started right at that time to describe and classify the various lures and ruses used by the Vietcong in springing their traps. Oddly, it had not been done before.

The larger fault I found in First Cavalry operations was that G-2 had not brought along a terrain and location file. Trails, Vietcong bases, landing zones, and other pivotal points in our brushes with the enemy were not being mapped, sketched, or photographed for future reference, though in the nature of irregular warfare we would be fighting over this same ground time and again. Curious about how anything that important could be overlooked, I checked it out. Early in the game Kinnard had directed his G-2 section to initiate the process. Then someone slipped up, and Kinnard had not later raised the question. I discovered that the void was there only when I asked for graphics on the going operations. Finding there were none, I went after my own to shape up a model for the archive, doing the sketching and directing the air photography that would give us coverage of the kind needed.

Once again, while a civilian, I was working de facto as a soldier. The 1st Brigade of the 101st Division, under General Will Pearson, had its main base at Dak To in the far west of the Central Highlands. Due to my prior service, I was as much at home there as when serving with the Cav. For the rest of my tour I moved mainly between Norton's and Pearson's forces, according to where the heavy action developed. The shuttle to and fro was always by Huey, and it was over that route, flying usually at around 1,500 feet, that I first began to marvel at the beauty of Vietnam and the abundance of running streams threading fertile valleys that had never known cultivation.

Out of the sixty-seven hours that I spent flying in Hueys on that first tour, more than half were burned away hopping to forward landing zones either next to an infantry perimeter or adjoining an artillery base, the greater number of which were secured only by gunners playing riflemen. Some of the flights had the object of contacting a patrol at some point where there was good observation all around. Every move made was for the purpose of collecting more data while memories were fresh. The average critique afield lasted about two hours. The nasty part was that the Chinooks, coming in with cargo, or taking off with casualties, kept burying us under the dust storm.

There was always the chance that we would get hit while holding these formations, though it happened only once. Toward the end of the Toumorong battle, I needed to talk to Dave Hackworth and his staff to get a few points pinned down. Dave's command post was spotted deep in jungle and had been there only three hours. The day was hellishly hot even after the rain came in early morning, and the jungle fairly steamed. On setting up his new stand, Dave had had a detachment of engineers hack out a landing zone (LZ) immediately—just a funnel sunk into the two-canopied bush so that a Huey could corkscrew down to the duff- and boulder-strewn hillside.

There hadn't been time for anyone to measure the LZ, much less name it, when my ship popped through the cloud bank above the ridge next door. From atop the slope on which the LZ was located, a heavy machine gun cut loose on us. The burst whistled well overhead, and within two seconds we had dropped below the gun's line of sight. But we knew Charlie was there before the friendlies below us sensed it, the pounding of the Huey having drowned out the chatter of the gun. The rude clearing had been cut too tight, and the pilot had to hover just a few feet above ground while I jumped off. Then he was to lift and get away, leaving me there, rather than taking a chance on getting shot up.

In those few fleeting seconds, the hillside crackled and boomed like a full-drawn battlefield. I thought Charlie had closed in to give me welcome. Then I saw what was happening. The chopper's rotor blade was shearing off bamboo stalks and mahogany saplings all around the clearing. Some of those bamboos were three to four inches thick. They snapped off with the explosive sound of a 37 mm gun. The mahogany made more of a crump. There wasn't much time to think on that or to marvel that the rotor blade could take it. The slashed and jagged-edged shafts of bamboo were whizzing about that LZ like so many spears.

The ship was up and away. Dave Hackworth came rushing to greet me, the usual boyish grin on his face. "Oh, Sir," he said, and that expression, when Hack uses it, has the soothing effect of a mother calming her infant. Before we could settle to work, there came a new rattle, again as close as the next second. This time it was for real. A group of North Vietnamese skirmishers had closed in on us; the firing came from the higher ground. In the next thirty minutes, before the incident closed, there were seven dead Charlies on the hill, against two Americans so slightly wounded that they wouldn't leave the hill. Hack and I worked on for another hour. Then it began pouring rain so hard I knew that to continue would wash out all of my notes. I folded the book and we had coffee. The Huey returned to lift me out just before dark fell. I was as surprised as I was overjoyed that the pilot was able to find the funnel again. Though there were other incidents in moving about, no ship that I rode during my first tour was struck by a bullet or anything else, and I never again flew with a pilot who used his Huey to chop wood.

Dave's battalion had been the first to enter the battle. In fact, that campaign had pretty much evolved out of a meeting in the sky between Dave and me and a twenty-minute conversation on top of Toumorong Mountain one Sunday afternoon, as is explained in *Battles in the Monsoon*. Through two quite different lines of reasoning, we had both concluded that the enemy was present in great strength somewhere close by, though a prolonged sweep by several battalions had failed to flush him. Of those hunches came brutal, bloody, and bizarre combat. When three criss-crossing B-52 strikes put the crusher on NVA resistance, Dave's was the last battalion to leave the battle zone. General Will Pearson and I reviewed them as they marched into Dak To, bearded, sweated-through, overburdened, and filthy, but still heads up. One hour later, after they had bathed, shaved, and donned fresh uniforms, every sign of fatigue had miraculously vanished from them.

Vietnam was different in that respect from other wars. Men didn't seem to age from the strain of combat. The hollows under the eyes, the drawn lines in the cheek, the look of utter weariness, and the shambling gait were somehow missing. I often pondered why. Many of my friends who had campaigned in Europe and Korea also noted the difference and credited it to the one-year tour. This I doubted, since to the average fighter, a commitment of even that length to the hazards of the field seems like infinity. I believe the explanation of the difference was much more subtle. Unlike Korea and the world wars, Vietnam was not monotonous. The problem, like the scene, changed from day to day. After every hard trial of the unit in threshing out the boonies, there would follow a shift of more relaxed and reasonably good living in the base camp. Like a small homecoming, this halfway house on the road to normalcy afforded an uplift to the spirit.

For another thing, division and brigade commanders worked closer to their men and were more concerned about morale building. One evening I sat with Jack Norton and his chief of staff, Colonel George Beatty, Jr., talking about a small logistical problem. Norton thought it would give his soldiers a real fillip if he could arrange to get two cans of beer to his fighters soon after they broke contact at the close of campaign. Instead of holding the beer in base camp, he would have it in readiness at the LZ as they emerged from the jungle or bush.

"The real problem," he said, "is the icing, first getting the ice here, then making sure that the can is practically frosted when they drink."

"Before you're too certain of that," I said, "you better poll your people to see how many of them want beer." He did. The poll showed that 37 percent would like beer; the great majority preferred coke or soda pop after a fight. Funny army.

Pearson, Norton, Kinnard and the others tried as hard with the natives as with their own soldiers. They were generals with a regard for humanity and a commitment to values far removed from the miserable job of killing people. Pearson worked as a missionary among the Montagnards toward elevating their status, helping them with health programs, and teaching them sanitation. At An Khe, Jack Wright organized ten Boy Scout troops from among the village waifs, paying for their uniforms and kit from his own pocket and the contributions of the Cav soldiers. It cost $6.37 to set up each Scout. Wright made it a rule that the Montagnard kids would get equal treatment with the Vietnamese youngsters.

The scope of problems taken on by the Cavalry Division having nothing to do with fighting was almost without limit. Ever since the ambushing of French Mobile Unit 100 in 1954 some seven miles westward of An Khe, that village had been a hamlet of about 2,500 persons, disease-ridden, near starvation, and directly under the heel of the Vietcong. Then, in the fall of 1965, First Cav moved in, chopped down the jungle that spread from the edge of the village to cover nearby Hon Kon Mountain, and constructed a barricade, eighteen kilometers in circumference, to enclose the division camp, the mountain, and the U.S. Air Force runways. The Cav's presence made the valley secure. Within six months what had been a village of 2,500 became a city of nearly 18,000 that daily grew larger. Yet the people of the community were not capable of organizing and energizing the institutional and economic requirements of such a community. The district chief was willing to try but couldn't get the requisite financial backing from the Saigon government.

The Cav took on the task by default, and because one thing led to another, a young captain-surgeon who had interned at Tulane moved into An Khe and stayed there unguarded, first treating the sick, later initiating immunization programs that would extend the length of the valley. Pretty much on his own, being a man of courage, he blazed the trail. Other soldiers had to follow. Doc won the support of the whole division because he was voluntarily taking great risks unattended.

Empirically, Norton and his people proceeded with the task of city-building. Each hamlet was given a course in how to make itself productive and self-sustaining. Furniture repair, laundering, souvenir making and vending, green vegetable raising, along with barbering, food and drink dispensing, and tailoring were activities that fitted easily into the pattern of helping the community to help itself. The division and its individuals became its best customers. The chicken-raising hamlets could proceed on their own. More complex was the problem given the one hamlet that had a monopoly for providing pork. The division built the feeding pens, but Vietnamese pigs lacked quality; so the division brought in breeding stock from the United States.

The intrepid medico's aid station at center of An Khe was expanded to a hospital, built on the basic structure of what had been a morgue during the Japanese occupation in World War II. I talked to the builder of its two wings, an army medical corps sergeant who had been a carpenter's helper in his youth and had had to teach six other corpsmen carpentry before construction could begin. A public library had been started; its few hardcover books, all in French or Vietnamese, were from the nineteenth century. The third institution, set up in town center with the help of the division, was an orphan asylum, the young inmates of which were kept tending vegetable gardens and rice paddies.

So far I have rather roughly described what community help the division provided in its first eight months before I came to An Khe. My attention was drawn that way on a Saturday morning in late May when, with Jack Norton and the province chief, I attended the ceremonial opening of the first public school ever built in the valley. The Cav band provided the music and the Boy Scout troops formed for inspection. The school was a solid structure of four rooms, rock walled with a red tile roof, complete with blackboards, chairs, and desks. There were no doors or window panes. Still, in that climate, the building could accommodate 200 students nicely, and the total cost had been $3,700. More than 700 An Khe children of grade school age would remain shut out.

While the band played, I asked Norton, "Where's the money coming from?"

"From my troops," he replied, "and we put no pressure on them. A pail is put up in each mess with a sign on it. A buck here and a buck there keeps these projects going."

I heard that with mixed feelings, glad that our soldiers cared that much, annoyed that other Americans cared so little about them. Here the same young fellows who were taking the risks of the war were paying out to help the Vietnamese solve their basic problems.

My last several days in Vietnam were spent with Bill Westmoreland so that we might talk things over. The man who was chief during the most trying years of the war inevitably became the main target of every critic who would try to shift the burden of blame to the military. The fact is that the war was run from the White House; the president and his coterie shaped its strategy. Though as a tactician Westmoreland was not without fault, I remind myself that the perfect field general has yet to be born. Westy was steady as a rock in his job, ever concerned for the welfare of his troops. In an unpopular war he managed to keep spirit in an army that was nigh abandoned and too often vilified by its people. This is generalship.

At Westmoreland's request, I spent my last morning going over a psywar operation with the four top men in his General Staff section. From what I had observed afield, psywar was consistently missing fire at the point where its work should have been most effective. During that conference I learned why. The top man was a dunderhead, outblimping Blimp. He reminded me of the story of the gent who sprinkled talcum powder on his lawn.

A neighbor asks, "Why are you doing that?"

"To keep away sabertooth tigers."

"There hasn't been a sabertooth around since the ice age."

"That's my point; it works."

All this Blimp could talk about was the millions of leaflets he sprinkled around over the countryside every week. He had no apparatus far forward with troops to bring about surrenders when the enemy force became beaten and scattered. When I pointed this out, and his three assistants supported what I said, he simply blew a fuse. He had yet to visit any fighting zone.

Hardly had I reached home when letters began coming from Norton and Pearson urging me to return. Jack did better than that; he wrote Cate to the same effect—that I was needed to carry on my kind of field work and give it a future. I was well aware that the gap was there. The army had no system for collecting and collating combat data other than the raw statistics on body and weapons count, heavy weapons expenditure, and so forth. Hence, there could be no meaningful tactical analysis. There were no specialists in this work, and if it was to be a continuing thing, the officers would have to be trained. My answer had to be yes. First, however, I had to write my book *Battles in the Monsoon* and do the pieces for *Harper's*. That gave me a busy autumn.

I had already talked over the problem with the army chief of staff, General Harold K. Johnson. He felt I should go back. I asked him not to put me on orders lest the secretary's office interfere once again. Getting to Vietnam and back would be my private business. Once there, my schedule and my right of way as a serving officer would be arranged through back-channel communications. One general can get on the phone to another general anywhere in the world and set up what is in the overall interests of the army.

Dave Hackworth had meanwhile finished his combat tour in Vietnam and taken over a desk in the Pentagon, where he was miserably unhappy. On hearing that I was taking on the mission, he volunteered to go along as my exec. It was the ideal arrangement, immediately approved by General Johnson. Dave knew me, the army, the country, the pattern of tactics, and the nature of the work, besides having a first-class writing talent. When we teamed, smooth sailing and success became assured. Hackworth would do the managing, deciding what operations we would cover, setting up the schooling sessions, and taking care of transportation and communications. We would base on An Khe instead of Saigon, that is, make Norton's headquarters our message center and storage depot as we moved about from one zone of operations to another. For me, the tour promised to be pie and ice cream.

Chapter 25
Hiawatha Hardison and Other Tales

Major General Bill Depuy had a problem on his hands. Three of his soldiers wouldn't talk, and the best efforts of the commander of the Big Red One and of his staff couldn't get them to open up.

A few days earlier there had occurred an ambush of a rifle platoon while on patrol, a particularly tragic and messy affair out of which only three men survived, one white 2nd lieutenant of artillery who had been the forward observer, and two black enlisted men.

The lieutenant and one of the blacks had not resisted interrogation. They pleaded that they could remember nothing. It was different with the other black. Put under charges for some minor offense not connected with the fight, he was outright hostile and uncooperative.

Depuy thought I might be able to work them over and establish what had happened to the patrol. As I was then conducting a training course for eight combat historians at headquarters of the 1st Infantry Division in Di An, it looked like a worthwhile experiment.

Such were the circumstances that led to my meeting Private First Class Hiawatha Hardison, the recalcitrant black, along with Lieutenant Alfred G. Carter and Private First Class Eugene Hicks, the two survivors who claimed they had lost their memories due to shock. The date was December 18, 1966, one week after the ambush, and the place was the commanding general's mess shack. The three men sat there saying nothing. Their eyes were dead, their features expressionless.

The stirring of recollection in such cases almost invariably requires gentle handling, and because I reckoned that Hardison must be the key figure, I opted for the indirect approach. Hardison had expected me to address the officer first. Instead, for the first thirty minutes, I ignored Carter and Hicks and talked to Hardison about his home town, Winston Salem, the conditions of his boyhood, what his parents were like, and why he had enlisted in the army. He began to unfold like a morning glory. When at last

279

he told me on his own that he had an illegitimate son, age three, and that his mother was caring for the child with money that he sent home, I knew that he would go with me all the way. Carter and Hicks had listened but were acting a bit restive.

At that point I switched to questioning about activities within the company on the day before the ambush, but again, for the first five minutes I talked to Hardison only. Then, because I wanted confirmation of some detail Hardison had brought up, still staying with the day before the fight, I began to question first Carter, then Hicks.

Thereafter, stage by stage, I brought them along to assembly, the movements of the patrol on the trail, their personal experiences during the approach, their hopes and their fears. We went right from there into the movement across the clearing where they had been trapped, and all that happened after the scene exploded around them.

It is as terrible a story of infantry slaughter as I have ever put together. The one redeeming feature is the incredible courage of a few men, including these three, in a starkly hopeless situation. How it happened, and what came of it, is fully reported in my book, *Ambush*. Later, I got in a chopper and flew low over the clearing and the trail approach so that I might sketch the scene adequately.

Carter and Hicks, the two who claimed to have lost their memories, were as articulate as Hardison. Their descriptions of what they had experienced and what they had seen were painfully graphic and replete with shocking detail. Otherwise, no connected narrative would have taken shape. One witness, be he ever so observant, cannot account for the destruction of a platoon. Three, if they were rightly placed, may do so.

How then explain the phenomenal recovery of memory by Carter and Hicks? Elementary. They had not lost it. Their studied but futile effort to forget had become a mental block that, unless broken, would do them more harm than good. They needed the emotional release for its purging effect. Once they were maneuvered into a conversation that denied them any convenient cutoff point, they had to talk things out to the finish. They had not been faking it with their general. To them, the hiatus was real enough until someone proved to the contrary.

Our concern here, however, is with Hiawatha Hardison rather than with seat-of-the-pants psychology. Though he was a rough, tough, and habitually surly soldier whose expression shifted seldom from scowl to smile with nothing in between, I liked him very much. He had been of tremendous help to me, and of the three survivors, he had fought most valorously.

For three years I lost track of him. Then in early December, 1969, I received a letter from Hiawatha which he had addressed to "General S. L. A. Marshall, New York City," which by some miracle was rerouted correctly. The return address was Drawer A79, Fort Leavenworth. That signalled that he was doing time in the disciplinary barracks* for some military offense. His message was a simple request that I send his parents in Winston Salem a copy of *Ambush* so that they would know he had done his duty in combat. He said nothing about being in prison or why.

One week later, after I had sent the book, I heard from his mother. She had read about how her "baby boy" had performed in battle. Would I help him? His application for parole was coming up in January. Right after her letter came one from Hiawatha. He had been given three years and a dishonorable discharge by a court-martial at Fort Hood for committing assault when ordered to do duty in Chicago in restraint of race riots. He said he had done violence to no one, that he had fired a gas grenade in the air without injury to any other person, and that for so doing, he had been crowned royally with a billy club and had spent three weeks in hospital, the only casualty out of the incident. As to the truth of his statements, I cannot vouch.

I had already written to the people at Leavenworth, telling them what I knew of Hardison, his experience in combat, and his obvious desire to re-establish his credit in the military. It had impressed me that Hardison had a sense of honor and some feeling for the country or he would not have wanted his folks to know that he had done well under pressure. The people at Leavenworth were most responsive. They said he had been a good prisoner, and they welcomed my support for him, but consideration of his application for parole would be under the secretary of the army, Stanley Resor, and I should deal directly with him.

Though I know Secretary Resor, from knowledge of the army I try to save executive time by going the most direct route, though one may become too cute about this. I wrote his military executive officer, stating the problem and why I was interested, and my wish that he would afford guidance to the appropriate channels. I reiterated my faith in Hardison as a man and as an American soldier and my feeling that if there is a chance to save a person, it is worth taking.

About February 8, 1970, I received a reply from a lawyer, the general counsel of the Army, whose name I have forgotten because, like Carter and Hicks, I would rather obliterate that which is obnoxious. I was told that he had reviewed the Fort Hood case and saw no reason to change the sentence. I had not even raised such a question: the counsel had proved himself totally unresponsive.

Four days later, there came a second letter from an assistant secretary, bless him. He had read what I said and the general counsel's recommendation. He went with me. Hiawatha would be paroled almost at once and given a general discharge.

---

*Army name for penitentiary.

So, suddenly the day brightens. Something has happened for good, the heart leaps up, and you say to hell with earthly cares. That evening as Cate and I sat having our martinis, the drink seemed to have an extra tang. We discussed whether I should wire or phone Hardison the good news, or at least talk to the PMG captain with whom I had corresponded. Otherwise, something might slip.

I reread the letter, which had reached me on February 13. It said that the secretary had reached a firm decision on February 11 and that the prisoner would be notified "in due course." I decided there must be some reason for all of this red tape, and so I did nothing.

On the morning of February 18 I flew to Washington to hear a special report on the prospects for the volunteer army. As I passed Bill Westmoreland's office, one of his aides called me in, handed me a wiregram addressed to the chief of staff and said, "Sir, please read it, your name is in it." It reported the death of a military prisoner. My friend, Hiawatha, had hanged himself in his cell with his own shoelaces the night before. The wire said that prior psychiatric examination had indicated there was nothing wrong with him except a short temper and a tendency to be moody. Pending report on the parole, the prison authorities had put him in a separate cell to protect him from molestation by homosexuals. Maybe he had taken that special confinement as a sign that all hope was gone.

Oh, yes, Hiawatha was buried with full military honors. A white-gloved escort took his body back to Winston Salem. Relatives and friends turned out. The bugler blew taps, the firing squad did its stuff, his mother was given the flag. There was no choice in this matter. He had been restored to grace, and his sins had been washed away six days before he died. To all of that, well, *merde!*

Another story of Cock Robin. Who killed Hardison? Not I, say the bungling bureaucrats who failed to notify Leavenworth. Not I, say the careless guards who made the wrong move and left him in ignorance with his boot laces handy. Not I, say I, who took too much for granted. The truth is we are all guilty and the blood of this poor man is on us.

★

Christmas overseas in time of war has never been for me a day for cheerless reflection. I have known six such Christmases, a fair number for an amateur soldier. Lucky the man who has a solid bank of precious memories of home to draw on when the holidays come round. Even in the salt mines of danger and duty they lift the spirit and ease the grind.

For no reason that I can explain, however, our troops in Vietnam in 1966 faced Christmas with lighter hearts than any army with which I had served in earlier years. The prospect of a holiday truce that everyone knew the enemy would break at will had nothing to do with it. At the field bases, decorations were up in the messhalls ten days before Christmas Eve. At LZ Hammond, the Cav's forward base just off the China Sea, there was one small Christmas tree contrived of plastic with one twist of tinsel and a few colored balls. Troops queued up to have their pictures snapped alongside this forlorn little object.

Hackworth and I passed Christmas at Di An, the main base of the 1st Infantry Division, which was about a fifteen-minute chopper ride out of Saigon. We kept our operation mobile. If a patrol got into a fight while we were in session, we mounted up in Hueys, flew to the scene of engagement, and interviewed the men on the ground.

With the start of the truce, people seemed to feel a bit edgier. As we settled to the game of liar's dice that invariably followed dinner in Depuy's mess, he told me the word had come through that the Vietcong would stage an attack somewhere in the division area at 2100. I wished him Happy Christmas Eve.

He said: "If they hit, I'll be heading that way, naturally. Would you like to come along?"

I said: "At 2100 or any time of night, count me in."

I had already tabbed Bill as one of the overly brave, something of a spurred bantam, and so I wanted to see more of him in action.

Nothing happened that night.

Next morning at 1100 the Bob Hope show played to a roaring crowd of Depuy's soldiers under a broiling sun. That was a Christmas feast lovely beyond description. We went for a laugh and a tear, and we came away charged with a wonderful fire.

The show over, we gathered in the general's mess with Hope and his principals for cocktails, prior to the turkey and trimmings. I stood talking to Phyllis Diller and another old friend, General Rosie O'Donnell, and I hadn't yet touched my drink.

Right then Depuy exploded into the scene, grabbed for his steel pot, and said, "They've shot up one of my patrols." He headed for the door.

I legged after him, yelling, "You said we'd go together."

His TOC chopper was not more than 200 feet from the door. Within five minutes we were over the ambush site, a wet rice paddy not more than 2,000 meters from where that tremendous crowd had been gathered a few minutes before.

A rifle platoon, which had been outguarding the assembly, had headed straight across that paddy trusting to the truce. A Vietcong mortar squad, covered by a machine gun, lay concealed by the far dike. When the Americans were halfway into the paddy, the gun opened fire and caught them square on. Stretched out below us in muck were seven dead and three wounded. Two soldiers were missing. For the next ten minutes we orbited a hundred or so feet above them until the medevac ship arrived, landed, and made off with the casualties.

Depuy meanwhile ordered two rifle companies and one battery of 105s up to the crossroads nearest the ambush site. By the time we landed among them the two missing soldiers had rejoined the patrol.

The infantrymen and gunners were all jammed together in the angles formed by the two dirt roads. From the ambush site, a spread of brush stretched to within one hundred meters of the intersection. Looking at that fat target, I worried about mortars and told Depuy so.

Bill answered: "There won't be any. They've cleared away by now."

I asked: "Then why call up the troops, if there's nothing to hunt?"

Depuy grunted. Still, he had the measure of it. In war, certain things have to be done, though they make little sense. Had Depuy not reacted, his troops, like his guests of the day, would have rated him a dull, unthinking commander. Even so, the arid reality of the situation made that afternoon wholly frustrating. We marked time at the intersection until sunset. When we made camp again, the Hope troupe had been gone for hours. The turkey was cold, the ice cream melted. Nothing really tasted good.

When I next talked to Depuy several days later, he was in a temper. General Jack Seamon, the commander at III Corps, had suddenly pre-empted all of the Big Red One's choppers without explaining why, which kept Bill's troops pretty much grounded. Two days later the Hueys were returned. Depuy still didn't know the reason for the move. That night I got it direct from Seamon. Corps had needed the choppers to put on a little show of its own, an operation of such a sensitive nature that Seamon decided to keep it as secret as possible.

First, an ARVN soldier who had escaped from a Vietcong prison camp had told this story: A large number of American POWs were being held in a base camp right next to the Cambodian border beyond War Zone C. He gave an exact fix on the location and said the place was heavily guarded. Within twenty-four hours an NVA deserter turned himself in at a Special Forces outpost and told the same story, embellished with a description of some of the prisoners.

Seamon swung into action at once, borrowing Depuy's choppers so that he could mount up a battalion. The run was made in beautifully clear weather, and the choppers touched down exactly on the spot given. There wasn't a sign any American had ever been there. There was no prison camp. There was abundant overgrowth but not a sign of human habitation within miles. That left Seamon feeling like the man who watched the mystery show on TV and figured out everything but the commercial.

At the beginning of the new year, I was back with Jack Norton. One morning, I heard him talking in low tones to his chief of staff, Colonel Wolff, about an operation of some sort that was to be launched soon after dark. I paid little attention until I caught the word "prisoners" and then I asked: "What's it all about?"

Norton said: "We have a fix on a group of about thirty of our POWs held by the Vietcong this side of the Soui Ca. We know the spot. The first information came to us from an ARVN who had just escaped from the same camp."

"And I guess that was followed up by a North Vietnamese deserter confirming the story and adding more details."

"That's just the way it happened. Funny thing. He told of a Negro sergeant being there, one of our guys, a quite fat man, wears a Cav patch. But we haven't lost any such soldier. Who told you about the NVA deserter?"

"No one. I just took a shot in the dark. Now, what are you going to do about it?"

"We're lifting out one company from the First Brigade to liberate the group."

"Jack, don't do it. Either send a battalion, or send nothing. If you send a battalion, you will probably get nothing. Send a company, and you'll get it ambushed and chewed to pieces. This is just one more of Charlie's cute tricks."

Having until then talked in riddles, I told them all about Jack Seamon's high hopes and mystifications of just four days before. Norton had heard nothing of that incident. Now, hearing the tale and noting that the scenarios were identical, he realized it could not be coincidence. He took my advice.

His choice was to send forth a battalion, and again, the operation was all waste motion. No prisoners were found, there was not a sign of a camp, and the battalion was neither engaged nor fired upon. Was it Charlie trying to give us the razzle-dazzle and run our legs off? Or was it Charlie baiting an ambush large enough to take on a rifle company, but too small to risk the engaging of a battalion? I would still like to know.

Whereas our field work brought me few surprises, since I had done the same kind of thing so many times before, the tour was for Hackworth a journey into disillusion ending in cynicism. Even as a battalion commander in Vietnam, he had had an almost childlike faith in the soundness and accuracy of the reports system. As he traveled from base to base with me, I was holding to the same SOPs that I had found useful in other wars.

On the operation under study, I would first get a debriefing from the division commander and his staff. This was done orally. I would do the questioning and write the report in full. We would then do the same at brigade and battalion. Last, we would get down to the troops who had fought the battle, and from them we would learn what really had happened. It was a terrible shock to Hackworth to discover that the stories from these several levels had little in common, that the division's story was only vaguely related to the reality, and that the average general's ideas of what had happened to his men in battle were almost invariably painfully distorted. The misinformation was not the consequence of deliberate self-deception or the desire to put the best possible face on things, and it was not a condition peculiar to the war in Vietnam. The same thing happens every time. It happens because too little solid information moves rearward from the combat field, higher commands try to fill in the bare spots, and their guesses much of the time are on the wild side. Ironically, the reality is almost always more dramatic, more sensational, than the scenario contrived by some scribbler from the staff for the enlightenment of visiting VIPs.

On pioneering this line of field work in the Central Pacific in 1943, I at first fretted about the repetitive pattern of my combat narratives. Each action, as I reconstructed it, seemed to have almost perfect dramatic form or story structure, the prolonged build up of suspense, the crashing climax, the brief anticlimax. The question that fretted me was whether I was letting my sense of story take charge and was shifting emphasis to heighten effect. It seemed unlikely, since for the most part I was following verbatim the continuity in my note books.

Then gradually I came to realize that the dramatic form was almost inevitable. Each fight carried through either to triumph or defeat or to some mystifying frustration. The plot was always man's struggle against death, its grandeur and its terror, sure-fire theater down through the ages. In this one field of writing, fact is ever stranger than fiction. The combat correspondent or historian who has to strain for effect to hold reader attention thereby indicates that he has missed the most vital details of the action. It is a resort to nature-faking. My 1966–67 winter tour in Vietnam provided all of the source material for four public books, *Ambush*, *Bird*, *West to Cambodia*, and *The Fields of Bamboo*. The total time spent on doing finished manuscript at my mill was less than five months, with no rewriting. There could have been a fifth book spun out of what happened in Operations Cedar Falls, El Paso II, and Geronimo II, but by that time I was weary of the subject and had put my notebooks away. All of which is to say that writing any such book is no great feat. The book almost writes itself.

By chance we were in Saigon during the Tet holiday, and we moved with the street throng until early morning. As with every main city in Vietnam, it was like being on a battlefield. Added to the roar and writhing of the monstrous crowd were the blasts and chatter of cannon crackers, torpedoes, and kiddy-size automatic firearms exploding right at one's heel and unto the far edges of the city. Perfect cover for a Vietcong attack, it continued through the night and next day. Hack and I talked it over at the Oriental, the small native hotel where we stayed because we liked the people. The enemy was bound to use this cover sometime. The following year they proved my hunch correct in the Tet Holiday Battle of the Cities.

Chapter 26
The Last Hoopla

My first time under fire was in November, 1917, when I had still eight months to go to reach legal military age, and my last such experience was in June, 1968, one month before I turned sixty-eight. That was a few days after Bill Westmoreland had turned over the MACV command to another old friend, Creighton Abrams. If I said other than that I was less jumpy, less concerned, the last time around than during my baptism, I would be lying, though the first brush was fleeting, and my final venture with bullet fire and bombardment was fairly prolonged. One can get hardened to that kind of danger, and in old age its consequences not only seem to matter less; they are intrinsically unimportant.

The eventuality, however, was not of my seeking, and the fact that my last tour in Vietnam worked out more explosively than all of the others put together was just one of those things, a sheer accident of numbers, the work of fate playing strange tricks.

On returning home in March, 1967, after having wintered with our line forces and the Green Berets in the forward areas, I had told Cate that I was not only through with Vietnam but with war itself and would never again go overseas to have a look at it. We called it a deal, shook hands, and were glad. There is no reason why life should lead a man or a family anywhere in particular; yet in our case we were pretty much held to a course whereon it was fatal to fail and dangerous to succeed. In our fourteen years of marriage until then, Cate had packed me off for the Sinai, Lebanon, China's offshore islands, the Congo, Algeria, and Vietnam three times, and as the children grew older every such absence imposed a heavier strain of suspense upon the household.

Our noble resolve to call quits on this kind of trekking lasted all of three months. It was washed out by the Six-day War in the Middle East. We probably would not have made the compact had we foreseen that Israel would go to war again, that land and its people being very dear to us. As it worked out, I got there too late for the shooting except for some moderate gunfire along the Suez on the day I visited the Israeli positions there. That brief shelling marked the very beginning of the Arab renewal of sustained harassment. Neither concern for Israel nor curiosity about the war had impelled my return to the Sinai. I went because the American Heritage wanted a book written, and the Columbia Broadcasting Corporation wanted a one-hour movie made, and the money made it worth doing.

When early in the following May I received a cable from Bill Westmoreland inviting me to Vietnam on orders to take a fresh view and arrive at an overall estimate of situation prior to his leaving the command, we did not mull it over very long. I handed the message to Cate and asked, "What do we say?"

She answered: "I don't see how you can reply 'no' without violating a rule you have followed all of your life."

The decision was made that simply. Again, David Hackworth volunteered to go with me as my escort, and Westmoreland honored the request. Then at the last minute Hack backed away. For the moment he was feeling a bit spooked, and no wonder. Hack, who started soldering at fourteen, had seen more battle than any American of his years or time. Later, he returned to the war in Vietnam, took a battalion in the delta, and was again shot up. As he was hospitalized, this time with his ninth wound, the army specifically directed that he would never again enter combat. Then he was put in for his eagles; and he immediately returned to the fighting line.

A charmed life, that one, and curiously contradictory and intertwined with my own. When we first met, in 1951, he was a kid sergeant in Captain Lew Millett's company of Wolfhounds in Korea. There soon followed the one great bayonet charge of that conflict, staged by Millett, which I witnessed from the lee side of a tank. Out of that one action Hack won a commission, Millet won a Medal of Honor, and I won a wife, my first acquaintance with Cate having come of my search for stenographic help so that I could write a proper citation for Millett.

Though among other virtues that need to be balanced against his sins Hack has the cheeriest uplift in his voice of any companion I have known in my travels, not getting him on this jaunt worked out as a break for me. In his place as my escort, after I reached Saigon, I was assigned Navy Commander Billups Lodge. A new arrival in the country, as chief PIO at the U.S. information center in the heart of the city, Lodge had volunteered to go with me, just for the experience. His bid had been approved by his boss, Brigadier General Winant Sidle, only to have Westmoreland object. Westy thought that a navy type wouldn't be to my liking. Sidle stood his ground, and so Lodge was there waiting when I arrived. I couldn't have had it any better.

Saigon was under attack in the hour I set down. Several Vietcong battalions were banging away at the Y-bridge area. The thrust was making big headlines in the United States: "Saigon Reeling Under the Blow," "City Imperiled," "Populace in Panic." That kind of thing was being written. It was outright nature faking. The attack was piddling, a mere fleabite, contained by one battalion from the 9th Division and a handful of national police, but correspondents love to write whoppers, particularly when the hair-raisers put them at the seat of danger.

We had some good ones over there, a few who understood war and wrote honest copy about it. Some months after Sidle was no longer on that job, we were discussing that subject. He asked how many correspondents I could remember from Vietnam that I would rate competent. I listed seventeen, including three women. He named nineteen, this out of hundreds of men and women.

Though most of my time was to be spent in the field on this last trip, I was basing at the guest house in the compound next to Westmoreland's palatial quarters, which with its grounds covered one city block. My extra baggage would be left there.

That evening, as the four of us—Westy, Bill Hall, Bill MacMillan, and I—were having the conversation over cocktails that brought about the naming of these papers, quite suddenly came revelation.

I had asked Westmoreland, "Were you shocked when in late March the president made his TV announcement that he would not run again?"

"No, and at last I can say why. I had known it was coming for four months."

Then he poured out the story. He had been a guest at the White House the previous November. In a room in the president's private quarters late one night, President Johnson had told Westmoreland of his tentative decision to retire. He said that his main reason was that he feared for his health. He talked of Woodrow Wilson's last months and Eisenhower's serious illness while in office. The thought that he might break similarly and become wholly incapacitated agonized him. Conscience required him to disclose his intentions to Westmoreland. He was concerned mainly that his action might be demoralizing to soldiers in Vietnam. To that, Westmoreland replied that the troops over there had taken so many jolts that one more wouldn't faze them.

Extending the conversation, Mr. Johnson said that McNamara was quitting as secretary of defense to take "a big job." What did Westmoreland think about Clark Clifford as his replacement? Westmoreland's reply was that he did not know Mr. Clifford, and that in any case, the question was not one that as an army commander he could answer with propriety.

Westmoreland concluded his recital to us: "No secret that I have ever kept has been a greater strain on me, if only because what I have known all along is at odds with the way history is being written."

The dinner lasted long, and we broke up about an hour before midnight.

En route to my quarters I could hear the rumble of artillery in the direction of Cholon. The night was starlit, and the air oddly balmy for mid-May. Ninety minutes after hitting the sack I was roused by a sharply crackling blast just outside the wall that surrounded our square, or about fifty feet from my bed. As I sat up, there came a second explosion, no less close. No whine had preceded it, and the blast was like that of a cannon cracker many times amplified. It was not particularly nerve-wracking. The noise was wholly unfamiliar to my ear, and I knew it had to be the Russian 122-mm rocket. One round hit a filling station just outside the wall, killing the attendant, and the other knocked off two policemen. The target was undoubtedly Westmoreland's quarters. It was the first such attempt.

Next morning, as we met for breakfast on the patio, Westmoreland remarked rather bitterly, "If we were playing the game according to the rules, we would retaliate on their cities. It doesn't make sense."

No, it didn't make sense. Almost two years earlier, I had been at dinner in the same quarters. Other guests were Ambassador Henry Cabot Lodge, Lieutenant General Joseph H. Moore, USAF, and Lieutenant General John A. Heintges, Westmoreland's deputy. That was the day in June, 1966, that Moore's pilots laid the heavy and successful raid on the petroleum refineries and tank nests at Hanoi. We heard the news over cocktails and raised our glasses high. Westmoreland was called twice to the telephone, to talk first to Defense Secretary McNamara and then to President Johnson, and to hear their congratulations. We sat down to dinner, and by the time we were topping it off with liqueurs, the pilots who had led the raid were with us. I debriefed them in front of the others. We were all happy as hell, and reacting like a pack of schoolboys. The wraps were off. It was to be a new deck and a new deal. Fighting with one hand tied was at last ended. We truly believed it, and we whooped it up. What we cheered turned out to be a flash in the pan, a lapse into brief resolution by the crisis managers who were too soon frightened by their own daring.

I should have understood that the manner of my reception when I got back to Saigon was a portent of things to come when I took to the field, but it never occurred to me. Westmoreland had personally laid out my schedule, and Commander Lodge and I would simply go along with what he had programmed. I was to visit and confer with all major commands from top to bottom in Vietnam and also get into as many forward bases as possible. As a favor, he had mailed a copy of my itinerary to Cate. Though I would be continuously on the move, with not as much as one full day in any one place, the month ahead did not look too tough. That's what I thought, and so did Westy.

As things worked out, the Charlies must have been reading our mail. The corniest of all soldier sayings, used to describe any action, from an ambuscade that misses fire to the dropping of an A-bomb, is "then all hell broke loose." That isn't what happened to us. We were merely rocketed and shelled from hell to breakfast, with a little sniping for good measure. Somehow we took two bullet hits through the rotor blade of a chopper on one of our rides from base to base, though we were wholly ignorant of how it happened.

Peculiarly, all runs to forward bases, including Khe Sanh, were bucolically peaceful, though we made about thirty of them. We hardly heard a shot fired in anger, except for distant shelling or the roar of friendly artillery, when we were puttering about in enemy country. It was when we settled into the comforting protection of main base camps that the flit hit the shan, and it happened invariably.

Camp Evans, the temporary home of the 1st Cavalry Division in the far north, was hit by only two rockets, which was just enough to blow the works. One round exploded the ammunition dump, which was much too close to the chopper corral, with the result that fifty-seven Hueys were destroyed in a flash. At Camp Eagle, the base of the 101st Division to the south of Hue, a battalion of Vietcong sappers from that ruined city attacked the artillery positions at midnight. In relation to the main base area, the guns were situated as is the tail of a tadpole to its blob. While the sappers were trying to cut off the guns, more than 450 Russian rockets and heavy mortar shells were laid on the main base to drive troops to the bunkers and keep the sapper attack isolated. The loss of life was mournful, and the base camp looked like it had been worked over by a twister.

Next day Lodge and I flew to Khe Sanh with Major General Ray Davis, who was taking over the command of the 3rd Marine Division. Six of his battalions were still tied down in that junkyard, the worst rubbled field I ever gazed upon. There was practically nothing to salvage. The siege had left it one vast rectangle of piled-up, twisted metal, shattered timbers, torn sandbags, and frayed sheets of camouflage cloth and plastic. It was a real crime against nature, for the surrounding hills were majestic, wondrously green, and the day was heavenly.

We walked around and about this foul acreage for the better part of an hour while Ray explained things. We happened to be old friends. I had known him in Korea and had written the citation that finally got him the Medal of Honor for a night attack in thirty-below-zero weather.

Not a shot was fired during our Khe Sanh stay. As we returned to the chopper, Ray asked me what I thought. I said: "The position no longer makes sense, if it ever did. It is simply a waste of troop strength better used elsewhere. This is not key ground."

Ray said: "I'd already figured that one out."

Shortly we were airborne, to keep a luncheon date at Camp Carroll, another marine base about ten minutes flying time to the east. The position, which was about seven miles from the well-tagged and cairnlike battlement known as the Rockpile, had nothing in common with that place. It was a fire base plunked down on a nakedly exposed shelf of red earth, barren of natural cover in any form. An improvisation from the ebb and flow of operations, it made little military sense.

As we first saw Camp Carroll that fine morning from two thousand feet up, we knew that we were in trouble. It was performing like a Roman candle. Earth flew upward. A fuel dump was ablaze. Flashes of bright light from the ground ahead came every few seconds. Due to the roar of the chopper, we couldn't hear the racket ahead, but we could see that our spot for a noontime rendezvous was fairly jumping under heavy attack from Russian rockets, mortars, and long-range artillery based in the demilitarized zone. Nothing looks more incongruous than the earth exploding underneath one on a bright blue day. From a blazing fuel dump, black smoke moved up thickly in oily ropes just off the landing strip.

We headed for that nasty plume. There was no way to get out of it. We were stuck with the luncheon engagement. I could not say to my friend Ray: "This doesn't make sense; by landing now we simply compound their problem; let's not play it stupid." For the same reasons, he couldn't say it to me, had it been on his mind to do so. We were like juvenile motorists playing the game of chicken, and there was no honorable way to reverse what circumstance had made a fool commitment. Stuck with the code, we corkscrewed down to the rendezvous.

The chopper didn't even touch earth. Shells were breaking on the runway as it hovered for a split second. We jumped from the skids two feet or so to the tarmac. Even as we hit, the Huey pilot—a more intelligent type than his passengers—was up and away. Davis and Lodge, setting the mobile example, were yelling for my edification, "Run! Run!" and they were not looking back.

They were legging it for the nearest bunker, about sixty yards from our touchdown, no marathon for a brace of athletic young sprouts. Being a coronary case, I could not share the urge. Better to go out quick from a shell burst than linger on with a heart attack. I could think that problem out instanter; so I put one foot in front of the other, proceeding at a normal gait.

When I made the bunker and the marine colonel commanding the base reached out to pull me in, Lodge, who had reached it a half-minute earlier and then looked back, yelled, "Damn it, sir, but you are calm."

I said: "Bill, that's what you think," and there was no time for more conversation than that. A 122-mm rocket exploded into the bunker next to us, and the blast burst two oil drums on its roof, emptying the fuel into the blazing wreckage. The base executive officer was showered with the stuff. He crawled out of the ruin looking like Tar Baby, dripping oil from head to foot, and when he got to us, we could see that he was horribly burned around the head, shoulders, and back.

Still, when he saw me, he braced, and brought that right hand up with a parade ground snap, saying, "Happy to meet you, sir." It was a salute to be remembered.

Within a few minutes we had him aboard a medevac ship, bound for hospital. We lunched fifteen feet below ground on the lower deck of the two-tier command bunker. The bombardment went on, adding no zest to my appetite.

One-half mile to the east of Camp Carroll, atop a bald hill shaped like a miniature volcano, was a marine outpost. The road to it ran along the spine of a gradually ascending and coverless hogback which put any vehicle right on the skyline throughout the slow run. Davis had set it up early that morning that we would visit the outpost at 1300.

Again we were stuck with it, though Carroll was still under intense shelling. When we arose to go, Lodge said, "Sir, I forbid it. General Westmoreland told me—"

I said: "Bill, you can forget all about that. You're not on the bridge."

It was a smooth, uneventful run along a conciliatory slope, and the outlook from the outpost toward the demilitarized zone was magnificent. By the time we returned the barrage had stopped, and the garrison was fighting the fires.

We flew that afternoon for Da Nang and visited a battalion of the 7th Marines, one company of which got mauled patrolling the rocket belt while we were watching a demonstration by a Long Range Reconnaissance Patrol. That night at corps headquarters I bunked in the trailer of another old friend, General Dick Stilwell. When we were on our second highball, the alert sounded. The camp was being mortared.

Getting away from I Corps Zone was sheer pleasure. It was one of the stickiest periods of the war. We were losing an average of 430 Americans killed weekly, and most of these casualties were in the far north. My impression was that too much of this toll came from our commanders pressing too hard. We were suffering, in a sense, from overexposure. Companies were sent forth to do the work that was better consigned to small patrols. In effect, we were setting up too many fat targets. At the same time, the base camps were half-organized and wretchedly secured. More troop time should have been spent getting the house in order.

Yet these overly massive deployments responded to an almost irresistible temptation. At this time, May and June of 1968, North Vietnamese by the thousands were sifting south out of the demilitarized zone along the coastal plain. For the most part, these were not tactical units but armed packets of replacements. Where they were intercepted and engaged, they fought poorly. The discipline and cunning of earlier years were lacking. Fields were left strewn with their dead. Weapons were no longer policed. The withdrawals were awkward. Camouflage was neglected or poorly done. In the high country to the west, our patrols were coming across batteries of heavy artillery in perfect condition, ready for firing. No attempt had been made to conceal them, and they were wholly unattended.

These signs said that the enemy was mounting one last great lunge out of desperation. The NVA was running out of trained military manpower. The killing opportunity was there right enough, and the slaughter of that spring was grim and great. Still, we were paying too high for the mop-up.

At the end of the flight south I had a luncheon date with General Bruce Palmer, Westmoreland's deputy. There was never better timing. As I entered his office, Bruce said: "Washington is on the wire and asking for you." The caller was General Harry Kinnard and he came on as clear as if he were in the next room. "I'm calling for Cate," he said. "She's worried sick. She hasn't heard a word from you, and she says the lightning is hitting every place you go."

My wife, my Cate, getting the wind up? I felt like the farmer when his cow died. I couldn't understand it. No such thing had ever happened to her before. I told Harry to assure her that I was above ground and in one piece and that Charlie couldn't possibly continue aiming his whole war at me.

Over lunch Bruce Palmer and I discussed the NVA drive in the north. I said: "I think it's the last great gasp. And I don't believe they can keep the pressure up until July." Bruce, who should have had the inside dope, replied: "I figure they can keep it up until late fall." I bet him a buck and that is one he lost.

There followed for Bill Lodge and myself a brief but blessed interlude of tranquillity where we had least expected it. We were inspecting a grid of far forward bases of the 4th Infantry Division to the west of Dak To and almost overlooking the Cambodian border. Everything was so beautifully serene that we felt as if we had lost touch with reality. The quiet ended when for the first time I heard the booming voice of the 4th's commander, Major General Charley Stone, who could out-blast Stentor. Stone is an original soldier.

He sat me down and said: "Marshall, I know exactly how to fight this war, and I'm going to do it my way. If higher authority doesn't like it, then it can relieve me." Since that jibed with my own feeling about command responsibility, I took in every word.

By the end I couldn't fault anything Stone had said. He didn't believe in random sweeps. He thought there should be offensive deployments only when a correlation of various intelligence forms, such as agents' reports, electronics, and air photos, definitely pointed to the presence of enemy forces. He held, further, that his forward bases should be as sedulously secured as Camo Enari, the main base at Pleiku. What he was doing was a model for all others, and Crate Abrams later told me that he thought it the ideal tactical pattern. It got results, and it kept casualties low.

The irony is that Stone proved right on both counts. Sound though his operating method, he was shortly relieved when the press skinned him for disciplining soldiers who failed to salute at Camp Enari. Flawed when he should have been supported, Stone at that point turned in his suit, and the army lost a top-grade fighter.

We flew from there to the headquarters of the 1st Infantry Division located in an abandoned rubber plantation, a most melancholy setting. The next day was spent inspecting the fire bases of the division with another old friend, Major General Keith Ware. A Medal of Honor winner who had entered the army as a draftee, Keith had few of the lesser graces that make a soldier popular with troops; the man had quiet modesty and never worked for reputation. His son, Spec 5 Keith Ware II, said of him: "Dad was always his own man," and it was true. This was to be the last time that I would see him. A few weeks later, in the same command chopper in which we moved about, with his friendly scout dog at his knee, he would be shot down and meet crashing death in the company of a group of his riflemen.

The Iron Triangle was in 1st Infantry Division country. When I had last viewed it, this Vietcong forwarding and assembly area was all verdure, a stream-bound flat so densely overgrown with palms, vines, and forest that from above one could not observe the paths, bunkers, and hooches. Keith's engineers had Rome-plowed that scene into rubble. The triangle had become tawny wasteland. The houses were gone. The trees were flattened and leafless. From above they looked like burned matchsticks. Below us there was not one sign of life stirring or of anything green. One viewed this ruin but to shiver, though the day was warm.

Quickly, the harsh earth of the triangle was under our feet. As we walked about amid the devastation, Keith said: "That story about a vast tunnel system underlying this place is all bunk. We have probed and found only a couple of small holes."

At first I thought he must be joking, but his face was deadpan serious. I answered: "You couldn't be more wrong. They're here—about four klicks [kilometers] of nigh-indestructible tunnels. I have the plat of the whole system in my desk at home, all of it done to scale. I'll send it to you."

It had not for one moment occurred to me that the engineer light colonel whose battalion had explored and mapped the tunnels was giving me the only copy and had not taken steps to make such vital information of use to future commands. This is the sort of lapse that occurs under rotation with too frequent changes of command. On return home I sent him the plat. His last letter reached me after he died. It said he had discovered that the Cong was still using the tunnels.

From 1st Division we flew to the delta to rendezvous with Major General Julian Ewell of 9th Division at the command post of Colonel Hank

Emerson's brigade. There are no better fighters in the army than these two. Hank was his usual gusty self, boasting about his men—"the guttiest studs to be found in any brigade." Some of these nonpareils were brought to the adequately sandbagged CP so that we could look them over. Their arrival coincided with a few incoming mortar shells.

From Emerson I first heard that North Vietnamese replacements were beginning to flood into the delta via Cambodia and the Plain of Reeds. This was something decidedly new. The delta had always been exclusively Vietcong territory, but Vietcong recruiting had dried up, and Hanoi was acting to fill the gap. That same morning Hank's soldiers had dragged an NVA prisoner from a bunker. He had lost a hand during the fire fight and was too weakened to get away. Age fourteen, he told a story of having been drafted for the war. His superiors had told him that the fight for the delta had been won, and he would simply do occupation duty. During its nine weeks on the trail, his column had half withered away from malaria, bombings, and desertions. His story was at least as believable as was the article published in the New York Times more than a year later which said that for the first time NVA replacements were present in the delta.

In late afternoon, with Ewell's chopper leading the way, we flew for Saigon, covered by gunships. Julian wished me to see his dispositions at the Y-bridge. According to G-2, the Vietcong would again hit that sensitive target early the following morning, which information proved to be right on the button. We talked to the national police and visited with Ewell's soldiers on the outpost line. There was not one grim lip in the crowd. Damage to the area was relatively light. Troops were thronging to the big PX near the bridge as usual; yet the threat to that quarter was being described to the American public in the most harrowing terms.

Ewell flew on ahead of us to Camp Bear Cat, the 9th's main base, eight or so kilometers outside the rim of Saigon. When we put down, Julian and staff were drawn up in formal array, all scrubbed and polished.

Julian greeted me warmly. "Slam, welcome to Bear Cat. I'm told you've had it rough. With us you are perfectly safe. Bear Cat has never been hit."

"Then get ready, Julian," I replied. "You have just said a few words too many. The hex is on."

It was. The early evening passed off pleasantly, the later evening more so. About midnight the party broke up. I next saw Julian an hour later. We were having a pajama party in his command bunker, this in response to the wailing of the siren. Bear Cat was being mortared for the first time. We sat there for five minutes laughing at one another like a brace of idiots while the bang-bang went on. It was too silly to last.

Julian said: "Nuts to this. Leave us repair to the trailer and take on some bourbon." We two hardy warriors had practically won the Battle of the

Bulge unassisted. Sporting around in pajamas because of a few mortar rounds was simply *infra dig.*

I was certain when I left Saigon that the war was making its final turning in our favor. We had topped the rise. From here on, we needed but to continue what we were doing, while striving for greater efficiency and true economy of force. Far too much artillery shell was being blown off in wasteful harassing and interdictory fires. Random sweeping of the country by companies operating in detachment led to carelessness, counter-ambushing, and excessive cost in casualties. More moderation and less headlong effort would get better results. We had learned these lessons perhaps too slowly, but at least we were learning, while the NVA obviously was rapidly deteriorating. Putting one graph against the other warranted a reasonable expectation that, barring further mistakes by our policy makers, the enemy power would be so far diminished by year's end that we would get some action in Faris before the next spring.

On return to the United States, being lengthily interviewed by Dean Brelis for the NBC network, I said just these things. There would be no more large-scale enemy offensives, North Vietnam no longer being capable of mounting them. Several days later I got word through Dr. Victor DeLuccia and Rose Mary Wood that Richard Nixon would like to talk over the Vietnam situation with me.

Cate and I met with Mr. Nixon at his New York apartment, the conversation lasting a little more than an hour. My report was roughly what I have said here, though with more data and more emphasis on the declining state of the Vietcong and the marked improvement in the ARVN and popular forces, especially in the Central Highlands and I Corps Zone. On the main point I was more than an advocate, I was a fanatic. We had to continue the pattern. There was no choice but to hit North Vietnam at both ends. Stop the bombing of the north, and every calculation would go by the boards. It would be as a reprieve to the condemned.

Mr. Nixon said: "You astonish me."

I asked why.

He said he had been in Washington the day before for talks with the president and Secretary Rusk. "They hung crepe all of the way," were his words. The war was all but lost. There was no way to bring off anything really favorable to our side.

In a very real sense, they were right about it. When the leaders of any nation at war come to that sad mental and emotional condition in which they see only blackness ahead, its cause is already more than half defeated. Not only is their faintheartedness all too clearly conveyed to the opposing camp. It is evident to all antiwar elements in their own.

That was the trouble all along in Vietnam. Of it came purely wishful decisions at the highest levels and disillusion at all others. When attention is no longer paid to those details that more hardy spirits do not consider beneath them, one may gamble that further official foolishness, if not catastrophe, is not far off. The White House did indeed try to manage the war, all along knowing that its people could not devote more than a small fraction of their time to the business. It was impossible, impossible.

Three days after being with Mr. Nixon, I was to appear before the Republican Platform Committee in Washington to discuss the draft and the much trumpeted but illusory alternative, the all-volunteer armed force. I asked Mr. Nixon if he wished me to give the committee the same estimate on Vietnam that he had heard. He said: "Do so, and tell them that it is at my request."

So I tried to impress them with my reckoning, and I failed. The one member who seemed to take my views seriously was Governor John Chaffee. I knew that the late Senator Everett Dirksen discounted my judgment heavily because he so implied as we sat together during lunch. General Jim Gavin had preceded me as a witness. It was one of his crepe-hanging days and he was at his soft-spoken though eloquent best.

The only point here worth making is that, when policy becomes shaped out of a fundamentally mistaken evaluation of situation, then decisions will almost inevitably be wrong. Mr. Johnson's next try at finding a way out was not just wrong but ruinous. We had a military victory within reach, and he washed out that prospect by his decision to stop bombing the north. Even now, it is almost inconceivable that in taking that action he could have believed that Hanoi would reciprocate and there would be some offsetting advantage gained by our side. The connotation is that he did not understand the enemy mind whatever, though he had been up against it from the hour that he became president. Any line captain who had been fighting the NVA for six months could have told him that he was fatally mistaken, that optimism had gripped him like an opium eater's dream.

None of this is rationalizing after the fact. I wrote and said on TV when it happened that there would be no Communist quid pro quo, and that the president had monumentally blundered. I might better have burped into a whirlwind. Because this action was taken on the eve of the national election, the interest of press and public was concentrated on the partisan debate over whether he had made the move to help Hubert Humphrey rather than on the fundamental question of whether he had sold short the national position.

Immediately following Mr. Nixon's election, I wrote him about the outlook. There would be no change in the Communist attitude in Paris. His delegation would be treated with the same contempt as Mr. Johnson's. The only chance to end the stalling would be to hand the other side an ultimatum on truce talks, give them ten days to get down to meaningful negotiation under threat of resuming full-scale operations, the meaning of which phrase need not be spelled out. To remove the curse from that action and make it publicly palatable, he could at the same time announce that 100,000 U.S. troops would be withdrawn from Vietnam over the next fourteen months. We could trumpet it that we were so far ahead that we could well afford to take that gamble. Not only would it make good propaganda; it would respond to political necessity. Public pressure would in any case compel troop withdrawals, and by anticipating, there was an advantage to be won.

In mid-May, 1969, I was called to Washington for a conference at the Pentagon. Over the phone it was explained to me that the analyst group in the Department of Defense was in agreement with my findings that between 35 and 40 percent of our casualties in Vietnam came of our own mistakes, chief among them a general carelessness among troops toward all security matters. They wanted me to talk over what steps could be taken toward reducing casualties without loss of combat effectiveness.

We batted the ball back and forth on that subject through all of one day and managed to score now and then. Then, wholly unexpectedly, on the second day I found myself dealing with another group of men, some civilian, some military.

This was the White House *ad hoc* committee that was advising the president on how to withdraw troops from Vietnam and in what numbers. Clark Clifford's sound-off had made this a hot subject, though his much-lauded proposals were a military absurdity and wholly impractical. It is astonishing that a man may serve as secretary of defense and know so little about the factors of main problems.

We were meeting on a Friday and the committee had to have its recommendations on the president's desk by the next Tuesday. They wanted my views about troop withdrawals, what ceiling would be reasonably safe, what size contingents should be pulled back to begin, where the first displacements should be made, and all of that. Also, I was to discuss what overall tactical pattern we should aim for to compensate for the shrinkage, conserve force, cut costs, and reduce casualties.

We talked along for six hours. They questioned and I answered. Their inquiry ranged far and wide: What sized packets should be redeployed to begin? Where should the displacements start? How should the combat force be balanced with support force during the contraction? What changes in tactics would bring about an optimum adjustment as the field army thinned out?

Through that afternoon of grilling, I was baffled that, while I was given a cordial response and an active working over, there was little or no objection to any of my recommendations, though I thought some of them were rather radical. At the end I felt quite pleased with myself.

Several weeks later a great light dawned. In the presence of the committee I had simply come up with the school solution. What I had proposed was consistent with all that they had tentatively concluded, and I was but reaffirming the positions they would take in the paper to be laid on Mr. Nixon's desk five days later. The realization was more than a little deflating. Though I had gone over big, it was strictly as a yes man.

★

According to Jack Benny, one of the main problems in humor is knowing what to leave out. In any such summing up as this, that is joined with the other problem of knowing when to call a halt and stack arms.

While grinding out these pages, I have felt warned by the story of the heckler who shouted at Al Smith, "Tell 'em all you know, Al, it won't take long," to which Smith replied, "I'll tell 'em all we both know, it won't take any longer." Hence, halfway along in the writing I strategically set a terminal point for myself, not in space but in time. I would write along until my seventieth birthday and then call quits.

The glitter of the planned sitdown vanished almost as swiftly as I had passed the mark. Within three weeks after coming to my seventieth, I could smell a new world crisis brewing in the Middle East. The hijacking of several commercial jets to the Jordan desert was the tipoff. It was pikestaff plain that King Hussein would have to go after the Palestinian guerrillas, or with help from the army they would get him. A shooting war seemed inevitable. Amman definitely was not the place to go, though. If hostilities eventuated, all newsmen at the center would be locked up and would see nothing.

In mid-August I booked passage to Israel for mid-September. On the appointed day, with Cate's blessing, I shoved off with a companion, my friendly dentist, Colonel Carl Rasak. Being of Arab blood and speaking Arabic fluently, Carl burned with curiosity about how he would be received, hardly believing when I told him that these very qualifications would make him a member of the club.

Our timing was right on the nose. When we touched down in Paris, the *Trib* headline screamed: "AMMAN IS BURNING." We were burning, too. In the interests of air safety, the gendarmes at Orly Field were dashing around and poking all passengers in the gut with machine pistols. Nothing hairier came later.

At Tel Aviv I found that, except for the army spokesman, all doors at Zahal were closed to us. As I had never been shut out before, I sensed that the army had to be on the move. We rented a Fiat and scouted the Jordan Valley and the Galilee and the Israeli armored concentration on the Golan Heights, which was to be thrown at the Syrians if the army of Jordan failed to contain their thrust. Jordan succeeded, and another bickering in the Middle East flamed out with no one noting that it had been a second Six-day War.

So subtly had Zahal marshaled the spearhead on the Golan that the public remained unalerted. Throughout the crisis, Israel stayed wondrously calm despite the tension elsewhere. Once the shooting died, all of my old friends were available, and we together did our Monday morning quarter-backing. These things made it the best kind of holiday.

On our return flight we spent a week in West Germany, visiting and inspecting the forces under General Jim Polk, a highly companionable soldier. As John Masefield said, no mortal ever does anything consciously for the last time without some feeling of sadness, and I reckoned this would be my final touchdown with the United States army.

Then the My Lai tragedy unfolded, and I could not sit still. My old friend, Lieutenant General Ray Peers, made his TV presentation in which he said how many officers were involved and gravely compromised. Listening, I felt certain that the army was in deep trouble, some of its own making.

I spoke to Westmoreland about it. "When you try to get all of the fish, the net breaks. There will be collusion. The question of the very nature of loyalty is at issue here. In the end, there will be only one lieutenant convicted, and it will be said that the army contrived to make him a scapegoat."

Westy would always hear me out. He asked me to spend the afternoon with Peers and his staff, including legal counsel, which I did. Peers was cordial as ever, and his counsel listened, but we got nowhere.

My argument was that most of the officers in the net did not have guilty knowledge of a crime but only hearsay. The legal beagle retorted that, even so, most operations in the field proceed by hearsay, that is, by telephone and radio. My rebuttal was: "That has nothing to do with it. No case based purely on hearsay will stand up in the Court of Military Appeals or the Supreme Court. Why accuse when you cannot finally convict?"

To my lasting regret, I could not shake them. I believe the army also now regrets the course taken. That the intentions were righteous made it no less of a blunder.

The stigma of My Lai hits hard. Too many Americans believe that this terrible affair was typical of our soldiers in combat and hence no cause for self-flagellation. Yet in covering forty-eight operations in Vietnam from patrol to multidivision size, I found nothing that even faintly compared with My Lai. Knowing combat in four wars, in three of which I was the chief analyst of soldier nature, I was impressed mainly by the decency and humanitarianism of our average fighter. Today it seems almost idle to bear such witness. That which is most scandalous and sordid is so much easier to believe.

In April, 1971, I was appointed special consultant to the chief of staff of the army. My task was to advise him on how the new army was coming along, with special reference to its receptivity to the programs designed to bring about the all-volunteer force. I possibly spent more time in that season interviewing troops, inspecting bases, and noting problem areas than did Westmoreland. It was a lulu of an assignment. While I realize that "new" is a battle-weary word, veteran of a thousand campfires and still more campaigns aimed to increase the sales of lotions and cereals, I did find that the army was making substantial progress, almost none of which was reflected in the press.

Later in the year I was named a member of a nine-man board of generals to advise on the reform of army training to make it more efficient. To take that on, I asked for a study period of the training at Forts Bragg and Benning to rid myself of the blur of intervening years. The happiest thing about the detail was that all other members of the board were retired four- and three-star generals of the regular army, most of them ex-theater commanders. So there was I, the lone former reservist, the only retired brigadier, with Jim Polk as my working partner.

★

Hardly of my own volition, I move higher in my seventies because the years now spin by, still not leaving enough hours in one day. There has come to me no surge of ripened wisdom or awakened interest in manners. Little is changed, though I may no longer play golf as well as I used to. I am already tired until next year, though I felt that way last year. I have my own teeth and enough of my thatch to deceive myself that I would not look better with a hairpiece. Shaving is the same infernal bore it ever was, though having lost the sight of one eye I see my face in a softer light. Martinis mean less because I drink them more. I stay mobile by walking rapidly away from anyone who suggests that I join him in vigorous exercise. Though I long since lost the battle against weight, I reflect that I might ease that problem by resolving to eat hearty only on days when the land rings with good news. Ours is a dieting household, not even the dog and cat being spared, and since some balance is needed, I provide it.

May it never be said that I wrapped up these papers because I became bored with the subject. Be the next one ever so vast and noble, it will seem trivial to me by comparison. My life was no big thing, but it was my own.

While I never valued it so highly that risking it seemed important, it was that feeling precisely that gave it worth to me.

I would like to be rated not by what I wrote but by how I lived, for I wrote to live and not the other way around. Having tried in this accounting to bestride the various periods in my journeying as if they were so many stages along a road, largely with the hope of explaining fortune that I hardly understand myself, I find on looking back that there is little to lament and much to cheer. Good companions were always alongside to help me through trial; I needed them as they in turn needed me. My yesterdays were the best the country ever knew, or so I believe, for in living them to the hilt I helped make them.

I think I will let it go at that.

Index

305